T0235364

Communications in Computer and Information Science 534

More information about this series at http://www.springer.com/series/7899

Hamid Jahankhani · Alex Carlile
Babak Akhgar · Amie Taal
Ali G. Hessami · Amin Hosseinian-Far (Eds.)

Global Security, Safety and Sustainability

Tomorrow's Challenges of Cyber Security

10th International Conference, ICGS3 2015
London, UK, September 15–17, 2015
Proceedings

 Springer

Editors
Hamid Jahankhani
GSM London
London
UK

Alex Carlile
SC Strategy Limited
London
UK

Babak Akhgar
Sheffield Hallam University
Sheffield
UK

Amie Taal
Deutsche Bank
New York
USA

Ali G. Hessami
City University
London
UK

Amin Hosseinian-Far
Leeds Beckett University
Leeds
UK

ISSN 1865-0929   ISSN 1865-0937 (electronic)
Communications in Computer and Information Science
ISBN 978-3-319-23275-1   ISBN 978-3-319-23276-8   (eBook)
DOI 10.1007/978-3-319-23276-8

Library of Congress Control Number: 2015948766

Springer Cham Heidelberg New York Dordrecht London

Springer International Publishing AG Switzerland is part of Springer Science+Business Media
(www.springer.com)

Foreword by Lord Carlile of Berriew

'Tomorrow's Challenges of Cyber Security'

'The World Wide Web is a wide-area hypermedia information retrieval initiative aiming to give universal access to a large universe of documents'. Since 6 August 1991 when these words headlined the first online website, the W3 as it was first labelled and what we today most associate with the Internet has expanded at an astronomical rate. Today the Internet exists with nearly 1 billion webpages, close to 3 billion users and global Internet traffic per year of 966 Exabytes – the equivalent of 15 billion iPads.

Sir Tim Berners-Lee's aim of a 'large universe of documents' is indeed well on the way. It is now integrated into almost all electronic systems, speaking to each other in real time, which we endeavour to develop as we push forward with the Internet revolution.

This hyper-connectivity has brought with it opportunity and benefit, connectivity and freedoms. But this is not without its costs. We have also seen a rapid growth in cyber crime, activism and espionage. The cyber threat is rapidly becoming ever more present, disruptive and destructive.

The growth of cyber threats has plunged the world of today into a serious deliberation over how the threat can be overcome. How do we restore the necessary international sense of order whilst defending the freedoms and rights of individuals around the globe? It is an ongoing battle without an end in sight.

This year alone hacks have hooked headlines. To see their impact one must only look at the hack of the US Office of Personal Management in June 2015 which Joel Brenner, a former head of CIA counter-intelligence described as 'not the end of American human intelligence, but a significant blow'.

Therefore it was excellent timing that the ICGS3-15 this year provided a platform to debate 'Tomorrow's Challenges of Cyber Security'. As Governments, corporations, security firms, and individuals look to tomorrow's challenges of cyber security this conference reminds us of the importance of this debate and discussion.

The ICGS3 conference entered its 10th year of bringing together international experts from all fields to examine the issues we face in the future. This year's conference provided expert and forward thinking analysis at a time when the debate over how we plan for the cyber security of the future has become a leading concern.

It is with great pleasure and appreciation that I thank ICGS3-15 for having brought us together to debate and formulate an effective strategy today. In doing so, ICGS3-15 guided us as we aim to defend and overcome the ever-present and ever-growing cyber threats of tomorrow.

Lord Carlile of Berriew CBE, QC

Conference Organising Committee

General Chair

Hamid Jahankhani   GSM London, UK

Program Chairs

Mathews Z. Nkhoma   RMIT International University Vietnam, Ho Chi Minh City, Vietnam

Amin Hosseinian-Far   Leeds Beckett University, UK

Workshop Chairs

Cyber Infrastructure Protection Workshop

Sufian Yousef   Anglia Ruskin University, UK

Intelligence Management Workshop

Sérgio Tenreiro de Magalhães   Universidade Católica Portuguesa, Braga

Vitor Sa   University of Minho, Braga, Portugal

Digital Forensics Workshop

MsAmie Taal   Deutsche Bank, NY, USA

IT and Cyber Crime Law Workshop

Michael Reynolds   GSM London, UK

Security Audit, Risk and Governance Workshop

Gianluigi Me   University of Rome Tor Vergata, Dipartimento di Informatica, Sistemi e Produzione (DISP), Italy

Systems Security, Safety and Sustainability

Ali Hessami   Vega Systems, UK

Ethical Hacking Workshop

Bobby L. Tait   University of South Africa, South Africa

Secure Software Engineering Workshop

Christos Kalloniatis	University of the Aegean, Greece
Stefanos Gritzalis	University of the Aegean, Greece

Publicity Chair

Clark McPhee	GSM London, UK

Webmaster

Duncan MacIver	GSM London, UK

Programme Committee

Babak Akhgar	Sheffield Hallam University, UK
Ameer Al-Nemrat	University of East London, UK
Samir Al-Khayatt	Sheffield Hallam University, UK
Omar S. Arabiat	Balqa Applied University, Jordan
Muhammad Ali Babar	IT University of Copenhagen, Denmark
Ali Chehab	American University of Beirut, Lebanon
Xiaochun Cheng	Middlesex University, UK
Mohammad Dastbaz	Leeds Metropolitan University, UK
Ken Dick	Nebraska University Center for Information Assurance, USA
Christos Douligeris	University of Piraeus, Greece
Orhan Gemikonakl	Middlesex University, UK
Carlisle George	Middlesex University, UK
Christos K. Georgiadis	University of Macedonia, Greece
Valiantsin Hardzeyeu	Ilmenau University, Germany
Ali Hessami	Vega Systems, UK
Amin Hosseinian-Far	Leeds Metropolitan University, UK
Lazaros Iliadis	Democritus University of Thrace, Greece
Hossein Jahankhani	University of East London, UK
William Kapuku-Bwabwa	Metropolitan Police, Special Operations, Counter Terrorism Command, UK
Konstantinos Kardaras	Technical Consultant, Greece
Sin Wee Lee	University of East London, UK
George Loukeris	Scientific Council for Information Society, Greece
Sérgio Tenreiro de Magalhães	Catholic University of Portugal, Braga, Portugal
Gianluigi Me	Luiss University, Italy
Siavosh Haghighi Movahed	Sheffield Hallam University, UK
Ali Mansour	University of Bedfordshire, UK
Hamid R. Nemati	The University of North Carolina at Greensboro, USA

Contents

Security Audit, Risk and Governance

Secure Software Engineering

Intelligence Management

Processing Social Media Data for Crisis Management in Athena

Babak Akhgar and Helen Gibson[✉]

CENTRIC, Sheffield Hallam University, Sheffield, UK
{b.akhgar,h.gibson}@shu.ac.uk
http://research.shu.ac.uk/centric/

Abstract. During a crisis citizens turn to their smartphones. They report what they see, they comment on other's reports, they offer their help, support and sympathy and, in doing so, they create vast amounts of data. Meanwhile, law enforcement agencies (LEAs) and first responders including humanitarian relief agencies are desperately trying to improve their own situational awareness, but can struggle to do so, especially in places that cannot be easily, quickly or safely reached. Since this user-generated content is often posted to social media, LEAs can tap into these resources by analysing this data. However, making sense of this data is not straightforward. In this paper we present a system that is able to process and analyse this data through categorisation and crisis taxonomies, classification techniques and sentiment analysis. This processed data can then be presented back to LEAs in informative ways to allow them to enhance their situation awareness of the current crisis.

Keywords: Social media · Crisis management · Disaster response · Information processing · Athena

1   Introduction

During a crisis situation citizens frequently turn to their smartphones. In doing so, they are both generating and consuming crisis related content, and, while some of this content may simply be a commentary on the unfolding events from afar, others are generating this content live at the scene. These citizens are in the unique (albeit often dangerous) position of witnessing these crisis events and if they are updating their social media pages with what they are seeing, hearing and experiencing then much of this information is available for anyone to view [11].

Law enforcement agencies (LEAs) see the data this generates as an opportunity: an opportunity to improve their own situational awareness of the crisis [21] and an opportunity to strengthen their relationship with citizens by also improving a citizen's understanding of the crisis. However, if vast amounts of data are collected but not effectively analysed these large repositories can quickly become silos where data is dumped but never used to its full potential. There are two phases to realising the potential of this data: (1) implementing robust and meaningful data processing and

© Springer International Publishing Switzerland 2015
H. Jahankhani et al. (Eds.): ICGS3 2015, CCIS 534, pp. 3–14, 2015.
DOI: 10.1007/978-3-319-23276-8_1

analysis techniques specifically designed for crisis data and (2) presenting relevant data in an easily understood and interpretable manner for by LEAs, first responder and citizen users.

Project Athena[1] is an EU funded FP7 project that aims to develop a system that can be used by citizens, first responders and LEAs during a crisis. The complete system will use sophisticated data processing techniques to transform incoming data from social media and a dedicated Athena mobile application into structured, informative reports that can be presented to LEAs in the form of a crisis dashboard used by command and control in order to enhance their situational awareness and to distribute information back to the public via social media the Athena mobile application.

This paper first discusses some background to social media and methods for processing of social media data from crisis situations. Section 3 presents a number of information processing components including crisis taxonomies, a method to aggregate and classify output from the taxonomies and an exemplar use case for sentiment analysis. The front-end components are briefly discussed to place the information processing context. Section 4 concludes the paper and discusses future developments for Athena.

2 Background and Related Work

2.1 Social Media in Crises

The use of social media in crisis situations is becoming increasingly prevalent and the information posted can provide actionable information in real-time [12]. The use of social media has already been explored in a number of different crisis settings such as hurricanes [14], earthquakes [23], floods [3], the riots in London in 2011 [8], and the aftermath of the Boston (USA) Bombings [6]. So much so that, the public now expect crisis response organisations to be using social media [1]. Despite this prevalence, the use of social media is often ad-hoc or does not reduce the information overload. This can result in conflicting reports, the spread of malicious information, cause panic and overwhelm the blue light services.

A good example of LEA use of social media was the 2011 Queensland (Australia) Floods. The @QPSMedia (Queensland Police Service) Twitter account became a trusted source for situational information while the #qldflood hash-tag generated discussion and support for the coordination fundraising and relief efforts [5]. However, this style of linear communication relies on having the man-power to read and respond to each post and the bigger the crisis becomes and the more people who participate in the crisis discussion on social media the more difficult managing the flow of information becomes.

Thus, despite the success in Queensland, many organisations are still searching for quick and easy ways to make sense of these vast amounts of data [10]. These problems include how to get access to the data, how to filter out the information not relevant to the crisis, how to process these text streams and create meaningful information from

---

[1] http://www.projectathena.eu/.

them and, finally, how should this information be presented to users in order for it to be useful to them.

2.2 Analysing Crisis-related Data

Twitter is one of the main sources of real time crisis information since tweets are usually publically available and easily accessible via the Twitter API (up to a limit). However, using Twitter directly is not considered to be a good platform for crisis management [9] but the information itself posted on Twitter is valuable hence the continuing efforts to collect and organise that information in a meaningful way. Therefore, a number of methods have been developed to process, organise, structure and subsequently represent that data in such a way that it is meaningful to users (including both citizens and LEAs).

Most of the methods for classifying and extracting information from crisis text tend to centre around two main methodologies: ontology or taxonomy based methods and machine learning methods.

Machine learning methods have been used by Imran et al. [7] to extract 'information nuggets' from crisis messages using Vieweg's [21] categorisation ontology as a basis for the categories and then training the data using a Naive Bayes classifier to assign posts to one of those categories. Imran et al. [14] use conditional random fields to classify messages using the same ontology. AIDR (Artificial Intelligence for Disaster Response) [12] also performs a similar ma- chine learning based classification process but on a larger scale. A further set of crisis classifications, called crisis dimensions, were defined by Olteanu et al. [19] based on previous research.

Olteanu et al. [18] developed a crisis lexicon containing crisis related terms extracted from a number of crisis messages and tested these terms against a further crisis dataset. They found that augmenting a set of expert related terms with the crisis lexicon was able to significantly improve their detection of crisis related tweets. While crisis ontologies include Vieweg's [21], the humanitarian exchange language (HXL) [16], the management of a crisis ontology (MOAC) [15] and the Integrated Data for Events Analysis [4]. However, while both a lexicon and ontologies exist there is not a mapping of particular lexicon to specific ontology classes. For a full review of methods of processing social media information in crises and emergencies see Imran et al. [13].

In addition to classification some applications try to extract sentiment from crisis related information. Nagy et al. [17] looked at a number of different methods that combine both machine learning and sentiment word lists and found that a hybrid approach seemed to detect sentiment most accurately. Torkildson et al. [20] went beyond simple positive and negative sentiment and looked to classify also based on emotions such as joy, anger, fear, disgust, etc. It is common in elections to see sentiment associated to particular parties thus in a crisis event there may also be sentiment directed towards particular actors in the scenario, for example the police or government. Thus enabling LEAs to be aware of the mood of the public towards these actors would provide an additional facet to their situational awareness.

3   Information Processing in Athena

Athena [2] is a current EU FP7 funded project aiming to bring citizens, first responders and LEAs together to tackle crisis situations using various types social media. One of the key outcomes from the project will be a suite of prototype software tools that will support citizens, first responders and LEAs in achieving these goals. A crisis dashboard for LEAs and a mobile application for citizens and first responders will be the two front facing components of the system. Both of these components are underpinned by a sophisticated data information pro-cessing engine. We will briefly cover the features of the mobile application and dashboard later, but the main focus of this section will be the underlying data processing and analytics techniques.

3.1   The Athena Pipeline

Athena has three main components: an information processing centre, a mobile application and a crisis dashboard. Fig. 1 demonstrates how information moves around the Athena system. Data is pulled in through social media APIs, such as those provided by Twitter[2], as well as receiving reports directly from the Athena mobile application. Data from these sources is then federated, aggregated, analysed and processed before being sent to the crisis command and control intelligence dashboard (CCCID). This dashboard presents the information it receives as textual reports, maps and visualisations to those in command and control. Here they are able to verify the information coming in, which, once verified, is sent back out to users of the mobile application. The CCCID can also post information directly to social media. This process continues in a loop as citizens send in more information the dashboard is constantly updated and the CCCID user's situational awareness is enhanced. Consequently increasingly accurate information can be disseminated back to citizens, which ultimately helps to ensure their safety and security in times of crisis.

Within the information-processing centre there are a number of data processing steps. Data is first imported from social media and the mobile application and then federated into a structured format. Reports are then categorised according to a crisis taxonomy (as described in the next sections) and are then further examined to extract more specific information, such as locations, people, groups and organisations. Formal Concept Analysis (FCA) will use the results of the categorisation and concept extraction to create aggregated reports that can be sent to the dashboard for presentation to LEAs. Alongside this reports are analysed for sentiment so that LEAs can be provided with the mood of the public overall and towards specific aspects of the crisis such as the actions of the police or government. The next sections will present each of these analysis components in turn and discuss their development and contribution to the Athena system.

---

[2] https://dev.twitter.com/.

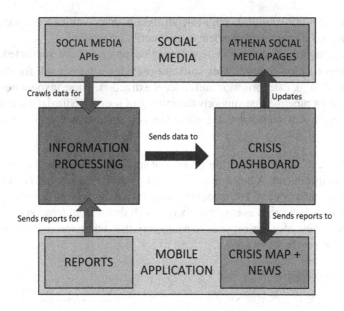

Fig. 1. Overview of the Athena components

SydneySiege. As a running example throughout this section we will present the results of the data processing techniques used in the context of the Sydney Siege. On the 15th December 2014 Man Haron Monis entered the Lindt Cafe on Martin Place, Sydney, Australia. Monis then initiated a situation where several of the cafe's staff and customers were taken hostage. The police are informed of the situation and send tactical operational units to Martin Place. During the siege a number of hostages are able to escape and images of this are posted to social media. Gunshots are also heard from inside the cafe during the siege. Eventually police storm the cafe which results in the death of Monis and one other hostage. We collected data from Twitter during the siege; however, a data collection failure meant that the tweets from the final few hours of the situation were not captured. Nevertheless, approximately 470,000 tweets were collected about the crisis using the keywords sydneysiege, sydney siege, sydneyseige, sydney seige, martinplace, martin place and lindt. By removing duplicates, such as retweets, this was reduced to 110,000 unique tweets. The following sections discuss methods for processing these messages.

3.2 Crisis Taxonomies

Given the unstructured nature of most social media posts, it was recognised that sophisticated natural language processing techniques would be required to in order to extract meaning from text. It has been shown that social media data used from one crisis for machine learning based activities does not necessarily apply effectively to another crisis even if they appear similar in nature [14], therefore taxonomies that have been developed do not depend on past crisis data but rather they are formed from a complex set of boolean rules. Initially, posts are simple categorised into one or more crisis categories and, secondly, the posts are examined in more depth and a number entities are extracted based on their context, i.e., context dependent named-entity extraction.

Both the categorisation and concept extraction processes are supported by SAS Content Categorization Studio[3]. This software provides a framework for developing rule-based models for categorisation and concept extraction. These taxonomies can then be plugged into a pipeline that supports the mining of social media data, the automatic mark-up of each post with the categories, concepts and, as will be discussed later, sentiment.

Categorisation. Categorisation is the process of applying one or more labels to a document based on its content. A taxonomy for identifying crisis events has been generated for use in the Athena system. The category hierarchy, as can be seen in Fig. 2, identifies a number of top-level crisis events that then branch down in to more specific events. Each top-level event also corresponds to a category that a user can select if they opt to send a report in via the crisis app.

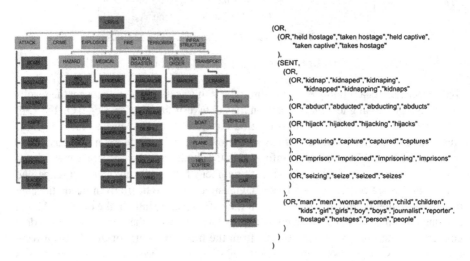

Fig. 2. The taxonomy of categories that each post or report can be categorised into. The top level of categories match those categories that can be select by the user when they make a report in the mobile application.

Each category is defined by a number of terms or a combination of terms that must appear in a post in order for it to be given a match to that particular category. Figure 2(b) shows an example of a single rule defining the 'Hostage' category. In this case, the category is applied if the any of the phrases are matched in the upper rule ('held hostage', etc) or, if in the same sentence, a mention of a verb related to a hostage taking plus the mention of 'someone' who has been taken hostage occurs. Similar rules are created for each entity in the hierarchy.

---

[3] http://www.sas.com/enus/software/analytics/enterprise-content-categorization.html.

Contextual Extraction. Running concurrently to the categorisation process is a second taxonomy that is used to extract specific crisis events known as contextual extraction. In this case, rather than applying a whole category to the text, certain information is instead extracted from it. This specified information may include named entities such as locations or the identification of people, groups or organisations. In Athena we go further than just entity extraction, instead, entities are only extracted when they occur in a specific context. That is, a context relating to an event happening during the crisis. These events include the large crisis events such as a plane crash or an earthquake but they also include smaller events such as people being injured (for which we then try to extract an associated location), or damage (which may have an associated location or entity that has been damaged).

Figure 3 shows a real tweet posted about the Sydney Siege. From this single tweet we are able to extract the category (i.e. it is a hostage situation), the location of the siege (a cafe in Sydney), that it is a gunman that has done the hostage taking and that a number of people who have been taken hostage.

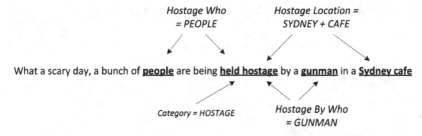

Fig. 3. Example of contextual extraction from a sentence about the Sydney Siege

However, simply extracting these concepts on their own is still not particularly informative and nor do they lend themselves to being presented to LEAs or the public. Further, they do not reduce the number of incoming posts by aggregating those which provide similar information. Therefore a further processing step is required to reduce this information overload.

3.3 Formal Concept Analysis (FCA)

Formal Concept Analysis (FCA), has been proposed as a method of classifying crisis data [2]. Briefly, FCA takes a binary feature-value matrix where here the rows (objects) would be social media posts and each column (attributes) represents a category or entity that has been extracted. It then classifies these posts into object-attribute groups where every object in the group has that particular set of attributes (although some objects may have further attributes). The classification is hierarchical so that an object A with attributes 1, 2, 3 could be in the groups that contain all objects with attributes 1 and 2, the group with all objects with the attributes 2 and 3 and the group with all objects with the attributes 1, 2 and 3. (For a gentle introduction to FCA see Wolff [22]). Each of these sets of groupings is called a formal concept.

For Athena it is not only useful to know which concepts are generated but also how many objects are associated with each concept and how it changes over time. Each chart in Fig. 4 represents a single concept found from applying the categorisation and contextual extraction techniques discussed in the previous section and creating formal concepts from the data extracted from the Sydney Siege. Initially there is a peak in people simply mentioning the hostage situation alongside a location such as Sydney or the cafe or Martin (which refers to Martin Place). Throughout the duration of the crisis there is steady stream of posts referring to the people trapped in the cafe while midway through the crisis we see a sudden burst of tweets that make reference to the hostages that were able to escape. The advantage of using the FCA approach is that the relevant information is still captured (through events, locations, people, categories, etc.) but by grouping tweets which contain the same information it reduces the information overload and provides a method of corroboration.

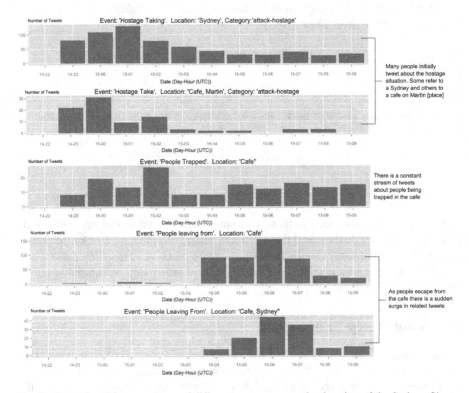

Fig. 4. Example of the prevalence of different concepts over the duration of the Sydney Siege

3.4 Sentiment Analysis

Sentiment analysis is the process of analysing a document's content for the feelings and emotions expressed within it.

In Athena we aim to classify sentiment based on the reports and data collected about the current crisis. We aim to detect overall sentiment for the crisis as it progresses and sentiment towards specific entities such as the police, first responders or the government, for example. Based on this idea we have constructed a rule-based sentiment taxonomy that uses rules similar to those in the categorisation and concept extraction to detect the sentiment. This includes a number of positive/negative words or phrases which determine overall sentiment but when appearing in certain contexts may be used to identify the sentiment towards a specific aspect of the crisis.

Figure 5 shows how overall sentiment about the Sydney Siege crisis changes over the duration of the crisis alongside how sentiment towards the government and police changes. As can be seen initially, negative sentiment towards the government and the police is quite high but as the crisis progresses there are fewer negative tweets. In particular, for the police towards the end of the crisis the number of positive tweets overtakes the negatives ones.

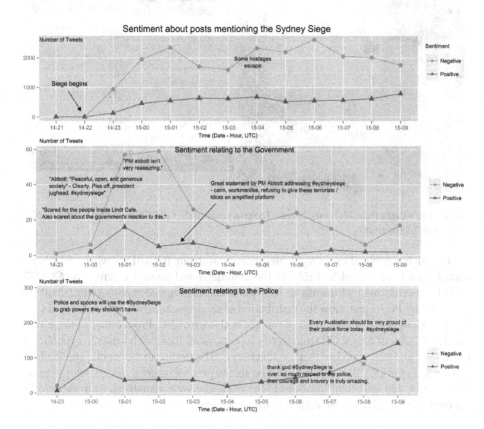

Fig. 5. Graphs of tracking positive and negative sentiment over the Sydney Siege Crisis

3.5 Athena Front-End Components

The two main front-end components for Athena are the Athena mobile application and then crisis command and control intelligence dashboard (CCCID).

The Athena mobile application is a tool for both citizens and first responders. Its key features are the ability to send reports directly to Athena (currently these appear directly on the map but in the final version they will go through the full processing pipeline) and the presentation of these reports on a mobile crisis map or alternatively as a crisis news feed. The aim of the application is to enable citizens that wish the participate in the crisis response to do so and for those in command and control to be able to post information out directly to citizens. Figure 6 shows some screenshots of the prototype Athena mobile application.

Fig. 6. The Athena front-end components. The crisis map of the CCCID on the left and the mobile application on the right.

The crisis command and control intelligence dashboard (CCCID) is where all Athena related data is presented to LEAs in the command and control centre. The CCCID provides a crisis map with links to individual and aggregated reports (which will be generated by FCA) that show the distribution of crisis events across the crisis area (see Fig. 6). Alongside this map a list of reports is also provided. From either of these two interfaces users of the CCCID may verify reports, mark them with a user tier (public or restricted), and edit or update them so that they can be pushed to the mobile application. From within the CCCID a user will also be able to post messages to social media, create new reports, add important locations to the map, and view visualisations associated to the crisis data (such as those related to the sentiment).

4 Conclusion

This paper has presented some of the data processing components used in the Athena system and shown how they are able to provide meaningful information from social media sources specifically in the context of the Sydney Siege. These have been presented in a time dependent context that enables users to assess how the crisis is changing over time and react accordingly. Future work on the Athena system will include further integration of these back-end and front-end components so that Athena truly is an end to end system. This will include presentation of the concepts created on the map and visualisation of the sentiment that can be fully explored by users alongside other crisis visualisations and querying methods. Additional text processing will also be implemented in the back so that when the social media messages are imported they can also be ranked for credibility and priority thus providing more contextual information to LEAs.

Acknowledgments. This project is co-funded by the European Union Seventh Framework Programme SEC Call 1 - FP7-SEC-2012.6.1-30.

References

1. Abbasi, M.-A., Kumar, S., Filho, J.A.A., Liu, H.: Lessons learned in using social media for disaster relief - ASU crisis response game. In: Yang, S.J., Greenberg, A.M., Endsley, M. (eds.) SBP 2012. LNCS, vol. 7227, pp. 282–289. Springer, Heidelberg (2012)
2. Andrews, S., Yates, S., Akhgar, B., Fortune, D.: The ATHENA project: using formal concept analysis to facilitate the actions of crisis responders. In: Akghar, B., Yates, S. (eds.) Strategic Intelligence Management, pp. 167–180. Elsevier, Oxford (2013)
3. Bird, D., Ling, M., Haynes, K.: Flooding Facebook-the use of social media during the Queensland and Victorian floods. Aust. J. Emergency Manage. **27**(1), 27–33 (2012)
4. Bond, D., Bond, J., Oh, C., Jenkins, J.C., Taylor, C.L.: Integrated data for events analysis (IDEA): an event typology for automated events data develoment. J. Peace Res. **40**(6), 733–745 (2003)
5. Bruns, A., Burgess, J., Crawford, K., Shaw, F.: #qldfloods and @QPSMedia: Crisis communication on Twitter in the 2011 south east Queensland floods. Technical report, ARC Centre of Excellence for Creative Industries and Innovation, Brisbane (2012)
6. Cassa, C.A., Chunara, R., Mandl, K., Brownstein, J.S.: Twitter as a sentinel in emergency situations: lessons from the Boston marathon explosions. PLoS Currents Disasters 1–10 (2013). Edition 1
7. Imran, M., Elbassuoni, S., Castillo, C., Diaz, F., Meier, P.F.: Extracting information nuggets from disaster-related messages in social media. In: Proceedings of ISCRAM. Baden-Baden, Germany (2013)
8. Denef, S., Augustin, S., Bayerl, P.S., Kaptein, N.: Social media and the police: tweeting practices of British police forces during the August 2011 riots. In: Proceedings of the SIGCHI Conference on Human Factors in Computing Systems, pp. 3471–3480. ACM, New York (2013)
9. Goolsby, R.: Social media as crisis platform. ACM Trans. Intell. Syst. Technol. **1**(1), 1–11 (2010)
10. Hughes, A.L.: Supporting the social media needs of emergency public information officers with human-centered design and development. Ph.D. thesis, Boulder, CO, USA (2012)
11. Hughes, A.L., Palen, L.: Twitter adoption and use in mass convergence and emergency events. Int. J. Emergency Manage. **6**(3/4), 248–260 (2009)

12. Imran, M., Castillo, C., Lucas, J., Meier, P., Vieweg, S.: AIDR: artificial intelligence for disaster response. In: International Conference on World Wide Web (WWW), pp. 159–162 (2014)
13. Imran, M., Castillo, C., Diaz, F., Vieweg, S.: Processing social media messages in mass emergency: a survey. CoRR (2014). http://arxiv.org/abs/1407.7071
14. Imran, M., Elbassuoni, S., Castillo, C.: Practical extraction of disaster-relevant information from social media. International Conference on World Wide Web (WWW), pp. 1021–1024 (2013)
15. Limbu, M., Wang, D., Kauppinen, T., Ortmann, J.: Management of a crisis (MOAC) vocabulary specification (2011). http://observedchange.com/moac/ns/
16. Kessler, C., Hendrix, C.J., Limbu, M.: Humanitarian eXchange Language (HXL) situation and response standard (2012). http://hxlstandard.org/
17. Nagy, A., Stamberger, J.: Crowd sentiment detection during disasters and crises. In: Proceedings of the 9th International ISCRAM Conference (2012)
18. Olteanu, A., Castillo, C., Diaz, F., Vieweg, S.: CrisisLex: A lexicon for collecting and filtering microblogged communications in crises. In: Proceedings of the AAAI Conference on Weblogs and Social Media (2014)
19. Olteanu, A., Vieweg, S., Castillo, C.: What to expect when the unexpected happens: social media communications across crises. In: Proceedings of the ACM 2015 Conference on Computer Supported Cooperative Work and Social Computing (CSCW 2015), Vancouver, BC, Canada (2015)
20. Torkildson, M.K., Starbird, K., Aragon, C.: Analysis and visualization of sentiment and emotion on crisis tweets. In: Luo, Y. (ed.) Cooperative Design, Visualization, and Engineering. LNCS, vol. 8683, pp. 64–67. Springer, Heidelberg (2014)
21. Vieweg, S.: Situational awareness in mass emergency: a behavioral and linguistic analysis of microblogged communications. Ph.D. thesis, University of Colorado Boulder (2012)
22. Wolff, K.E.: A first course in formal concept analysis. StatSoft **93**, 429–438 (1993)
23. Yates, D., Paquette, S.: Emergency knowledge management and social media technologies: a case study of the 2010 Haitian earthquake. Int. J. Inf. Manag. **31**(1), 6–13 (2011)

Online Surveillance Awareness as Impact on Data Validity for Open-Source Intelligence?

Petra Saskia Bayerl[1](✉) and Babak Akhgar[2]

[1] Rotterdam School of Management, Erasmus University,
Rotterdam, Netherlands
pbayerl@rsm.nl
[2] CENTRIC, Sheffield Hallam University, Sheffield, UK
B.Akhgar@shu.ac.uk

Abstract. Online surveillance, especially of open sources such as social media (OSINT/SOCMINT), has become a vital source of information for decisions made by public institutions such as law enforcement agencies. This keynote discusses the concept of online surveillance awareness (OSA) as a possible long-term threat to the quality of OSINT-relevant online sources. An interdisciplinary research agenda to systematically investigate the links of OSA to the reliability and validity of OSINT sources and thus the quality of OSINT more generally is outlined.

Keywords: Online surveillance awareness · Online surveilliance · OSINT · Data reliability · Data validity · Law enforcement agencies · Research agenda

1   Introduction

Open source Intelligence (OSINT) is increasingly being utilized by Law Enforcement Agencies (LEAs) and public authorities in order to enhance a wide range of their functions. These include investigative capabilities, situation awareness, the management of public disorder, responses against criminal threats, responses to crises, as well as understanding public perceptions of security and safety [1–3].

Examples of OSINT applications by LEAs can be found in their public announcements, news broadcasts and in the professional literature. Most prominent amongst them are cases such as the 'Arab spring' in 2010–2011, the riots in London and other English cities in summer 2011, the 2012 London Olympics, FBI-hostage negotiations in Pittsburgh in 2012, the murder of British soldiers in the streets of London in 2013 or the abduction of Nigerian girls from their school by Boko Haram in early 2014. These events have seen a considerable reliance on the processing of OSINT, and more specifically social media intelligence (SOCMINT) by LEAs, security agencies and public authorities in particular. OSINT can support tasks such as the creation of situational awareness, intelligence gathering, sentiment analysis and communication with and from the public.

LEAs gathering information from open sources depend on the monitoring, collection and analysis of often very large amounts of data. These are activities, which happen

© Springer International Publishing Switzerland 2015
H. Jahankhani et al. (Eds.): ICGS3 2015, CCIS 534, pp. 15–20, 2015.
DOI: 10.1007/978-3-319-23276-8_2

generally unbeknownst to the producers of the data, i.e., the citizens using the internet. However, since the Snowden revelations knowledge about online surveillance has become ubiquitous. Our question is what happens, when internet users are aware of the presence, type and degree of online surveillance? In what way does this influence their behaviors and in which ways and to what degree does this impact the quality of OSINT sources, if at all?

Issues in the quality, i.e., reliability and validity of open data sources, threaten the dependability, effectiveness and efficiency of decisions made using it. These may result in critical mistakes for deployment of resources and actions by LEAs and other authorities, for instance, during a criminal investigation or the management of crises. We argue that online surveillance awareness (OSA), i.e., the knowledge or at least assumption of users that their behavior and information online is monitored, collected and analyzed, threatens the quality of OSINT and OSINT-based decisions. This issue has so far received little attention in discussions of OSINT, and even less empirical efforts have been undertaken to systematically investigate the concrete effects of OSA on OSINT quality for LEAs. In this keynote we will reduce introduce the concept of online surveillance awareness presenting a research framework and agenda to investigate the links of OSA to the reliability and validity of OSINT sources and thus the overall quality of OSINT.

2 Online Surveillance and OSINT Effectiveness

Surveillance of online behavior is a vital aspect of efforts to fight crime as well as in the response to and management of crises. We argue that two elements affect the quality of OSINT: (1) awareness of online surveillance and (2) public attitudes towards surveillance.

A first indication for this link can be found in a recent study by Marthew and Tucker, which investigated the shift in Google search patterns prior compared to after the Snowden revelations in ten different countries [4]. As they demonstrated, in most countries keywords became less 'contentious', i.e., users avoided searches "they believe might get them in trouble with the [U.S.] government" [4]. Although the study does not allow a direct causal link, it provides strong indications of OSA and subsequent modifications of online user behavior. In our own research, we have investigated assumptions of online surveillance and the tendency for falsification of personal information [5]. We found that OSA in the form of online surveillance assumptions increased the acceptance of falsification in others as well as the propensity to falsify our own personal information.

Our study on information falsification introduces two possible contingencies to the effect of OSA on OSINT: perceived usefulness and acceptance of online surveillance and type of organization conducting the surveillance (in our case state agencies versus private companies). On a conceptual level this leads a possible Effects Model of OSA for falsification of personal information, which links online surveillance with falsification moderated by usefulness perceptions and user trust in the organizations conducting online surveillance (see Fig. 1).

Together these studies provide first empirical indications that OSA can change user behavior on a large scale. This link between OSA and changes in online user behavior creates not only social, legal and political implications but also critical practical

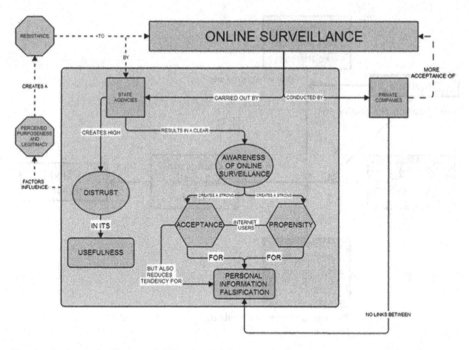

Fig. 1. Suggested effects model for the link between online surveillance and falsification of personal information based on [2]

implications for LEAs and other organizations basing operational decisions on OSINT, starting with the design and development of relevant tools and platforms. Similarly, OSA is also likely to affect citizens' acceptance of the tools and applications put forward by LEAs for use during situations such as natural disasters or help and advice services (e.g., "ask the police" applications).

As the debates and reactions in the aftermath of the Snowden revelations demonstrate, online surveillance awareness threatens citizens' trusts in state authorities and LEAs. Critically, trust is one of the main factors that determine whether citizens use online services provided by LEAs [6]. In our opinion, it is thus crucial to systematically investigate the impact of online surveillance awareness on the multitude of sources and information types LEAs use in OSINT-based analyses and operations. In the following, we put forward a road map and agenda for future research efforts into this area.

3   A Research Road Map and Agenda

In order to further explore the relationship between OSINT quality and online surveillance awareness and to create a 'reference architecture' for the development of future OSINT applications, we sketch a research road map outlining possible topics and methodologies. Our agenda is based on the generic framework presented in Fig. 2.

As demonstrated in Fig. 2, several areas require investigation to understand the link between OSA and possible implications for OSINT quality. Firstly, the features of online

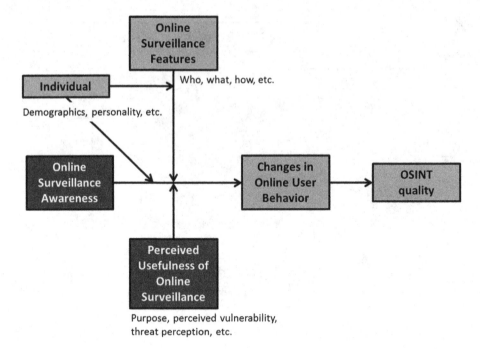

Fig. 2. Generic research framework for the link between online surveillance, online user behaviours and OSINT quality

surveillance (e.g., type of information collected, implicated organizations, and collection process) may influence how intrusive or problematic online surveillance is perceived. We hypothesize that the more problematic the surveillance is considered, the stronger the relationship between OSA and behavioral changes will be. Connected to this is the perceived usefulness of the surveillance [5], which will also depend on personal variables such as perceived vulnerability to the threats address in the surveillance (cyber-grooming, financial fraud, terrorism, crises, etc.). Moreover, features of the individual may play a role in shaping the relationship between OSA and behavioral changes, for instance, in terms of gender, online experiences, political orientations, etc. For example, men seem more critical about online surveillance than women, while less experienced internet users seem less critical than users with longer online experience [5]. Individual features may also play a role in determining the impact of surveillance features on the OSA-behavioral link, in that demographics, personalities, national contexts, etc. may influence judgments about the what, who and how of the surveillance process. Of course the behavioral changes are only relevant in as far as they impact OSINT-relevant information. It is therefore also vital to determine which relevant behaviors may be more or less influenced by OSA.

Our research agenda combines elements of big data analytics with psychological, organizational and criminological perspectives. We thus envision research on OSA-impacts as an interdisciplinary endeavor. Accordingly, methodologies will span the range from observations and experimentation to sentiment analysis and behavioral modelling. These methodologies will be adapted depending on the specific parts of the model under investigation (e.g., investigation inter-individual differences versus investigating impacts of behavioral changes on different quality parameters).

We propose this research framework as a possible road map to inform newly established, but also existing research projects. Below we use an example from the context of crises management to illustrate how it may be integrated into more traditional research efforts on OSINT applications.

4 Application Scenario: OSINT Quality in Crises Management

One of the key elements for the management of crises is a clear understanding of the situation to enable decision makers to take appropriate actions in often volatile conditions. OSINT is one of the channels which can act as information source for decision makers. To avoid wrong decisions during fast developing critical situations, the reliability and validity of information is of special concern.

The use of OSINT in crisis response and management is addressed in several research projects, among them the EU-security project ATHENA. ATHENA explores how the huge popularity of new communication media, particularly web-based social media such as Twitter and Facebook, and the use of OSINT can be harnessed to provide efficient and effective communication and enhance situational awareness during crises. Its aim is to enable and encourage users of social media to contribute to the security of citizens in crisis situations by developing a suite of software tools to enhance the decision-making capabilities of LEAs, crisis management command and control centers, first responders, and citizens during and in the aftermath of crises ('ATHENA platform') [7]. Athena outputs will then feed into a Command and Control Centre for decision making authorities (e.g., LEAs and emergency planners).The effectiveness of the ATHNEA platform relies heavily on the quality of its source information, which is obtained from open sources in the public space [8]. Its success further depends on the trust between citizens, LEAs and other organizations involved in crisis management efforts.

As part of our research agenda we will investigate the proposed framework (see Fig. 2) during the live exercise of Athena in collaboration with UK and European LEAs and other crisis management authorities. Amongst others, these exercises can focus on investigating in more detail the role of OSA for the willingness of citizens to provide information on social media during crises, the quality of this information (e.g., level of detail) and the role of trust in these situations.

5 Challenges to be Addressed in Current and Future Research on OSA-OSINT Links

While we firmly believe that systematic research into the costs and benefits of online surveillance awareness is a vital addition to current discussions of OSINT-use and application design. In addition there are also challenges to develop a unified research agenda as suggested in this paper. We have identified the following closely interlinked challenges for the development and deployment of the research agenda:

(1) The speed of technological change
(2) The evolution of internet regulatory, societal and technological frameworks, which are and may remain scattered across EU and international regions and institutions
(3) The lack of a clear strategy to address the multi-disciplinary dimension of online surveillance by member states and authorities. The OSINT domain is addressed by many different organizations, research disciplines and approaches. The dialogue among these stakeholders remains too localized and needs to be coordinated in order to identify consensus on what is consider to be OSINT from ethical and legal standpoints.
(4) A lack of a common terminology across disciplines, which hampers the development of a multidisciplinary approach.

All these challenges explain the need for a comprehensive, multidisciplinary research agenda elaborated through a citizen centered multidisciplinary and multifaceted methodological approach. Research on OSINT needs to evolve towards concrete solutions governed by citizens' rights to freedom of speech and the full spectrum of ethical concerns while maintaining national security of each country. In this context we believe that the consequences of online surveillance and the awareness of online surveillance for citizens' online behaviors and the relationships with each other as well as state authorities are of vital concern. In our research agenda we aim for a systematic investigation of these effects to create actionable knowledge for LEAs, designers of OSINT-tools and platforms, and decision makers relying on the quality of their data.

References

1. Akhgar, B., Yates, S.J.: Strategic intelligence management for combating crime and terrorism. In: Akhgar, B., Yates, S.J. (eds.) Intelligence Management, pp. 145–157. Springer, London (2011)
2. Bell, P., Congram, M.: Intelligence-Led Policing (ILP) as A Strategic Planning Resource in the Fight against Transnational Organized Crime (TOC). Int. J. Bus. Commer. 2(12), 15–28 (2013)
3. Steele, R.D.: Open source intelligence. In: Johnson, L. (ed.) Handbook of Intelligence Studies, pp. 129–147. Routledge, New York (2007)
4. Marthews, A., Tucker, C.: Government surveillance and internet search behavior. In: SSRN (2014)
5. Bayerl, P.S., Akhgar, B.: Pitfalls for OSINT investigations: Surveillance and online falsification tendencies. Communications of the ACM, August 2015
6. Bayerl, P.S., Horton, K., Jacobs, G., Akhgar, B.: Who wants police on social media? In: Proceedings of the 1st European Conference on Social Media, pp. 42–49 (2014)
7. Andrews, S., Yates, S., Akhgar, B., Fortune, D.: The ATHENA project: using formal concept analysis to facilitate the actions of responders in a crisis situation. In: Akhgar, B., Yates, S. (eds.) Strategic Intelligence Management: National Security Imperatives and Information and Communication Technologies, pp. 167–180. Elsevier, Amsterdam (2013)
8. West Yorkshire Police: Athena Project: Latest News, 29 April 2014

Improving Cyber Situational Awareness Through Data Mining and Predictive Analytic Techniques

Sina Pournouri[(✉)] and Babak Akhgar

The Cultural, Communication and Computing Research Institute,
Sheffield Hallam University, Sheffield, UK
{Sina.pournouri,babak.akhgar}@shu.ac.uk

Abstract. Due to the widespread usage of computer resources in everyday life, cyber security has been highlighted as one of the main concerns of governments and authorities. Data mining technology can be used for prevention of cyber breaches in different ways and Cyber Situational Awareness (CSA) can be improved based on analyzing past experiences in terms of cyber-attacks. This paper aims to investigate and review current state of CSA improvement through data mining techniques and predictive analytic and offers possible methodology based on data mining techniques which can be used by cyber firms in order to secure themselves against future cyber threats.

Keywords: Cyber security · Cyber threat · Cyber situational awareness · Data mining techniques

1 Introduction

Nowadays computers play crucial role in everyday life. Private and public organizations, banks, governments, Law enforcement agencies, intelligence services benefit from using computers in order to fulfil their business objectives. However this dependence to computer systems and digital resources also gives opportunity to cyber criminals in order to fulfil their aims too.

Cyber-attacks have huge implications on companies and governments. For instance unknown hackers targeted Sony Pictures and as a result some of their production including movies, contracts and market plans were leaked. Analysts predicted Sony financial loss was around 83 million dollars. (Savov 2014) Damages caused by cyber-attacks are not only always financial but also can lead to loss of reputation, customers and partners.

Prevention is always better than curing, so managers and authorities are always attempting to find an efficient way to be prepared and stay secured against current and future cyber-attacks. One of the common methods is applying security standards and policies including cyber security awareness programs. "How to improve cyber security awareness" is a significant challenge for security experts.

Understanding trends of cyber security can be divided into 2 different levels as follows:

© Springer International Publishing Switzerland 2015
H. Jahankhani et al. (eds): ICGS3 2015, CCIS 534, pp. 21–34, 2015.
DOI: 10.1007/978-3-319-23276-8_3

(1) Detection of weakness and bugs in the system: This step can be taken by security specialists by examining systems using penetration tests in order to find security bugs and weaknesses. By detection of weaknesses in the system, security managers can implement and design effective and solid security standards and procedures. In addition in order to fill technical bugs and gaps, security patches and equipment will be installed.

(2) Identifying cyber hackers and their methods: This level completes previous stage and it aids security managers to be aware of cyber-attacks recent methods. The concept of cyber-attack analysis will be highlighted in this stage in other words by analysing past historical cyber-attacks to cyber firms and finding relationship between different involved factors, a better landscape will be obtained and let managers to make effective decisions based on recent cyber threats.

2 Cyber Security

In order to understand the concept of cyber security, threats and possible breaches should be defined. Cybercrime is not a new phenomenon and all of cyber firms must be aware of that threat. Not only previous cyber-attacks should be taken into consideration but also there is always need for an efficient strategy against future cyber-attacks as they are getting more and more sophisticated.

FBI and Department of Justice in January 2012, Sony in May 2011 (Aspan and Soh 2011) and Citi Bank in June 2011 were victims of cyber-attacks and it proves that any organizations and businesses regardless of their size can be a potential target for cyber attackers (Das et al. 2013).

There are different categorization of cyber threats but mainly they are divided in following categories (Nikishin 2004):

1. Virus: a piece of malicious program which attacks to computer systems and spreads itself to different parts including disk without users' knowledge.
2. Worm: a malicious program which penetrates to the system and causes interruption in the process of computers.
3. Trojan horse: a program which has no sign of threat to computer systems in first place but can cause destruction and damage to systems.
4. Logic bomb: a piece of malicious program that penetrates to the systems and executes and damages at a specific date and time.
5. Key logger: key loggers are used to save key strokes and have multi usages. On one hand organization and companies use them for safety and monitoring employees and on the other hand cyber criminals install them on the victim's system to steal information.
6. DOS: Denial of Service attack is a malicious method targeting availability of the victim's server by sending too many request to it. After a while the server will be taken down by cyber attackers.
7. SQL injection: a piece of malicious codes that tries to compromise the database of a system and steal stored information.

8. Zero day threat: this threat refers to an unknown bug in a system which security experts are not aware of it or have not patched it yet and cyber attackers use it as a penetration gateway.

9. Phishing: refers to a malicious method tries to steal sensitive information such as credit card information and so on by tricking a victim through an electronic communication.

Above, cyber threats have been defined and cyber attackers and cyber role should be defined. According to Awan and Blakemore (2012) cyber attackers are divided into following groups:

1. White hat: This group also is defined as cyber security experts where they are hired by organizations and businesses to test their security standards and demands. The task of white hackers is identifying current and potential weaknesses of the computer and network systems through various approaches such as black box test or white box test. After identification of those weaknesses they present efficient solution in order to address them.

2. Black hat: This group refers to those hackers who use their abilities to attack systems and obtain unauthorized and sensitive information. Although Black hat hackers' motivations do not always focus on stealing information, sabotage and damaging to the systems are other motivations. (Jaishankar 2011). Cyber terrorists can be a subgroup of black hats whereas their motivations are illegitimate. According to Lewis (2002) those cyber attackers targeting critical infrastructure such as power, government operations in order to make public fear, are defined as cyber terrorists. There is some disagreements and dissimilarities between sociologists' definition of "cyber terrorism" term. Some authors like Aviksoo (2008) and Pollit (1998) define cyber terrorists as type of cyber attackers who follow political and social interests and carry cyber-attacks to achieve them. On the other hand some authors such as Cox (2015) the term of cyber terrorism makes sense when human casualties are the main risk as a result of cyber-attacks. However all of them agree on the type weapon for this act which is a computer and type of target which is critical infrastructures.

3. Grey hat: grey hat hackers can be a categorized in both previous groups. In other words they are judged based pn the result of their performance whether is peaceful and leading to improvement of security standards or harmful and leading to security breaches.

3 Data Mining

According to Ledoltar (2013) data mining is increasingly used in everyday life when customers and data have become strategic goals. Data mining is a method of analysing, extracting and discovering useful information form huge amount of raw data. Ahlemeyer-Stubbe and Coleman (2014) suggest that managers try to use data mining methods for prediction of future behaviour business. Therefore cyber security is not an exception between those subjects which benefit from data mining techniques.

According to Dean (2014) and Odei Danso (2006) data mining methods are divided into two main categories; supervised and unsupervised.

Supervised method attempts to measure relationship and similarity between from known input and output. A threshold will be defined and based on first result and the comparison between threshold and error level, some changes will be applied to learning process to get better output. On the other hand unsupervised method tries to discover hidden pattern in input set and there is no need for modification. Figure 1 shows difference between unsupervised and supervised learning.

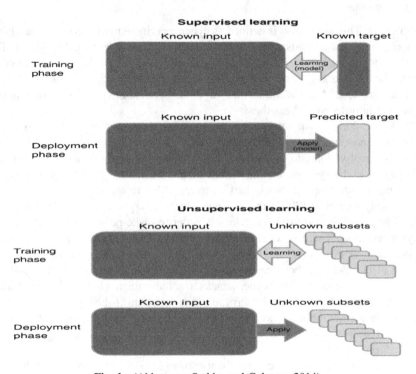

Fig. 1. (Ahlemeyer-Stubbe and Coleman 2014)

Data mining also includes different knowledge discovery techniques as follows (Dean 2014):

1. Regression analysis: This technique tries to establish a function leading to model the data.
2. Association rules: Refers to a technique used to discover interesting relationship among different variables in a data set.
3. Classification: Classification techniques are mainly used to classify data set into different subgroup and the result can be interpreted as a predictive model.
4. Clustering: This technique tries to arrange similar object in a specific groups based on their similarity factors.

4 Cyber Situational Awareness

According to Dua and Du (2011) in order to fill the present gaps in cyber security and deal with recent threats, an effective collaboration between cyber specialists and agencies is needed. These days cyber security researchers intend to design a solid and efficient framework maintaining confidentiality (the effort of keeping information secret between eligible and authorized parties and protecting it from unauthorized parties), Integrity (the ability of compatibility and accuracy of information) and Availability (Accessibility to cyber infrastructure and information) to protect computer and network systems (Dua and Du 2011). Cyber situational awareness is one of the frameworks designed by cyber security experts in order to preserve cyber security's interest and prevent from any sort of security breaches.

The definition of Situational Awareness should be taken into consideration. Situational Awareness is often described as an understating different factors in an environment which leads to predict and precept the near future events and trends for decision makers (Antonik 2007). In other definitions from other authors such as Tada and Salerno (2010) and Harrison et al. (2012) the factor of time plays crucial roles, in other words the time in situational awareness is coming with past information and learning from failures in order to analyse and extract any possible relations among them for a deeper and clearer understanding of future condition and situation. Situational Awareness (SA) is mainly divided to 2 different aspects as follows:

1. Cognitive aspect: from cognitive point of view, SA is mainly concerned with human perception. Endsley (1995) suggests that SA comes down to three main criteria: Basic perception of important data, Interpretation and conversion the data to knowledge and capability of using found knowledge for prediction of near future.
2. Technical aspect: In terms of technical according to Bryrielsson (2006) and Arnborg et al. (2000) SA is a combination of three main factors; arrange, analyse and integrate information as Arnborg et al. (2000) concentrates on arrange meaning collecting the data which suits the main demands and Bryrielsson (2006) reports that analyse and integration are two significant criteria in SA.

Franke and Bryielson (2014) and also Weick et al. (2005) suggest that Cyber Situational Awareness (CSA) can be a sub group of SA where the environment is cyber space and also in order to CSA, Data from IT equipment will be gathered and converted to suitable format for processing stage and that leads to better decision making. According to the study conducted by Weick et al. (2005) cyber sensors play prominent role gathering data for CSA improvement purposes in a deeper and detailed condition such as logs and data recorded by Intrusion Detection Systems.

Barford et al. (2010) categorizes existing methodologies for improving CSA into two main categories:

(1) Low level: Low level of improvement of CSA includes more technical factors rather than other factors including human factors. Vulnerabilities assessment, damage assessment and alert correlation are significant factors in the low level. For example security experts can correlate alert extracted from IDS and

vulnerabilities of their system in order to better understanding of current situation and predicting future issues occurring in the network.

(2) High level: High level of CSA is more general than low level in other words it is the combination of human elements and technical factors. Human elements includes human resources and human interference.

5 Existing Approaches

Ahn et al. (2014) suggest that big data analytic using machine learning, Artificial Intelligence and so on can benefit the improvement of CSA. Future and unknown attacks can be predicted by 3 main approaches:

(1) Classification: cyber experts use classification techniques to classify past cyber-attacks in order to define level of current and future threats in terms of cyber security.

(2) Regression analysis: regression analysis can help prediction of future cyber-attacks by probing similar behaviour among collected data from past. In other words regression analysis is a type of data mining technique which tries to find any possible patterns between different data based on their similarity and extends that pattern in order to predict the future.

(3) Relation rules: association techniques can find relationship between collected data and detect anomaly behaviour. For instance IDS alerts can be collected and by using association techniques anomaly behaviour can be detected from collected packets in the network.

Figure 2 shows the architecture of their approach. In the first step, event data from IDS, log files and network devices will be collected and then they will be formed into suitable and usable appliance for processing purpose. The third step includes applying various data analytic methods including regression analysis, association rules and classification techniques and so on. The result of third step feeds to fourth stage which is the process of interpretation for managers and make the valuable information meaningful for decision makers.

Although Ahn et al. (2013) do not purpose a real time algorithm, they introduce significant framework for obtaining valuable information raw collected data in order to improve CSA.

i-Hope framework is another approach presented by Das et al. (2013) trying to improve CSA by predicting cyber threats through formulation of goals as hypothesis and corroboration of them with mathematical and statistical analysis. Das et al. (2013) use CSI/FBI survey as their main resource of raw data and try to prove their hypothesis by applying Generalized Linear Model and it is a mathematical model used to predict uncertainty.

Das et al. (2013) formulate four main hypothesis as follows:

(H1) By increasing defence equipment within the system, the probability of cyber breach will be reduced.

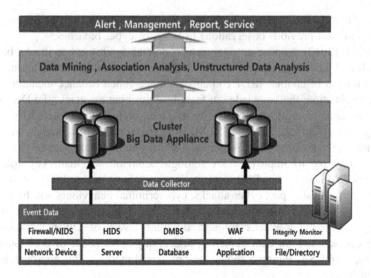

Fig. 2. Big Data analysis system architecture (Ahn et al. 2014)

(H2) By reporting the first attack to law enforcement agency, the probability of second or future attacks can be reduced.

(H3) Increasing IT budget leads to decreasing the chance of cyber-attacks.

(H4) By Increasing IT security outsourced, the probability of cyber-attacks will be decreased.

Das et al. (2013) apply chi-square and Deviance values to their data into a GLM and by interpretation of obtained models following answers are concluded to their hypothesizes:

Specify type of attack can be stopped only by installation of specify security equipment.

Reporting the first cyber-attack to Law enforcement agency does not have any influence on probability of future attacks.

The chance of security breach in a firm can be reduced by increasing ITO and IT budget.

Bayesian network has been suggested by Wu et al. (2013) in order to predict abd prevent cyber-attacks. Wu et al. (2013) take environmental criteria in target side into consideration and correlate them through Bayesian network analysis. These criteria are as follows:

Identify vulnerabilities and weaknesses: in order to this task in the system, powerful scanning tools such as Nessus are needed to identify security bugs.

The Usage Situation of Network: through this criterion, the usage condition of the network can be measured. The usage condition means the load of traffic which each node or device should deal with or number calls any of them received.

The Value of Asset in the Network: this can be done through an examination of each node in the network. Type of contained data and type of the task of each node will determine the value them.

Attack History: this attribute shows which nodes are more likely to be targeted by attackers based on previous observations in terms of cyber breaches.

Dut et al. (2012) propose an approach to defend against cyber-attacks based on Instance Based Learning Theory (IBLT). IBLT is a method providing accurate prediction of human behaviour. IBLT contains a storage called Instance including 3 main factors: (A) situation: the knowledge of features describing an attack. (B) Decision: an action taken against an attack. (C) Utility: the measurement of expected result of an action against an attack. Dut et al. (2013) reports that IBLT focuses on 3 main behaviours; Defender behaviour, Adversarial Behaviour and Tolerance level to threats. Therefore they try to improve CSA through behaviour of main key roles in a cyber-attack. Although this PhD project does not have accessibility to defenders behaviour, by analysing past cyber-attacks, cybercriminal behaviours will be analysed.

Morris et al. (2011) proposed an approach based on collecting intelligence and predicting future cyber-attacks through different levels of cyber missions. This approach concentrates on data gathering and giving solid result to decision makers level to improve CSA. Figure 5 shows their proposed method. This approach includes 8 different levels:

Mission tools: in this level regarding to type of attack, tools and general policies will be defined.

Mission need: based on outcome of level one, needs and different requests will be determined in order to combat against the cyber-attack.

Mission question: in order to identify weakness of the system, various questions will be brought up.

Mission area: it includes monitoring, Indication and warnings and counter intelligence. Based on questions which parts of cyber defence system should be activated.

Mission activity: in this level more specific activity against the cyber-attack will be agreed on.

Mission capability: in this level capabilities will be discussed based on taken actions.

Mission resources: type of resources needed by decision makers will be considered in this level.

Mission sources: the main concern of this level is where raw data comes from.

Musliner et al. (2011)'s approach is based on fuzzy logic which is an Artificial Intelligence technique. They divide the model into two various parts:

Proactive: Identification of weaknesses and vulnerabilities within the system in real time is the main task of this part.

Reactive: Identification of possible prevention techniques against cyber-attacks is the concern of reactive part.

The result of these two parts will be encoded into the fuzzy logic interference system as facts and rules. The outcome of the fuzzy system will build an automatic cyber shield against cyberattacks. Figure 3 shows Musliner et al. (2011)' s approach.

Schreiber-ehle and Koch (2012) suggest using JDL model of data fusion for improvement CSA in cyber defence. Data fusion is the process of combination different pieces of information in order to make them meaningful for better understating of different issues. Data fusion includes different sub-processing stages such as recording,

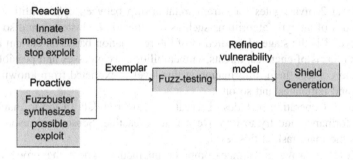

Fig. 3. (Musliner et al. 2011)

storing, filtering, analysis and suitable projection of result of analysis. The JDL model of data fusion is a cohesive model showing each components of data fusion in a organised form helping manages to comprehend valuable information. Schreiber-ehle and Koch (2012) apply JDL model to cyber defence factors. Figure 4 Shows proposed JDL model of their methodology which has 6 levels as follows:

Level 0: is a component accepting input from monitoring sensors within the system. IDS is one of those sensors which monitors activities in the system and in case of suspicious one, it will notify the system administrator.

Level 1: level 1 aims to refine inputs from level 0 in other words those raw data extracted by level 0 needs to be pre-processed and allocated to specific objects on the system. For instance log files and IP addresses recorded by IDS need to map to relevant nodes or objects in the network.

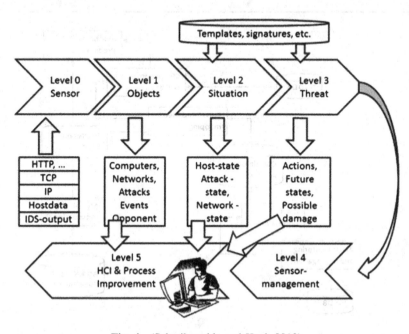

Fig. 4. (Schreiber-ehle and Koch 2012)

Level 2: level 2 investigates for current relationship between cyber entities through different types of analytic algorithms such as classification, clustering and so on.

Level 3: level 3 is the stage of prediction of future situation based on current and past condition in terms of enemies, threats, vulnerabilities, weaknesses and possible future operations to combat them. Information at this level is extracted from known attacks, signatures and templates and so on.

Level 4: level 4 operation includes observation of overall data fusion to maintain the system performance and try to improve it if it is feasible. Sensor and resource management is the main task at this level.

Level 5: level 5 provides Human-computer interaction where the process can be modified and refined by human experts.

Basically Schreiber-ehle and Koch (2012) draw general model of improvement of CSA and it can be suitable for projects in big scale.

Fayyad and Meinel (2013) design a methodology for prediction of new attack scenarios leading to improve CSA. Figure 5 shows their methodology. Fayyad and Meinel (2013) use three main resources of data; IDS data base, Attack graphs and vulnerability data base. IDS records all of the alerts and by applying clustering and aggregation algorithms, they will be formed into suitable format for correlation process. After correlating alerts, they will be stored in another built data set. Now it is time for processing attack graphs data. Fayyad and Meinel (2013) defines attack graph as "is a directed graph has two types of vertices, exploit and condition. An exploit is a triple (hs, hd, v), where hs and hd represent two connected hosts and v a vulnerability on the destination host".

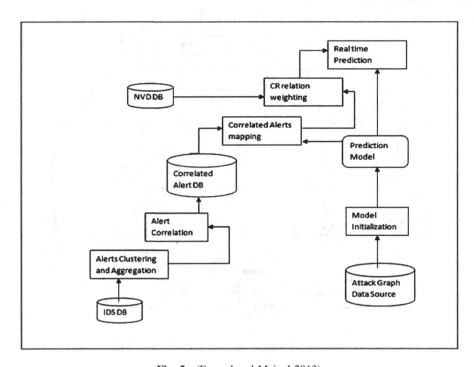

Fig. 5. (Fayyad and Meinel 2013)

By this definition attacks model will be initiated and then in another stage they will combined with correlated alerts. The next stage is processing vulnerability data base and trying to find relationship between them, attack graphs and correlated alerts. The result of this model provides a real time protection. The advantage of this methodology is staging each part of attack scenario which means defense indicators can have specific plan for each stage of ongoing attack when it happens.

5.1 Summary

To sum up, the following relations have been concluded between literatures and the possible methodology offered by this paper:

1. Framework: framework is highly important in any project and this research paper seeks to to make an effective framework which it not only fulfils the purpose of this paper but also delivers an operative method dealing with improvement of CSA. By reviewing above literatures, it can be understood that all of them, same principle in designing their framework where they have same blocks in their framework with different names and same operations, however, all of them do not look for same result and performance. Ahn et al. (2013) and Wu et al. (2013) and Schreiber-ehle and Koch (2012) do not propose a real time algorithm and their system mainly was designed for decision makes to improve CSA and protect their network through those solutions. Also the study by Das et al. (2013) follows same path but in different way. In other words they combine decision making process with financial issues in their approach of improvement of CSA. On the other hand Morris et al. (2011), Musliner (2011) and Fayyad and Meinel (2013) try to present real time framework of combating cyber breaches by probing technical elements in cyber security. This PhD can be a combination of both types of proposed models where by analysing past cyber breaches incidents in terms of not only type of attacks and methodology but also cyber attackers motivations and behaviours, it aims to present deeper understating of current situation of cyber environments and its players and predict future conditions based on current and past state.
2. Type of data and its collection: All of the literature mentioned in this paper focus on using Open Source Intelligence because they are publicly accessible and do not raise any ethical issues.
3. Type of analysis: All of proposed frameworks in this paper use statistical and data mining techniques.

6 Proposed Framework for Improving CSA

This paper aims to design a framework applying data mining and predictive analytic techniques to past historical data in terms of cyber-attacks to predict future cyber threats which will help to a deeper understanding of cyber situational awareness. This Paper is an ongoing research and it will be developed in near future.

The proposed framework includes following steps as it is showed in Fig. 6:

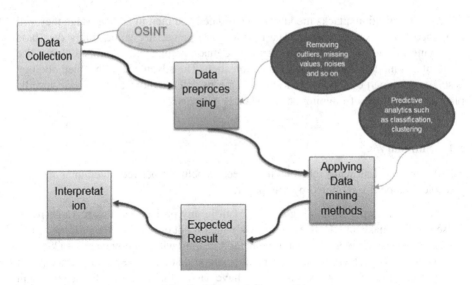

Fig. 6. (Proposed framework)

1. Data collection: as it mentioned this research paper will focus on cyber-attack historical data and the data will be collected from Open Source Intelligent (OSINT). Therefore it has been decided to use sources such as news and websites and any other sources which is publicly accessible and also their information does not raise any ethical issues.
2. Data type and attributes: the collected data initially will be nominal and categorical, however, based on requirements and type analysis they can be transformed into nominal and other formats. Data will include attributes such as type of attack, attacker, type of target, cyber motivation and so on.
3. Data pre-processing: sometimes because of operational errors and implementation of system, obtained data from real world has some errors, contradictions, incompatibility and missing values. This stage is based on Al-Janabi (2011) method which consists of following tasks to make the data ready for analysis purposes; dealing with missing values, removing noises, fixing incompatibilities and removing outliers.
4. Data mining techniques: Based on literature review, in order to find patterns among the data, data mining techniques will be applied. According to Ahn et al. (2014) using classification techniques can help cyber experts to find current patterns and based on findings try to predict the future patterns. Naïve Bayes and decision tree algorithms are two suitable techniques can extract valuable information from uncertain knowledge. (Bhardwaj and Pal 2011)
5. Expected result: after applying data mining techniques, the suitable result will be obtained including patterns relationships between different attributes and features of past cyber-attacks.
6. Interpretation of result: This stage is a crucial stage, Schreiber and Koch (2012) report that making the result meaningful to managers and decision makers is the

most significant stage of CSA improvement. For instance it should be determined which attributes or elements have more effect and cyber-attacks or which factors are weakest or strongest in the CSA.

7 Conclusion

Cyber Situational Awareness helps cyber defenders to adopt operative solutions dealing with cyber-attacks. This paper aims to review current frameworks improving CSA and propose an effective method to help cyber experts to understand their cyber situation deeply and combat cyber-attacks through implementation of security policies and countermeasures. The proposed framework is an ongoing and developing research which is based on data mining and predictive analytic techniques and it intends to highlight current issues in cyber firms through analysis of past cyber-attacks and predict future trends. This research will contribute to cyber managers to identify which attack methods are more favorable and help them to prioritize cyber security demands based on current and predicted future trends.

References

Aaviksoo, J.: Cyber-terrorism. Vital Speeches Day **74**(1), 28 (2008)

Ahlemeyer-Stubbe, A., Coleman, S.: A Practical Guide to Data Mining for Business and Industry. Wiley, New York (2014)

Ahn, S., Kim, N., Chung, T.: Big Data Analysis System Concept for Detecting Unknown Attacks (2014)

Al-janabi, K.B.S.: A proposed framework for analyzing crime data set using decision tree and simple k-means mining algorithms. J. Kufa Math. Comput. **1**(3), 8–24 (2011)

Antonik, J.: Decision management. In: Military Communications Conference (MILCOM 2007), Orlando, FL, USA, October 2007, pp. 1–5. IEEE (2007)

Aspan, M., Soh, K.: Citi says 360,000 accounts hacked in May cyber attack. Reuters (2011)

Awan, I., Blakemore, B.: Policing Cyber Hate, Cyber Threats and Cyber Terrorism. Ashgate, Farnham (2012). MyiLibrary

Barford, P., Dacier, M., Dieterich, T.G., Fredrikson, M., Giffin, J., Jajodia, S., et al.: Cyber SA: situational awareness for cyber defense. In: Jajodia, S., Liu, P., Swarup, V., Wang, C. (eds.) Cyber Situational Awareness, pp. 3–14. Springer, New York (2010)

Bhardwaj, B.K., Pal, S.: Data Mining: a prediction for performance improvement using classification. Int. J. Comput. Sci. Inf. Secur. **9**(4), 136–140 (2011)

Cox, C.: Cyber capabilities and intent of terrorist forces. Inf. Secur. J. Global Perspect. **24**, 1–8 (2015)

Das, S., Mukhopadhyay, A., Shukla, G.K.: i-HOPE framework for predicting cyber breaches: a logit approach. In: 2013 46th Hawaii International Conference on System Sciences, pp. 3008–3017 (2013)

Dean, J.: Big Data, Data Mining, and Machine Learning: Value Creation for Business Leaders and Practitioners. Wiley and SAS Business Series. Wiley, Hoboken (2014)

Dua, S., Du, X.: Data Mining and Machine Learning in Cybersecurity. CRC Press, Boca Raton (2011)

Dutt, V., Ahn, Y.-S., Gonzalez, C.: Cyber situation awareness: modeling detection of cyber attacks with instance-based learning theory. Hum. Factors J. Hum. Factors Ergon. Soc. **55**(3), 605–618 (2012). doi:10.1177/0018720812464045

Fayyad, S., Meinel, C.: Attack scenario prediction methodology. In: 2013 10th International Conference on Information Technology: New Generations, pp. 53–59 (2013). doi:10.1109/ITNG.2013.16

Franke, U., Brynielsson, J.: Cyber situational awareness – a systematic review of the literature. Comput. Secur. **46**, 18–31 (2014). doi:10.1016/j.cose.2014.06.008

Harrison, L., Laska, J., Spahn, R., Iannacone, M., Downing, E., Ferragut, E.M., Goodall, J.R.: situ: situational understanding and discovery for cyber attacks. In: 2012 IEEE Conference on Visual Analytics Science and Technology (VAST), pp. 307–308 (2012). doi:10.1109/VAST.2012.6400503

Jaishankar, K.: Cyber Criminology: Exploring Internet Crimes and Criminal Behavior. CRC, Boca Raton, London (2011). Dawsonera

Ledolter, J.: Data Mining and Business Analytics with R. Wiley and SAS Business Series. Wiley, Hoboken (2013)

Lewis, J.A.: Assessing the Risks of Cyber Terrorism, Cyber War and Other Cyber Threats, 1–12 December 2002

Morris, I., Mayron, L.M., Smith, W.B., Knepper, M.M., Ita, R., Fox, K.L., Corp, H.: A perceptually-relevant model-based cyber threat prediction method for enterprise mission assurance, pp. 60–65 (2011)

Musliner, D.J., Rye, J.M., Thomsen, D., McDonald, D.D., Burstein, M.H., Robertson, P.: FUZZBUSTER: towards adaptive immunity from cyber threats. In: 2011 Fifth IEEE Conference on Self-Adaptive and Self-Organizing Systems Workshops, pp. 137–140 (2011). doi:10.1109/SASOW.2011.26

Nikishin, A.: Malicious software–past, present and future. Inf. Secur. Tech. Rep. **9**(2), 6–18 (2004)

Odei Danso, S.: An exploration of classification prediction techniques in data mining: the insurance domain. Master Degree Thesis, Bournmouth University (2006)

Pollitt, M.M.: "Cyberterrorism — fact or fancy?". Comput. Fraud Secur. **1998**(2), 8–10 (1998)

Savov, V.: Sony Pictures hacked: the full story (WWW Document). The Verge (2014). http://www.theverge.com/2014/12/8/7352581/sony-pictures-hacked-storystream. Accessed 6 April 15

Schreiber-Ehle, S., Koch, W.: The JDL model of data fusion applied to cyber-defence—a review paper. In: 2012 Workshop on Sensor Data Fusion: Trends, Solutions, Applications (SDF), 4–6 September 2012 (2012). doi:10.1109/SDF.2012.6327919

Wu, J., Yin, L., Guo, Y.: Cyber attacks prediction model based on Bayesian network. In: 2012 IEEE 18th International Conference on Parallel and Distributed Systems, pp. 730–731 (2012). doi:10.1109/ICPADS.2012.117

Detecting Deceit – Guessing or Assessing?
Study on the Applicability of Veracity Assessment
Methods in Human Intelligence

Marko Uotinen[✉]

Department of Leadership and Military Pedagogy, National Defence University,
Helsinki, Finland
marko.uotinen@mil.fi

Abstract. Intelligence from a human source, that is falsely thought to be true, is potentially more harmful than a total lack of it. In addition to the collection the veracity assessment of the gathered information is one of the most important phases of the process. Lie detection and veracity assessment methods have been studied widely but a comprehensive analysis of these methods' applicability is lacking. Multi Criteria Analysis was conducted to compare scientifically valid lie detection and veracity assessment methods in terms of accuracy, ease of use, time requirements, need for special equipment and unobtrusiveness. Results of the analysis showed that Studied Features of Discourse and Nonverbal Communication gained the highest ranking. They were assessed to be the easiest and fastest to apply, and to have required temporal and contextual sensitivity. Plausibility and Inner Logic, MACE and CBCA were also found to be useful, but with some limitations.

Keywords: Lie detection · Veracity assessment · Applicability · Human intelligence

1 Introduction

"The use of the CIA's enhanced interrogation techniques was not an effective means of obtaining accurate information or gaining detainee cooperation [...]. While being subjected to CIA's enhanced interrogation techniques and afterwards, multiple CIA detainees fabricated information, resulting in faulty intelligence" [1].

A professionally operating intelligence community is expected to produce reliable intelligence that is based on true facts. In many cases the gathered background information and other supporting data may be incomplete and the actual intelligence is based on deduction and assessments. The intelligence that is based on false facts or biased observations is misleading and can be more harmful than a total lack of it [2]. Today, in the 21st century, plenty of different collection methods and intelligence disciplines are available [3]. Some of them are more prone to the source's deliberate manipulation than others and thus offer better chances for deception. The recognition of erroneous

© Springer International Publishing Switzerland 2015
H. Jahankhani et al. (Eds.): ICGS3 2015, CCIS 534, pp. 35–49, 2015.
DOI: 10.1007/978-3-319-23276-8_4

facts, distorted observations and biased assessments are critical steps towards more reliable and reality based intelligence. Still it must be recognized that 100 % accuracy might never be achieved.

When defining the value of the intelligence from a human source, in this case accuracy and usability it is essential to assess the truthfulness of the source itself and the veracity of the information obtained from him or her. Collected intelligence can be incomplete or misleading for various reasons that are not only related to the human source's deception. A human source might possess only a limited amount of information, might recall it incompletely or the scheme could be somehow distorted. These limitations are naturally occurring due to the nature of memory, recollection processes, high level of stress or overload of cognitive processes [4, 5]. The interviewer is also a possible source of error. Correct observations can lead to incorrect interpretations if the interviewer's training is insufficient and if the information assessment methods are based on beliefs rather than knowledge [5, 6]. Interviewer's pre assumptions, coercive methods and manipulation can lead to either totally false statement or true statement which veracity cannot be correctly assessed [7].

Sometimes interviewing and interrogation techniques, lie detection techniques and veracity assessment methods are confused to be synonyms or are thought to serve the same purpose. That is not the case, though closer examination has revealed that in some cases they are overlapping. There have also been multiple efforts to create a Swiss Knife types of techniques that combine all of the above mentioned areas into one. In a way these efforts reflect the need to diminish the ever rising working load that is inherent to human intelligence collection and related veracity assessment. Despite the efforts, one such overly efficient and accurate method has not been developed yet.

A lot of scientific studies have been conducted to address the challenges that are related to different interviewing and interrogation techniques and veracity assessment methods. Based on their validity and usability in different information collection situations they are not seen as equal. Some of them are more valid and reliable than others and some of them are more prone to errors which derive from the interviewer's lack of skills [6]. The level of required expertise and other supporting technical equipment also varies depending on the method and situation [8].

Although accuracy and reliability of different veracity assessment methods have been studied broadly, a thorough analysis of these methods' applicability is lacking. The aim of this study was to examine different methods for assessing the veracity of the information obtained from a human source and to analyze these methods in terms of applicability in the context of the intelligence interview.

1.1 Research Problem

A few problems are related to the discussion of the different veracity assessment methods. There is a conventional belief that an almighty, almost 100 % accurate, methods to detect lies exists. It is also believed that these methods can be applied rapidly during any social encounter. A layperson often uses those methods that are easiest to adopt and most convenient to reach. Nowadays very popular television series such as "Lie to Me" and "The Mentalist" give an easy access to the secrets of lie detection. Both of these television series are in many respects professionally made and are mostly based on actual behavioral science. However in order to create good entertainment for the audience methods are sometimes presented as quick wins with inadequate background information.

From the scientific point of view popular approaches are often over simplified. Cutting the edges straight make methods easier to apply but in the end oversimplification can start to work against the original goal – getting information that is based on true facts.

The main research question was: *What is the applicability of veracity assessment methods, which are reliable and are based on scientific proof, in terms of the following criteria: Accuracy, i.e. probability of detecting deception successfully, Ease of Use, to apply the method correctly, Time Required to apply the method reliably, The Need for Special Equipment and Unobtrusiveness of the method?*

In order to get the answer for the main research question, the following supporting research questions were first answered: What kinds of interviewing and interrogation techniques exist and how they could be used in the intelligence interview context, what kinds of veracity assessment methods exist that are reliable and are based on scientific proof and what kind of uncertainty and other limitations are included in these methods?

1.2 Scope, Context and Exclusions

In this study the information collection was examined within the frame of intelligence interview. Intelligence interview as a term was chosen because emphasis was put on the non-coercive methods. Although officially interrogation in both law enforcement and intelligence refers to something that essentially is a dialog between two persons, the term interrogation carries a slightly coercive connotation. Events in the history, questionable accusatory or guilt-presumptive interrogation methods in law enforcement and enhanced interrogation methods used in Iraq and Afghanistan are perhaps the main reasons for that [9].

The research problem was approached from the social interaction's point of view. The interviewer can be supported or accompanied by other persons but in the context of this study they were thought not to interfere with the interview. This means that successful interviewer is forced to multitask constantly in order to lead the conversation, listen to the interviewee, monitor interviewee's reactions, control own behavior and plan ahead the interview based on the intelligence requirements and interviewee's feedback. Different detailed scenarios, where intelligence interviews could take place, were excluded. Emphasis was on the methods, their logic of operation and especially on the analysis of their applicability. The results and findings of this study may be applied to different kind of situations but that consideration is left for the reader or the future studies.

Situations, where interviewees are antagonistic, mute or otherwise uncommunicative, were excluded. Persuasion and other methods of influence that could be used to enhance communication between the interviewer and interviewee were also excluded.

Since this study was about detecting deception it was fair to assume that interviewees are not totally honest in their statements. The motives behind lying were not discussed.

It was recognized that there are multiple reasons for interviewees not to tell the truth or make their version of the truth look as nice as possible [5]. However it is worth mentioning that some motives behind lying include higher stakes and stronger emotions than others and that way may have a more noticeable effect on the interviewee's communication [10]. It must also be emphasized that some people are comfortable with lying and show very little traditional signs of deceit [11].

2 Method

2.1 Meta-analysis

In the beginning of this study a meta-analysis was conducted to build understanding of the existing interviewing, interrogation, veracity assessment and lie detection methods. The focus of the literature search was in scientific papers that covered these topics. Google scholar web search and Science Direct online database searches were used for the initial document collection. It was assessed that these two major date bases cover the most part of published scientific articles and studies.

After the search phase a meta-analysis of the gathered studies and other papers was conducted. The content of the document about a certain method was analyzed in order to find out the scientific principles and the logic of operation. Reliability and validity of the results were also assessed. Finally the results from all of the papers concerning a certain method were compared with each other and conclusions from the synthesis were drawn. At this stage a general understanding of the methods that were available for further analysis was starting to develop.

From this point on the documentation was started by describing, analyzing and discussing the questioning techniques and veracity assessment methods in detail. The aim of this phase was to create an overall view of the questioning techniques and veracity assessment methods in order to answer supporting research questions. The main goal was to present the theoretical background in required detail so that the reader would have an easy access to all relevant information that was needed before and during the analysis of the methods' applicability.

2.2 Multi Criteria Analysis

Multi Criteria Analysis (MCA), utilizing Analytic Hierarchy Process (AHP), was used to assess different interviewing and interrogation techniques and veracity assessment methods. Although the emphasis of the preliminary analysis was in qualitative assessment, MCA was used to create a second opinion.

To rate the Interviewing and Interrogation Techniques the following criteria were used: A preferred technique should (1) produce longer and narrative answers, (2) support accurate memory retrieval, (3) challenge inconsistencies in a constructive manner and (4) should not promote leading or suggestion.

MCA regarding the applicability of veracity assessment methods was conducted in two phases. The first round of applicability analysis was based on the information provided by the scientific studies and other papers. During this preliminary analysis the traits of the studied veracity assessment methods were described and documented in written form to support quantitative assessment that was done with a three-point scale. The question regarding the preliminary analysis was: Does the method present limitations in this field of criterion?

The selected applicability criteria were:

- Accuracy: Does the method work and is it reliable?
- Ease of Use: Is it likely that the method is used incorrectly or the outputs are misinterpreted?
- Time Required: How time consuming is the method?
- No Need for Special Equipment: Can the method be applied only by using special equipment?
- Unobtrusiveness: Can the method be applied covertly?

The following scale was used for preliminary analysis: 1 "Presents noticeable limitations", 2 "Presents some limitations" and 3 "Presents no significant limitations".

The result of the preliminary analysis was a list of veracity assessment methods that were carried on to the second round of analysis. At this point veracity assessment methods that had evident limitation in their scientific background, in terms of "Accuracy", were excluded.

The actual applicability analysis was conducted using an AHP comparison table with relative weighting [12]. Every veracity assessment method was rated in terms of each five applicability criteria listed above. The rating was a pairwise comparison answering the question: "Which one of these compared methods is preferred over the other one in terms of current criteria?" In addition to choosing the preferred one a relative weight or importance of the choice was given with a nine-point scale, one meaning equal importance and nine meaning extreme importance in favor of the chosen one. After completing the comparison of the veracity assessed methods, in terms of all of the five criteria, a total sum of applicability was calculated.

The aim of the above described comparison was not to highlight the ultimately best alternative but to create a relative order of the alternatives in terms of the used criteria. In the scope of this study the result of the comparison would be the assessed applicability of the veracity assessment methods in relation to the others.

3 Results

3.1 Interrogation and Interviewing Techniques in Information Collection

The intelligence interview or interrogation is essentially a controlled dialog where the interviewer asks questions and the interviewee answers them. Prerequisite for the information collection is that the interviewee is willing to cooperate and gives relevant answers. The answers can only be as relevant as the questions are. It is reasonable to assume that in some cases the interviewee does not exactly anticipate what kind of matters the interviewer is exactly interested in. It is relevant what questions are asked and how they are delivered.

Closed questions offer an opportunity to give very short answers and open-ended questions potentially promote longer answers. It has been noted that leading and suggestive questions can produce false or misleading recollection of information [5]. From the information gathering point of view leading or suggestive questions are not preferred.

It becomes more difficult to assess the veracity of the given information if there is only a little of it. Common to all veracity assessment methods is that they are based on observations. Observations become statistically more reliable when their number increases. Even the application of the more advanced technical methods requires two-way communication to take place. It has been suggested that such questioning technique that produce longer answers should be preferred. These techniques potentially produce more information and also more opportunities for verbal cues of deception to occur [11].

Interviewee's memory plays an important role in this kind of information gathering setup. Human memory does not work like a camera that records and stores every observed event as it originally occurred [4]. Observations are distorted, human brain stores them incompletely, memories decay over time and memorized events or details could get corrupted during the retrieval process [5]. Interviewing technique that makes memory retrieval processes easier and produces undistorted recollections of past events or other details should thus be preferred.

Among others, one way of resisting the interrogation or intelligence interview is "not remembering" [5]. As mentioned above poor memory is not a definite sign of deceit. To make a difference between these two possibilities is not a simple task. An effective questioning technique should also take this factor into account. Questioning technique should challenge the interviewee in a constructive manner if interviewee's statement indicates inconsistency, is not plausible or is in contradiction with the known facts. Emphasis is in the constructiveness to avoid possible suggestion, diminished willingness to talk and excessively increased stress that could handicap memory.

To conclude, questioning techniques that are: "not leading or suggestive", "produce longer and narrative answers", "support accurate memory retrieval" and "challenge inconsistencies in a constructive manner" should be preferred.

The following interrogation and interviewing methods were assessed against the above mentioned four criteria: Direct Questions and Repeated Questioning, Accusatorial Questioning, Kinesic Interview and Interrogation, Elicitation, Information-gathering Questioning, Cognitive Interview, Strategic Use of Evidence and Polygraph [5, 7, 9, 11, 13–17].

It was assessed important to include Accusatorial Questioning technique and Polygraph in the analysis because they are widely used in North-American law enforcement and publicly known through the entertainment industry.

3.2   Ranking of Interviewing and Interrogation Techniques

The AHP comparison showed that all of the information gathering oriented methods were on the top of the ranking. This result was more or less expected on the basis of the ranking criteria. When calculated weights were taken into consideration a clear top three was highlighted. Cognitive Interview, Elicitation and Information-gathering Questioning all promote values that improve the collection in terms of the quantity and quality of the information. This result should not be interpreted in a way that Direct Questioning is usable. It is the most straightforward method of the top four and perhaps the easiest to apply. Its usability can be improved when potential confirmatory biases from the control and repeated questions are identified and good balance between goal orientation and information collection is found (Fig. 1).

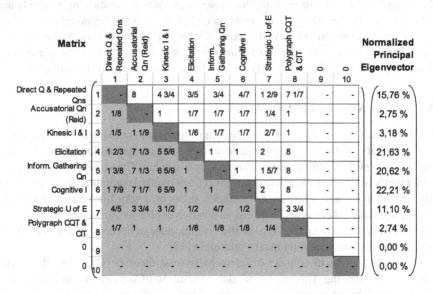

Fig. 1. Ranking of interview and interrogation techniques based on AHP

According to this analysis Cognitive Interview is the most recommended questioning method with a small marginal compared to the two others in top three. Information-gathering Questioning and Elicitation are potentially less suggestive than Cognitive Interview but on the other hand they lack CI's special methods for enhanced memory retrieval. Elicitation benefits from the concealment of the actual area of interest but at the same time the focus shifts towards irrelevant topics. It is fair to conclude that all of the top three methods are usable and serve their purpose. Which method to choose is more about the specific needs of the situation than method's absolute goodness. In some cases a combination of the three could be the most beneficial.

For the purpose of securing a confession or challenging the source for being deceptive the Strategic Use of Evidence shows the most potential. The foundation of this technique is based on the information superiority and it is used to achieve the goal step by step instead of rushing to the confession with heavy mental pressure. Due to the lesser amount of mental coercion and psychological trickery SUE is assessed to be more diagnostic and to produce less false confessions compared to Reid Technique or Polygraph. Current results strongly reflect the ranking criteria. If the criteria had been for example the likelihood of securing a true confession, the rating would obviously have been very different. However in the context of this study the information collection point of view is the most relevant.

The analysis of the interrogation and interview techniques highlight their difference not only from the information collection's point of view but also from the veracity assessment's point of view. Polygraph test is a lie detection test during which questioning is used to evoke physiological responses that indicate deception. Strategic Use of Evidence is based on an assumption that the content of the truth tellers' statement differ from the liars'. Guilt-presumption based accusatorial questioning methods are used to secure a confession with moderate mental pressure, and after initial questioning they pay very little attention to actual content of the statement or the veracity assessment. Whatever the embedded veracity assessment or lie detection method in the questioning technique is, it must be based on a theory that has got a solid scientific foundation.

3.3   Veracity Assessment Methods

Demeanor based credibility assessment, which is often thought to have a direct connection the veracity of the sender, is prone to sender's deliberate manipulation and has a very weak scientific background with low diagnostic value. The same limitations apply to other methods that rely exclusively on subject's nonverbal communication. Behavior Symptom Analysis, and other similar methods, relies on a very simple and short chain of deduction where there is no room for alternative explanations: Simply stated nervousness, avoidance, uncooperativeness and hesitation mean deception, and in criminal investigation context deception means guiltiness [18].

Despite the efforts to connect different behavioral theories (Orienting Response, Preliminary Processing Theory, Emotional Arousal and Cognitive Load hypothesis) with demeanor based methods the scientific proof and diagnostic value is still low. However real life and laboratory studies have found reduced hand/finger movement to be connected to lying. Increased amount of blinking and decreased amount of illustrating hand gestures are additional but potentially less reliable cues. On the other hand gaze aversion, self-adapting gestures, smiling and increased leg movement have not been found to be reliable signs of deception [6, 16, 19–21].

Evidence based sender credibility assessment offers a systematic way to analyze items of information provided by a human source. Method for Assessing Credibility of Evidence (MACE) recognized the negative effects of observatory biases and demeanor based credibility assessment and the emphasis is in an analytic approach to the source's competence and credibility. The competence evaluation focuses on the access, understanding or expertise, observatory capabilities, motivations and cooperation. The evaluation of credibility, which consists of veracity, objectivity and observational sensitivity under the conditions of observation, is based on seven categories: internal consistency of the source, support from other sources, source's motives to alter the facts, intentional external manipulation of the source, testimonial value of sensory information, ability to remember accurately and observations about source's nonverbal communication. The evaluation scale is set in a way that it acknowledges the lack of evidence as an approvable alternative. This method's strength is that it fosters objectivity, comprehensive evaluation and the use of alternative sources to confirm the veracity. The lie detection part in MACE is based on probabilities, plausibility, logic and multiple sources. The emphasis is in the content of the message not how it was delivered. Although no comprehensive results from field or laboratory studies were presented to back this method's claimed effectiveness it is included in further analysis because its scientific background comes from Baconian and Bayesian probability methods [2].

Any event that a statement describes must obey the laws of physics. Facts regarding the course of events, related people, surroundings and timeline must be able to exist in real world [13]. So it is fair to assume that logical inconsistencies or contradictions with the laws of physics indicate that there is something wrong with statement. Lying or a fabrication of a story could be a reason for that. There are also other explanations. Misunderstanding the question or the answer, errors in communication or negligent taking of notes can distort the statement and make it unbelievable. It is essential to first note the shortcomings in plausibility and logic, and then to find out what causes them. If no other explanation exists the probable cause is then deception. Goodness of this method relies on the disciplined application of deduction and bias free search for alternative explanations. When applied correctly and with good scientific working ethics this kind of deductive method could be reliable. The threat is that lying can become the only possible explanation for all inconsistencies and therefore too hasty judgments are done about source's veracity.

The content of the speech has been found to vary in relation to its veracity. Changes in the content can be identified within words, phrases, sentence structures and previously mentioned plausibility or logical consistency. In addition to that, according to Undeutsch's hypothesis (1967), the representation of self-experienced memories differs from the fabricated one in its verbal quality and content [22]. Statement Validity Assessment (SVA) offers a broader concept according which witness's testimonial credibility is assessed. In the core of the SVA is Criteria-Based Content Analysis (CBCA). To assess source's veracity CBCA's 18 evaluation criteria are applied to the transcription of the interview. The presence of a criterion is in favor of the statement's veracity [23].

It has been noted that some of the CBCA's criteria are more effective in their discriminating power. Studies show that in different scenarios "Unstructured Production", "Quantity of Details", "Contextual Embedding" and "Reproduction of Conversations" were found to be the most effective. All of the statements were also judged to be internally consistent and logical regardless of their veracity [20, 22, 23]. A true statement is expected to include the above mentioned elements along with Reality Monitoring (RM) related affective and perceptual information like visual, auditory, spatial and temporal details [19]. One major restriction with the CBCA and RM is that the statement is assessed as a whole. Instead of dividing the statement in different topics, themes, characters, paragraphs and items the whole statement is subjected to the overall analysis regarding the criteria. Although CBCA's validity in discriminating truthful and deceptive statements has been proven, it could be argued to what extent CBCA would be successful in identifying lies within otherwise truthful statement. In this kind of scenario CBCA's temporal diagnostic value could be questionable.

Discourse analysis in communication studies how people talk with each other, how they present themselves and persuade other people. The goal is to find out why speakers choose a certain way of talking, what purposes it might serve. According to theory personal motivations and goals reflect directly to conversational choices [24]. In the intelligence interview context, deeper thoughts, valuations, motives and speaker's position can be assessed through the discourse analysis. Changes in the speech can be identified, stored systematically and connected to the content. A successful analysis requires detailed and disciplined transcription of the conversation. Transcription and the actual analysis is a time consuming job that requires trained and skillful professionals.

Multifactor Model suggests that changes in speaker's vocal features could be explained by Arousal Theory, Cognitive Theory or Attempted Control Theory. Heightened stress, emotional arousal and cognitive load should increase the speaking rate and the amount of hesitation and errors. On the other hand hyperarticulation as a result of increased control over communication should decrease the amount of these signs [25].

In lie detection research indicators like increased pauses, increased latency periods, "ah" speech disturbances and slower speech rate have been found to have a reliable connection with lying [19, 21]. Potentially the most beneficial aspect of discourse analysis compared to the content analysis is that according to the theory vocal indicators appear almost simultaneously with the deceptive communication. This significantly would increase its diagnostic value over content analysis. It must be noted that most of the above mentioned cues are explained by different aspects of Multifactor Model. The judgment of the source being deceptive is based on deduction that situation related stress, arousal, cognitive load or self-control means lying. When applied with scientific discipline this kind of deductive method could be effective in identifying the parts of the statement where sender experiences unusual discomfort or is forced to think harder than usual. The threat is that lying can become the only possible explanation for observed deviant behavior and therefore a false judgment about source's veracity is made.

The polygraph and most of the other advanced technical methods of deception detection are used to enhance human's ability to detect different physiological signs of deception. These machines are undeniably effective in identifying and recording different parameters that are potentially caused by stress, anxiety, cognitive load or other psycho-physiological factors. They require the use of sophisticated and complex technical equipment which need special operating personnel with extensive professional experience [8, 11, 16, 25]. Despite their sensitivity to detect and measure different physiological artifacts these machines and protocols are only as reliable and valid as the underlying scientific proof that connects observed physiological phenomena to lying. Most of them can be classified as modern day lie detectors. Like with the polygraph, their highest value could be during the last stages of collection when the source's veracity regarding very specific topics is checked. It must be emphasized that they are not exceptionally good in promoting information gathering during an intelligence interview.

The biggest drawback of the polygraph test [8, 16, 17, 26], and possibly other lie detection tests with similar methodological background, is the comparative high rate of false assessments. Statistically one out of four or five sources would receive a false assessment of being deceptive (false positive) or truthful (false negative) on the contrary of their real status. It could be argued to what extent this becomes a problem. In the intelligence gathering context the source is always initially considered unreliable until proven otherwise. False negatives would enable one fourth or fifth of the liars to continue feeding lies and fabricated stories as their status is confirmed "reliable". Over time a "reliable" deceptive source would also start to decay the value of other intelligence that was collected from sincere sources. In return false positives would result in the rejection of one fourth or fifth of the truthful sources. In this context the effect of false positive is less concerning as it decreases the amount of potentially reliable information. From this point of view a false negative would be more harmful because deceptive source could earn extra credit over the other ones who perhaps did not go through the lie detection test. If the polygraph was used, the biggest threat would be a total reliance on the results and thus the locking of a source's status permanently as a liar or truth teller.

To conclude, veracity assessment methods that did not have evident doubts about their scientific background were carried to the applicability analysis. As a result gaze aversion, self-adapting gestures, smiling and increased leg movement as nonverbal signs of deception and Demeanor Based Credibility as an overall veracity assessment method were excluded.

3.4 Applicability of the Veracity Assessment Methods

Overall applicability assessment, which was based on five selected criteria, produced a ranking list presented in Fig. 2. Additional sensitivity analysis was conducted by giving high weight to one criterion that was described in a simple scenario. Weighting of the "Time Required" only accented the initial result. Weighting of the "No Need for Special Equipment" did not add any information to the initial analysis and returned the initial order with tighter margins.

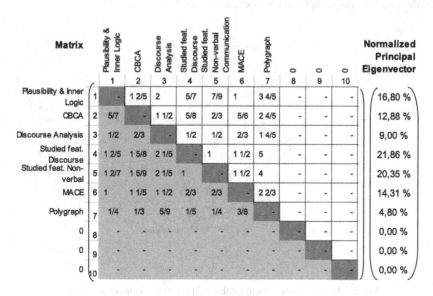

Fig. 2. Relative applicability of analyzed veracity assessment methods

Studied features of Discourse and studied features of Nonverbal Behavior share the first place as the most applicable veracity assessment method. The second place is also shared. Plausibility and Inner Logic of the statement, Method for Assessing Credibility of Evidence (MACE) and Criteria Based Content Analysis (CBCA) do not have any critical deficits but are assessed to have some limitations compared to the most applicable ones. Discourse Analysis and the Polygraph Test were assessed to be the least applicable.

Common to Plausibility and Inner Logic of the statement, studied features of Discourse and studied features of Nonverbal Behavior is that they can be applied during or right after the collection by the interviewer or other supporting personnel. A successful application evidently requires training and personal abilities for multitasking if the assessment is done alone by the interviewer. Available supporting personnel can be used simultaneously with the collection if access to audial and visual information is established. In addition audio-video recordings can also be used for post analysis.

Recording of the statement, at least audio, and transcription is imperative for the application of Criteria Based Content Analysis (CBCA). It is also assessed that reliable and valid application of Method for Assessing Credibility of Evidence (MACE) requires the recording of the statement and transcription.

The most significant limitation of Discourse Analysis is its labor intensiveness. A successfully application requires a full transcription of statement, both content and discourse, and highly trained personnel to do it. Polygraph was not particularly successful in the light of any criteria. In addition to its possible weaknesses regarding the unquestionable reliance on its result, especially false negatives, another drawback is that it must be applied as a secondary means of veracity assessment. The Polygraph Test must be preceded by traditional interrogation and preliminary veracity assessment until the need for polygraph becomes evident (Fig. 3).

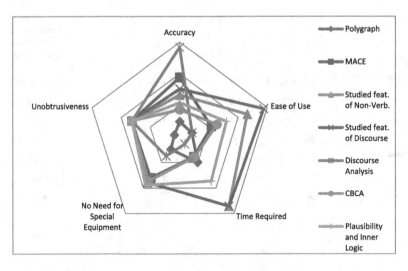

Fig. 3. Veracity assessment methods in relation to the used criteria

4 Discussion

Normally people base their opinions on their own observations, experiences or on the opinions of trusted people. Establishing a scientifically sound view of a phenomenon requires extra effort to avoid presumptions, biases and false believes of everyday thinking. This same rule seems to apply in lie detection and veracity assessment. A vast majority of people have adopted their views about lie detection from self-observed behavior, mass media, social networks or own personal behavior [27]. Not surprisingly most of the adopted cues to deception are the ones that do not have scientific support for being reliable signs of deception [27]. The need for continuous research that cumulates scientific understanding in the field of lie detection and veracity assessment could not have been highlighted better.

The findings of this study do not mean that the most applicable methods perform the best in every situation and for all purposes. The results do not either suggest that the least applicable methods are useless. All of the above mentioned seven veracity assessment methods have a scientific foundation and some of them have extensive amount of scientific studies to support that. The aim of the study was to highlight their pros and cons from the applicability's point of view.

Is the overall veracity assessment of the source, or the delivered content, the correct direction to head for in the future studies? In the intelligence interview, or some other human source intelligence gathering context it is not perhaps relevant to study whether the source is totally honest or not. Partial dishonesty should be the starting point for the veracity assessment.

From this point of view it is essential to assess which parts of the statement can be considered reliable and which parts of the statement are doubtful. Used veracity assessment methods should produce insight whether the source tries to control the delivery of content or personal behavior, leaves facts untold, uses avoidance strategies, embeds unrelated true facts, ads fabricated pieces of information, speculates, remembers facts incorrectly, tells what he/she really knows or presents a well prepared cover story with no connection to true events.

Since most of the lie detection studies are concentrated around the last scenario, where roughly half of the assessed people are liars and presents a well prepared cover story and the other half is totally truthful, it is proposed that in the future studies lie detection and veracity assessment methods are tested against partially truthful human sources.

References

1. Senate Select Committee on Intelligence: Committee Study of the Central Intelligence Agency's Detention and Interrogation Program, Findings and Conclusions. United States Senate, United States of America (2014)
2. Schum, D.A., Morris, J.R.: Assessing the competence and credibility of human sources of intelligence evidence: contributions from law and probability. Law Probab. Risk **6**, 247–274 (2007)
3. Headquarters Departments of the Army. Field Manual 2–0, Intelligence, Washington (2010)
4. Borum, R.: Approaching truth: behavioral science lessons on educing information from human sources. In: Fein, R.A., Lehner, P., Vossekuil, B. (eds.) Educing Information: Interrogation: Science and Art - Foundations for the Future, pp. 17–44. Intelligence Science Board, NDIC Press, Washington DC (2006)

5. Fein, R.A. (ed.): Intelligence interviewing, teaching papers and case studies. In: A Report from the Study on Educing Information. Intelligence Science Board, National Defence Intelligence College, Washington DC (2009)
6. Hart, C.L., Fillmore, D.G., Griffith, J.D.: Indirect detection of deception: looking for change. Curr. Res. Soc. Psychol. **9**, 134–142 (2009)
7. Neuman, A., Salinas-Serrano, D.: Custodial interrogations: what we know, what we do, and what we can learn from law enforcement experiences. In: Fein, R.A., Lehner, P., Vossekuil, B. (eds.) Educing Information: Interrogation: Science and Art - Foundations for the Future, pp. 141–234. Intelligence Science Board, NDIC Press, Washington DC (2006)
8. Heckman, K.E., Happel, M.D.: Mechanical detection of deception: a short review. In: Fein, R.A., Lehner, P., Vossekuil, B. (eds.) Educing Information: Interrogation: Science and Art - Foundations for the Future, pp. 63–94. Intelligence Science Board, NDIC Press, Washington DC (2006)
9. Meissner, C.A., Redlich, A.D., Bhatt, S., Brandon, S.: Interview and interrogation methods and their effects on true and false confessions. The Campbell Collaboration, Norway (2010)
10. Frank, M.G., Svetieva, E.: Lies worth catching involve both emotion and cognition. J. Appl. Res. Mem. Cogn. **1**, 131–133 (2012)
11. Vrij, A., Granhag, P.A.: Eliciting cues to deception and truth: what matters are the questions asked. J. Appl. Res. Mem. Cogn. **1**, 110–117 (2012)
12. Goepel, K.D.: BPMSG AHP Excel Template with multiple Inputs. Business Performance Management Singapore, Singapore (2012). http://bpmsg.com/new-ahp-excel-template-with-multiple-inputs/
13. Headquarters Departments of the Army. Field Manual 2–22.3, Human Intelligence Collector Operations, Washington (2006)
14. Memon, A., Higham, P.A.: A review of the cognitive interview. Psychol. Crime Law **5**(1–2), 177–196 (1999)
15. Memon, A., Meissner, C.A., Fraser J.: The Cognitive Interview: a meta-analytic review and study space analysis of the past 25 years. Department of Psychology, Royal Holloway College, University of London (2010)
16. Palmatier, J.J., Rovner, L.: Credibility assessment: Preliminary Process Theory, the polygraph process, and construct validity. Int. J. Psychophysiol. **95**, 3–13 (2015)
17. Iacono, W.G.: Accuracy of polygraph techniques: problems using confessions to determine ground truth. Psychol. Behav. **95**, 24–26 (2008)
18. Hirsch, A.: Going to the source: the "New" Reid method and false confessions. Ohio State J. Crim. Law **11**(2), 803–826 (2014)
19. Vrij, A., Edward, K., Roberts, K.P., Bull, R.: Detecting deceit via analysis of verbal and nonverbal behavior. J. Behav. **4**, 239–263 (2000)
20. Vrij, A., Evans, H., Akehurst, L., Mann, S.: Rapid judgements in assessing verbal and nonverbal cues: their potential for deception researchers and lie detection. Appl. Cognit. Psychol. **18**, 283–296 (2004)
21. Vrij, A., Mann, S.A., Fisher, R.P., Leal, S., Milne, R., Bull, R.: Increasing cognitive load to facilitate lie detection: the benefit of recalling events in reverse order. Law Hum Behav. **3**, 253–265 (2008)
22. Gödert, H.W., Gamer, M., Rill, H.-G., Vossel, G.: Statement validity assessment: inter-rater reliability of criteria-based content analysis in the mock-crime paradigm. Legal Criminol. Psychol. **10**, 225–245 (2005)
23. Blandón-Gitlin, I., Pezdek, K., Lindsay, D.S., Hagen, L.: Criteria-based content analysis of true and suggested accounts of events. Appl. Cognit. Psychol. **23**, 901–907 (2009)

24. Tracy, K.: Discourse analysis in communication. In: Schiffrin, D., Tannen, D., Hamilton, H.E. (eds.) The Handbook of Discourse Analysis, pp. 725–749. Blackwell Publisher Ltd., Oxford (2001)
25. Kirchhübel, C., Howard, D.M.: Detecting suspicious behaviour using speech: acoustic correlates of deceptive speech – an exploratory investigation. Appl. Ergon. **44**, 694–702 (2013)
26. Ford, E.B.: Lie detection: historical, neuropsychiatric and legal dimensions. Int. J. Law Psychiatry **29**, 159–177 (2006)
27. Hurley, C.M., Griffin, D.J., Stefanone, M.A.: Who told you that? uncovering the source of believed cues to deception. Int. J. Psychol. Stud. **1**, 19–32 (2014)

Human Factors of Social Engineering Attacks (SEAs) in Hybrid Cloud Environment: Threats and Risks

Reza Alavi[1]([⊠]), Shareeful Islam[1], and Haris Mouratidis[2]

[1] University of East London, London, UK
{reza,shareeful}@uel.ac.uk
[2] University of Brighton, Brighton, UK
H.Mouratidis@brighton.ac.uk

Abstract. Conventional patterns of the ways information systems run are rapidly evolving. Cloud computing undisputedly has influenced profoundly in this direction by providing many benefits such as accessibility and availability of resources to organisations. But the economical advantage and the cost impacts are far more attractive to organisations than anything else when it comes to cloud computing. This convenient and attractiveness comes with new phases of security and risk challenges for both cloud providers and clients which requires investment for managing and mitigating them. The challenges get more complicated as the service itself passes geographical and national boundaries which create a completely new paradigm for security, risk, privacy, and more importantly cost implications. Social Engineering Attacks (SEAs) are example of those risks that are very attractive way for attackers for accessing classified data. There are certain constraints for employees when they use LAN. These limitations reduced greatly by the introduction of Cloud and off-site services. This allows attackers to use any compromised passwords from any web-connected device. This paper discusses main issues in migrating to a cloud environment by organisations regarding the human factors of SEAs threats and risks related concepts. The approach provides a set of recommendations for appropriate control actions to mitigate related risks.

Keywords: Social Engineering Attacks (SEAs) · Human factors · Risks · Threats · Hybrid cloud · Threat assessment

1 Introduction and Related Work

Nowadays the cloud computing is becoming a necessity part of organisations. Simultaneously, fulfilling its security becomes a nightmare. Continuity of business is greatly depends on a secure platform of cloud system because securing organisations' information assets must be given highest priority. SEAs can compromise any steps organisations take to secure the cloud platform. This is getting more challengeable when the hybrid cloud is adopted. A hybrid cloud is a cloud-computing environment in which an organization provides and manages some resources in-house and has others provided

© Springer International Publishing Switzerland 2015
H. Jahankhani et al. (Eds.): ICGS3 2015, CCIS 534, pp. 50–56, 2015.
DOI: 10.1007/978-3-319-23276-8_5

externally [1]. Human factors are an important part of any information security system and cloud is not different from any computing system [2]. SEAs are presenting real danger to the hybrid cloud computing. There are several SEA methods such as Advanced Persistent Attack (APT), Phishing and revers social engineering which demonstrate a compromise to the integrity of a hybrid cloud system [3]. National Institute of Standards and Technology of US Department of Commerce's (NIST) cloud computing standards roadmap provided a set of guideline and recommendations to deal with privacy as a standards issue that is narrowly dealt with confidentiality as a subset of information security [4]. In which confidentiality includes preserving authorised restrictions on access and disclosure, including means for protecting personal privacy [4]. However, this is a general approach with less concentration on human factors and SEAs as one of the main issues around cloud computing.

2   A Background of Cloud Computing

Cloud computing is a model for isolating applications and information resources from the key IT infrastructure and allowing a global and timely access to those resources whilst they require very little supervision. Cloud computing model can be provided in three main different sub-models in which Applications (A), Operating System (OS) and Infrastructure (I) resources are divided between cloud operators and clients.

1. Software as a Service (SaaS): Provider owns A, OS and I
2. Platform as a Service (PaaS): Provider owns OS, I and client owns A
3. Infrastructure as a Service (IaaS): Provider owns I and client owns A and OS

NIST in its standards road map of cloud computing provided four deployment models consists of private, community, public and hybrid cloud. In this study we are interested in hybrid cloud deployment model because many organizations use this model [4]. Even those organizations adopted private cloud, the employees may use privately other sort of cloud services in which data and information moving from one to another without firms notice it.

3   Social Engineering Attacks (SEAs) and Cloud Computing: The Relationship

Social Engineering Attacks (SEAs) have been a central point of crimes in all forms and formats but their prime concern were in information security matters. These crimes have one important common issue in which to manipulate people in order to access to target whether a hard or soft system. Cloud deployment created a heaven for attackers using socially engineered techniques. Cost efficiency is one of the major drives for organisations to adopt cloud services. But organisations required analysing threats and keeping up with day-to-day security operations in regards to off-site cloud services. However, despite the best intentions the lack of in-house expertise result in security strategies fail to meet their goals and leave organisations vulnerable just as threats of SEAs become more sophisticated. Attackers have advantages such as, login from anywhere, no physical security, simple credentials, and trick a user, in the cloud environment. Therefore SEAs can be simply orchestrated by various techniques such as impersonate, using emails and a phone to get the credentials of a system. The Advanced Persistent Threat (APT) is very suitable in the cloud environment as the attacker intends to steal data by gaining access to a network, using spear fishing and staying there undetected for a long time. In this technique the attackers has no intention of causing damages but stealing data. The attacker exploits various human weaknesses such as lack of awareness and training and unauthenticated communication channels [5].

4   SEAs Cloud Taxonomy

Figure 1 demonstrates the taxonomy of SEAs in the cloud environment. An attacker socially engineered human and plan and initiate a SEA, using various methodology. Attacker is gaining system's credentials that compromises cloud services in regards to availability and privacy of data and other information assets. This will result in loss, disclose and the corruption of data. Finally, the attacker gains his/her goal/s whether financial or political.

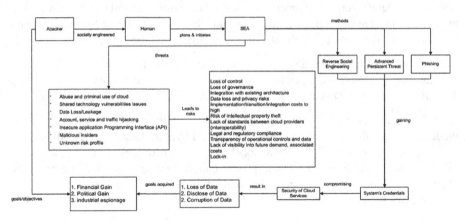

Fig. 1. Social engineering attacks taxonomy in the hybrid *cloud environment*

5   Associated Risks and the Mitigation Process

Cloud computing still involves many risks concerning security, integrity and network dependency. Extending on-sites data centre architectures to the cloud is what organisations search for to deliver additional value from hybrid cloud to increase the business agility. But they face grave risks from SEAs. The threats to assets, application performance and critical business data, creates risks such as availability, authentication and virtual exploit risks through virtualisation. Regardless of cloud delivery and deployment model, risk can be originated from the followings:

- People
- Organisation
- Cloud environment
- Cloud Provider
- Network Provider

These sources feeding the following types of risks: CIAAA (Confidentiality, Integrity, Availability, Audibility and Authenticity) in cloud environment.

5.1 Threat Assessment

In order to identify the probability and nature of risks a threat assessment should be established. The purpose of threat assessment is to provide recommendations and maximising the safeguarding of assets. Threat assessments take into account a broad range of issues. The following main threats are relevant to the cloud environment.

- Abuse and criminal use of cloud: taking advantage of many IaaSs services is quite simple. Registration and payment provide access to their services. A great number of IaaSs have limited fraud detection capabilities that allow attackers targeting cloud services by using the relatively weak authentication and identification process.
- Data Loss/Leakage: lack of protection of data leads to its compromise. Data can be either accidently or maliciously deleted and altered. Attackers may compromise data integrity by accessing the server in the Cloud. It is also possible data to suffer from damage during transition operations from or to the service provider.
- Shared technology vulnerabilities issues: cloud computing provide a wide range of powerful services for multiple clients. However, many of the clients do not necessarily belong to the same organisation. Various clients' data can result in co-residing in the dense virtualisation as they may use same CPU subsystems. Attackers may acquire unauthorised access to underlying platform, using only an isolated software mechanism despite having virtual machine manager that allows multiple operating systems to share a single CPU.
- Account, service and traffic hijacking: attackers use methods such as phishing to steal the credentials and accessing critical parts of cloud and potentially eavesdrop on transactions, falsify and/or manipulate data and in some cases re-direct customers and clients to illicit websites.
- Insecure application programming interfaces (APIs): APIs are keys used by Web and CSPs to pin down third-party applications using the services. In the absence of adequate security consideration by CSPs, attackers could access to the key and then cause a DoS or rack up fees on behalf of the target.
- Malicious insiders: security is in a greater risk from an insider if cloud services only depend on CSPs. It is important that the encryption keys are kept with clients at all time rather than being available to them at the time they would need to access to data.
- Unknown risk profile: the lack of knowledge of a CSP security protocols, procedures and policies. Clients should have a fairly good knowledge about CSPs security software, update and patch procedures, intrusion detection and alerting and overall

security design. Releasing control of data to a CSP has important security consequences. Without a comprehensive understanding of CSP's security practices, organisations may be open to hidden vulnerabilities and risks.

Whilst clients benefit from CSPs but the threats and risks are important players that resist the development of any hybrid cloud environment [3]. Based on the above threat assessment now the risks around the hybrid cloud environment can be defined.

5.2   Risks

Risks are functions of the probability of the threats that organisations are confronting. For the purpose of this study, only related threats have been defined for establishing an understanding of the risks around the role of human factors in SEAs in hybrid cloud environment. The following risks to the assets in a hybrid cloud environment can be perceived in scenario of SEA:

– Loss of control
– Loss of governance
– Integration with existing architecture
– Data loss and privacy risks
– Implementation/transition/integration costs to high
– Risk of intellectual property theft
– Lack of standards between cloud providers (interoperability)
– Legal and regulatory compliance
– Transparency of operational controls and data
– Lack of visibility into future demand, associated costs
– Lock-in

There are certain technical steps can be taken to ensure the risks are minimised in the cloud environment:

– Reviewing access control protocol
– User-limited based access
– Reviewing encryption protocol and monitoring
– Patch management agent on mobile devices
– Intelligent network protection

However, for the purpose of this study we look at the security-soft issues, dealing with human factors and the role of people. The main and major issue to deal with human factors of are training and awareness. There have been many studies around these issues but there are two main sub-factors of awareness:

– Situational Awareness (SA)
– Self-awareness

The importance of security awareness that highlighted by several researches requires a special focus in cloud environment [5, 6]. Improving people situational awareness of current types of SEAs and the critical understanding of security awareness would enhance soft approaches to the risks in cloud computing. Maceachren et al. (2011) looked at the SA in crisis management which can be extended to the analysis of role of human awareness in the process of SEAs in the cloud environment. SA can create a platform to deal with such incidents to ensure the agility of business is being served. It also assists in the process of business impact analysis (BIA) in the cloud deployment and migration.

6 Related Human Factors

One of the biggest challenges in cloud computing is people. A frequently overlooked issue in cloud computing is the human, and more specifically the manipulation of a person to compromise cloud environment. Human factors are critical areas of focus in cloud computing. Whilst the blame for an security incident cannot be attributed to a single individual but vast majority of causes of incidents in the cloud environment contributed by various human factors [9]. There are many human factors related to the compromise of a hybrid cloud service. They can be as a result of the following psychological affects as result of social engineering manipulation process:

- Personal affection
- Excessive responsibilities
- Deceptive association
- Dissemination of duties
- Moral duty
- Authority
- Personal integrity
- Consistency

They assist attackers to exploit the cloud system using various tactics such as reverse social engineering, advanced persistent threat, phishing and so on. Whatever the nature of attack, the human factors are the majority of reasons for both problem and solution phases. Therefore, the reasons behind most information security incidents as result of SEAs generally are contributed by human factors or the combination of people and technology. But the human factor will have been the most significant of.

7 Soft-Risks Mitigation Process

There are key steps require by organisations to ensure all risks related to human factors can be mitigated and addressed [8]. The key issues they need to consider include:

- To remove all inactive assigned users. They increase the attack surface of the organisation whilst have cost implications.
- To minimise a number of administrative access because they represents a real and present risk to the organisation.
- To disable ex-employees and contractors' credentials as they real threats

- To ensure employees can't bypass identity and access management controls by rebalancing the organisation's security portfolio from exclusively preventative controls to harmonised risk management based.
- To certify organisation's private files are not publicly accessible
- To control the liability and accountability of the distribution of enterprise data, especially privileged data.
- To manifest that employees do not share organisations files with their personal email accounts
- To observe files in cloud services are not orphans which created by users outside the organisations, such as terminated employees or former contractors.

8 Conclusions

The causes of SEAs in cloud such as in hybrid cloud environment are varied. IT organizations can fight back with strong identity and access management, including two-factor authentication where possible, strong password requirements, and proactive monitoring for unauthorized activity. However, human factors are paly a major role in them. This study looked at the relationship between SEAs and hybrid cloud computing as a perspective of human factors, risk and threat. It provided a set of recommendations to address the main human factors in the process of addressing SEAs in the cloud environment.

References

1. Pearson, S., Yee, G.: Privacy and Security for Cloud Computing. Springer, London (2013)
2. Alavi, R., Islam, S., Jahankhani, H., Al-Nemrat, A.: Analyzing human factors for an effective information security management system. Int. J. Secure Softw. Eng. (IJSSE) **4**, 50–75 (2013)
3. Ryan, M.D.: Cloud computing security: the scientific challenge, and a survey of solutions. J. Syst. Softw. **86**(9), 2263–2268 (2013)
4. Hogan, M., Sokol, A.: NIST cloud computing standards roadmap. In: Commerce, U.D.O. (ed.) National Institute of Standards and Technology (NIST) April 2014 (2011). http://www.nist.gov/customcf/get_pdf.cfm?pub_id=909024
5. Alavi, R., Islam, S., Mouratidis, H.: A conceptual framework to analyze human factors of information security management system (ISMS) in organizations. In: Tryfonas, T., Askoxylakis, I. (eds.) HAS 2014. LNCS, vol. 8533, pp. 297–305. Springer, Heidelberg (2014)
6. Yin, X., Yurcik, W., Treaster, M., Li, Y., Lakkaraju, K.: VisFlowConnect: netflow visualizations of link relationships for security situational awareness. In: Proceedings of the 2004 ACM Workshop on Visualization and Data Mining for Computer Security. Washington DC, USA, ACM (2004)
7. Maceachren, A.M., Jaiswal, A., Robinson, A.C., Pezanowski, S., Savelyev, A., Mitra, P., Zhang, X., BlanfordL, J.: SensePlace2: GeoTwitter analytics support for situational awareness. In: IEEE Conference on Visual Analytics Science and Technology (VAST), pp. 181–190. 23–28 Oct 2011, IEEE (2011)
8. Heiser, J., Nicolett, M.: Assessing the Security Risks of Cloud Computing, March 2014 (2008). http://www.gartner.com/id=685308
9. Lacey, D.: Managing the Human Factor in Information Security: How to win over staff and influence business managers. Wiley, New York (2011)

Digital Forensics

A Consideration of eDiscovery Technologies for Internal Investigations

Amie Taal[1]([✉]), Jenny Le[2], and James A. Sherer[3]

[1] Deutsche Bank, New York, NY, USA
amie33_uk@yahoo.co.uk
[2] Evolve Discovery, New York, USA
jle@evolvediscovery.com
[3] Counsel in the New York Office of Baker Hostetler LLP, New York, USA
jsherer@bakerlaw.com

Abstract. Internal incidents that implicate security or data privacy considerations require present-day forensic scientists and investigators to craft a narrative
that explains both "what" happened within the system during the incident, and
"why" it matters to the organization. To explain the "why," investigators are
increasingly utilizing tools outside of the traditional forensic and investigatory
practices. One such tool set is comprised of techniques used and refined in the
practice of eDiscovery. This paper examines those techniques and presents
instruction and advice on their application within forensic and investigatory
practices.

Keywords: Computer forensics · eDiscovery · IT law · Incident response

1 Introduction

Systems falter and fail. Many of those failures, especially those that implicate security
or data privacy considerations, require subsequent investigations, and present-day
failures—whether mechanical or personnel-driven—now require a heavily technology
dependent approach for a successful investigation. There is more to the investigation
than the technology, of course; in all such investigations an investigator is also tasked
with identifying the "What, How, and Why" of the incident. This identification asks
such questions as: What was the method of wrongdoing within the network? What was
the point of the incident—was it itself an attempt to cover-up some *other* wrongdoing
within the network or the environment? How might the incident affect a single or
multiple jurisdictions, data privacy issues, or raise litigation considerations? And how
does the incident and its investigation matter politically within the organization? These
questions are integral in understanding how to both prevent and preempt future incidents, and certainly factor into their mitigation. Since global organizations are retaining
larger and larger volumes of structured and unstructured data due to legislative, regulatory, and procedural requirements, investigators face increasingly complex challenges in how to analyze and answer these "What, How, and Why" issues.

More specifically, these investigations are aimed at finding out "what" happened
and "why" it happened, but perhaps even more importantly—and where there may be

© Springer International Publishing Switzerland 2015
H. Jahankhani et al. (Eds.): ICGS3 2015, CCIS 534, pp. 59–73, 2015.
DOI: 10.1007/978-3-319-23276-8_6

immediate repercussions within the organization, "why" it matters that the incident happened? This latter "why" issue can often be addressed (in part) by the data itself. Academics have called this analysis "a process of reciprocal interaction between bottom-up exposure to data on the one hand, and the top-down application of inter-pretations on the other;"[1] however, within the context of an investigation, these analyses need to occur much more quickly than traditionally required by the timeline of a litigation. In a litigation, the practice of electronic discovery (eDiscovery) seeks to find electronically stored information (ESI) that supports a conjecture, thereby estab-lishing evidence for that conjecture,[2] but the same technologies that unearth infor-mation in litigation can be equally useful in unearthing the factual underpinnings that lead to those technological or personnel failings (the "what" and "why" it happened) that are often the root cause of those failings that lead to investigations.

Here, we return to the requirements of technology for these investigations. The integration of computing and ESI at every stage of nearly every corporate process requires technology to support the definition of the "why," and eDiscovery technolo-gies have been developed with exactly that goal in mind. We surmise, therefore, that these technologies can also help investigators answer that lasting question, the question that helps determine the broader institutional impact of an incident: *why* it really matters that the incident happened. Plainly put, while the investigator needs enough of the factual underpinnings of the failure to tell the story of what happened, the inves-tigator also needs to know enough of the *context*—and, in this paper's case, enough about the *information* potentially affected—to determine why the failure does or does not matter outside of the incident's boundaries; and, if it does matter, how far that concern extends outside of the event itself. And eDiscovery technologies can help.

2   eDiscovery Practice and the Development of the Investigator's Tool Chest

For those unfamiliar, the practice of eDiscovery involves processes where electronic data is "sought, located, secured, and searched with the intent of using it as evidence in civil or criminal proceedings, or as part of an inspection ordered by a court or sanc-tioned by a government."[3] As such, eDiscovery is concerned with the entirety of the so-called 5 W's: Who, What, When, Where, and Why.[4] Further, the techniques of eDiscovery analysis aim to capture a sufficient understanding of the information contained in a dataset to "support decision-making"[5] and to answer those 5 W's.

[1] Chapin et al., *Predictive Coding, Storytelling, and God - Narrative Understanding in e-Discovery*, DESI V Workshop (Jun. 14, 2013), at 5.

[2] Oard & Webber, *Information Retrieval for E-Discovery*, Foundations and Trends in Information Retrieval, Vol. 7, Nos. 2-3 (2013), at 121.

[3] Attfield & Blandford, *Discovery-led refinement in e-discovery investigations: sensemaking, cognitive ergonomics and system design*, Artificial Intelligence and Law, 18.4, 387-412 (2010).

[4] Oard & Webber, *supra* note 2, at 121.

[5] Grossman & Cormack, *A Tour of Technology-Assisted Review*, Perspectives on Predictive Coding and Other Advanced Search and Review Technologies for the Legal Practitioner (ABA 2015).

This practice of eDiscovery has also been considered a combination of the sciences of "information retrieval (IR) and information extraction (IE),"[6] recognizing that these technologies can be employed in areas other than "discovery alone, as [they are] capable of much, much more" suggesting that predictive coding (where machine learning makes decisions about data) can also be used to identify potential risks to a company before these risk develop into litigation.[7] In fact, answers to questions asking "why" as a means of telling a story is already well within the scope of the eDiscovery world, where "the human understanding of what matters in any one case may very well rest upon how well the human reviewers apprehend the case as a narrative or a series of narratives."[8] This, of course, makes sense, as litigation and the presentation of a case to a jury or fact finder is, at heart, the development of a convincing story.

As more and more of these internal incidents provide enough considerations to raise the specter of a reasonable anticipation of litigation (RAL),[9] forensic scientists and investigators are increasingly being asked questions by traditional legal practitioners, and exchanging their own questions in return. This is an important factor in this new state of investigation, where a root-cause analysis is no longer only the purview of information technologists. Instead, attorneys and other interested parties are asking not only what happened, but what information was affected, what it means in the course of the investigation, and what it might mean if litigation follows after the fact. These questions of "why" in eDiscovery investigations, as in other kinds of investigation, spur new discoveries and "cue new human theories which then become a theme for further investigation in a process of 'discovery led refinement'"[10] This recursive system, alive and well within eDiscovery, works as follows: eliminating the wheat from the chaff allows a better focus on what is most likely to matter at the beginning of an investigation. Once some of the wheat is examined, further refinement aids the next set of examination, and so on.[11]

Within the framework of this paper, we consider the point-of-view of an organizational decision maker who must determine the steps to take based on an event occurring within the organization and the data associated with the event, and who will likely interact with attorneys and other legal professionals when preserving information related to the event, and perhaps when developing the narrative as well. We suggest that eDiscovery techniques may be incorporated into the investigative context as improvements occur, and that, as evidenced by the hope of one author, that all of "these advances, and several others, will have effects that reach far beyond e-discovery."[12]

---

[6] Graus et al., *Semantic Search in E-Discovery - An Interdisciplinary Approach*, DESI V Workshop (Jun. 14, 2013), at 1.

[7] White & Nichols, *Predictive Coding 2.0*, Westlaw Journal Computer & Internet, Vol. 32, No. 6 (Aug. 28, 2014), at 1.

[8] Chapin et al., *supra* note 1, at 2.

[9] *Zubulake v. UBS Warburg LLC*, 220 F.R.D. 212 (S.D.N.Y. 2003); *Pension Comm. of the Univ. of Montreal Pension Plan v. Banc of Am. Sec., LLC.*, 685 F. Supp. 2d. 456, 473 (S.D.N.Y. 2010).

[10] Chapin et al., *supra* note 1, at 5.

[11] Attfield & Blandford, *supra* note 3.

[12] Oard & Webber, *supra* note 2, at 217.

3   The Implications of the Strategy

The transition to active searching, including (sometimes) enterprise-wide search and the incorporation of advanced information governance techniques, has also led orga- nizations to incorporate what they have learned from eDiscovery into their approaches to investigations.[13] Some consider the initial application of eDiscovery technologies to be the practice of sensemaking[14] in that textual *corpora*[15] or environment where search is exploratory to begin because "it is not exactly clear beforehand what is sought in the eDiscovery setting."[16] Other authors consider eDiscovery to include a search "for that needle-in-the-haystack" in these big data volumes that incorporate structured and unstructured electronic data in "new and evolving forms, and identifying that com- paratively small set of documents that are relevant to the matter at hand, and from among those, finding the rare documents that really matter, that truly mean something."[17]

Investigations present unique additional challenges where datasets are typically large and disparate, and where data resides in a number of various locations and file types. Further, in an investigation—and unlike other approaches which might allow for time for a strategic look at how to manage data sets as part of a considered, well-thought-out plan—investigations (as opposed to audits, perhaps) are usually *ad hoc* and singular in nature. While there may be a strategy as to how to do investigations generally, each specific investigation is its own creature, and may draw out issues relating to different data sources and locations among other considerations.

This paper evaluates and considers different types of eDiscovery applications and approaches to determine the best tools for an investigation, and how their application, in whole or in part, might assist an investigator in developing a plan for developing a narrative and answering the "why" of why a particular incident matters. This may also include some additional assistance in the normal course of business associated with a root-cause analysis, but this is not the primary focus of this examination. This is also not the first time the use of eDiscovery tools have been considered within a different application, as prior research has included views on how to "support forensic analysts in their broad line of work."[18] However, this paper aims to survey some eDiscovery tools and their development within both the eDiscovery and investigatory spaces, and also examine how a similar and sometimes overlapping use has grown within the information governance realm.

---

[13] Scholtes, *Next-generation Deployment for Enterprise Search Tools*, KM World (Apr. 2006).

[14] Attfield & Blandford, *supra* note 3.

[15] Graus et al., *supra* note 6, at 1.

[16] *Id.*

[17] Chapin et al., *supra* note 1, at 1.

[18] Graus et al., *supra* note 6, at 1.

4 Early Case Assessment and First Steps and Considerations

In litigation, "parties must assess the strength of their position, determine their strategies, and negotiate with their opponents, including on the terms of the production itself—a stage known as 'early case assessment' (ECA)."[19] This is not unlike what happens during the early phase of an investigation. Typically, the ECA process involves "separating data into critical and non-critical groupings, and identifying and narrowing the number of actual key players and search terms . . . involv[ing] a process of searching, foldering, clustering, email threading and topic grouping."[20] This should be unsurprising, as eDiscovery began as the exercise of applying "paper methods to electronic information, amassing all data from relevant custodians and displaying it page by page on screen, or even printed out on paper."[21] This process migrated to keyword search, and onto concept searches, which may include "query expansion to clustering documents for more focused review,"[22] much of which will be covered later in this paper.

Within an investigation's ECA, the investigator should include common-sense implications of her analysis in defining the scope of the investigation: for example, if the location of the data investigated is outside a period of concern and this is evident by viewing the metadata such as the (verified) file's last modified date(s), an investigator may be able to take the same position she would have taken had she found a broken lock to a shed containing outmoded product brochures. This is also an opportunity to reinforce the concept that investigators should not, in any way, shape, or form, abandon traditional considerations associated with investigation; these may include forensic considerations, chains-of-custody, and the use of investigative tools (such as forensic software data capture and the examination of a variety of file types not normally implicated within the practice of eDiscovery).

5 Early Forensic Case Assessment

Those eDiscovery considerations that also incorporate *forensic* considerations include "a full range of auditing and analysis tools, plus tools for workflow, digital signatures, and the recovery of deleted files and lost clusters, are all very important aspects of any e-discovery software solution."[23] The importance of forensic considerations such as evidence handling procedures among others cannot be stressed enough, especially since forensic considerations form the basis of defining the scope of an investigation. But regardless of the technologies used for analysis in an investigation, the story cannot be told by data that was not captured or identified. And neither traditional search terms nor concept or predictive analytics can identify deleted data or data stored on removable media that has not been recovered or collected.

---

[19] Oard & Webber, *supra* note 2, at 212.

[20] White & Nichols, *supra* note 7, at 2.

[21] Oard & Webber, *supra* note 2, at 109.

[22] *Id.*

[23] Scholtes, *supra* note 13, at 2.

It also bears keeping in mind that there may be specific limitations associated with investigations that include time and resources that prevent the fullest application of some eDiscovery tools.[24] Because the eDiscovery toolset has its own considerations (and is imperfect in its own right), the investigator must find her comfort level for which components of this practice she incorporates into her checklist, and should continue to evaluate that mix based on the particulars of the incident. For instance, the integrity of evidence is and will always be at the forefront of an investigator's mind when planning and undertaking an investigation. While there may be an overlap between eDiscovery and existing forensic investigation tools (such as current market leaders EnCase and Forensic Toolkit (FTK)), this need not be a choice between ostensible competitors. We present that these technologies and techniques may work better in concert, and this holds true even when the manner in which investigations, collections, reviews, and analysis are carried out varies significantly according to the investigator's direction.

Even eDiscovery practitioners and commentators note specifically that "ESI provides only one part of a rich collection of sources; other potential sources include physical documents from various sources, statements and depositions from people involved, and information that is on the public record or that is otherwise available to the requesting party (e.g., from its own information systems)."[25] Further, application of certain algorithm sets may give rise to the "tank detector" problem, where a misunderstanding as to what meaning—or the why—means within a given data set, even if results seem promising at first, may give rise to a "sunny day detector" —rather than the tank detector originally ordered.[26] This problem is well-noted, where it is an acclaimed "absolute myth that you can send an algorithm over raw data and have insights pop up."[27]

6   The Mechanical Automatic

The first approach that practitioners may incorporate into their review of information may be the easy steps that eDiscovery practitioners consider as cost-limiting measures: culling of data (eliminating non-relevant data by file type, date, location, metadata, or other means); eliminating duplicates (deduplication); identifying "key" custodians and associated custodial data. Next steps may then include working on so-called near-dupe or similar document detection,[28] so that the same (or nearly similar) document need not be reviewed by a practitioner or investigator multiple times, but a judgment about the document may be spread out across all the examples of the document within a dataset or data environment.

---

[24] Graus et al., *supra* note 6, at 2.

[25] Oard & Webber, *supra* note 2, at 122.

[26] Chapin et al., *supra* note 1, at 4.

[27] Lohr, *For Big-Data Scientists, 'Janitor Work' Is Key Hurdle to Insights*, The New York Times (Aug. 17, 2014) (quoting Jeffrey Heer).

[28] Sperling et al., *Similar Document Detection and Electronic Discovery So Many Documents, So Little Time*, DESI V (Jun. 14, 2013), at 1.

This approach to finding duplicates also helps present a consistent approach to reviewing large sets of documents, where the technologies may use "redundancy and placement of language to identify relevant documents within a review set."[29] This may rely upon both the organization of the documents as well as the associated metadata; this metadata step and its use will continue throughout the process, as some authors note that there is a clear showing that, the "promise of incorporating metadata into the machine learning process in ways that more effectively tap the added layer of information intrinsic to the values in these fields and that more effectively capture the complementary perspective metadata contributes to document classification endeavors."[30] This step in the process may also use "fast and highly automated text classification using sophisticated machine learning algorithms [to liberate] users from junk email [and like files] through "spam" filtering."[31]

A further early consideration for datasets whether litigations or investigations benefit from properly identifying which types of data should be processed for review. Investigators can do this by identifying or compiling an inclusionary file list or an exclusionary list for data processing. A common exclusionary list used within the practice of eDiscovery is compiled by the National Institute of Standards and Technology (NIST). In a process known as DeNISTing, practitioners can remove files "which are 'known' system files – files that are installed as a consequence of running a certain program or operating system"[32] that a practitioner may know can be easily and properly excluded from review.

Investigators may wish to combine this type of objective DeNISTing step with their own personal development of a similar list specific to their organization in those instances where proprietary tools or operations give rise to a separate set of non-usable files. Of course, as elsewhere, the investigator should continue to incorporate her own knowledge of hidden files, and use forensic techniques to confirm that a wrongdoer has not hidden one file within the cover (or filename) of an otherwise innocuous file type.

7   A Consideration of Search Terms

The second approach that many practitioners utilize, especially those unfamiliar with technology assisted review technologies and the possibilities, is the employment of simple search terms, such as those used in the now-ubiquitous internet search window. Unlike many internet searches, practitioners typically use a combination of search terms, because a "single search term is rarely sufficient to capture substantially all relevant documents in a collection."[33] Two or more search terms may then be combined together

[29] Horrigan, *RenewData focuses on both services and software for legal e-discovery*, 451 Research (Aug. 13, 2014), at 3.

[30] Jones et al., *The Role of Metadata in Machine Learning for Technology Assisted Review*, DESI VI Workshop (Jun. 8, 2015).

[31] Paskach, *The Case for Technology Assisted Review and Statistical Sampling in Discovery*, DESI VI Workshop (Jun. 8, 2015) at 2.

[32] Xact Data, *"DeNISTing" - What It Is and Isn't*, Xact Data Discovery Newsletter (Aug. 2011).

[33] Grossman & Cormack, *supra* note 5, at 5.

with Boolean operators such as "AND," "OR," "NOT," or "AND NOT" as well as proximity operators, which would locate words within specified distances from one another.[34] This initial step of search terms is familiar to everyone using now-traditional search engines, and while this can provide valuable analysis (including capturing unique names where individuals are at the heart of a given investigation), there are a number of improvements available even within this initial step.

One such search improvement technique focuses on the use of "fuzzy" logic, which recognizes that search terms can be misspelled or spelled differently within a document. The use of fuzzy logic, which is the equivalent of placing wildcards within a term to account for differences in spelling, can often specify the degree of fuzziness within a term.[35] A technique called "stemming" is also frequently used, which recognizes that search terms can have various alternate endings (like "ed," "ing," "ly," or "ion"[36]). Search terms are familiar to investigators and eDiscovery practitioners alike, and as indicated above, are in most cases the very first line of active search efforts (as opposed to the filtering and categorization efforts also discussed).

However, one issue associated with search terms quickly arises, where the "challenge of traditional keyword formation is to identify which search words will capture the relevant documents without dragging in a bunch of extraneous ones."[37] How can an investigator do a competent and capable job of determining the vocabulary of the incident, especially in those instances of intentional obfuscation? The eDiscovery practitioners struggle with the same issue, and linguists practicing within the space refer to this problem as "polysemy, or the coexistence of many possible meanings for a word or phrase."[38]

The challenge of weeding out the false positives (where a search term exists but the document is not relevant), and accounting for the false negatives (where a search term does not exist but the document is relevant) arises when using only search terms to define a potentially useful dataset. There are, however, some relatively simple steps that can help before bringing in additional technologies. Using a thesaurus to develop synonym lists can improve search term success. Search term results can also be further analyzed across data types or sources to access their applicability. But a caution remains regarding their use; if a court subsequently evaluates keyword use, especially in those instances where their evaluation is fundamental to an investigation that terminates in litigation, considerations regarding keyword quality control and testing will be considered as well.[39]

---

[34] *Id.*, at 7.

[35] The Sedona Conference, *Best Practices Commentary on the Use of Search and. Information Retrieval Methods in E-Discovery*, 8 Sedona Conf. J. 189, 219.

[36] *Id.* at 218.

[37] Kraftsow, *Document Review Without Artificial Intelligence*, The National Law Journal (Sept. 1, 2014).

[38] *Id.*

[39] *William A. Gross Construction Associates, Inc. v. American Manufacturers Mutual Insurance Co.*, 256 F.R.D. 134, 134 (S.D.N.Y. 2009) (Reiterating the "need for careful thought, quality control, testing, and cooperation with opposing counsel in designing search terms or 'keywords' to be used to produce emails or other electronically stored information.").

Finally, the use of search terms does not need to be abandoned altogether in favor of the conceptual or predictive analytics we discuss later, and search term practices can also be improved substantially by other means. In some instances, search terms can be vetted through a process called "Key Word Expansion" which uses a conceptual analytics index so a practitioner or investigator can see other words or concepts that may also be useful in addition to the terms already known.[40] Other technologies allow practitioners an in-depth look at their search term results—without running real time searches—allowing investigators to identify false positives and generating a tree containing the terms with a listing of all wildcard and proximity search results automatically.[41] This provides investigators with the ability to quickly identify important topics, group related documents according to concepts, and further refine terms by incorporating other useful terms gathered from the search index.[42]

8   Basic Pattern Recognition and Automated Presentment

Data analysis and review in litigation has matured over time, moving from traditional linear review of each document (and a document-by-document-*by-document* process) to traditional Boolean searches, to concept searching, and grouping activities using "pattern matching, clustering, categorization, and 'find similar' capabilities" that can provide practitioners with "a 50,000-foot view of data, including groupings of 'like' documents"[43] or "visualization and social network analysis"[44] to technology assisted review (also called computer-assisted review, predictive coding, suggested coding, or automated review). This may also include such issues as "ranked retrieval, clustering, summarization, information extraction, data mining, gap analysis (e.g., to detect missing parts of e-mail threads), and visual analytics."[45]

Technologies that enable the analysis of relationships across individuals and entities may be exceptionally useful for an investigator who needs to come up to speed quickly with the data subjects of a collection, especially where a narrative is necessary to understand just what an incident represents. This type of relationship analysis technology allows an investigator to quickly identify the "who," "what" and "when" of complex email communication between custodians with simple graphic visualizations and maps.[46] The presented information may also allow an investigator to examine both "spikes" and "valleys" in communication between custodians without the need to review unnecessary data, and identify communications between known custodians and unknown parties or entities. Relationship analysis can also unearth who sent and

---

[40] *The Grossman-Cormack Glossary of Technology-Assisted Review*, Fed Courts Law Review, Vol. 7, Issue 1 (2013).

[41] Lateral Data, *Viewpoint Review and Analytics*, Xerox Whitepaper (undated).

[42] *Id.*

[43] Wood & Babineau, *Review Acceleration - Leveraging Language to Streamline e-Discovery*, Enterprise Strategy Group White Paper (Oct. 2012), at 3.

[44] Grossman & Cormack, *supra* note 5, at 2.

[45] Oard & Webber, *supra* note 2, at 122.

[46] Lateral Data, *supra* note 41.

received important documents within specific timeframes, and present a window into communication patterns of interest among various custodians.[47] Data visualization of this type provides both an easy and seamless way to understand or grasp concepts embedded in large datasets, and also quickly identifies important information that may be critical in taking the next step in a given investigation.

9   User-Involved Keyword Searching and Recursive Analysis

Language-Based Analytics (LBA),[48] in the context of technology-assisted review or predictive coding offerings, claims to provide the best of both of those worlds by combining "the technological ability to reduce and analyze datasets with the inherent human ability to comprehend language" by taking language from documents reviewed and coded by attorneys and using the redundancy and placement of language to identify relevant documents within a review set.[49] This approach focuses on unstructured data ("mostly text, but also dates, numbers, facts, and so on")[50] and may build off of an integral part of the data indexing process, where "large volume search-based classification systems often depend for efficiency on an inverted index, comparable to the index in the back of a book or a concordance"[51] and such "inverted indexes can also support ontology-based classification."[52] Tools create these indices by extracting the vocabulary of the collection, and often reduce the collection to a 25,000 root-word vocabulary (at least in English document collections).[53]

Another technology involves the use of anagram automatic keyword builders which may be used to develop keywords "into a multiple choice exercise from a 'fill-in-the-blank' exercise—taking logical expressions of an issue and helping investigators quickly build queries with synonyms based on the actual language of the case"[54] as well as their understanding of how the synonyms work in the context, and limiting them to the available words in the inverted index or concordance.[55] This approach may be qualified as a technological approach employing a rule base, itself comprised of forms "of complex Boolean queries, specifying combinations of words and their order or proximity, that indicate relevance or non-relevance, exceptions to those rules, exceptions to the exceptions, and so on, until nearly all documents in the collection are correctly classified."[56]

---

[47] Id.

[48] Horrigan, *supra* note 29.

[49] Id.

[50] Wood & Babineau, *supra* note 43, at 3.

[51] Oehrle & Johnson, *The Structure of Predictive Coding - A Guide for the Perplexed*, DESI V (Jun. 14, 2013), at 8.

[52] Id.

[53] Kraftsow, *supra* note 37, at 3.

[54] Wood & Babineau, *supra* note 43, at 6.

[55] Kraftsow, *supra* note 37, at 4.

[56] Grossman & Cormack, *supra* note 5, at 2.

Similar tools include keyword expansion, described above, where key terms can be further informed by other terms or concepts that relate to those of interest.[57] Investigators may also consider the use of "hit-highlighting,"[58,59] where once key terms are identified, they are highlighted for the reviewer to ensure that the reviewer does not miss the potential import of the document—or at least the reason why a given document was flagged for subsequent human review.

10 Technology Assisted Review (TAR) and the Rise of the (Sometimes User-Directed) Machines

TAR tools are perhaps the most novel and current category of technologies in both the context of eDiscovery and for use in investigations. These conceptual and predictive analytic technologies can provide practitioners with both a bird's eye view of large and disparate datasets common to investigations as well as offering a method of bucketing these large datasets for immediate prioritization and contextual understanding without the investigator looking at many—or in some cases, any—documents. Conceptual analytics can even be used in concert with search terms and even inform better search terms through concept searches, underscoring the continual need for the investigator to think of these tools as working together and in combination, rather than in a checklist-type fashion. And their continued and growing use is recognized in a number of related arenas, where these types of analytics are trumpeted as ways to improve decisions, "minimize risk, and unearth valuable insights that would otherwise remain hidden."[60]

Within the practice of eDiscovery, TAR tools have been defined as a "process for prioritizing or coding a collection of documents using a computerized system that harnesses human judgments of one or more Subject Matter Expert(s) on a smaller set of documents and then extrapolates those judgments to the remaining document collection."[61] This process focuses on the power to "generalize human relevance decisions from a relatively small set of exemplars to a larger collection."[62] The way in which these decisions are extrapolated across documents takes terms that the system understands, often from the judgments made by reviewers, and then determines relevance according to the computer model employed, which may map specific document characteristics, "such as the presence and absence of text tokens, to locations within a multidimensional parameter space"[63] in a vector-type relationship similar to that seen in the glyph encoding discussed above.

---

[57] Pappas, *Easy Workflow Wins with Text Analytics*, Kcura Blog (Dec. 18, 2014).

[58] Scholtes, *supra* note 13, at 2.

[59] Kcura, *What's new in Relativity 9*, Kcura.com (April 29, 2015).

[60] Manyika et al., *Big data - The next frontier for innovation, competition, and productivity*, McKinsey Global Institute (MGI) (May 2011), at 5.

[61] Grossman-Cormack Glossary, *supra* note 40.

[62] Chapin et al., *supra* note 1, at 1.

[63] *Id.*, at 4.

Within this specific framework of analysis, practitioners and mathematicians have proposed a number of different supervised learning algorithms. Among the most effective are support vector machines (SVM), logistic regression (LR), bagging, boosting, random forests, and k-nearest neighbor (k-NN). Other, but avowedly less effective, methods include the naïve Bayesian searches discussed above; nearest neighbor (NN) or similarity searches; and Rocchio's vector-space, relevance feedback method.[64] Again, this is the math of the computer programming and its manifestation; the investigator will still have to examine the data presented, make value judgments that the computer is incapable of providing, and ultimately determine the narrative that fits the facts most closely. And if the math seems not to work, the work of the algorithms should not necessarily usurp the narrative judgment of the investigator. While the results of a given algorithm may not lie, they may mislead in the same way improperly presented statistics can.

In this context, it is important to distinguish *supervised* learning methods from *unsupervised* learning methods. Unsupervised methods do not use a training set or any other human input as to what constitutes relevance. Such methods, which automatically group documents or document features *without human oversight*, include clustering, latent semantic indexing (LSI) or analysis (LSA), and probabilistic latent semantic indexing (PLSI) or analysis (PLSA).[65] Further, these types of semantic search capabilities work as a compliment to text retrieval or search hit results by applying "structured knowledge, e.g., discussion structure, topical structure, or entities and relations as a complement to text retrieval" that may "provide guidance in analysts' search or sense making process."[66]

Some of these methods are not true TAR tools in their own right, but can be components of more complicated analysis, perhaps as a component of a similarity search, or as a measure by which an investigator may derive features of documents that could be used in further types of analysis, such as a supervised machine-learning method.[67] The use of these techniques within investigations is still under development, where there is less focus on a determination of relevance and more on root-cause analysis, the prevalence of a particular activity, and narrative development; however, with increasing frequency, investigators are finding opportunities to incorporate these automated processes for document review within their matters as one more perspective for their overall considerations.

11   Pulling Meaning from Paper

While the majority of techniques presented in this paper focus on ESI created and stored as such, an investigator cannot forget that there is still a universe of paper documents within every organization, and much of that paper has ended up as scanned,

---

[64] Grossman & Cormack, *supra* note 5, at 16.

[65] *Id.*

[66] Graus et al., *supra* note 6, at 2.

[67] Grossman & Cormack, *supra* note 5, at 16.

now-electronic data. When an investigator encounters a copse of PDF, TIFF, or other scanned data, rather than examining that data on a page-by-page basis, the investigator should consider whether automated practices associated with "document image retrieval are applicable, such as Optical Character Recognition (OCR), statistical correction of OCR error effects, and character n-gram indexing (to accommodate moderate character error rates)."[68] While OCR has steadily improved as a common practice, and its improvement has led to its increasing incorporation into both the basic Boolean search process as well as the more advanced techniques described further below, there are some additions to the traditional paper-as-electronic-document tools investigators might consider.

One such approach is called glyph encoding,[69] which has its underpinnings in standard vector models for review in which the model "represents each individual document as a vector in a high-dimensional vector space V," but the dimensions of V may be labeled "with many different kinds of data."[70] Here, instead of using words within a *unigram* model, or even word sequences (such as a *bigram* two word sequence), the technology instead relies upon graphic depictions of issues that may turn out to be words, but until (or even after) proven such, will be considered unique track-able objects to use in subsequent analyses and determinations. In the same fashion as the basic pattern recognition analysis provides a sum of the whole document collection for an investigator's consideration, this type of image-based analysis works across the collection and identifies "like" information, which can then be bundled together for group decisions, rather than on a page-by-page basis.

12 Considering eDiscovery Tools in Digital, Criminal Forensic Investigations

The possibilities of these tools are recognized in areas other than internal investigations and civil cases, especially in those instances where "the requirement for such tools has come from both the defense and prosecution as the cost of data review is inevitably a point of contention."[71] With exactly this concept in mind, in 2014, the United Kingdom performed an assessment of eDiscovery options for digital investigations carried out by the Metropolitan Police Service (MPS) and the Centre for Applied Science and Technology (CAST). This assessment focused on criminal investigations involving digital evidence and a sampling of a small selection of eDiscovery tools.

While this investigation found gaps in functionality (in particular with the range of sources faced by digital investigators such as cloud storage, audio and visual material analysis, voice data, and some information traditional forensics provided for) the

---

[68] Oard & Webber, *supra* note 2, at 131; *see also* Doermann, *The indexing and retrieval of document images: A survey*, Computer Vision and Image Understanding, Vol. 70, 287-298 (1998).

[69] Beyond Reconition, *Technical Overview Visual Classification*, (Jan. 21, 2015).

[70] Oehrle & Johnson, *supra* note 51, at 8.

[71] Lawton et al., *eDiscovery in digital forensic investigations*, Home Office, CAST Pub. No. 32/14, 1 (Sept. 2014).

conclusion was still that of improvements over traditional, forensic-only practices. Even the acknowledgement of these gaps did not overshadow the recognized potential of applying eDiscovery tools in forensic standard workflows, especially where they provided "a strong capability in text searching."[72] This is especially important where a given investigation incorporates additional concerns related to investigations of certain types of covered issues, where the potential destruction of evidence during these investigations could run afoul of federal regulation.[73] In sum, where there is a proven improvement, or even the possibility of the same, practitioners adapt to that practice and begin incorporating it into existing workflows. Here it is clear those eDiscovery tools that have matured (somewhat) within the context of litigation and U.S. discovery are rapidly finding purchase in a variety of investigatory settings, with implications in both the civil and criminal contexts.

13 Conclusion

Most active, informed eDiscovery practitioners understand that the techniques and technologies presented in this paper are useful as part of an eDiscovery "analytical 'toolbox'"[74] whose operation will depend on both the information at hand and the import of the matter. That is, there is no one-size-fits-all approach, and a given tool may "support a variety of tasks and legal scenarios effectively" even while these tools often function "even better in combination."[75] In fact, most practitioners note that a "broad range of tools might be employed to support this sensemaking process."[76] This is commonly understood within the data analysis space, and the state of the art is still comprised of eDiscovery approaches that employ "ad-hoc, hybrid methods that move in iterative cycles between search, analysis, and review"[77]

Further, when addressing existing shortcomings, an incorporation of different approaches, like "linguistic approaches requiring limited *a priori* knowledge such as information extraction and ontology evolution may go some way to bridge the mismatch."[78] But in the end, the result of this combination of processes—not just of eDiscovery processes, but also forensic practices and technologies—is still "almost always storytelling of some kind—whether to another party sitting across a table, or a

---

[72] *Id, at 23.*

[73] *See* Sloan, *The Compliance Case for Information Governance,* 20 RICH. J.L. &TECH. 4 (2014) at 18, (citing Sect. 802 of the Sarbanes Oxley Act: Whoever knowingly alters, destroys, mutilates, conceals, covers up, falsifies, or makes a false entry in any record, document, or tangible object with the intent to impede, obstruct, or influence the investigation or proper administration of any matter within the jurisdiction of any department or agency of the United States or any case filed under title 11, or in relation to or in contemplation of any such matter or case, shall be fined under this title, imprisoned not more than 20 years, or both. 18 U.S.C. § 1519 (2012)).

[74] Wood & Babineau, *supra* note 43.

[75] *Id.*

[76] Oard & Webber, *supra* note 2, at 122.

[77] Grossman & Cormack, *supra* note 5.

[78] Chapin et al., *supra* note 1, at 5.

decision-maker sitting behind a bench."[79] The key is determining the right tools for the job, relying on standardized and proven technologies where available to "automate as many steps in the process as possible"[80] and still presenting a cohesive narrative and appropriate basis for making determinations and solving problems. The investigator must not forget, however, that investigative techniques may differ in application depending on the jurisdiction, and while "a U.S. multinational may feel tempted to pull out [her] domestic-U.S. kit of state-of-the art investigation tools and strategies" when conducting an overseas investigation, "employment and data protection laws differ widely outside the U.S., which means American investigation strategies need significant retooling before export."[81]

While new technologies, such as glyph encoding for paper, visualization techniques for ECA, and TAR for review demonstrate the benefits technological advances present, investigators (and eDiscovery practitioners) should not forget that, until data management and information governance improve dramatically, "because of the diversity of data, you spend a lot of your time being a data janitor."[82] But being a janitor is not all bad. Janitors are often best placed to know and develop the true narrative of an organization,[83] and while sifting through the digital detritus is time intensive, it is the root of the analysis and the basis for the story of "why" the incident matters. For that reason, and for the others discussed in this paper, eDiscovery tools have gained a place in the investigator's tool chest, because they give the investigator additional opportunities to manipulate the data in meaningful, hands-on ways; because of the ease in which they can be integrated into existing investigative workflows; and their promise where, as these tools advance, they will provide great value for all those involved in investigations—including, of course, digital forensic investigators.[84]

---

[79] *Id.*, at 12.

[80] Lohr, *supra* note 27.

[81] Dowling, *Conducting Internal Employee Investigations Outside the U.S.*, NYSBA Labor and Employment Law Journal, Vol. 35, No. 1 (2010).

[82] Lohr, *supra* note 27.

[83] Bristol, *Why Successful CEOs Must Think Like the Janitor*, Fast Company – Leadership (Dec. 17, 2014) ("Never underestimate how much your janitor knows. I have personally seen instances where the janitor was the most knowledgeable and insightful team member when discussing overall employee morale.").

[84] Lawton et al., *supra* note 71.

Cloud Forensics Challenges Faced by Forensic Investigators

Wakas Mahmood, Hamid Jahankhani^(✉), and Aykut Ozkaya

GSM-London, London, UK
Hamid.jahanhani@gsm.org.uk

Abstract. Cloud computing has generated significant interest in both academia and industry, but it is still an evolving paradigm. Cloud computing services are also, a popular target for malicious activities; resulting to the exponential increase of cyber attacks. Digital evidence is the evidence that is collected from the suspect's workstations or electronic medium that could be used in order to assist computer forensics investigations. Cloud forensics involves digital evidence collection in the cloud environment. The current established forensic procedures and process models require major changes in order to be acceptable in cloud environment. This paper, aims to assess challenges forensic examiners face in tracking down and using digital information stored in the cloud and discuss the importance of education and training to handle, manage and investigate computer evidence.

Keywords: Cloud computing · Cloud forensics · Digital evidence · Cyber security strategy · Computer misuse act · Anti-forensics · Challenges of cloud forensics

1 Introduction

In a fully connected truly globalised world of networks, most notably the internet, mobile technologies, distributed databases, electronic commerce and E-governance E-crime manifests itself as Money Laundering; Intellectual Property Theft; Identity Fraud/Theft; Unauthorised access to confidential information; Destruction of information; Exposure to Obscene Material; Spoofing and Phishing; Viruses and Worms and Cyber-Stalking, Economic Espionage to name a few.

According to the House of Commons, Home Affairs Committee, Fifth Report of Session 2013–14, on E-crime, "Norton has calculated its global cost to be $388bn dollars a year in terms of financial losses and time lost. This is significantly more than the combined annual value of $288bn of the global black market trade in heroin, cocaine and marijuana." [1].

Since the launch of the UK's first Cyber Security Strategy in June 2009 and the National Cyber Security Programme (NCSP) in November 2011, UK governments have had a centralised approach to cybercrime and wider cyber threats.

Until recently E-crimes had to be dealt with under legal provisions meant for old crimes such as conspiracy to commit fraud, theft, harassment and identity theft. Matters

© Springer International Publishing Switzerland 2015
H. Jahankhani et al. (Eds.): ICGS3 2015, CCIS 534, pp. 74–82, 2015.
DOI: 10.1007/978-3-319-23276-8_7

changed slightly in 1990 when the Computer Misuse Act was passed but even then it was far from sufficient and mainly covered crimes involving hacking.

Over the years, the exponential growth of computing era has brought to light many technological breakthroughs. The next radical wave of this growth appeared to be outside the traditional desktop's realm. An evolving terminology that can describe this paradigm is cloud computing. Smith [2] and Martini & Choo [3] argued that cloud computing has recently become a prevalent technology and currently is one of the main trends in the ICT sector. In cloud computing several tangible and intangible objects (such as home appliances) surrounding people can be integrated in a network or in a set of networks [4].

Migration to cloud computing usually involves replacing much of the traditional IT hardware found in an organisation's data centre (such as servers and network switches) with remote and virtualised services configured for the particular requirements of the organisation. Hence, data comprising the organisation's application can be physically hosted across multiple locations, possibly with a broad geographic distribution [5].

As a result, the use of cloud computing can bring possible advantages to organisations including increased efficiency and flexibility. For instance, virtualised and remote services can provide greater flexibility over a physical IT infrastructure as they can be rapidly Re-configured to meet new requirements without acquiring a new or potentially redundant hardware [6]. Further, Khajeh-Hosseini et al. [7] found that cloud computing can be a significantly cheaper alternative to purchasing and maintaining system infrastructure In-house.

Though, the other side of the coin supports that cloud computing services are a popular target for malicious activities; resulting to the exponential increase of cyber-crimes, Cyber-Attacks [8]. Consequently, this phenomenon demonstrates the need to explore the various challenges and problems of cloud computing in the forensics community to potentially prevent future digital fraud, espionage, Intellectual Property (IP) theft as well as other types of concern.

2   Challenges Raised by Cloud Computing with Respect to Existing Digital Forensics Models

It has been observed that use of cloud computing currently presents several challenges to its users (i.e. individuals, organisations, regulatory and law enforcement authorities).

In 2006 two new laws were passed to tackle E-crime namely the Fraud Act 2006 which came into force in 2007 which "the new law aims to close a number of loopholes in proceeding Anti-fraud legislation, because, the Government said was unsuited to modern fraud", and the Police and Justice Act 2006 (part 5) which prohibits "unauthorised access to computer material; unauthorised acts with intent to impair operation of computer and the supply of tools that can be used for hacking" [9].

Documented guidance, practices and procedures were outdated and wholly inadequate to help tackle electronic evidence in a forensic manner, until first E-crime publication by ACPO in July 2007 and subsequently revised in November 2009 and 2012. This is recognised as the best guidelines ever produced to assist law enforcement in handling digital evidence [10]. On one hand these guidelines seem sustainable and functional; however on the other hand it is still yet practically unclear how digital evidence used in courts produced by a digital forensic investigation could be gathered by such guidelines in a cloud environment.

Digital evidence is the evidence that is collected from the suspect's workstations or electronic medium that could be used in order to assist computer forensics investigations.

There are basically two types of evidences that could support a digital forensic investigation, which are, physical evidence and digital evidence. Physical evidences are categorised as touchable and substantial items that could be brought to court and shown physically. Examples of physical evidence that could assist in the investigations are computers, external hard disk drives and data storage (memory sticks and memory cards) handheld devices including mobile phones/smart phones, networking devices, optical media, dongles and music players. Digital evidence would be the data that is extracted from the physical evidence, or the computer system.

In order to perceive a bit of information or data as evidence, it needs to satisfy the 5 rules that are;

(1) The evidence should be admissible and excepted in the court of law
(2) The evidence needs to be authentic and not contaminated
(3) The evidence needs to the whole piece, not just indicative parts
(4) The evidence has to be reliable, dependable
(5) The evidence needs to be believable

Digital evidence, as compared to hard evidence, are difficult to find, in terms of defining the nature of the data, and classifying it as a digital evidence that is worthy to be presented in court.

Proving evidence which is reliable has been proven to be a difficult task, not just because the nature of evidence, but also the wide scope and environment in which the evidence are extracted from.

In a corporate environment, the forensic investigator team will need to identify, contain and maintain the integrity of the evidence, and differentiate whether the piece of evidence is relevant or not to the current crime being investigated, and whether it would stand a chance in finding the culprit and charging them through legal proceedings.

Among the considerations that need to be evaluated by the investigators when dealing with collecting digital evidence are the expenses, cost and loss incurred and the availability of the service during and after the incident.

However, the question here is, can we investigate a crime in the cloud using the existing computer forensics models, frameworks and tools?

According to Grispos et al. [5], the available digital forensic practices, frameworks and tools are mainly intended for Off-line investigation, therefore if an investigation is conducted in a cloud computing environment new challenges come to light since the potential evidence that arises is likely to be ephemeral and stored on media beyond the investigator's immediate control.

In addition, digital forensics investigation processes heavily rely on theoretical frameworks and enhanced Digital Investigation Process Models which are practically not very useful for the current available cloud technologies as they were developed prior to their advent; and mainly assume that the investigator has physical access and control over the storage media of the targeted network, system or device [5].

As a result, it is apparent that the current cloud technologies face numerous significant challenges as the majority of available forensic process models do not respond adequately to the requirements of a digital forensic investigation and therefore they do not meet the needs of a complex cloud environment. All of the assumptions of the suggested forensic process models are likely to be invalidated when investigating forensic activities in a cloud environment as the majority of them strictly follow tactics of a physical investigation.

Roussev et al., [11] argues that, although the digital forensics models comprehensively reviews the stages of a digital forensic process and analyses the cloud forensics' impact on this process; most of its assumptions are not yet valid in the context of cloud computing and the problem will only get worse with the explosive growth of data volumes. As a result they proposed the Distributed Digital Forensic (DDF). This of course is not new and several researchers have already proposed models for DDF services for cloud computing paradigm. However, Roussev et al., [11] proposal is based on the MPI MapReduce (MMR) framework.

Grispos et al. [5], have summarises the challenges of cloud forensics in Table 1 below.

Table 1. Summary of challenges to digital forensics in cloud environments. [5]

Phase	Action	Challenges
Identification	Identifying an illicit event	Lack of frameworks
Preservation	Software tools	Lack of specialist tools
	Sufficient storage capacity	Distributed, virtualized and volatile storage; use of cloud services to store evidence
	Chain of custody	Cross-jurisdictional standards, procedures; proprietary technology
	Media imaging	Imaging all physical media in a cloud is impractical; partial imaging may face legal challenges
	Time synchronization	Evidence from multiple time zones
	Legal authority	Data stored in multiple jurisdictions; limited access to physical media
	Approved methods, software and hardware	Lack of evaluation, certification generally, but particularly in cloud context
	Live vs. Dead acquisitions	Acquisition of physical media from providers is cumbersome, onerous and time consuming data is inherently volatile
	Data integrity	Lack of Write-Blocking or enforced persistence mechanisms for cloud services and data
Examination	Software tools	Lack of tested and certified tools
	Recovery of deleted data	Privacy regulations and mechanisms implemented by providers
	Traceability and event reconstruction	Events may occur on many different platforms
Presentation	Documentation of evidence	Integration of multiple evidence sources in record
	Testimony	Complexity of explaining cloud technology to jury

Dykstra & Shermann [12], introduced FROST which is three new tools for the OpenStack cloud platform. These tools are integrated into the management plane of cloud architecture; hence, forensic investigators can obtain trustworthy forensics data independent of the cloud providers. OpenStack [13] is an Open-Source cloud computing platform and users includes many large organizations such as Intel, Argonne National Laboratory, AT&T, Rackspace and Deutsche Telekom.

Legal requirement for cloud forensics is currently uncertain and presents a challenge for the legal system. These challenges arises from the fact that cloud environment consists of distributed shared storages so there is a level of necessary interactions forensic examiners and law enforcement officers require from the cloud provider in order to conduct their investigations. This means they are at the mercy of their public cloud providers to assist in an investigation. In cloud investigation this lack of physical access due to the decentralized nature of the data processing cause enormous technical and legal disruptive challenges [14]. There are two legal issues:

(1) Validity-Of-the-Warrant – Establishing a specific location for search warrant that evidence is believed will be found together with the specifics required in the warrant.
(2) Authenticity – Making sure that the data is of the suspect (defendant) alone when searching shared storages.

The National Institute of Standards and Technology released a draft report in 2014 [15], highlighting the requirement for cloud forensics standards to aid law enforcement. In that report NIST identified 65 challenges in 9 major groups that forensics investigators face in gathering and analysing digital information stored in the cloud. The nine major groups are architecture, data collection, analysis, Anti-forensics, incident first responders, role management, legal, standards, and training. Figure 1, is the NIST mind map of forensic challenges.

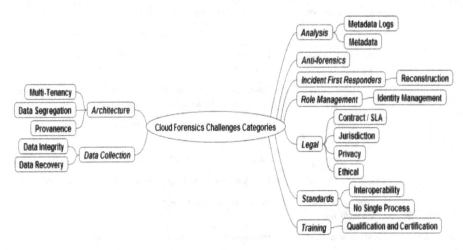

Fig. 1. NIST mind map of forensic challenges. [15]

3   Anti-forensics

Anti-forensics as a concept is as old as the traditional computer forensics. Someone that commit a punishable action use any possible way to get rid of any evidence connected with the prohibited action. The traditional forensics can have a range of Anti-forensics that start from a trivial level (e.g. wiping fingerprints from a gun) and to a level where our fantasy can meet the implementation of an Anti-forensic idea (e.g. alteration of DNA left behind in a crime). In digital Anti-forensics the same rules exists, with the difference that they are fairly new with little research and development [16].

There are number of techniques that are used to apply Anti-forensics. These techniques such as obfuscation, data hiding, and malware are not necessarily designed with Anti-forensics dimension in mind.

While in theory the forensics investigator should monitor everything available around the suspect, in reality the post incident response could end up quite dramatically. This could be due to; ignorance regarding the network activity logs, legal barriers between the access point and the forensics acquisition, non – cooperative ISP's, etc.

Anti-forensics is a reality that comes with every serious crime and involves tactics for "safe hacking" and keeps the crime sophistication in a high level. Computer forensic investigators along with the forensic software developers should start paying more attention to Anti-forensics tools and approaches.

If we consider the Computer Forensics as the actions of collection, preservation, identification and presentation of evidence, Anti-forensics can affect the first three stages. Because these stages can be characterized as "finish to start" between them from a project management point of view, the failure of one of them could end up as a failure of the lot. Thus, there is a high impact of Anti-forensics to the forensics investigations.

Officially there is no such thing as Anti-forensic investigations because the Anti-forensic countermeasures are still part of the investigator's skills.

4   The Main Difficulties Faced by Law Enforcement Officers Fighting Cyber-Crime

It is evident that cybercrime is no longer in its infancy. It is 'big business' for the criminal entrepreneur with potentially lots of money to be made with minimal risks. Cloud computing has generated significant interest in both academia and industry, but it is still an evolving paradigm. Confusion exists in IT communities about how a cloud differ from existing models and how its characteristics affect its adoption. Some see cloud as a novel technical revolution, some consider it a natural evolution of technology, economy, and culture [17]. Nevertheless, cloud computing is an important concept, with the strong ability to considerably reduce costs through optimization and increased operating and economic efficiencies. Furthermore, cloud computing could significantly enhance collaboration, agility, and scale, thus enabling a truly global computing model over the Internet infrastructure. However, without appropriate security and privacy solutions designed for clouds, this potentially revolutionizing computing paradigm could become a huge failure. Several surveys of potential cloud adopters indicate that security and privacy is the primary concern hindering its adoption. At the same time cloud creates unique challenges for digital forensic investigators, and one of the areas which have been recognised as the contributory elements in the failing by law enforcement officers is lack of proper training.

From law enforcement point of view the task of fighting Cyber-Crime is a difficult one. Although crime is irrespective of how big or small, a decision has to be made on the merits of each case as to whether investigating and prosecuting is in the public's interest and therefore, It is becoming necessary to understand and manage the Computer Forensics process in the cloud.

Computer Forensics is no longer a profession where training on the job to get experience is sufficient, especially when dealing in cloud environment. Most other professions require one to have a degree before one can progress to train in their vocation i.e. teachers, lawyers, forensic scientist and doctors etc., the same should be with Computer Forensic as the work done is as important as those in other fields and be it positive or negative does affect people's lives.

Numerous universities in in UK and abroad are offering Computer Forensic and Information Security courses to graduate and Post-Graduate level which will help those taking on the courses to have a good grounding in computer science, a better understanding of computer forensic theories and most of all help them develop to be more innovative in coming up with new forensically sound ways of fighting E-crime and to "think outside the box".

It is time for the government to actively work in partnership with universities to encourage people to take on these courses especially those already working in the field in the public sector.

A degree is now a prerequisite in the private sector as well as experience, as it is becoming a lot more difficult for one to claim to be an expert in the field of computer forensics and an expert witness in a court of law. Gone are the days where Do-It-Yourself forensics will be accepted [18].

This leads us to another area a lot of experts in the field of computer forensics have been reserved about and that is the idea of accreditation. It is an area that is very difficult to make decisions on. Most agree and recognize that a board should be set up, but what cannot be agreed upon is who should lead it. Some have suggested that it should be lead by universities, by government, by their peers or jointly by universities, government and businesses.

If it is government lead, without set of standards the situation will be no different from what we have at present. It will also involve those working in the profession to give it some direction and it is still doubtful as to whether those people are in a position to decide what form of accreditation to be embarked upon.

This brings us to the option of, a joint partnership with government, universities and businesses. This is the most feasible option but a lot of joint effort will be required to come up with a credible accreditation that will be accepted by all.

One thing is for sure having a form of accreditations will force government, academics, researches and those working in the field of computer forensics to set more appropriate standards and controls for those who handle, analyse and investigate computer evidence.

5 Conclusions

Cloud computing is still an evolving paradigm and has already created challenges for law enforcement around the globe to effectively carry out cloud forensics investigations. Although the digital forensics models comprehensively reviews the stages of a digital forensic process and analyses the cloud forensics' impact on this process; most of its assumptions are not yet valid in the context of cloud computing and the problem will only get worse with the explosive growth of data volumes.

Legal requirement for cloud forensics is currently uncertain and presents a challenge for the legal system. These challenges arises from the fact that cloud environment consists of distributed shared storages so there is a level of necessary interactions forensic examiners and law enforcement officers require from the cloud provider in order to conduct their investigations. One of the areas, which have been recognised as the contributory element in the failing by law enforcement officers, is lack of proper training. Education and training will help to provide good grounding in computer science, a better understanding of computer forensic theories and most of all help to develop to be more innovative in coming up with new forensically sound ways of fighting E-crime and to "think outside the box".

References

1. House of Commons, Home Affairs Committee, E-Crime, Fifth Report of Session 2013–14, http://www.publications.parliament.uk/pa/cm201314/cmselect/cmhaff/70/70.pdf
2. Smith, D.M.: Hype cycle for Cloud Computing (White Paper). Gartner Inc., Stamford (2011)
3. Martini, B., Choo, K.: An integrated conceptual digital forensic framework for cloud computing. Digital Invest. 9, 71–80 (2012)
4. Cook, T.: The Cloud of Unknowing, 1st edn. Harcourt Inc, Orlando (2007)
5. Grispos, G., Storer, T., Glisson, W.B.: Calm before the storm: the challenges of cloud computing in digital forensics, 1–25 (2012)
6. Sammons, J.: The Basics of Digital Forensics, 2nd edn. Elsevier, Waltham (2015)
7. Khajeh-Hosseini, A., Greenwood, D., Sommerville, I.: Cloud migration: a case study of migrating an enterprise IT system to IaaS. Paper presented at the IEEE International Conference on Cloud Computing, CLOUD 2010, Miami, USA (2010)
8. Blumenthal, M.S.: Hide and Seek in the Cloud. IEEE Secur. Priv. 8(2), 57–58 (2010)
9. Police and Justice Act (2006). http://www.legislation.gov.uk/ukpga/2006/48/contents
10. ACPO Guidelines (2009). http://www.acpo.police.uk/documents/crime/2009/200908 CRIECS01.pdf
12. Roussev, V., Wang, L., Richard, G., Marziale, L.: A cloud computing platform for large-scale forensic computing. In: Peterson, G., Shenoi, S. (eds.) Advances in Digital Forensics V. IFIP Advances in Information and Communication Technology, vol. 306, pp. 201–214. Springer, Heidelberg (2009)
12. Dykstra, J., Sherman, A.T.: Design and implementation of FROST: digital forensic tools for the OpenStack cloud computing platform. Digit. Invest. 10, S87–S95 (2013). Elsevier
13. OpenStack: OpenStack open source cloud computing software (2012). http://www.open stack.org/

14. Orton, I., Alva, A., Endicott-Popovsky, B.: Legal process and requirements for cloud forensic investigations. In: Ruan, K. (ed.) Cybercrime and Cloud Forensics: Applications for Investigation Processes. IGI Global, Hershey (2012)
15. NIST, Cloud Computing Forensic Science Challenges, Draft NISTIR 8006, NIST Cloud Computing Forensic Science Working Group Information Technology Laboratory (2014). http://csrc.nist.gov/publications/drafts/nistir-8006/draft_nistir_8006.pdf
16. Jahankhani, H., Anastasios, B., Revett, K.: Digital anti forensics: tools and approaches. In: 6th European Conference on Information Warfare and Security Defence College of Management and Technology, Shrivenham, UK, 2–3 July 2007 (2007)
17. Takabi, H., Joshi, J.B.D., Hn, G.J.A.: Security and privacy challenges in cloud computing environments. IEEE Comput. Reliab. Soc. (2010). http://www.cs.ru.nl/~jhh/pub/secsem/takabi2012security-privacy-cloud-challenges.pdf
18. Jahankhani, H., Hosseinian-far, A.: Digital Forensics education, training and awareness. In: Cybercrime and Cyber Terrorism Investigators' Handbook, pp91–100. Elsevier (2014) ISBN 978-1447126829

Integrated Computer Forensics Investigation Process Model (ICFIPM) for Computer Crime Investigations

Reza Montasari[1]([⊠]), Pekka Peltola[2], and David Evans[1]

[1] Derby University, Derby, UK
{r.montasari,d.f.evans}@derby.ac.uk
[2] Nottingham University, Nottingham, UK
pekka.peltola@nottingham.ac.uk

Abstract. Contrary to traditional crimes for which there exists deep-rooted standards, procedures and models upon which courts of law can rely, there are no formal standards, procedures nor models for digital forensics to which courts can refer. Although there are already a number of various digital investigation process models, these tend to be ad-hoc procedures. In order for the case to prevail in the court of law, the processes followed to acquire digital evidence and terminology utilised must be thorough and generally accepted in the digital forensic community. The proposed novel process model is aimed at addressing both the practical requirements of digital forensic practitioners and the needs of courts for a formal computer investigation process model which can be used to process the digital evidence in a forensically sound manner. Moreover, unlike the existing models which focus on one aspect of process, the proposed model describes the entire lifecycle of a digital forensic investigation.

Keywords: Computer forensics · Digital forensic investigations · Process model · Computer crime · Formal framework · Incident response

1 Introduction

Nowadays, the nature of evidence presented in courts of law tends to be less likely paper-based considering the ubiquitous nature of information technology [1, 16]. Evidence of computer crime differs from that related to traditional crimes for which there are well established standards and procedures [1, 16, 17]. There does not exist a comprehensive digital investigation process model that is widely accepted by the digital forensic community and courts of law and which covers the entire lifecycle of digital forensic investigation processes. In many cases, digital forensic practitioners rely mainly on ad-hoc tools to carry out digital investigation. Examples of ad-hoc models include models developed by authors in [1–6]. The lack of a standardized digital investigation process model is not an isolated flaw within the field of digital forensic science. Cohen [7] states that the entire field of digital forensic still lacks agreements in fundamental areas. This might be due to the fact that the digital forensic field is still a very new discipline. A study conducted by Cohen [7, 8] on the level of

© Springer International Publishing Switzerland 2015
H. Jahankhani et al. (Eds.): ICGS3 2015, CCIS 534, pp. 83–95, 2015.
DOI: 10.1007/978-3-319-23276-8_8

consensus in foundational elements of digital evidence investigation revealed that the use of common definitions and common language are lacking.

The fact that there exists a lack of common definitions and language is also pointed out by other researchers such as [1–3, 9, 10]. Moreover, many other researchers in the field have increasingly been calling for scientific approaches and formal methods for describing the computer investigation processes [8, 11–14]. By implementing an integrated and comprehensive computer investigation process model, this paper will be of great value to the computer forensic practitioners. Moreover, as Adams et al. [1] state, the development of such a model will establish a starting point from which other investigators and researchers in the field will be able to continue to advance the field's scientific credentials.

2   Related Work

2.1   Background

The main objective of a Computer Forensic Investigation Process Model or CFIPM is to assist the investigator in explaining how particular digital evidence is found on a device [1, 9, 20]. Although various CFIPMs exist in the current literature, the CFIPM processes and terminology have not been formally standardized up to date. Previously attempts to standardize the computer investigation process models appear to have failed due to various reasons. The main rationale behind these failed attempts is the fact that the authors have utilised their own terminology without attempting to identify the most common language that can be accepted unanimously by the digital forensic investigators.

The Table 1 describes the phases covered within the conducted research up to date. Like any other types of evidence, courts of law do not assume that digital evidence is valid and reliable without some empirical testing in relation to theories and techniques associated with its production [1, 18]. Courts of law take a careful notice of the way and process in which the digital evidence acquisition and storage were carried out [7, 18, 19]. The concept of admissibility refers to the fact that the courts need to verify whether the digital evidence is sound to be placed before a jury and will help to deliver a solid base in terms of making a decision in the case [20]. Courts in the U.K. and U.S. require the investigators and "proponent" of digital evidence to lay the proper foundation for its admissibility. They are concerned with the reliability and authenticity of such digital evidence [20, 21]. However, if forensic investigator is not able to present his/her evidence in a coherent and understandable way to the layperson such as judge and jury, the case may be lost [22]. The complexity of methodologies and software used to extract digital evidence requires the digital investigator to explain the evidence in such a way that judge and jury understand it [19].

Authors in [20, 23, 24] argue that while the actual mechanics of digital forensics are different from the better-known physical and medical forensics, the processes of all forensic sciences are fundamentally the same. Cohen [7, 8] states that judges need to keep out the poor-quality digital evidence from the courtroom. Regardless of the digital evidence or physical evidence, a forensic report must contain conclusions that can be reproduced by independent third parties. Reports based on accurately documented digital sources are much more likely to withstand the judicial scrutiny than opinions based on less reliable sources [25]. In the absence of something better, judicial systems might apply methods used to test scientific evidence into digital evidence presented before them [19, 26]. The digital forensic discipline was developed without any initial research required for a thorough scientific ground essential for permitting digital forensic evidence [27–29]. In 2004, Meyers et al. [28] warned that digital forensics is branded as "junk science" because of the absence of certifications, standards or peer-reviewed methods. Although this reference dates back to 2004, the issue of the lack of standardisation and consensus concerning process models regarding terminology, phases and types of activities within a process model still remain. This is pointed out by the latest reference such as [1, 7–10].

A careful and detailed examination of the literature has revealed a gap that there does not exist a comprehensive digital investigation process model which is widely accepted by the digital forensic community and courts of the law. The existing models are considered to be ad-hoc tools as opposed to formal models [1–3, 7, 8, 23, 24, 30–35]. For instance, Beebe et al. [33] state that a more comprehensive and generally accepted framework is needed to enhance scientific rigor and to facilitate education, application and research. Referring to the level of consensus in foundational elements of digital investigation process amongst researchers in the field, Cohen [8] states that the use of common language is lacking, and the consensus can be found present only after the definitions are made explicit. The United States Computer Emergency Readiness Team [30] states, "Because computer forensics is a new discipline, there is little standardization and consistency across the courts and industry." Ciardhuáin [34] states that a complete and inclusive model should have general advantages for IT managers, auditors and others who are not necessarily implicated with the legal process because of growing occurrences of crimes implicating computers. Ciardhuáin [34] further states, "A comprehensive model of cybercrime investigations is important for standardising terminology, defining requirements, and supporting the development of new techniques and tools for investigators". This is further supported by the authors in [1, 9]. Moreover, Zainudin et al. [10] state that one of the most significant problems that digital investigators encounter is the absence of standardisation in the field of computer forensics. Karyda et al. [36] state that utilising ad-hoc methods and tools for the extraction of digital evidence can undermine the reliability and credibility of digital evidence.

Therefore, to deal with these shortcomings and to fill the gap, we propose an Integrated Computer Investigation Process Model ICFIPM which deals with the process of digital evidence in computer crime investigations. Very few researchers have previously attempted to develop standardised computer investigation process models. These attempts have failed due to various reasons [1–3, 9, 10]. One of the reasons is due to the fact that researchers tend to use their own terminology and different types of activities in the models. Moreover, the existing models are not complete by covering the entire processes involved in a computer crime investigation. For example, the model developed by Adams et al. [1] is based only on the "Analysis" phase and partially on the "Preparation" phase. The model does not include phases related to Preparation, Incident Response or Documentation.

2.2   Review of the Existing Models

Due to the space constraint, it is not possible to present a description of all the previously developed Computer Forensics Process Models which were reviewed by the authors prior to developing the proposed model. Although a description of only four reviewed models is provided in this paper, it should not be denoted that the proposed model is based on only these four models. On the contrary, the proposed model is the integration of almost all the existing developed models. Nevertheless, a comprehensive analysis of these models is represented in Table 1.

Carrier et al. (2003). The model proposed by Carrier et al. [15] is called "An Integrated Digital Investigation Process". This model is organised into 5 groups consisting of Readiness, Deployment, Physical Crime Scene Investigation, Digital Crime Scene Investigation and Review. Although this model dates back to 2003, it is still one of the most prominent DFPMs to date [1, 9]. This is due to the fact that it included physical crime scene investigation in the model and drew a clear distinction between physical crime scene and digital crime scene investigation. However, the model's practicality in real life has been challenged by other digital forensic experts such as authors in [9, 37]. This model has not differentiated the primary crime scene (where the digital crime initiates) from the secondary crime scene (the target computer). This is not part of the physical or digital forensic investigation in this model. Therefore, computer forensic investigation based on this model will not consist of the outcome of the nefarious activity; this will affect the reconstruction of events and subsequently results in incomplete findings in the presented report [9].

Baryamureeba et al. (2004). Baryamureeba et al. [37] proposed "The Enhanced Integrated Digital Investigation Process (EIDIP)". This model is built upon the previous model proposed by Carrier et al. [15]. The phases of this model include: Readiness, Deployment, Traceback, Dynamite and Review phases. In their model, Baryamureeba et al. [37] aim to address the flaw in Carrier et al.'s [15] model by including an investigation of the primary and secondary crime scenes. Baryamureeba et al. [37] adds a new sub-phase in which the primary crime scene is identified in the Traceback phase [9]. Moreover, in this model, reconstruction is conducted after all the evidences have been collected. Apart from differentiating between primary and secondary crime scene, this model offers no other contributions.

Beebe et al. (2005). Beebe et al. [33] proposed a model, "A Hierarchal, Objectives-Based Framework for the Digital Investigation Process". This model consists of Preparation, Incident Response, Data Collection, Data Analysis, Findings Presentation and Incident Closure Phases. Beebe et al. [33] suggest the concept of objectives-based tasks in which the investigative goals are utilised to select the analysis tasks.

Although in contrast with other models, this model is more detailed by introducing sub-phases and objectives-task hierarchical structures, it still has various shortcomings. These include the fact that its first-layer phases are mainly non-iterative not allowing the investigators to return to the previous phases. Moreover, as the authors themselves state, the model's low level details is not complete as the model includes sub-tasks only

Table 1. Analysis of the existing digital investigation process models up to date.

No	Authors	Year	Digital Investigation Process Model
1	Pollitt	1995	Computer Generator: an Approach to Evidence in Outspace
2	Lee et al	2000	Digital Evidence and Computer Crime
3	Casey	2000	Model of Scientific Crime Scene Investigation
4	Palmer et al	2001	DFRWS - Investigative Process for Digital Forensic Science
5	Reith et al	2002	An Abstract digital Forensics Model
6	Mandia et al	2003	Incident Response & computer Forensics
7	Carrier et al	2003	An Integrated Digital Investigation Process
8	Stephenson	2003	End to End digital Investigation Process
9	Ciardhuáin	2004	An Extended Model of Cybercrime Investigation
10	Casey et al	2004	Digital Evidence and Computer Crime Process Model
11	Baryamureeba et al	2004	The Enhanced Digital Investigation Process Model
12	Carrier et al	2004	An Event-Based Digital Forensic Investigation
13	Beebe et al	2005	A Hierarchical, Objective-Based Framework for the Digital Investigation Process
14	Kohn et al	2006	Framework for a Digital Forensic Investigation
15	Kent et al	2006	Guide to Integrating Forensic Techniques into Incident Response
16	Ieong, R	2006	FORZA - Digital Forensics Investigation Framework That Incorporates Legal Issues
17	Freiling, F	2007	Common Process Model for Computer Forensics and Incident Response
18	Grobler et al	2010	A Multi-Component View of Digital Forensics
19	Zainudin et al	2010	A Digital Forensic Investigation Model for Online Social Networking
20	Alharbi et al	2011	The Proactive and Reactive Digital Investigation Process: A systematic Literature Review
21	Yusoff et al	2011	Generic Process Model of Computer Forensics Investigation Models
22	Cosic et al	2011	Chain of Digital Evidence Based Model of Digital Investigation Process
23	Agarwal et al	2012	Systematic Digital Investigation Process Model
24	Roger et al	2012	Multi-Perspective Cybercrime Investigation Process Modeling
25	Valjarevic et al	2012	Harmonised Digital Investigation Process
26	Sabran et al	2014	Detect and Abstract Digital Forensics Model with Prosecution and Protection at Umbrella Principles

Phases analysed (column headers of the matrix): Readiness, Identification, Detection, Preservation, Evidence Collection, Examination, Analysis, Evidence Acquisition, Preparation, Approach Strategy, Forensic Duplication, Recovery, Survey, Interview, Deployment, Approved Methods, Authorisation, Harvesting, Organisation, Classification, Sampling, Seizure, Data Reduction, Compression, Presentation, Documentation, Live Data Collection, Trace Back, Dynamite, Decision/Resolution, Returning Evidence, Physical Crime Scene Investigation, Digital Crime Scene Investigation, Review, Operational Readiness, Infrastructure Readiness, Notification, Evidence Search, Event Reconstruction, Awareness/Report, Hypothesis, Proof & Defence, Confirm, Record, Package, Transport, Store, Communication, Incident Response, System Restoration, Evaluation, Incident Closure, Dissemination.

for the Analysis phase. Beebe et al. [33] call for their model to be extended by including sub-phases for other first-layer phases included in the model.

Ciardhuain (2004). The model developed by Ciardhuain [34] is considered to be the most comprehensive model proposed to date [1, 7, 9, 13]. This model consists of Awareness, Authorisation, Planning, Notification, Search for and identify evidence, Collection of evidence, Transport of evidence, Storage of evidence, Examination of evidence, Hypothesis, Presentation of hypothesis, Defense of hypothesis, Dissemination of information phases. The terminology used in this model is similar to the terminology used in the previously proposed models. Although this model is considered to be the most comprehensive model proposed to date, it has various shortcomings. The model is mainly aimed at information flow and the digital investigations within the field of commerce. It is not designed in a way which can be implemented in different settings. Moreover, the model does not allow the investigators to return to the previous phases.

2.3   Discussion of the Existing Models

The existing DFIPMs are not complete in that they do not cover the entire digital investigation processes. Moreover, they have differing approaches by lacking common terminology, language and the types of activities that are widely agreed upon by the digital forensic community. For example, a comparison of the set of activities included under Examination phase in Casey's [20] model and Cohen's [9] model respectively revels the problem in terms of standardization.

Casey:
Examination: Recovery → Harvesting → Reduction → Classification
Cohen
Examination: Analysis → Attribution → Reconstructing

As seen, clearly not a single sub-process within the two identified sets has the same meaning. A possible explanation for this discrepancy is that the interpretations of the terms examine and analysis has been exchanged by the authors [9]. Therefore, in order to acquire the digital evidence in a forensically sound manner, it essential to develop a model based on scientific and formal methods.

3   Methodology

In order to create a consistent research environment and to carry out a successful research, various methodologies were considered. The reason for selecting Design Science Research Process (DSRP) methodology over other alternatives lies in the fact that it is especially suited for the task of designing and developing a new process model. Armstrong [38] states that design science is an ideal approach in the problem domain of digital forensic evidence with its focus on designing solutions [1]. Researchers within information system research have been widely applying the DSRP. Moreover, this methodology has been previously adopted by other researchers in similar situations and has proved to be effective [1, 39, 40]. The DSRP is related to the development and subsequent evaluation of IT artefacts within an organisational environment in order to solve specific problems [39, 41]. The artefacts in question can consist of models, constructs and methods [1].

Also, in order to represent the proposed Integrated Computer Forensic Investigation Process Model (ICFIPM) discussed in this paper in a uniform and consistent manner, we considered various visual and formal representations. These consisted of UML Activity, Use Case Diagrams and Finite State Machines. However, we decided to use Sequential Logic formulated by More et al. [42]. The reason for choosing this representation is due to the fact that ordering of the phases and sub-phases are critical in the proposed model. Kohn et al. [9] state, "In order for the circuit to evaluate true, all the conditions of the previous states must be true." This means that the circuit will fail if the current state is not positively completed [9, 42]. This will enable the investigator to revisit previous steps in the process; however, he or she will not be able to continue if a step is not complete or fails. The ordering of the phases and sub-phases are critical in the proposed model. This is because the circuit outcome is dependent on the input and the current internal state – note that in this context, we refer to a phase or sub-phase as a circuit. This methodology has been previously applied in Kohn et al. [9] work and has proved to be effective. In their work, Kohn et al. [9] adapt the sequential logic notation formulated by More et al. [42] in order to represent each of the DFPMs in which Kohn et al. [9] replace the list values with the process steps. We aim to utilize the sequential logic notation adapted by Kohn et al. [9].

4 Contribution of the Paper

This paper proposes a computer forensics process model which rationalizes terminology as well as synthesizes phases and activities included in a process model. The model is simple enough to use, by having generalised methods that the judicial members or company management can use to relate technology to non-technical observers.

5 Proposed Computer Forensics Model

All the prominent models developed since 1997 up to 2014 have been critically analysed. This was to identify and integrate the essential components and terminology agreed upon by the digital forensic community to include in the proposed model. The rationale in doing so is multifaceted. Firstly, we aimed to leverage the benefits and advantages of previously proposed models. Secondly, in any type of community, it is important to create synergic interaction between different points of view. As the authors in [1, 7–9, 33] state, any framework institutionalized through subsequent intellectual discourse and practical use must take into account differing perspectives, approaches and vernacular. Therefore, we have integrated the previously proposed models to the new uniform model. The soundness of a digital investigation process model is "a function of usability and acceptability" [33]. Therefore, in order to acquire usability and acceptability, we integrated phases, sub-phases, principles and objectives. Phases and sub-phases are obvious; they are individually separate steps in the process which can sometimes be a function of time and are inevitably sequential or sometimes iterative approach. In contrast, principles are encompassing procedures, guidelines and methodological approaches that encompass some or all the eight specified main phases of the proposed model as well as its sub-phases. Principles as opposed to phases are not distinct and discrete steps in the process. Rather, they are aims and objectives needed to be achieved throughout the process. Chain of custody and proper documentations are examples of principles. The phases of a model are tied together through the process model flow accompanied by its investigative principles such as information flow and case management [15, 20, 33, 34].

The proposed model (Fig. 1) shows information flow through phases. Case management and investigative objective are the general factors defining the nature of the phases within the model. First layer phases are distinct and discrete. They are clearly defined, and obvious delineation exists between them. In other words, each given phase has a clear event which initiates it and clear output as the conclusion of the phase [33]. Phases occur in order and are chronological. Some first layer phases are non-iterative within the extent of a single accident.

5.1   Readiness Phase

Forensic Readiness is the ability of an organisation to maximise its potential to use digital evidence whilst minimising the costs of an investigation [9, 43, 44]. Organisations need to take certain important steps to prepare to use digital evidence. These include: improved system and staff monitoring, physical and procedural equipment and means to preserve data to evidential standards of admissibility, processes and procedures to ensure that the staff recognise the importance and legal activities of evidence, and appropriate legal advice and interfacing with law enforcement.

5.2   Identification Phase

Identification phase is where the incident or a digital crime is detected and reported either to the incident response team in an organisational context or to the police in the case of ordinary individuals.

5.3   Incident Response Phase

Various activities are involved in this phase. It is the first responders who typically arrive at the crime scene. Every investigation is different, and it is unlikely to decide what the first responders will encounter at the crime scene. In this phase, the potential suspects need to be detained. The first responders will then need to assess and confirm the incident and notify the incident to the right authority i.e. management in the company or police. Based on the result of this phase right equipment and personnel are deployed and a response strategy is drawn.

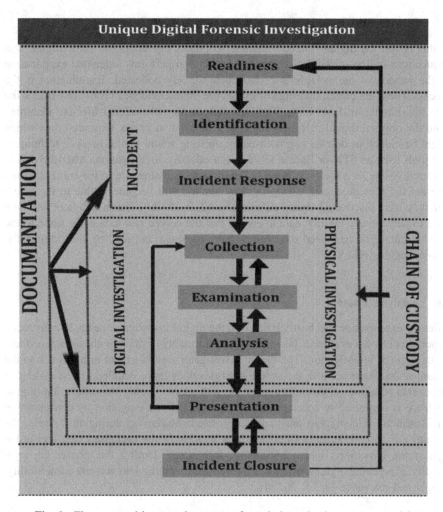

Fig. 1. The proposed integrated computer forensic investigation process model

5.4   Collection Phase

The collection phase involves searching the physical crime scene and identifying the digital media containing potential digital evidence. Upon the identification, the examiner performs a live digital data acquisition by imaging the volatile data and authenticating it using checksum verifications (MD5 and SHA1). This is to ensure the legal validity of the digital evidence. If the digital media cannot be seized in cases of server in large organisations, then the examiner also needs to perform a live digital data acquisition of the logical drive of the server. If the search warrant permits the removal of the digital media, the media is seized and taken away for laboratory digital data acquisition.

5.5   Examination Response

In this phase, the digital forensic examiner conducts the laboratory static digital data acquisitions on the seized digital media. He/she then performs a detailed examination of the images of the volatile and static data already collected. Examination is the process where the digital investigator makes the digital evidence visible or extracts the data into human readable form [9]. Files such as partially deleted files are identified from the original digital media through the Examination phase. Obscured data which might be hidden or deleted is processed by utilizing sound digital forensic techniques and tools such as FTK or Encase to carry out effective investigation. After the data is rendered visible, it is then harvested by giving a logical structure to the entire data set. The deleted files processed during the examination will become visible to the extent that they were discovered during examination [7, 9, 15, 20]. The investigator will then need to authenticate the raw data to ensure that the copied raw data is the same as the original data. The harvested data can then be mounted and read by the original file system such as NTFS.

5.6   Analysis Phase

After the examination has been carried out, the digital investigator needs to construct a hypothesis of what occurred. The extent of the formality of the hypothesis is dependent on the type of investigation. The digital investigator should expect to backtrack to the Examination phase because the investigator develops more detailed understanding of the events resulting in investigation in the first place. During this phase, the digital evidence is organised to accelerate the digital forensic investigation by concentrating on identified incident type and data categorised. Moreover, during this phase, the investigator should perform a detailed investigation of the organised data and test it against the hypothesis which he/she has formulated. During this phase, the legal validity of potential digital evidence is questioned by taking into account admissibility, weight and relevance [9, 15, 20, 34].

5.7   Presentation Phase

The developed hypothesis needs to be presented to people other than the investigators. For a law enforcement case, the hypothesis will be placed before a jury whereas as an internal company investigation puts the presentation before the management for a decision to be taken. Other activities involved in this phase include proof and defence. Often the hypothesis will be challenged; the defence will provide a contrary hypothesis before the jury. The investigators will need to prove the validity of their hypothesis and defend it against criticism and challenge. If the challenges are successful, the digital investigator will then need to backtrack to earlier stages in order to acquire and examine more evidence and to develop a better hypothesis.

5.8   Incident Closure

The final phase of the proposed model is the Incident Closure phase, where the case is officially closed. The result of the investigation is utilised to review the existing policies and procedures of the organisation. The original digital evidence either must be destroyed or must be returned to its rightful owner. In this phase, lessons should be learnt, and recommendations be made. A case study should be developed to assist future investigations. The case study can consist of i.e. the type of attack and perpetrator's skills set etc. Dissemination is an important activity in this phase; some information might be made available within the organisation whereas other information might be more widely disseminated. This information also will influence future investigations as well as policies and procedures.

6   Conclusions and Future Work

Various digital investigation process models in the literature were identified and compared. The results revealed that none could be considered standard since they all have differing approaches. The essential and most agreed-upon components of the existing models were identified and incorporated into the new model. Although the model is represented in its first-layer phases, the final product of this research will be a model which represents the detailed model consisting of sub-phases and activities. We contend that our model is not just a merging of the existing models. We have clarified the terminology and have added further essential phases to the model.

The proposed model will be standardized by identifying and incorporating into the proposed model the terminology and activities that the researchers and practitioners in the field of digital forensic community agree upon. Similarly, in order to make the model generic in a way which it can be used in different fields of digital forensic and for any type of cybercrime, we will combine different models developed separately for different fields of digital forensic including law enforcement, third party providers of digital forensic services and incident response. The proposed model in this paper has been presented in its high level phases (first-layer). As a future work, the authors are in the process of extending the proposed model to consist of the lower lever sub-phases. This is to conduct further research in order to determine components and activities which are widely accepted by the computer forensics experts for inclusion in the extended process model.

After the extension of the proposed model, it will then be evaluated and tested in two stages in order to assess its usability and utility. The first stage involves using two sets of digital forensic experts within academia and industry, and the second stage involves carrying out a closed network attack and apply the proposed process model to a case study.

References

1. Adams, R., Hobbs, V., Mann, G.: The advanced data acquisition model (ADAM): a process model for digital forensic practice. J. Digit. Forensics Secur. Law **8**(4), 25–48 (2014)
2. Bulbul, H., Yavuzcan, H., Ozel, M.: Digital forensics: an analytical crime scene procedure model (ACSPM). Forensic Sci. Int. **233**(1), 244–256 (2013)
3. Agarwal, A., Gupta, M., Gupta, S., Gupta, C.: Systematic digital forensic investigation model. Int. J. Comput. Sci. Secur. **5**(1), 118–130 (2011)
4. Ieong, R.S.C.: FORZA–digital forensics investigation framework that incorporate legal issues. Digit. Investig. **3**, 29–36 (2006)
5. Grobler, C.P., Louwrens, C.P., Sebastiaan, von Solms, H.: A multi-component view of digital forensics. In: ARES 2010 International Conference on Availability, Reliability, and Security. IEEE (2010)
6. Ademu, I., Imafidon, C., Preston, D.: A new approach of digital forensic model for digital forensic investigation. Int. J. Adv. Comput. Sci. Appl. **2**(12), 175–178 (2011)
7. Cohen, F.: Putting the science in digital forensics. J. Digit. Forensics Secur. Law **6**(1), 7–14 (2011)
8. Cohen, F.: Update on the State of the Science of Digital Evidence Examination. In: Proceedings of the Conference on Digital Forensics, Security & Law, pp. 7–18 (2012)
9. Kohn, M., Eloff, M., Eloff, J.: Integrated digital forensic process model. Comput. Secur. **38**, 103–115 (2013)
10. Zainudin, N., Merabti, M., Liwellyn-Jones, D.: Online social networks as supporting evidence: a digital forensic investigation model and its application design. In: International conference on Research and Innovation in Information Systems (ICRIIS), Kuala Lumpur, 23–24 November, pp. 1–6. IEEE (2011)
11. Garfinkel, S., Farrell, P., Roussev, V., Dinolt, G.: Bringing science to digital forensics with standardized forensic corpora. Digit. Investig. **6**, S2–S11 (2009)
12. Carlton, H., Worthley, R.: An evaluation of agreement and conflict among computer forensic experts. In: 42nd Hawaii International Conference on System Sciences (HICSS), Hawaii, 5–8 January. IEEE, Hawaii (2009)
13. Pollitt, M.: Applying traditional forensic taxonomy to digital forensics. In: Ray, I., Shenoi, S. (eds.) Advances in Digital Forensics IV, vol. 285, pp. 17–26. Springer, New York (2008)
14. Leigland, L., Krings, A.: A formalization of digital forensics. Int. J. Digit. Evid. **3**(2), 1–32 (2004)
15. Carrier, B.: Defining digital forensic examination and analysis tools using abstraction layers. Int. J. Evid. **1**(4), 1–12 (2003)
16. Stanfield, A.: Computer Forensics, Electronic Discovery and Electronic Evidence. LexisNexis Butterworths, Chatswood (2009)
17. Smith, R., Grabosky, P., Urbas, G.: Cyber Criminals on Trial. Cambridge University Press, Cambridge (2009)
18. Mason, S.: Electronic Evidence: Disclosure, Discovery & Admissibility. LexisNexis Butterworths, London (2007)
19. Kessler, C.: Judges' awareness, understanding, and application of digital evidence. Ph.D. thesis. Nova Southeastern University (2010)
20. Casey, E.: Digital Evidence and Computer Crime Forensic Science, Computers and the Internet, 3rd edn. Elsevier, San Diego (2011)
21. The Law Reform: The Admissibility of Expert Evidence in Criminal Proceedings in England and Wales (2009). http://lawcommission.justice.gov.uk/docs/cp190_Expert_Evidence_Consultation.pdf. Accessed 20 Jan 2015

22. Wiles, J. (ed.): The Best Damn Cybercrime and Digital Investigations Book Period: Syngress Publishing Palmer, Gary (2001). A road map for digital forensic research. First Digital Forensic Research Workshop, Utica, New York (2007)
23. Turnbull, B.: The adaptability of electronic evidence acquisition guides for new technologies. In: Proceedings of the 1st International Conference on Forensic Applications and Techniques in Telecommunications, Information and Multimedia and Workshop
24. Calhoun, C.: Scientific Evidence in Court: Daubert or Frye, 15 Years Later, vol. 23(37). Legal Backgrounder, Washington, DC (2008)
25. Peisert, S., Bishop, M., Marzullo, K.: Computer Forensics. In: Forensis', Third International Workshop on Systematic Approaches to Digital Forensic Engineering, Oakland, California, USA (2008)
26. Meyers, M., Rogers, M.: Computer forensics: the need for standardization and certification. Int. J. Digit. Evid. 3(2), 1–11 (2004)
27. Carrier, B.: Open source digital forensic tools: the legal argument' (2002). http://www.digital-evidence.org/papers/opensrc_legal.pdf. Accessed 6 Jan 2014
28. US-CERT: Computer Forensics (2012). http://www.us-cert.gov/reading_room/forensics.pdf
29. Yussoff, Y., Roslan, I., Zainuddin, H.: Common phases of computer forensics investigation models. Int. J. Comput. Sci. Inf. Technol. 3(3), 17–31 (2011)
30. Trcek, D., Abie, H., Skomedal, A., Starc, I.: Advanced framework for digital forensic technologies and procedures. J. Forensic Sci. 55(6), 1471–1479 (2010)
31. Beebe, N., Clark, J.: A hierarchical, objectives-based framework for the digital investigations process. Digit. Investig. 2(2), 147–167 (2005)
32. Ciardhuáin, O.: An extended model of cybercrime investigations. Int. J. Digit. Evid. 3(1), 1–22 (2004)
33. Reith, M., Carr, C., Gunsch, G.: An examination of digital forensic models. Int. J. Digit. Evid. 1(3), 1–12 (2002)
34. Karyda, M., Mitrou, L.: Internet forensics: legal and technical issues. In: 2nd International Workshop on Digital Forensics and Incident Analysis, Samos (Greece), pp. 3–12 (2007)
35. Baryamureeba, V., Florence, T.: The enhanced digital investigation process model. In: Proceedings of the Fourth Digital Forensic Research Workshop (2004)
36. Armstrong, C., Armstrong, H.: Modeling forensic evidence systems using design science. In: IFIP WG 8.2/8.6 International Working Conference, Perth, Western Australia (2010)
37. Hevner, A., Chatterjee, S.: Design Research in Information Systems. Springer, New York (2010)
38. Peffers, K., Tuunanen, T., Gengler, C., Rossi, M., Hui, W., Virtanen, V., Bragge, J.: The design science research process: a model for producing and presenting information systems research. In: Design Science Research in Information Systems and Technology (DESRIST 2006), 24–25 February, Claremont, CA (2006)
39. Rogers, M., Goldman, J., Mislan, R., Debrota, S., Wedge, T.: Computer forensics field triage process model. In: Conference on Digital Forensics, Security and Law (2006)
40. Nair, B.S.: Digital Electronics and Logic Design, 6th edn. Prentice Hall, New Delhi (2006)
41. Rowlingson, R.: A ten step process for forensic readiness. Int. J. Digit. Evid. 2(4), 1–28 (2004)
42. Tan, J.: Forensic Readiness (2001). http://isis.poly.edu/kulesh/forensics/forensic_readiness.pdf. Accessed 20 Jan 2015

Computer Forensic Analysis of Private Browsing Modes

Reza Montasari[1](✉) and Pekka Peltola[2]

[1] Derby University, Derby, UK
r.montasari@derby.ac.uk
[2] Nottingham University, Nottingham, UK
pekka.peltola@nottingham.ac.uk

Abstract. This paper investigates the effectiveness of the private browsing modes built into four major Internet browsers. In examining the phenomenon of the private browsing modes built into four widely used Internet browsers, this paper aims to determine whether one can identify when a private browsing mode has been utilized by a suspect to perform a criminal or illegal act and to what extent the forensic examination of a computer can expose evidence of private browsing use.

Keywords: Private browsing · Incognito · InPrivate · Computer forensics investigation · Digital analysis

1 Introduction

Web browsers are used on a daily basis to perform many various online activities, such as searching for information, shopping and conducting payment transactions. Web browsers log and store a large amount of data concerning users' browsing activities, including caching files, visited URL's, search terms and cookies. These are retained on the user's computer and are easily located by other users. The use of a browser's public mode therefore facilitates a digital forensic investigator's examination of a suspect's internet activities, as is needed in cases where questionable web sites were visited or criminal acts were conducted through the Internet. However, over the past few years, vendors of the major web browsers have expressed concern over users' privacy while browsing the Internet. This has entailed their development of a new feature, the "private browsing" mode, with the aim of enabling users to browse the Internet whilst leaving no trace of their browsing activity. Although private browsing modes may be deployed by some users for a variety of respectable reasons, such as buying a surprise gift, they can also be exploited by cyber criminals for nefarious activities. The endeavours of these criminals to thoroughly erase any evidence of their Internet browsing activities seem to be facilitated by the private browsing modes. For example, they can prevent the inscription of an individual's private browsing data on the hard drive, assisting criminals by leaving none of the evidential artifacts which can be vital in a court of law.

This paper aims to investigate the effectiveness of the private browsing modes built into four major Internet browsers: Google Chrome Incognito, Mozilla Firefox Private Browsing Mode, Internet Explorer InPrivate and Apple Safari Private Browsing Mode.

© Springer International Publishing Switzerland 2015
H. Jahankhani et al. (Eds.): ICGS3 2015, CCIS 534, pp. 96–109, 2015.
DOI: 10.1007/978-3-319-23276-8_9

To achieve this, a set of identical experiments is carried out on private browsing mode of each of the four web browsers, using selected pre-defined web browsing activities. The forensic analysis is conducted in two stages. Firstly, the analysis is performed on both "common" and "uncommon" locations on the hard drive; and the second stage involves investigating Physical Memory (RAM). This is to investigate whether each browser, while in private mode, leaves browsing artifacts or not in these locations.

2   Literature Review

Private browsing modes have different names according to the browser. It is called "Incognito Mode" in Chrome [1], "InPrivate Browsing" in Internet Explorer [2], "Private Browsing" in Firefox [3] and "Private Browsing" in Safari [4]. "Private Browsing" was first released by Apple Safari in 2005 [5]. Following the same principle Google Chrome and Microsoft introduced "Incognito" and "InPrivate" respectively in 2008 [6]. Mozilla's "Private Browsing" was introduced in 2009 [7]. The most common reasons cited by vendors for providing private modes are to enable shopping for surprise gifts on a family PC [2] and the planning of surprise parties [1]. However, through their research work, Aggarwal et al. [8] revealed that in reality the searching of adult websites was the primary reason for utilizing private modes [8]. Using a particular technique, Aggarwal et al. [8] posted advertisements on ad-networks to target various categories of websites including adult and gift websites "to correlate the use of private mode with the type of website being visited". This experiment revealed that private browsing was more popular at adult sites than gift buying websites.

Two distinct goals must be met in order for a private mode to be considered safe and secure. The first goal is security against a local attacker ("an attacker who controls the user's machine") and the second goal is security against a web attacker ("an attacker who controls websites the user visits") [8]. Regarding the local attacker, while in private mode browsers should be able to prevent the sites visited from placing browsing artifacts on the user's machine. For web attackers, browsers should make it impossible for websites to find out whether a particular user has previously visited them by preventing websites from linking users' activities whilst in private and public modes. Although the web attacker model has been previously researched to some extent [8–10], the concept of the local attacker has not been addressed adequately. No paper was found that investigates private browsing modes except the research conducted by Said et al. [12]. However, Said et al's [12] results cannot be considered accurate as they conducted their experiments on a polluted system. Moreover, they carried out their experiments on older versions of the web browsers' private modes. Therefore, it was decided to conduct new experiments to provide a better understanding of this phenomenon and to find out how this feature could affect digital forensic investigations.

3   Testing Methodology

Web browsing activities plan detailed below was designed to emulate a realistic scenario in which a cyber-criminal or suspect carries out one of the following actions:

1. Use of the browser to visit www.youtube.com; entering the search term "jessie ware wildest moments" and watching the video.
2. Use of the search engine 'Google' to find and visit the "Pirate Bay Proxy," then searching for "Ubuntu" on this website, but taking no further action.
3. Visiting www.facebook.com and downloading a profile picture.
4. Visiting www.amazon.co.uk and searching and viewing "Casio F-91W".
5. Using Google, searching and viewing, but not saving, a PDF file titled "Doppelganger: Better Browser Privacy without the Bother."

The aim of these tests was to investigate the effectiveness of the private browsing modes of the four widely used web browsers and to find out whether artifacts of the tests carried out could be found. Experiments on the "private" modes were conducted on the below versions of the four browsers as follows. Note that although the experiments were conducted on the private modes of the older versions of the browsers, the problem associated with the security of these private modes still remain.

- Incognito – Google Chrome Version 26.0.1410.43.
- Private Browsing – Mozilla Firefox Version 20.0.
- InPrivate – Internet Explorer Version 9.0.8112.16421.
- Private Browsing – Apple Safari Version 5.1.7 (7534.57.2).

The presented set of browsing activities was run identically on the snapshots of the virtual machine in the private browsing modes in order to determine whether any of the following browsing artifacts could be recovered; cached web pages, web browsing history, download history, visited URLs, search terms used in the Google search engine or website search options. In the search for browsing artifacts, images of Physical Memory (RAM) were also captured for analysis. Physical Memory contains volatile data which can be lost once the machine is switched off. Therefore, the decision to investigate RAM was made with a view in emulating a realistic police raid scenario, where officers must carry out a live investigation of the suspect's machine before turning it off and removing it for further analysis.

3.1 Platform Options - Virtualization

In order to ensure that the experiments would be conducted on a clean system to avoid polluting the research by mixing browsing artifacts, various options were considered. It was decided to utilize virtualization, and VirtualBox was selected as it is freely available and has open-source software and a virtual hard disk which can be forensically imaged using AccessData's FTK Imager. It was decided to utilize snapshots as the preferred method and was adopted for all the experiments conducted for this project. The reason for this choice was because snapshots would require the setting up of only one base virtual machine from which multiple snapshots could be taken each taking only a few seconds. Once each experiment was completed, the snapshot of the virtual machine was closed and the snapshot was restored to its preceding, original state.

In order to prevent the pollution of the experiments, each web browser was installed in separate virtual machines using its installer, which was transferred without using another browser to download (such as Internet Explorer). This ensured that no browsing artifact was left behind when experimenting on other browsers. Using VirtualBox, it was possible to set up a shared folder between the host machine (the physical machine on which VirtualBox ran) and the guest machine (the virtual computer running inside VirtualBox). In order to carry out the hypothetical digital forensic investigation, various software and tools were utilized. These included: (1) FTK Imager version 3.1.2, (2) Autopsy 3.0.4, (3) FTK 1.81.6 and (4) WinHex.

4 Results

Identical test was performed on each web browser's private mode inside its respective snapshot of the virtual machine. Upon the completion of each experiment and prior to closing down a particular web browser's private mode, RAM was imaged and verified through matching MD5 and SHA1 checksums using FTK Imager 3.1.2. The private mode session was then terminated by closing down the private browsing window. Using FTK Imager again, the virtual hard drive of the snapshot was then imaged and verified through corresponding MD5 and SHA1 checksums.

The first part of the analysis involved the examination of different locations on the hard drive image. The hard drive image of each snapshot was separately imported to Autopsy and FTK for examination. Four different cases were then built for four different experiments on the private browsing modes. Both "common" and "uncommon" locations on the hard drive were analyzed to identify whether traces of the browsing activities carried out in private mode could be found.

The second part of the analysis required examination of the captured image of the RAM of each snapshot for each particular experiment on the private browsing mode. As with the hard drive examination, four different cases were built for four different experiments on the private browsing modes. FTK 1.81.6 and WinHex were deployed for the examination of the RAM images due to their useful and powerful capabilities. In this way, the RAM images were analyzed to search for any browsing artifacts from the experiments on the private mode sessions.

4.1 Common and Uncommon Locations

The first part included the examination of different locations on the captured image of the hard drive including "common" and "uncommon" locations where the browsers store web browsing history and cache. Neither "common locations" (Cache folder, Web history) nor "uncommon locations" ("$MFT", "$LogFile", "Favicons", "etilqs", "Manifest.json", "pagefile.sys.", "unallocated space" and "slack space") revealed any trace of browsing artifacts in Chrome browser. In Firefox, no traces were found in "common locations" or "uncommon locations" (including "places.sqlite", "webapps-store.sqlite", "sessionstore.bak", "search.json" and "nssckbi.dll"). However, on investigating the "pagefile.sys", some entries were discovered relating to pre-defined web browsing search terms used during the private browsing session. The findings were as follows (Table 1):

Table 1. Entries related to search terms discovered from pagefile.sys.

Search term	Entries
'Pirate Bay Proxy'	1
'Ubuntu'	3

A profile picture downloaded from "www.facebook.com", while in Mozilla Firefox's private browsing mode, was discovered. Firefox had unexpectedly retained this picture. Using the "data carving" technique, profile picture was recovered. This finding contradicts the claims of Mozilla's vendor that Firefox deletes any downloaded item after the termination of a private browsing session [7].

Unlike the tests of the first two web browsers, examination of Internet Explorer's "Cache" records revealed many traces of the pre-defined web browsing activities, despite the browsing activities being undertaken in its "private" browsing mode. All the traces of the browsing artifacts from private browsing session had leaked into the "Cache" folder. For example, the visited URLs, search terms, downloaded picture and PDF file viewed could all be seen in the "Cache" folder.

Although many of the files containing the web browsing artifacts within the "Cache" folder were intact, Internet Explorer had deleted some of them. It appears that Internet Explorer caches the browsing artifacts on the hard drive and "deletes" them when the private browsing session is terminated. However, it does not "erase" the browsing data, thus files remain on the hard disk until they are overwritten by other files. Therefore, a forensic investigator would be able to recover those files if he were analyzing a machine at the state where the files containing the browsing data had been deleted but not yet overwritten. This was confirmed by the recovery of the deleted files using the "data carving" technique on the entire "Cache" folder. Executing data carving on the "Cache" folder using the FTK surprisingly recovered all the deleted artifacts that

Table 2. Entries for visited URLs and search terms used in InPrivate mode found in Cache.

Visited URL	Entries
www.youtube.com	19
www.facebook.com	27
www.google.com	132
www.amazon.co.uk	276
Search term	Entries
'jessie ware wildest moments'	84
'Pirate Bay Proxy'	102
'Ubuntu'	32
'Casio F-91 W'	96
'Doppelganger: Better Browser Privacy…, the entire PDF file could be found in the "Cache"'	6
Picture downloaded from www.facebook.com	Entries
"Profile Picture"	1

were contained in those files. Below are the findings after analyzing the "Cache" folder (Fig. 1 and Table 2):

Next "common location" investigated was Internet Explorer's "Web History". Although this was not as rich as the "Cache" folder in terms of browsing artefacts, an analysis nevertheless revealed some traces relating to a search term for the PDF file and an entry for the downloaded picture during the private browsing session. Entire PDF file could be seen, despite the fact that it had only been viewed and not downloaded, as specified in the pre-defined web browsing activities. Indeed, the full PDF file was recovered. Below shows the findings after analyzing the "Web History" of Internet Explorer (Table 3).

Table 3. The analysis of Web History revealing the full path to the location of the downloaded picture and PDF on the hard drive image.

Downloaded picture	Entries
/img_HDImage-Internet-Explorer-Private-Mode.001/vol_vol3/Users/XXXX/Downloads	1
PDF file	Entries
/img_HDImage-Internet-Explorer-Private-Mode.001/vol_vol3/Users/XXX/AppData/Local/Microsoft/Windows/TemporaryInterneFiles/Low/Content.IE5/X1DMOQG2/doppelganger-ccs06 [1].pdf	1

The next stage in analyzing the hard drive image was an examination of the "uncommon locations". These included "ntuser.dat", "$Unalloc" "$MFT", "pagefile. sys", "search.js", "iframe.js" and "schema.dat". The followings are the findings after analyzing these "uncommon locations" (Tables 4 and 5).

Table 4. Search terms used in InPrivate mode discovered in uncommon locations $MFT and unallocated spaces.

Search term discovered in $MFT	Entries
'jessie ware wildest moments'	19
'Casio F-91 W'	3
'Doppelganger: Better Browser Privacy without the bother'	1
Search term discovered in pagefile.sys	Entries
'Ubuntu'	2
Search term discovered in search.js	Entries
'jessie ware wildest moments'	23
Search term discovered in unallocated spaces	Entries
'jessie ware wildest moments'	65
'Pirate Bay Proxy'	59
'Ubuntu'	148
'Casio F-91 W'	52

Table 5. Internet Explorer, while in private mode, had leaked the PDF file into $Logfile.

PDF file	Entries
doppelganger-ccs06[1].pdf	5

In Safari the hard drive image was examined by searching the "uncommon locations" which included "WebpageIcons.db", "pagefile.sys", "_k.cfs", "search.js", "ieframe.dll.mui", "schema.dat", "Data1.cab", "e4e8be02b8faeta7_blobs.bin" and "LastSession.plist". No trace of browsing artifacts was discovered in any of these "uncommon locations," except in "WebpageIcons.db" and "e4e8be02b8faeta7_blobs.bin". All traces of browsing artifacts regarding the "pre-defined web browsing activities" conducted in the private browsing mode of Apple Safari could be seen in this "uncommon location". The findings were as follows (Table 6):

Table 6. Search terms used in Apple Safari's private mode discovered in WebpageIcons.db and e4e8be02b8faeta7_blobs.bin.

Search term discovered in WebpageIcons.db	Entries
'jessie ware wildest moments'	6
'Pirate Bay Proxy'	18
'Ubuntu'	7
'Casio F-91 W'	7
'Doppelganger: Better Browser Privacy without the bother'	3
Search term and PDF discovered in e4e8be02b8faeta7_blobs.bin	Entries
'Casio F-91 W'	3
doppelganger-ccs06[1].pdf	1

A subsequent investigation of "unallocated spaces" revealed that they too were rich in their storage of the browsing artifacts left behind from Safari's Private browsing mode. The findings after analyzing "unallocated space" were as follows (Table 7):

Table 7. URLs visited and search terms used in the private mode recovered from $Unalloc.

Visited URL Discovered in $Unalloc	Entries
www.youtube.com	45
www.facebook.com	27
www.google.com	15
www.amazon.co.uk	1
Search term discovered in $Unalloc	Entries
'jessie ware wildest moments'	16
'Pirate Bay Proxy'	28
'Ubuntu'	18

Table 8. The number of entries found in the RAM for each pre-defined web browsing activity carried out in the private browsing mode of each web browser.

Web browsing activity	Chrome	Firefox	IE	Safari
Visited URL "www.youtube.com"	1,180	204	504	4,038
Visited URL "www.google.com"	1,611	210	1,053	2,142
Visited URL "www.facbook.com"	1,764	396	5,757	7,077
Visited URL "www.amazon.co.uk"	1,719	760	3,292	11,744
Search term *"Jessie ware wildest moments"*	412	412	488	1,416
Search term *"Pirate Bay Proxy"*	906	330	2,697	1,281
Search term *"Ubuntu"*	197	164	330	665
Search term *"Casio F-91W"*	268	216	780	8,253
Search term *"Doppelganger: Better ..."*	2,586	2,232	264	12,552
Downloaded *"profile picture"*	None	None	None	3

Additionally, entries for the "profile picture" downloaded while in the private browsing session of Apple Safari were also discovered. For example, the image itself was found in the "Download" folder on the hard drive. The full path to this folder is as follows: /img_HDImage-Safari-Private-Mode.001/vol_vol3/Users/xxx/Downloads". Moreover, there were enough traces left on the system to show that a Facebook profile "xxx" had been accessed during the private session. The traces of this browsing activity was found in many "uncommon locations" on the hard drive, such as "WebpageIcons. db" and "$Unalloc".

4.2 Physical Memory (RAM)

The second part of the investigation involved an analysis of the captured images of the "Physical Memory" (RAM). After running a string search, both WinHex and FTK returned many hits on the URLs and search keywords used during the private browsing test. The below are the findings of analyzing the captured images of RAM:

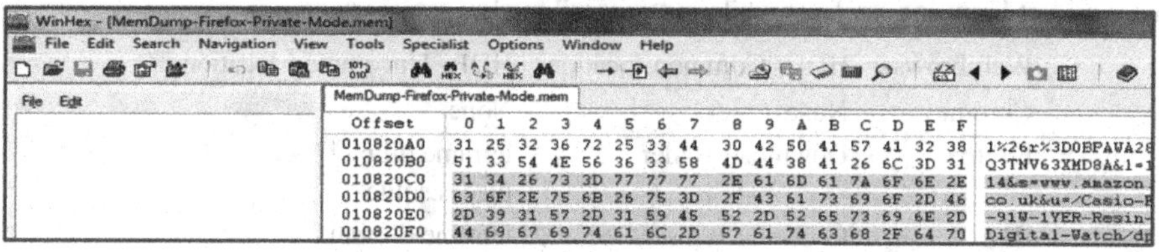

Fig. 1. Firefox browsing data from private browsing session recovered from the RAM, showing the website www.amazon.co.uk visited and the entered keywords "Casio F-91 W"

5   Evaluation and Comparison of the Results

The aim of this phase was to provide a consistent evaluation environment in which to compare the results of the experiments performed on the "private" browsing modes of the four widely used web browsers. For simplicity, statistics are presented in tables. To minimize the amount of these tables, the number of entries found for each item of the pre-defined browsing activities is not given individually for each location. Instead, the total number of entries found in the different locations for that particular activity is provided. The exact amount of entries is detailed under the relevant sub-headings. Table 9 outlines the total number of entries found for a particular pre-defined web browsing activity and Table 10 lists the "common" and "uncommon" locations on the hard drive in which those entries were found. It is the results presented in these two sets

Table 9. The total number of entries found in different locations on the hard drive for each pre-defined web browsing activity performed during the "private" browsing session of each web browser.

Browsing activity	Chrome	Firefox	IE	Safari
Visited URL "www.youtube.com"	None	46	74	63
Visited URL "www.google.com"	None	22	322	21
Visited URL "www.facbook.com"	None	7	259	47
Visited URL "www.amazon.co.uk"	None	3	514	19
Search term "Jessie ware wildest moments"	None	None	191	22
Search term "Pirate Bay Proxy"	None	1	161	46
Search term "Ubuntu"	None	3	182	25
Search term "Casio F-91 W"	None	None	151	10
Search term "Doppelganger: Better ..."	None	None	13	4
Downloaded "profile picture"	None	1	2	1

Table 10. Various "common" and "uncommon" locations on the hard drive where the four web browsers left browsing artefacts while in "private" mode.

Web browser	HDI - Common locations	HDI - Uncommon locations
Chrome	None	None
Firefox	Download folder	ieframe.dll.mui places.sqlite
IE	Cache Web history	ieframe.dll.mui pagefile.sys schema.dat search.js $Logfile and $Unalloc $MFT
Safari	Download folder	e4e8be02b8faeta7_blobs.bin WebpageIcons.db $Unalloc

of tables that are subsequently compared and evaluated to determine whether the private modes left traces of the pre-defined activities on the "common" and "uncommon" locations on the hard drive and whether traces were left in the same locations in the public and private modes.

5.1 Evaluation

While in the private mode, Google Chrome left no browsing artifacts in any of the "common" and "uncommon" locations on the hard drive. Consistent with Google Chrome, although Mozilla Firefox, while in private mode, avoided leaving browsing artifacts in the majority of locations, nevertheless it spread artifacts into one "common" location, the Download folder, and two "uncommon" locations, namely places.sqlite and ieframe.dll.mui. Analysis of these locations revealed traces of all of the pre-defined browsing activities performed in the private mode session, with the exception of the search terms "Jessie ware wildest moments", "Casio F-91 W" and "Doppelganger: Better Browser privacy without the Bother." In contrast, the number of locations in which Internet Explorer stored artifacts while in private browsing mode was astonishing. These entries represented traces of the entirety of the pre-defined web browsing activities performed. While in the "private" mode, Internet Explorer had stored browsing artifacts in "common" and "uncommon" locations such as Web History, Cache, ieframe.dll.mui, ntuser.dat, pagefile.sys, schema.dat, search.js, $MFT, $Logfile and $Unalloc and "e4e8be02b8faeta7_blobs.bin". Apple Safari, whilst in "private" mode, avoided leaving artifacts in most of those locations, leaving them in only one "common" location, Download folder, and three "uncommon" locations, "e4e8be02 b8faeta7_blobs.bin", "$Unalloc", "WebpageIcons.db".

5.2 Comparison

5.2.1 Common and Uncommon Locations

This sub-section compares and evaluates the "private" browsing modes of the four web browsers based upon the results of the analysis of the "common" and "uncommon" locations on the Hard Drive. Based on the figures in Tables 9 and 10, "Incognito" of Google Chrome is the most secure and private of the private browsing modes. Google Chrome left no browsing artifact from its "private" browsing session in the "common" and "uncommon" locations on the hard drive. These results accord with Google's claims that, "Web pages that you open and files downloaded while you are in Incognito aren't recorded in your browsing and download histories." [1]. Moreover, "Incognito" can be regarded as a "secure" and "private" mode based upon the definition of Aggarwal et al's [8] first goal of private modes, the "local attacker model". Aggarwal et al. [8] state that for a web browser's private mode to be considered "secure" it must provide security against a "local attacker" (a forensic examiner or user of the same machine) by not leaving any browsing artifact in any location on the hard drive while in "private" mode.

Although Mozilla Firefox leaked browsing artifacts from its "private" browsing session to some locations on the hard drive, the number of such locations was low, amounting to two "uncommon" locations and only one "common" location. The experiments therefore demonstrated that Mozilla Firefox offers the second most secure web browser, the first being Google Chrome. However, based upon the "local attacker model" [8], Firefox's "private" mode cannot be regarded as a "secure" and "private" mode, leaking some artifacts into locations on the hard drive which could be accessed by a forensic investigator. Therefore, Mozilla Firefox must not be regarded as a private browser due to the fact that browsing artifacts can be seen, albeit in relatively few locations. Such findings appear to be in contradiction with the claims of Mozilla that, "Private Browsing allows you to browse the Internet without saving any information about which sites and pages you've visited." [3].

In contrast to Google Chrome and Mozilla Firefox, traces of the entirety of the pre-defined browsing activities carried out in Internet Explorer's "InPrivate" mode were recovered from both "common" and "uncommon" locations on the hard drive. As Tables 9 and 10 highlight, the results of the experiments in the private browsing mode of Internet Explorer are astonishing. For example, while in private mode, Internet Explorer leaves browsing artifacts in many locations on the hard drive. The conclusion is that Internet Explorer offers no privacy at all. Therefore, Internet Explorer's private mode does not meet the criteria of the "local attacker model" in [8]. The results for private browsing using Internet Explorer are in conflict with the claims of Microsoft that, "InPrivate Browsing helps prevent your browsing history and temporary Internet files from being retained by the browser." [1].

Consistent with Internet Explorer's "private" browsing mode, Apple Safari also leaked onto the hard drive traces of all pre-defined web browsing activities carried out during its "private" session. However, based upon the figures in Tables 9 and 10, Apple Safari would appear to be more secure and private than Internet Explorer. For example, Internet Explorer left artifacts in many "common" and "uncommon" locations, whereas, Apple Safari left them in only one "common" location and three "uncommon" locations. Nevertheless, Apple Safari's private mode cannot still be regarded as "private" and "secure" based upon the "local attacker model" in [8], which asserts that in order for a private mode to be regarded as "private", it must provide security against a "local attacker" by leaving no browsing artifact in any location on the hard drive. It can be concluded that Apple does not fulfill the promises made to users in stating:

> When Private Browsing is on, web pages are not added to the history list, the names of downloads are removed from the Downloads window, and searches are not added to the search field's pop-up menu [4].

5.3 Physical Memory

This sub-section compares and evaluates the private browsing modes of the four web browsers based upon the results of the analysis of the "Physical Memory" (RAM). Table 8 provides the total number of entries discovered in "Physical Memory" (RAM) for each pre-defined activity carried out in the private browsing mode of the four web browsers. As Table 8 demonstrates, an analysis of the captured image of the "Physical Memory" (RAM) for each "private" mode reveals that each web browser's "private" mode places in the RAM a significant number of entries relating to the browsing activities. In those circumstances, it would not be appropriate to compare the number of entries to conclude which is the safest "private" mode as the deposit of so many artifacts in the RAM thoroughly undermines the privacy offered by each of the four web browsers, even Google Chrome, which is considered to be secure and private.

The results of the analysis of the RAM for "private" browsing activities carried out for this project accord with those of other forensic experts, including [8, 11, 12]. These forensic experts all agree that private browsing artifacts can be recovered from RAM as erasing all volatile memory after exiting the private mode is difficult for private browsers to achieve. However, the opinions of forensic experts then diverge. Said et al. [12] believe that forensic experts would be able to acquire data from RAM even if the user had exited the private mode session, provided that the computer was still running. In contrast, Aggarwal et al. [8] believe that a forensic investigator would be able to retrieve data only if he/she was able to access the suspect's computer before the private mode session was terminated. Aggarwal et al. [8] do state that although most of these artifacts are erased from the volatile memory once the user exits the private mode, the investigator could nevertheless find some artifacts even after exiting the private mode, as erasing all private browsing data from volatile memory is difficult to achieve.

The assertions of Aggarwal et al. [8] appear to be the more valid, being supported by others such as [11]. Aggarwal et al's [8] arguments are also supported by the experiments carried out in this project, where "private" browsing artifacts were recovered from RAM by imaging the RAM before closing down the "private" mode and shutting down the computer. Consequently, digital forensic investigators are advised to take advantage of "live" examinations, imaging and analyzing the RAM which has proved to be a rich source of browsing artifacts. Furthermore, there are cases where "private" browsing data left in the RAM was retrieved despite the fact that the computer was turned off after the termination of the "private" mode session. An "uncommon" location on the hard drive behaves as though it were the RAM in order to store data that RAM cannot accommodate when fully used. This "uncommon" location on the hard drive accommodating data from RAM is called the "pagefile.sys" file. This was confirmed in the experiments conducted for this project, the "pagefile.sys" file providing a substantial source of browsing artifacts in both the "public" and "private" browsing modes. For example, browsing artifacts were left in this "uncommon" location by all four of the web browsers. Internet Explorer alone placed browsing artifacts from the "private" browsing session in this file. Accordingly, based on its significant benefits for recovering browsing data, forensic investigators are recommended to examine this file to retrieve evidential artifacts left from "private" browsing sessions. However, this method is not infallible as a suspect with a good understanding of digital forensic techniques could manually erase from the memory any browsing artifact left from a "private" session.

6 Conclusion and Future Work

This project analyzed the effectiveness of the "private" modes of four widely deployed web browsers, resulting in the discovery of numerous weaknesses in their implementation which preclude them from meeting their desired security goals. As regards the "local attacker model", experiments carried out in this project exposed the reality that the "private" browsers of Mozilla Firefox, Internet Explorer and Apple Safari cannot keep browsing activities private from a local attacker, such as a forensic examiner. All three left behind various types of browsing data in both "common" and "uncommon" locations on the hard drive. Consequently, although the "private" modes of Mozilla Firefox, Internet Explorer and Apple Safari might offer regular users some degree of privacy against other regular users of the same machine at a local level of Internet information, they cannot conceal the user's private browsing activity from a dedicated computer forensic expert. Therefore, the level of privacy provided by these three major browsers is at best sufficient for only the average user. In contrast, this project's experiments on the "private" browsing mode of Google Chrome revealed that it is completely private, not leaving any browsing artifact in either "common" or "uncommon" locations on the hard drive. These results conflict with the results achieved by Said et al. [12], where Google Chrome is disregarded as a completely private mode. However, this could be explained by the fact that Said et. al's [12] experiment was conducted on an older version of Google Chrome. It is important to note that all four web browsers leave behind "private" browsing artifacts in the "Physical Memory" (RAM). Therefore, on seizing a suspect's computer whilst it is still turned on, a forensic examiner could recover from the RAM all browsing activities carried out during the "private" browsing session. The opportunity to recover such data if a computer is seized after the machine is turned off is greatly reduced, as the volatile nature of RAM may cause the data to be lost.

A dedicated computer forensic investigator is able to recover many forensic browsing artifacts by using effective forensic tools and techniques. This contradicts the professed advantages of "private" modes, making it arguable that "private" modes are not in reality private at all. Nevertheless, the prospect of reconstructing the suspicious behaviour of a person using a "private" mode is dependent on the variety of the "private" browser used and the skills of both the forensic investigator and suspect. For example, a forensic investigator would more easily retrieve evidential artifacts from a computer where a suspect had utilized the "private" modes of Internet Explorer or Apple Safari rather than Mozilla Firefox, as they are less secure. The difficulty of recovery increases in proportion to the suspect's knowledge of digital forensic techniques and tools, such as the methods of manually deleting any remaining data not effectively removed by the browser. However, even where a suspect had no such knowledge, a forensic investigator would be unable to recover "private" browsing data where Google Chrome had been used, as no such data is left in Google Chrome's "private" mode.

Future work should be extended to investigate the browser add-ons to determine whether these add-ons undermine the security of "private" browsers by leaking data onto the hard drive. This has not been verified by any experiment, being outside of the scope of this project.

References

1. Google: Incognito mode (browse in private) (2013). http://support.google.com/chrome/bin/answer.py?hl=en&answer=95464. Accessed 10 Mar 2013

2. Microsoft: InPrivate Browsing (2013). http://windows.microsoft.com/en-GB/internet-explorer/products/ie-9/features/in-private. Accessed 13 Mar 2013
3. Mozilla: Firefox 3.5 (2009). http://www.mozilla.org/en-US/firefox/3.5/releasenotes/. Accessed 11 Mar 2013
4. Apple: Safari 5.1 (OS X Lion): Browse privately (2013). https://support.apple.com/kb/PH5000. Accessed 10 Mar 2013
5. Fox, S.: 'Porn mode' browsing not really that private, NBCNews, 24 August 2010. http://www.nbcnews.com/id/38834872/ns/technology_and_science-security/t/porn-mode-browsing-not-really-private/#.UQl3Nh2EzTq. Accessed 11 Mar 2013
6. Keizer, G.: Microsoft Adds Privacy Tools to IE8 (2008). http://www.pcworld.com/article/150334/ie8_privacy_tools.html. Accessed 13 Mar 2013
7. Mozilla: Private Browsing- Browse the web without saving information about the sites you visit (2013). http://support.mozilla.org/en-US/kb/private-browsing-browse-web-without-saving-info. Accessed 11 Mar 2013
8. Aggarwal, G., Bursztein, E., Jackson, C., Boneh, D.: An analysis of private browsing modes in modern browsers. In: Proceedings of the 19th USENIX Security Symposium, Washington, DC, Stanford University (2010). http://static.usenix.org/events/sec10/tech/full_papers/Aggarwal.pdf. Accessed 10 Mar 2013
9. Eckersley, P.: How unique is your web browser? In: Atallah, M.J., Hopper, N.J. (eds.) PETS 2010. LNCS, vol. 6205, pp. 1–18. Springer, Heidelberg (2010)
10. Frowen, A.: How Private Is 'In Private' Browsing? (2010). http://www.intaforensics.com/Blog/How-Private-Is-In-Private-Browsing.aspx. Accessed 17 Mar 2013
11. Mahendrakar, A., Irving, J., Patel, S.: Forensic analysis of private browsing mode in popular browsers. In: Proceedings of the USENIX security symposium (2010). http://www.mocktest.net/paper.pdf. Accessed 2 May 2013
12. Said, H., Al Mutawa, N., Al Awadhi, I., Guimaraes, M.: Forensic analysis of private browsing artefacts. In: International Conference on Innovations in Information Technology (IIT), Dubai, 25–27 April, pp. 197–202 (2011)

IT and Cyber Crime

Searching the Web for Illegal Content:
The Anatomy of a Semantic Search Engine

Luigi Laura[1,2]([⊠]) and Gianluigi Me[3]

[1] Department of Computer, Control, and Management Engineering
"Antonio Ruberti", "Sapienza" University of Rome,
Via Ariosto 25, 00185 Roma, Italy
laura@dis.uniroma1.it
[2] Research Centre for Transport and Logistics (CTL),
"Sapienza" Università di Roma, Roma, Italy
[3] CeRSI - Research Center in Information Systems,
LUISS Guido Carli University, Roma, Italy
gme@luiss.it

Abstract. In this paper we describe the challenges in the realization of
a semantic search engine, suited to help law enforcements in the fight
against the online drug marketplaces, where New Psychoactive Substances (NPS) are sold. This search engine has been developed under
the *Semantic Illegal Content Hunter* (SICH) Project, with the financial
support of the Prevention of and Fight Against Crime Programme ISEC
2012 European Commission. The SICH Project specific objective is to
develop new strategic tools and assessment techniques, based on semantic analysis on texts, to support the dynamic mapping and the automatic
identification of illegal content over the Net.

1 Introduction

In the last decade we witnessed a large rise of New Psychoactive Substances
(NPS): according to a very recent report [15] of the United Nations Office on
Drugs and Crime (UNODC), synthetic drugs are taking an ever-greater share
of the illicit drugs market, and in particular they gained popularity among the
young: for example, in North America and Europe, certain NPS are now more
used by young consumers than traditional illicit drugs.

We cite Jean-Luc Lemahieu, Director for Policy Analysis and Public Affairs
at UNODC: *There is a dynamic and unprecedented global expansion of the synthetic drugs market both in scope and variety. New substances are quickly created
and marketed, challenging law enforcement efforts to keep up with the traffickers
and curb public health risks.*

In this context, it is important to support law enforcements, also against
the proliferation of online drug marketplaces, such as the famous Silk Road,
that has operated anonymously since 2011 [9]: it is accessible through the Tor
anonymizing software [14], that encrypts computer IP addresses, and payments
are made using the anonymous and untraceable Bit Coins crypto-currency [3].

H. Jahankhani et al. (Eds.): ICGS3 2015, CCIS 534, pp. 113–122, 2015.
DOI: 10.1007/978-3-319-23276-8_10

In this paper we describe the challenges in the realization of a semantic search engine, suited to help law enforcements in the fight against the online drug marketplaces. This search engine has been developed under the *Semantic Illegal Content Hunter* (SICH) Project, with the financial support of the Prevention of and Fight Against Crime Programme ISEC 2012 European Commission.

The SICH Project specific objective is to develop new strategic tools and assessment techniques, based on semantic analysis on texts, to support the dynamic mapping and the automatic identification of illegal content over the Net. Xenophobia/Racism, illegal online Gambling and Novel Psychoactive Substances (NPS) are the main areas of reference. In this paper we focus, for the sake of exposition, to the NPS related aspects of the search engine, and leave the other areas for the full version of the paper.

This paper is organized as follows: in the following section we describe the related work, whilst Sect. 3 details the internal organization of the SICH search engine, highlighting the differences with traditional search engines. Finally, Sect. 4 addresses concluding comments and remarks.

2   Related Work

The Internet investigations supporting technology research received full attention in the area of pedopornography and pedophile image files detection and analysis the last years. In particular, the FIVES[1], MAPAP[2] and I-Dash[3] projects, aiming at developing novel investigative tools specifically tailored for investigations involving images and videos of child sexual abuse. We also mention the iCOP[4], delivering a forensics toolkit to be utilized by law enforcement, to help filter and prioritize new instances of child abuse media on P2P networks, via a image/text analysis combined approach.

NPS in the dark/surface of web. The famous former version of 'Silk Road' online drug marketplace has been studied by Van Hout and Bingham from several perspectives: in [10] the authors aimed to describe user motives and realities of accessing, navigating and purchasing on the Silk Road marketplace. They used systematic online observations, monitored discussion threads on the site during four months of fieldwork and conducted anonymous online interviews with a convenience sample of adult Silk Road users. In [11] the authors explore the accounts of vendor subunits situated within the Silk Road marketplace: ten vendors, that completed an online interview via the direct message facility and via Tor mail, described themselves as intelligent and responsible consumers of drugs. These vendors explained the decisions to commence vending operations on the site centred on simplicity in setting up vendor accounts, and opportunity to operate within a low risk, high traffic, high mark-up, secure and anonymous Deep

---

[1] http://fives.kau.se/.

[2] http://antipaedo.lip6.fr/.

[3] http://www.i-dash.eu/.

[4] http://scc-sentinel.lancs.ac.uk/icop/.

Web infrastructure. Currently, malicious actors use anonymous networks (i.e. Tor, I2P, Freenet) to exchange information and goods and use the marketplaces available in the deepweb, along with the goods offered. Due to a large variety of goods available in these marketplaces (e.g. Mr Mice Guy, Agora, AlphaBay, BlackBank, Silkkitie, Babylon, Crypto Market, etc.), TOR represents a term of reference for exchanging goods in the black market which can be entered by different kinds (e.g. MultiSig And Trusted Marketplaces, Invite Markets etc.). Moreover, many NPS e-shops on the surface of the Web represent the point of contact with the anonymous networks, thanks to heterogeneous European member states legal frameworks, while, in our knowledge, there are not similar evidences regarding *fora* hosting manufacturers and end-users discussions. Finally, in [9] Van Hout and Bingham describe extensively a single case study: they recruited the participant following a lengthy relationship building phase on the Silk Road chat forum. Thus, the authors explored a Silk Road users motives for online drug purchasing, experiences of accessing and using the website, drug information sourcing, decision making and purchasing, outcomes and settings for use, and perspectives around security.

In [8] Deluca et al. present the outcome of the European funded Psychonaut Web Mapping Project[5], whose the aim was to develop a web scanning system to identify and categorize novel recreational drugs/psychoactive compounds, and new trends in drug use based on information available on the Internet.

In the two years period of the project (2008–2010) more than 200 discussion forums, social media, online shops, websites and other Internet resources (e.g. YouTube, eBay, Google, Google Insight) have been extensively and regularly monitored in 7 European countries (UK, Finland, Norway, Belgium, Germany, Italy and Spain) for emerging trends of NPS throughout the period of the study. In total more than 400 substances/products have been recorded.

The outcome of the closely related the Recreational Drugs European Network project (ReDNet[6]), also funded by the European Commission, are reported in the work of Corazza et al. [6]. The ReDNet was implemented to improve the information stream to young people and professionals about effects/risks of NPS by identifying online products and disseminating relevant information through technological tools. The ReDNet project also maintain a database of NPS.

From the point of view of a search engine, it is important to cite the paper of Corazza et al. [7]: here the authors study the marketing strategies, and, most notably, the brand names of NPS, designed to appeal young people. They also identified evolving strategies for the online diffusion and the retail of NPSs, including discounts and periodic offers on chosen products.

Search engine technologies. After the very famous paper *The anatomy of a large-scale hypertextual Web search engine* of Brin and Page [4], that describes a high level view of the architecture of the Google search engine, in the scientific literature is possible to find a huge wealth of works detailing every possible

---

[5] http://www.psychonautproject.eu/.

[6] http://www.rednetproject.eu/.

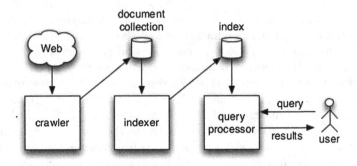

Fig. 1. A simple view of the main components of a web search engine: the crawler, the indexer, and the query processor (from [1]).

aspect inside a search engine. We refer the interested reader to the books of Baeza Yates [2] and Witten et al. [16].

3   The Anatomy of the SICH Search Engine

In Fig. 1 we can see a very simple and general view of the three main components of a Web search engine:

- **The crawler**, also called the spider, is the component that is in charge of collecting the web pages to be indexed.
- **The indexer** is the component in charge of parsing and storing data in order to facilitate fast and accurate information retrieval.
- **The query processor** is the component that interacts with the user: it parses the user query and return a list of the relevant documents.

In the following sections we detail each of the above components of the SICH search engine, highlighting the differences from a traditional web search engine.

3.1   The Crawler

The crawler is probably the most standard components inside the SICH search engine. It is important to clarify that, since we are not (yet) dealing with a massive amount of data, there is no need to use a complex parallel crawler, such as the ones described in the classical paper of Cho and Garcia-Molina [5].

In particular, the Web search and index process is achieved by ESCrawler, a customizable, proprietary spider, developed by Expert System[7], one of the partners of the SICH project. The ESCrawler is able to:

1. download documents from the Web;
2. search and extract parts of documents;

---

[7] http://www.expertsystem.com/.

3. generate documents composed by the parts of different documents;
4. filter non-core parts of documents;
5. populate HTML forms and to get the result;
6. catalogue documents or parts of them by calculating a hash signature.

Note that, differently from a traditional Web search engine, where sites' creators are eager to be crawled and indexed, in this NPS setting, as in the other illegal content setting, we cannot expect to users to provides the starting URLs of the sites to be explored, and therefore the list of URLs is build in a semi-assisted way, using manually collected data together with the data from available databases, such as the ones provided by the already mentioned ReDNet and Psychonaut projects.

3.2 The Indexer

In a traditional web search engine, the indexer builds, as its name suggests, an index of all the web pages. The index is used, together with the query processor, to retrieve the pages in an order provided by a ranking algorithm, such as the famous PageRank [13].

The main difference with a traditional Web search engine is, in some sense, the reversal of the game being played: in a traditional Web search engine the goal of all the sites' owners is to have their website ranked as high as possible, thus obtaining benefits such as visibility and, subsequently, money; here the sites' owners do not want their sites to be listed at all. In both the cases we are in the area of *Adversarial Information Retrieval* (see, e.g., [12]): the difference here is the goal; indeed, in the traditional settings the players (i.e., the sites' owners) cheat in order to be ranked high, whilst in this case they do the opposite: they cheat to be ranked low or, even better, not be ranked at all.

In order to establish an intermediate layer of data representation, in the SICH search engine has been defined an analysis process, able to discover knowledge and intelligence, focused on identifying NPS among unstructured information (stored in temporary repository created during acquisition phase). To achieve this goal, semantics overcomes the limitations of traditional systems which use criteria based on keywords, statistics or pattern matching. In such cases, we only examine text as a sequence of characters, ignoring the meaning of words and concepts. The applied methodology relies on a semantic engine, whose functionalities are based on linguistic analysis based on a semantic network, accomplishing a huge understanding of text. To implement this workflow, acquired files will pass through two processing phases, briefly described below.

- **Discovery.** From unstructured text, data content will be automatically extracted, normalized and then loaded into databases. In this way, its possible to extract from text key entities as NPS active principles, nicknames and specialized terms related to this domain.
- **Categorization.** Free-text documents will be grouped by applying automatic classification rules; these rules will be applied on text content as well as on many other details and on customizable taxonomies.

The implementation of the above mentioned process is based on the use of several integrated components. These components are able to process natural language and understand meaning of text content. We have three main components: Parser, Semantic Network and Memory.

- **Parser.** It performs a complete morphological, grammatical and syntactical analysis of the sentence, thus identifying every element of a text and assigning each to the appropriate logical and grammatical function.
- **Semantic Network.** It contains the representation of concepts and relationships between them. It is a lexical database structured by a conceptual framework. The semantic network consists of a combination of Lexicon and Knowledge Base, assigning a specific meaning to each word analyzed:
  - **Lexicon:** Knowledge of all of the possible meanings of words, and in their proper context, is fundamental for processing text content with high precision. Representing knowledge in a series of networks, semantic network represents the complex connections and associations between text essential for disambiguation. Searching for word "MDMA", the SICH system will return a set of documents containing words (or sequence of characters) as "ecstasy", "disco biscuit", "methylenedioxymethamphetamine", "love drug". In the NPS domain, the lexicon, as aggregation of different words/lemma having the same meaning; is a very crucial phase, due to continuous updates of blacklists and the introduction of new NPS in e-shops and fora.
  - **Knowledge Base:** Knowledge is a key element for understanding what is being read. A lack of specific knowledge on a subject or area may prevent a person from fully comprehending a text. The Knowledge Base within Semantic Network is organized and applied during analysis in a process that can be compared to what humans do when they apply their "common knowledge" to the reading of a text. In the same way our personal knowledge is improved when we learn new things, Knowledge Base may also be increased, enriched and improved by a mechanism of guided learning with current and domain-specific information.
- **Memory.** To extract meaning of the text, with the best approximation, we use a method that identifies its semantic context through a retention technique applied during document analysis.

Described processes shall transform text (downloaded during acquisition phase) in data. Data can be frequently and easily organized, managed and found by request. Therefore we have a Semantic Index that allow us to make deep search and exploring on our initial set of unstructured text and to identify patterns in the relationships between the terms and concepts contained. Finally we create a *conceptual map* of acquired information.

The conceptual map is a graphic view of the text elements analyzed, essentially a structured representation of previously unstructured text, where:

- each concept expressed in the text is uniquely identified regardless of which words of a language are used to represent it in the text analyzed;

– each agent is associated with the action carried out;
– each object is connected to the related action.

In this representation of content, a document's main topic, as well as other topics, dates, numbers and other meaningful information, may be stored. The map provides a document with structure, which enables it to be used in formal processing tasks such as indexing, classification, summarization and translation.

3.3   The Query Processor

In a traditional Web search engine, the user interface is quite simple: we have a text form in which the user can enter the text and obtain, as already mentioned, the list of the relevant results, sorted according to some ranking algorithm. These traditional Web search engines are designed for a generic user, and thus provide a simple and effective interface.

The SICH search engine must be able to support law enforcements' agents, and thus it provides its users with the ability of searching, downloading, filtering, clustering and organizing illegal content contained in unstructured text documents. Obtained information will be available to final users through a system able to search, navigate and display them, supporting, in this way, criminological analysis and investigation. Search and Exploring developed process allows us to find information, starting from different aspects. Therefore, it is possible to do different search type: *linguistic search* (based on lemma, concepts, entities or categories), *spatial search* (using GEO mapping), *events-based search* (configuring push notifications or alerts), and searches based on corpora selection (corpora are structured sets where logical similar information are grouped).

The SICH system offers to the users a web interface, that allows interacting with all the functionalities described above. In particular, in Fig. 2 we can see an image of the textual search results; most notably, beside the input search

Fig. 2. Textual search results in the SICH search engine.

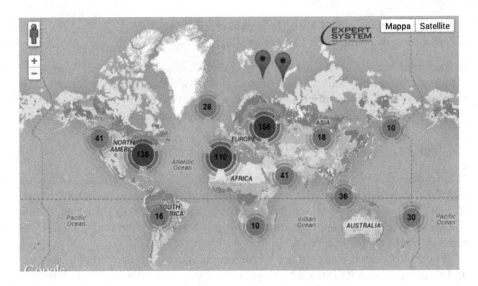

Fig. 3. Interactive World Map with Geolocalized Search Results.

form in the top center part, and the results shown, as usual, in a ranked list just below, two side panels that allow to refine and filter the search results. The left panel, indeed, allows users to access the elements of the NPS ontology already mentioned, whilst the right panel offers more classical filtering options based on time, language, source and corpora.

In Fig. 3 we can see the presented interactive world map, where the (geolocalized) search results are clustered based on their geographical proximity and shown in the map. It is possible to zoom in and out, with the clusters changing dynamically as a function of the zoom level, thus allowing an interactive exploration of the results.

4   Conclusions

In this paper we described the challenges in the implementation of a vertical search engine, designed to support law enforcements in the their fight against online drug marketplaces, and in particular those devoted to NPS drugs. In particular, we described the internal architecture of the SICH search engine, that is based on semantic techniques.

A search engine can be broadly divided into three distinct components: the crawler, the indexer, and the query processor. If compared against a traditional web search engine, there are several differences that makes the vertical search engines, such as the SICH one:

- The crawler component is simpler, since it has not to crawl a significant part of the web. Note, however, that the starting list of URLs to be visited cannot be built automatically, but it requires (at least) a human supervised approach.

- The indexer is a completely different: in traditional search engines the sites' owners try to cheat and rank their sites high, here we see the opposite: the site's owners try to have their sites ranked low, or, better, not ranked at all. We are still in the *Adversarial Information Retrieval* field, but the game is completely different and requires adhoc techniques.
- The query processor component is significantly more complex, at least from the users' perspective. This is mainly due to the difference in the target: the users of traditional search engines are generic users, that are nowadays used to the simple and effective text form where they can text their query; the users of vertical search engines, like the SICH one, are specialized agents of law enforcements, and they need an interactive system able to support them in different tasks, such as searching, downloading, filtering, clustering and organizing illegal content contained in unstructured text documents.

We are currently working on extending the user interface with a module that allows the interactive exploration of a graph obtained from the *conceptual map*: each concept is a node and there is a (n undirected) link between two nodes if the corresponding concepts have a similarity score bigger than a threshold. The user interaction allows to move the graph, explore it visually, and to select a subset of nodes and run the clustering algorithm on the subset, thus dynamically changing the visualization.

Acknowledgement. The EU ISEC programme has funded the 2 year national project SICH to the consortium formed by Expert System and RiSSC (Centro Ricerche e Studi su Sicurezza e Criminalità http://www.rissc.it/).

References

1. Arapakis, I.: System and user aspects of web search latency (2015)
2. Baeza-Yates, R., Ribeiro-Neto, B., et al.: Modern Information Retrieval, vol. 463. ACM Press, New York (1999)
3. Bitcoin. Bitcoin P2P digital currency (2011)
4. Brin, S., Page, L.: The anatomy of a large-scale hypertextual web search engine. Comput. Netw. ISDN Syst. **30**(1), 107–117 (1998)
5. Cho, J., Garcia-Molina, H.: Parallel crawlers. In: Proceedings of the 11th International Conference on World Wide Web, pp. 124–135. ACM (2002)
6. Corazza, O., Assi, S., Simonato, P., Corkery, J., Bersani, F.S., Demetrovics, Z., Stair, J., Fergus, S., Pezzolesi, C., Pasinetti, M., Deluca, P., Drummond, C., Davey, Z., Blaszko, U., Moskalewicz, J., Mervo, B., Furia, L.D., Farre, M., Flesland, L., Pisarska, A., Shapiro, H., Siemann, H., Skutle, A., Sferrazza, E., Torrens, M., Sambola, F., van der Kreeft, P., Scherbaum, N., Schifano, F.: Promoting innovation and excellence to face the rapid diffusion of novel psychoactive substances in the eu: the outcomes of the rednet project. Hum. Psychopharmacol. Clin. Exp. **28**(4), 317–323 (2013)
7. Corazza, O., Valeriani, G., Bersani, F.S., Corkery, J., Martinotti, G., Bersani, G., Schifano, F.: "Spice", "kryptonite", "black mamba": an overview of brand names and marketing strategies of novel psychoactive substances on the web. J. Psychoact. Drugs **46**(4), 287–294 (2014)

8. Deluca, P., Davey, Z., Corazza, O., Furia, D., Farre, M., Flesland, L.H., Mannonen, M., Majava, A., Peltoniemi, T., Pasinetti, M., Pezzolesi, C., Scherbaum, N., Siemann, H., Skutle, A., Torrens, M., van der Kreeft, P., Iversen, E., Schifano, F.: Identifying emerging trends in recreational drug use; outcomes from the psychonaut web mapping project. Prog. Neuropsychopharmacol. Biol. Psychiatry **39**(2), 221–226 (2012). New Drugs of Abuse

9. Hout, M.C.V., Bingham, T.: Silk road, the virtual drug marketplace: a single case study of user experiences. Int. J. Drug Policy **24**(5), 385–391 (2013)

10. Hout, M.C.V., Bingham, T.: Surfing the silk road: a study of users experiences. Int. J. Drug Policy **24**(6), 524–529 (2013)

11. Hout, M.C.V., Bingham, T.: Responsible vendors, intelligent consumers: silk road, the online revolution in drug trading. Int. J. Drug Policy **25**(2), 183–189 (2014)

12. Jansen, B.J.: Adversarial information retrieval aspects of sponsored search. In: AIRWeb, pp. 33–36 (2006)

13. Page, L., Brin, S., Motwani, R., Winograd, T.: The pagerank citation ranking: bringing order to the web. Stanford InfoLab (1999)

14. Tor Project: Anonymity Online (2011). https://www.torproject.org/

15. United Nations Office on Drugs and Crime (UNODC). Global synthetic drug assessment (2014)

16. Witten, I.H., Moffat, A., Bell, T.C.: Managing Gigabytes: Compressing and Indexing Documents and Images. Morgan Kaufmann, San Francisco (1999)

The Enemy Within: The Challenge for Business from Cyber-attack

Michael Reynolds[(✉)]

GSM-London, London, UK
`Michael.reynolds@gsm.org.uk`

Abstract. This paper presents an overview of certain risks posed by cyber abuse in the business context. It does not in any way represent a definitive study of **this** very complex area which is in a state of constant flux to the extent that the laws of nations cannot keep pace with the challenges of today let alone tomorrow. This paper therefore gives warning of this phenomenon and focusses on the role of business to its management and staff and others affected by its IT structure. The paper gives some analysis of the threats from cyber-crime and abuse from a variety of government agencies and other bodies. The underlying theme is one of caution and warning of the enemy within organisations and outside who use cyber-attack as a means to an end.

Keywords: Cyberattack · Risk · Cyber law

1 Introduction

These days anyone with a computer is liable to cyber-attack. It can be extremely frustrating and costly for academics as well as businesses. Even worse it can damage the country's economy and in many respects cyber war when global organized cybercrime can be as deadly as actual military hostilities. Cyber-attack can steal your identity, steal the money out of your bank account, destroy final business information, breach client confidentiality, and even destroy State security and vital intelligence that becomes useless when made public.

Whilst everyone has got a computer very few people know how computers work and even fewer people are aware of the very real security risks they run whether they use a mobile phone, a laptop computer or an iPad.

In a society like the UK where shopping on line is the increasing norm and where in 2008 the value of on line retail sales was £48 billion and 57 % of individuals ordered goods or services on line £328m was stolen from credit card holders. Theft of copyright in music and film was estimated at £180m. and the loss to the economy in terms of non-delivery issues was £55m per year.[1]

---

[1] Consumer Survey, Office of Fair Trading.

© Springer International Publishing Switzerland 2015
H. Jahankhani et al. (Eds.): ICGS3 2015, CCIS 534, pp. 123–136, 2015.
DOI: 10.1007/978-3-319-23276-8_11

The best description of the risk is probably that expressed by NW3C[2] who recently reported:

Criminal Use of Social Media (2013)

Defining social media is difficult because it is ever changing like technology itself, but for the purposes of this paper, social media will be defined as any website or software that allows you to receive and disseminate information interactively.

The tremendous rise in popularity of social media over the past seven years has led to a drastic change in personal communication, both online and off. Comparing to the world population clock, the total world population is around 7.06 billion. With that being said, the popularity of sites such as Facebook, (1.06 billion monthly active users). YouTube (800 million users), Twitter (500 million users), Craigslist (60 million U.S. users each month) and Foursquare (has a community of over 30 million people worldwide) has connected people from all over the world to each other, making it easier to keep in touch with friends, loved ones, or find that special someone. In addition to personal usage, businesses and the public sector use social media to advertise, recruit new employees, offer better customer service, and maintain partnerships. In fact, 65 % of adults now use social media. Social networking is the most popular online activity, accounting for 20 % of time spent on PCs and 30 % of mobile time. As social interactions move more and more online, so does the crime that follows it.

In countering this threat the United States is the world leader. Unique amongst many countries the US has extra territorial jurisdiction to enforce many of its laws that other countries may not or are unwilling to extend their court's jurisdiction. This is a highly contentious area of international law and one which requires considerable review and development, a subject for a far more detailed analysis which is outside the scope of this overview.

A key player in the United States and in the world is the Federal Bureau of Investigation (FBI). An organisation which became famous in the 1930s depression fighting gangsters and in the 1960s under Attorney General Robert Kennedy fighting organized crime.

The FBI states that: *The FBI has the authority and responsibility to investigate and enforce all violations of federal law that are not exclusively assigned to another federal agency.*

- *Title 28, USC Sect. 533 & 28 CFR 0.85*
- *"The Department of Justice and the FBI lead the national effort to investigate and prosecute cybercrime."*
- The President's National Strategy to Secure Cyberspace, 2003

The FBI further states that it:

"has a unique dual responsibility, to prevent harm to national security as the nation's domestic intelligence agency and to enforce federal laws as the nation's principal law enforcement agency. These roles are complementary, as threats to the nation's cybersecurity can emanate from nation-states, terrorist organizations, and transnational criminal enterprises; with the lines between sometimes blurred.

The FBI's unified mission brings all lawful investigative techniques and legal tools together in combating these threats. This approach facilitates information sharing and ensures

---

[2] The Internet Crime Complaint Centre. Partners: The Federal Bureau of Investigation, Bureau of Justice Assistance U.S. Department of Justice and the National White Collar Crime Centre.

responsible stewardship of resources by collocating talent, tools, and institutional knowledge in a single organization."

Whilst the FBI have oversight of such matters the specific IC3 is the partnering organisation that deals with cyber complaints in the United States and elsewhere.

In 2012 the IC3[3] reported that there were 289,874 consumer complaints when a loss of $525,441,110, an 8.3 % increase reported losses since 2011.The IC3 s success has led to the UK and other countries adopting similar centres.

Of those 289,874 complaints 114,908 reported losses. The average total loss overall to all complaints was $1,813. The average dollar lost to those reporting such loss was $4,573. What a United States the largest number of complaints was received from the state of California at 13.41 % and the lowest from Washington State at 2.72 %.

On a countrywide basis the percentage of victim complainants ranked as follows:

- United States: 91.2 %
- Canada:1.4 %
- UK: .9 %
- Australia: .7 %
- India: .6 %

2   Cyber-Crime Auto-Fraud

One key area of the cybercrime is auto-fraud. This is where criminals pose as car salesman selling stolen cars instructing their victims to send the payment to a third-party agent by wire transfer service. Usually the criminal pockets the money and does not deliver any vehicle. IC3 have reported that in 2012 there were 17,159 complaints where the victims lost the sum of $64,572,324.

2.1   Impersonation Email Scam

Government agencies in America do not send unsolicited emails. However IC3 received complaints at the rate of 47 per day resulting in victims losing more than $6,604 per day to this scam. These scams are dangerous and undermine confidence in the government agencies. The FBI identified this as including elements of Nigerian scam letters (419 scams) incorporating get rich inheritance scenarios, bogus lottery winning notifications and occasional extortion threats. In 2012, there was a total of 14,141 complaints with victims losing the sum of $4,672,985.

2.2   Frequently Reported Internet Crimes

(a)   Telephone Calls

A number of victims received unsolicited telephone calls from foreigners posing as representatives of software companies. The victims were advised that malware had been

---

[3] The Internet Crime Complaint Centre. Partners: The Federal Bureau of Investigation, Bureau of Justice Assistance U.S. Department of Justice and the National White Collar Crime Centre.

detected on their computers and was an immediate threat. The fraudsters pressured victims into logging onto their computers where they were directed to a utility area which appeared to demonstrate how their computer was infected. The fraudsters' then offered to rid the computers of the malware the fees ranging from $49-$450. When the victims pay the fees they are then asked to complete Western Union authorisation so the money could be taken out of their account. Thus, the fraudsters gained access to the computers and all the information on the computers as well as pocketing the proceeds. This is a very common crime and the criminals have been known to operate from Africa and Pacific region.

(b) Payday Loans

The payday loan scam reported by IC3 involves victims receiving harassing telephone calls from fraudsters claiming the victim is delinquent in payment. These criminals have accurate information as to social security numbers, dates of birth, addresses, employer information, bank account numbers and names and telephones of relatives and friends. All this may be obtained from any social media that the victim may have innocently visited. The victim is harassed and often subjected to threat of assault or legal action and often this is directed at relatives, friends and employers.

(c) The Grandparent Scam

Here the scan involves quite elderly individuals claiming to be a grandson granddaughter or whatever who happens to be a young relative in a legal or financial crisis. It generally involves claims being arrested in a car accident another country. The caller's great sense of urgency and make a desperate plea for money making the grandparents agree not to tell the parents and consequently often preventing potential victims from discovering the scam. These criminals have often impersonated embassy officials or attorneys and ask the victims to transfer money to a special or a specified individual. These criminals have been operating from Canada, United States, Mexico, Guatemala Peru and the Dominican Republic. They use telephone numbers generated by free apps so the burgers telephone number appears on the recipient's caller ID.

IC3 reported that for 2012 the loss incurred in these cases amounted to $10,624,427 for 8,324 reported instances.

Other Internet fraud involves real estate and IC3 reported that in 2012 the sum of $15,418,734 was lost to fraudsters rental scams, timeshare marketing scams and loan modification scams[4].

In 2012, IC3 processed 289,874 complaints representing more than half a billion dollars in losses.

In 2013, IC3 processed 262,813 complaints the losses recorded for that year amounted to $781,841,611. [2013 Internet Crime Report IC3] 90.63 % Of the complaints emanated from the US .85 % from the UK.

---

[4] 2012 Internet Crime Report IC3 p.15. www.ic3.gov.

3   EU/COE Joint Project on Regional Co-operation Against Cybercrime[5]

This report evaluated the cyber security policies of several countries in eastern Europe including Turkey Albania, Bosnia Herzegovina, Croatia, Kosovo, Serbia and the former state of Montenegro. Whilst some had taken effective steps to protect their networks many had not done so. Governments were encouraged to ensure that their national data protection legislation complied with the principles of the Council of Europe's data protection convention ETS 108 and to participate in the Convention's current modernization process. The same applied to the future data protection standards of the European Union. This could facilitate transborder sharing of data also for law enforcement purposes.

The report concluded (p.121):

In all countries and areas participating in the CyberCrime@IPA project, the creation or strengthening of police-type cybercrime units is in progress and the specialisation of prosecutors is under consideration in some. This process should be pursued. It is essential to understand that technology changes day by day and that the workload of cybercrime and forensic units is increasing constantly. The resourcing (staff, equipment, software) and maintenance of specialised skills and the adaptation of such units to emerging requirements is a continued challenge.

It also recommended that:

All law enforcement officers – from first responders to highly specialised computer forensic investigators – need to be enabled to deal with cybercrime and electronic evidence at their respective levels. Elements of law enforcement training strategies have been identified, but not yet fully implemented.[6]

Perhaps more importantly the report recommends the need for:

A Regional Pilot Centre for Judicial Training on Cybercrime and Judicial Evidence is being established. These achievements need to be institutionalised.

Enabling all judges and prosecutors to prosecute and adjudicate cybercrime and make use of electronic evidence in criminal proceedings should remain a strategic priority.

*Relevant authorities should consider the following actions: **Mainstream judicial training on cybercrime and electronic evidence.** Domestic institutions for the training of judges and prosecutors should integrate basic and advanced training modules on cybercrime and electronic evidence in their regular training curricula for initial and in-service training.*

Whilst this may be recommended for Eastern Europe it is surely essential that the judiciary in all countries attain this level of competence in this vital area.

Another vital suggestion in the report was that there should be:

Memoranda of understanding between law enforcement and Internet Service Providers are a fundamental tool in this respect. Regional coordination of such MOUs would facilitate the ability

---

[5]   Strasbourg, 18 June 2013, Data Protection and Cybercrime Division, Council of Europe, Strasbourg. Data Protection and Cybercrime Division Directorate General of Human Rights and Rule of Law Council of Europe, F-67075 Strasbourg Cedex (France).

[6]   http://www.coe.int/t/DGHL/cooperation/economiccrime/cybercrime/Documents/Cyber %20IPA%20reports/2467_LEA_Training_Strategy_Fin1.pdf.

of law enforcement authorities to conduct investigations across regional borders, with the knowledge that comparable standards have been adopted in other countries and areas. MOUs combined with clear rules and procedures may also facilitate the cooperation with multi-national ISPs and other private sector entities including in the disclosure of data stored in foreign jurisdiction or on cloud servers that are managed by these ISPs. [p.127]

Finally the Report concluded p.126:

"Governments should consider the following actions:

- **Exploit the possibilities of the Budapest Convention on Cybercrime and other bilateral, regional and international agreements on cooperation in criminal matters.** *This includes making full use of Articles 23 to 35 of the Budapest Convention in relation to police-to-police and judicial cooperation, including legislative adjustments and improved procedures. Governments (parties and observers to the Convention) should fully participate in the 2013 assessment of the international cooperation provisions of the Budapest Convention that will be undertaken by the Cybercrime Convention Committee (T-CY). They should follow up to the T-CY assessment of 2012 and promote the use of Articles 29 and 30 of the Budapest Convention regarding international preservation requests.*
- **Provide for training and sharing of good practices.** *Authorities for police and judicial cooperation should engage in domestic, regional and international training and the sharing of good practices. This should facilitate cooperation based on trust.*
- **Evaluate the effectiveness of international cooperation.** *Ministries of Justice and of Interior and Prosecution Services should collect statistical data on international cooperation requests regarding cybercrime and electronic evidence, including the type of assistance requests, the timeliness of responses and the procedures used. This should help identify good practices and remove obstacles to cooperation. They may engage with regional partners in an analysis of the issues adversely affecting international cooperation.*
- **Strengthen the effectiveness of 24/7 points of contact.** *Such contact points have been established in all countries and areas in line with Article 35 Budapest Convention, but their role needs to be enhanced and they may need to become more pro-active and fully functional.*
- **Compile statistics on and review the effectiveness of 24/7 contact points and other forms of international cooperation on a regular basis."*

All these measures seem entirely sensible in the light of the threats described by IC3 and other agencies. It expresses good intentions and it is easier for governments to give vague expressions of intent and declarations, but actions speak louder than words and what is missing is enactment and enforcement.

4   Cybercrime in the UK

In its Cyber Crime Strategy Report of March 2010 the Home Office reported:

The number, sophistication and impact of cyber crimes continues to grow. These threats evolve to frustrate network security defences, and many business systems and home computers do not keep what protection they have up to date. "Hacking" has evolved from the activity of a small number of very technical individuals to an increasingly mature marketplace where technical skills and data can be purchased by criminal groups to carry out specific attacks. The trend therefore is for growth in the threat to internet security, as evidenced by the following figures:[7]

- *In 2008, 55,389 phishing website hosts were detected, an increase of 66 % over 2007.*
- *A 192 % increase in spam detected across the internet, from 119.6 billion messages in 2007 to 349.6 billion in 2008. The most common type of spam detected in 2008 was related to internet or computer related goods and services which made up 24 % of all detected spam.*
- *Active bot-infected computers – an average of 75,158 per day, showing an increase of 31 % from the previous period. In 2008, bot networks were responsible for the distribution of about 90 % of all spam e-mail.*

The Government's Serious Crime Bill, Part 2, Computer Abuse factsheet considers how the Government plan to tackle cyber-crime in the Serious and Organised Crime Strategy, published in October 2013.

The factsheet discusses The Computer Misuse Act 1990 ("the 1990 Act") which sets out the offences associated with interfering with a computer (i.e. hacking) and the associated tools (such as malware) that enable computer systems to be breached. It does not contain any powers. The 1990 Act makes unauthorised access to, or modification of, computer material unlawful, creating four offences.

Section 1 provides that the basic offence is of unauthorised access to computer material, for example by logging onto a system or accessing parts of a system for which additional authorisation is required by using another person's user ID and password. This offence is triable either in a magistrates' court or the Crown Court, with a maximum sentence of 2 years' imprisonment.

More serious offences are committed where the purpose of the unauthorised access is to commit or facilitate the commission of another offence (Sect. 2) or to impair the operation of the computer or hinder access to the programmes or data it contains (Sect. 3).

Section 2 offences would include, for example, unauthorised access to transfer money and so commit theft, or theft of sensitive data to be used for blackmail.

Section 3 offences include circulating viruses, deleting files, inserting a "Trojan Horse" to steal data or mounting a Denial of Service attack. Sections 2 and 3 offences are both triable either way, with maximum sentences of 5 and 10 years' imprisonment respectively.[8]

Section 3A deals with making, supplying or obtaining articles for use in offences under Sects. 1 or 3. This offence is also triable either way, with a maximum sentence of 2 years' imprisonment.(Section 3A has only had two prosecutions in England and Wales over the last three years. The problem is that Sect. 3A does not meet the EU Directive Article 7 requirement regarding "the intentional production, sale, procurement for use, import, distribution or otherwise making available "of tools with the intention that it is used to commit any further offences.[9]

---

[7] Internet Security Threat Report" – Symantec, October 2009.
[8] Home Office June 2014.
[9] Home Office June 2014.

Part 2 of the Bill amends the 1990 Act to:

1. Create a new offence of unauthorised acts causing serious damage;
2. Implement the EU Directive on Attacks against Information Systems; and
3. Clarify the savings provision for law enforcement.

The new offence in clause 37 addresses the most serious cyber-attacks, for example those on essential systems controlling power supply, communications, food or fuel distribution.[10]

The new offence applies where an unauthorised act in relation to a computer results, directly or indirectly, in serious damage to the economy, the environment, national security or human welfare, or a significant risk of such damage (where damage to human welfare encompasses loss of life, illness or injury or serious social disruption). A significant link to the UK is required, so that at least one of the accused or the target computer at the time of the offence or the damage must have been in the UK, or the accused must be a UK national at the time of the offence and the conduct constitute an offence under the law of the country in which it occurred. The accused must have intended to cause the serious damage, or to have been reckless as to whether it was caused. This offence is more serious than the existing Sect. 3 offence and is triable only on indictment (in the Crown Court). Where the attack results in loss of life, serious illness or injury or serious damage to national security the maximum sentence is life imprisonment, where the attack results in serious economic or environmental damage or social disruption the maximum sentence is 14 years' imprisonment.[11]

The EU adopted a Directive on attacks against information systems in August 2013. The aim of the Directive is to establish a set of minimum rules within the European Union on offences and sanctions relating to attacks against information systems. It also aims to improve cooperation between competent authorities in Member States. The Government has until 4 September 2015 to transpose the Directive into UK law.

In 2013, the government introduced the Cyber Essentials Scheme providing a set of controls that organizations could implement demonstrating that they had met a recognised baseline.[12]

4.1 Common Forms of Cyber Attack

Cyber attacks coming for stages:

1. Survey
2. Delivery
3. Breach
4. Attack.

---

[10] Home Office June 2014.
[11] Home Office June 2014.
[12] Cabinet Office https://www.gov.uk/government/organisations/cabinet- office. Accessed: 10/02/15.

In 2013 the government reported 81 % of those companies that reported a breach of security suffered losses or between £600,000 and £1.15 million.[13]

When it is considered that the cost of IT is excessive and in many cases a scandalous waste of public money in terms of the IT systems provided for the Ministry of Justice and the NHS where the providers were paid millions of pounds of taxpayers money and the systems proved completely unworkable is learning how to ensure that many more millions of pounds are not wasted because the systems are totally insecure. What is worse is the amount of time and money that is expended with IT which is increasingly perceived as being manipulated by the manufacturers and so-called geeks who run the systems.

The time has come, if not long passed to stop this nonsense and produce systems that are not all things to all men, not play toys or gimmicks, and are specifically designed for business to satisfy its real needs and no other. Similarly for academics systems must be designed which are capable of precise measurement of statistics and scientific analysis meeting the demands required by science and industry. Today's computers and IT systems are just not up to this task and they are not fit for purpose. The dangers of all this and the lack of awareness are highlighted in the research undertaken by Professor Jahankhani.[14]

The measures one is advised to take seem pitiful when compared to the sophistication of global organized crime and states that sponsor cyber terrorism and attack.

The measures one is advised to take appear to be the only measures that can be taken and these include:

1. Risk management education outlined in the governments paper 10 Steps: User Education and Awareness;[15]
2. Patch management; this applies patches purchased at the earliest possibility to limit exposure to know software new vulnerabilities; therefore simpletons to keep software updated to deal with the potential of software bugs;
3. Secure configuration; it is advised to remove unnecessary software and default user accounts. It is advised that default passwords or changed and that automatic features that could activate malware are turned off.
4. Restrictions on user access to applications, privileges and data;
5. Monitoring and analyzing all network activity to identify any malicious or unusual activity; security monitoring will be necessary where the organisations more likely to be attacked to identify any unexpected suspicious activity; businesses should also having place and effective response to reduce the impact of an attack on the business.

---

[13] 2014 Information Security Breaches Survey sponsored by the Department for Business Innovation and Skills.

[14] Jahankhani, H., Al-Nemrat, A., Hosseinian-far, A. (2014) "Cybercrime classification and characteristics" in Cybercrime and Cyber Terrorism Investigators' Handbook, Elsevier, ISBN 978-1447126829. And in Jahankhani, H. (2013) "Developing a model to reduce and/ or prevent cybercrime victimization among the user individuals", in Strategic Intelligence Management, Springer, ISBN 978-0124071919.

[15] Cabinet Office https://www.gov.uk/government/publications/ 10 steps to cyber security advice sheet. Accessed: 10/02/15.

6.   It is important that all staff are properly trained in reducing the risks of successful social engineering attacks;
7.   Malware protection within the Internet gateway which can detect malicious codes in imported items;
8.   Network perimeter defences which can block insecure or unnecessary services what only now permitted websites to the access; this can be achieved by establishing web proxy, web filtering, content checking, and firewall policies to detect and block executable downloads, blocked access to known malicious domains, and prevent users computers from communicating directly with the Internet.
9.   Malware protection which can block malicious emails and prevent malware from being downloaded from websites;
10. Password policy which can prevent users from selecting easily guessed passwords and locks accounts after a low number of failed attempts;
11. Device controls within the Internet gateway can be used to prevent unauthorized access to critical services or inherently insecure services that may still be required internally;
12. Secure configuration and restricted System functionality to devices used in the business.
13. White listing and execution control can prevent unknown software from being able to run or install itself including auto run on USB and CD drives.

4.2   Business at Risk

Business can be at risk where does not establish clear security guidelines for employees. For example, many employees may download material from insecure sites, may use USBs or portable hard drives for their own uses which might potentially important malware and compromise business data.

Confidentiality is essential in most businesses. In the legal profession all client information and data, the Instructions to counsel, advice to client and any advice given privileged from disclosure. If such information comes into the public tonight there are serious consequences for the law firm not only is it a preacher client confidentiality, a breach of obligation to the client but a disciplinary matter.

4.3   Types of Cyber Attack Exposure

There are several types of attack to which businesses may be exposed. These may include:

(a) Connection to and trusted network;
(b) Denial of access to services and information;
(c) Compromising the system or the service.
(d) Unauthorised access compromising confidentiality, integrity and availability of systems, services and information.

A number of measures may be taken to reduce the risk of these attacks has referred to below in the security policy measures.

4.4 Security Policy

Each firm should adopt a security policy and special operating procedures with security control. Regular surveillance and monitoring is therefore essential to maintaining security and keeping client confidentiality. Government has reported that some individuals may release personal sensitive commercial information, or abuse the system or their privileges in gaining unauthorized information, they may also steal or damage the computer system.

4.5 Security Policy Measures

The government recommend that all businesses follow the network design principles of ISO/IEC 27033-1:2009 to help define the necessary security qualities for the perimeter and internal network segments and ensure that all networked devices are configured to the secure baseline build.[16]

Businesses should limit access to network ports, protocols and filtering, inspecting all traffic at the network perimeter to ensure that only traffic which is required to support business is being exchanged. Technical controls that should be implemented to scan for malware and other malicious content.

Businesses should install firewalls to form a buffer zone between interested external network and the internal network used by the business. A white list should be applied that only allows authorized protocols, Ports and applications to communicate with authorized networks and network addresses. This should reduce the exposure of the ICT systems to network-based attacks.

The government have warned in their 10 Steps: Network Security that untrusted networks expose corporate networks to attacks that can compromise confidentiality, integrity and availability of Information and Communications Technologies (ICT).[17]

Anti-virus and malware checking solutions should be utilized to examine both inbound and outbound Data at the perimeter in addition to antivirus and malware protection deployed on internal networks and on host systems.

There should be no direct network connectivity between internal systems and systems hosted on trusted networks. The business should identify a group and isolate critical business information assets and services and apply appropriate ductwork security controls to them.

Wireless devices may be especially vulnerable and therefore wireless devices should only be allowed to connect to trusted wireless networks. Wireless access points should be secured. Security scanning tills should have the ability to detect and locate unauthorized wireless access points.

The government further advises that the anti-virus and malware solutions use of the perimeter should be different to those used to protect internal networks and systems in order to provide some additional defence in depth.

---

[16] Cabinet Office https://www.gov.uk/government/publications/ 10 steps to cyber security advice sheet. Paras 3 and 3.1. Accessed: 10/02/15.
[17] Cabinet Office https://www.gov.uk/government/publications/ 10 steps to cyber security advice sheet. Accessed: 10/02/15 Summary.

4.6 Training

All staff should be trained, monitored, and given further periodic training in security. Staff should be aware that the users of the system are the weakest link as they are always the target for phishing attacks, social engineering etc. In many instances a successful cyber attack only requires one user to divulge log on credentials or open an email with malicious content. Ideally new staff should be inducted into the company's security policies and also made aware of their employment obligations with regard to information and cyber security whilst in the course of their employment. This should be subject of contract terms of engagement and also supervisory control and disciplinary sanction.

Regular briefings from the company's IT experts or updates with regard to current threats should be given.

The company should have on its staff persons who are qualified in information assurance (IA) skills such a system administrators, incident management team members, and forensic investigators. If there are any serious incidents investigation should be carried out in accordance with the companies security procedures. The incident needs to be fully recorded and reported and then properly investigated. Where serious information has been late all systems have been damaged in legal proceedings maybe necessary and therefore important that any hard or software be examined and produced in evidence.

Staff should be tested on their knowledge and asked what steps they vaguely take to prevent risk.

Staff should report any untoward incidents and to voice their concerns about poor security to senior managers and senior management should accept their responsibilities accordingly.[18]

All the above advice he Is critical to running a safe and secure business. In 2011 Ernst & Young published a report entitled: Ever-increasing fraud risks in the IT and ITeS sector. They looked at the reasons for fraud hand blazing means of preventing and deterring employees/vendors from committing fraud. One of the problems they found that although certain businesses had policies in place they were not communicated to staff.[19] Alarmingly they pointed to:

> *"an absence of dedicated efforts/specialised skill sets to prevent/detect fraud under pressure situations. The internal audit teams may not be equipped with the necessary skills/tools required to prevent and/or detect frauds by employees/others."*

They also pointed to the fact that over the last five years i.e. from 2006 to 2011 they had detected and noted:

> *that senior/middle management employees, who have obtained a higher level of trust and responsibility within a company, are more likely to commit fraud by misusing the authority and trust bestowed on them."*

---

[18] Cabinet Office https://www.gov.uk/government/publications/ 10 steps to cyber security advice sheet. Accessed: 10/02/15.

[19] Ernst & Young. Ever-increasing fraud risks in the IT and ITeS sector. (2011) p.4.

This is pretty much an indictment of business organisations in the UK is a dangerous time when the economy was on the brink of collapse. It is it begs the questions not only about corporate governance, not only about business efficacy, and not only about management efficacy, but also about professional and ethical standards in the UK at that time and even now.[20]

What Ernst & Young advise and what is entirely sensible is that businesses create an antifraud environment. Each business should have a code of business conduct and ethics policy and describe what will be considered as unethical or unacceptable behavior. Employees should be free to report any unethical behavior, misconduct, or criminal or fraudulent activity without fear of victimization or oppression or other disciplinary action or retaliation of some kind. The business should undertake a comprehensive fraud risk assessment and insure it has an effective framework and in place.

They also recommend that there should be adequate monitoring procedures in place to review and improve the effectiveness of anti-fraud programs and controls. The measures they suggest are:

(a) Employees annual declaration of 100 % compliance with the code of business conduct and anti-fraud policies;
(b) Adequate review/monitoring process to ensure that tipoff's/complaints made through fraud hotlines are investigated/I dressed appropriately;
(c) Oversight by audit committee of the risk of override of controls by management.

The questions that need to be asked are whether there is sufficient documentation relating to the full policy, code of conduct and ethics. Has the coping communicated, is there an effective whistleblower mechanism, is the management team trained sufficiently, is there a full prevention health check, does the risk assessment process specifically cover the risk of fraud, is the internal audit team adequately equipped to cover the risk of fraud, other adequate tools to detect suspicious unfortunate transactions, and does the business have the necessary skill sets to investigate fraudulent/dishonest acts?

5   Conclusions

In this paper we have noted that cyber-attack is an ever resent problem and that despite all efforts of various agencies to counter this phenomenon it remains an ever present danger to business. We have also noted however the concerted efforts and declarations of intent by many states, including those in Eastern Europe to act in concert against these threats. Regulation is being reviewed and revised, new laws are being introduced and judges are encouraged to have specialist training in this area. Be that as it may the fact is that according to the UK Home Office in 2010 there were 75,158 computers bot infected. In the 21st century it must therefore be asked whether business can afford such systems when so much time is wasted sorting out IT problems. Have we not reached the point where each profession should have its own system? Most computers are designed

---

[20] For an example of the concerns raised at the highest levels of international arbitration see; Michael Reynolds PhD (LSE) Ethics in International Arbitration. Legal Ethics December 2014.

for public use with entertainment a key component, social media etc. Does business require all this? Do academics? Perhaps the time has come for a critical re-evaluation of what we need these systems for and to limit their use for specific defined purposes which may be more secure. The rate and extent of abuse cannot be sustained in terms of time or cost because the preventative measures that were successful yesterday and which succeed to day may not succeed tomorrow.

Understanding Privacy Concerns in Online Courses: A Case Study of Proctortrack

Anwar ul Haq[1](✉), Arshad Jamal[2], Usman Butt[1], Asim Majeed[1],
and Aykut Ozkaya[1]

[1] GSM London, London, UK
{anwar-ul-haq, usmanjaved.butt, asim.majeed,
aykut.ozkaya}@gsm.org.uk
[2] QABS, London, UK
arshad.jamal@qa.ulster.ac.uk

Abstract. This study aims to investigate underlying causes of privacy concerns of online learners which emerged as a consequence from the launch of an automated proctoring technology by an educational institution. The privacy has become a vital issue in the modern age of information due to the complex, dynamic and fluid nature of privacy it is far from easy to define and understand what privacy means in certain situations. Consequently, designers of interactive systems often misunderstand privacy and even often ignore it, thus causing concerns for users. Using content analysis approach [1], qualitative data was collected and analysed from 130 online bloggers during the deployment phase of Proctortrack tool. The results and findings provide useful new insights into the nature and form of privacy concerns of online learners. Findings have theoretical as well as practical implications for the successful adoption of Massive Open Online Courses (MOOCs) and similar systems.

Keywords: Privacy · Security · Online verification · MOOCs · Online courses · Decision making · Design · Planning · Biometric scanning · Tracking

1 Introduction

Privacy in online environments has become critical given the recent advancements in information technologies. Open learning environment resources (OLEs) are an example of such online platforms which are becoming increasingly popular amongst the higher education institutions; offering courses and contents for free via the internet to anyone who is willing to dedicate a bit of time and energy in participating. These courses are designed to support most Internet browsers and the content is delivered via various multimedia tools most of which is available for free as inclusive of web 2.0. Most OLEs are designed with a combination of teaching and learning resources such as discussion forums, online video, audio, documents, pictures, simulations and quizzes. However availability of resources vary from institution to institution and course to course; according to the intended learning outcomes and learner's requirements.

Due the openness of the OLEs anyone can register with many accounts and some which may be used for malicious purposes including gaining academic advantage or

© Springer International Publishing Switzerland 2015
H. Jahankhani et al. (Eds.): ICGS3 2015, CCIS 534, pp. 137–150, 2015.
DOI: 10.1007/978-3-319-23276-8_12

disadvantaging others. However, some open systems such as Coursera developed an honour code; which is simple declaration of a set of rules setting out an agreement between the learner and the OLE providers during their participation [2]. With the emergence of new technologies and rapidly changing learner and technology interactions, organisations are looking to implement automatic verification tools to make sure that interactions are authentic so that the integrity of such system can be maintained. One U.S. university has implemented a new technology called automated remote proctoring [3]. The basic premise of a Proctortrack tool is to detect any suspicious behavior and report it to the concerned people. For example, if a student talks, uses mobile phone or browse on the web to find an answer during an online test or exam, then the Proctortrack tool which continuously tracks people will flag this and report it to the tutors.

The deployment of Proctortrack has caused privacy concerns amongst users of the system as complexity, nature and form of privacy concerns were not completely understood. Students have filed an online petition [4] and around 900 students have signed that petition to stop using this tracking tool on grounds of privacy. Because open learning environments are a recent phenomenon and the use of automated proctor tracking technology is the first of its kind of example and little is known about the nature and form of privacy concerns of learners of these systems. Understanding of privacy concerns of learners in OLEs here can provide useful insights into the complex and dynamic nature of privacy.

This paper is structured into four sections. First section provides literature review of privacy and security. The next section discusses the research methodology whereas data analysis and findings are presented in the third section. Finally, conclusion and further research are discussed.

2   Literature Review

The privacy of user's personal information and privacy leakage are extremely important themes when accessing the contents through online courses [5]. According to Boyd [6], the nature of online information is quite persistent and could be easily accessed invisibly so to identify the viewer is difficult. As stated by Rotenberg [7], the privacy has become a vital issue in the modern age of information whereas according to Solove [8], due to the complex nature of privacy it is far from easy to define what privacy means. Consequently, designers of interactive systems often misunderstand privacy and even often ignore it, thus causing dilemma for online learners' privacy.

Online courses are becoming increasingly popular amongst the higher education institutions. Whilst some researchers regard online courses are a natural evolution of technology others consider these as a novel technical revolution [9]. Albatch [10] states that online courses are considered to be an important paradigm with the potential to increase economic efficiencies through optimisation and significantly reducing costs. So online courses do not only enhance the agility and collaboration significantly but provide a globally accepted computing model and infrastructure. Thus, without appropriate security and privacy solutions designed for online courses, this potentially revolutionizing computing paradigm could lead to a huge failure.

2.1 Open Online Courses and Data Security

Online courses are becoming increasingly popular amongst the higher education institutions that even most prestigious universities are beginning to offer online courses using advanced technological platform by embedding audio, video and other media tools. Despite the growth of e-learning environment the data security measures referring to the digital privacy are applied to prevent accessing computers on unauthorized basis along with data being corrupted. This is meticulous for all organisations to secure their data as a priority.

The developments in e-learning technology have discovered and embraced a new shape called Open Learning Environments (OLEs) during the recent years. According to Briggs, [9], this new intervention is increasingly becoming popular within the higher education sector including the prestigious and leading universities who have also started offering online courses. The use of OLEs has been a centre of debates and discussions over the past few years, specifically in regards to their impact on data security and privacy issues within the higher education [10]. The contents available through OLEs are aimed at large-scale inclusions constituting the dispersed participants who can access the courses through the web. As stated by De Waard et al., [11], the population of the new and diversified students require that the courses are developed carefully absorbing and then satisfying the needs of them by the institutions respectively. The privacy of user's personal information and privacy leakage is an extremely important theme when accessing the contents through OLEs [5].

OLEs are still evolving but have generated significant interest and attention in both industry and academia. According to Rotenberg, [7], the essential theme behind OLEs transformation is to consolidate both the evolutionary development and economic utility model constituting various computing technologies including applications and distributed services. Some see OLEs as natural evolution of technology while others consider as novel technical revolution [9]. On the other side, Albatch, [10] states that OLEs are considered to be an important paradigm with the potential to increase economic efficiencies through optimization and significantly reducing costs. OLEs do not only enhance the agility and collaboration significantly but provide a globally accepted computing model and infrastructure. This leads to the confusion of how OLEs differ from the existing models in regards to adoption, security and privacy whereas the above indicates that security and privacy is the primary concern in its adoption. However, without appropriate security and privacy solutions designed for clouds, this potentially revolutionizing computing paradigm could become a huge failure.

2.2 Overview of Privacy

The concept of privacy has emerged and recognised since remote access is applied as e-learning where teaching material and participation is made available through various places. According to M. Koet al., [12], this modification does not only lead to privacy issues but also security and reliability of procedures and systems of e-learning. In relation to conceptual problems the principals of privacy should be decided by various online systems as the huge increase access of online resources requires an appropriate and adequate level of privacy on the basis of European and national data privacy legislation [7].

According to Warren and Brandeis, [13], the privacy of data has been considered as a vital notion especially since the emergence and evolution of the Chinese and Greek civilisations. A renewed interest has also been seen during the recent developments of information technology advancements.

2.3   Why Security and Privacy Are Important?

According to Solove, [7], the e-learning conditions have unique privacy and also solitude amounts that will depend on varieties of studying routines conducted through various e-learning systems, but each and every study process must protect the personalized facts of the individuals. This increases the importance of problems of privacy, reliability and security of e-learning systems and procedures. In the context of increasing global interconnections the privacy and security of e-learning could be ensured by using different encryption tools, but the main requirements should be defined as a part of data privacy policy [14]. Security Policy should be regarded as set of means and methodologies for preventing incidents, detecting attacks and restoring the system after successful attack. It includes rules, procedures and tools used on hierarchical layers [15].

The particular term "Privacy-preserving" is incredibly vital within e-learning because user's data is needed to be secured as well as to go over the primary principles connected with person's information and also system solitude [5]. Within the context connected with global interconnections the security and privacy connected within e-learning might be ensured by making use of unique encryption resources, but the primary demands need to be defined in facts privacy policy. Analysing e-learning solitude and also privacy demands, a study connected with more popular e-learning criteria can be made.

3   Research Methodology

This research adopted case study approach to investigate the phenomenon of privacy leakage concerns in online courses by specifically exploring privacy concerns experienced by learners during the launch of a tracking tool called Proctortrack [16]. Proctortrack tool provide an online proctoring service. It is used to verify if the student is legitimate and to monitor any misconduct. Proctortrack works by using the webcam on the device being used to give the exam, by capturing the facial features and being sensitive to any motion which may lead to any cheating.

Case study is one of the ways to conduct social science research. It is an analysis of people, group, event, policy, institution or a person. Whereas case study based research has been a feasible method for doing research because of its ability to examine in-depth, a "case" within its "real-life" context and it is a useful practice to illuminate a decision or set of decisions when investigator has little control over events e.g. why they were taken, how they were implemented, and with what result [17]. Case study research is also defined as exploratory or empirical method. It uses different sources of evidences with their strength and weaknesses, such as; documentation, archival records, interviews, direct observations, physical artefacts and participant observation [18]. Case study based research methodology can also be useful for both conducting a new research and provides hypothesis and solution to a problem [19], or when there is insufficient research in the existing literature and gives you the opportunity to improve the literature incrementally and provides insight to the research [20].

Virtual learning has been adopted by educational sector for long time using traditional media sources. However evolution of Internet, powerful computing capabilities, and web technologies, have shifted this idea on the Internet and transformed it to a new phenomenon called Massive open online course; MOOC [21]. A case study based research could be very useful to find out how higher education can make use of smart ubiquitous mobile devices to attract more educators and learners [22].

It is critically important to consider how to avoid misuse of data and protect privacy in case study based research. This starts with establishing and maintaining trust with people who you studying and how to provide equilibrium between knowledge and stakeholders [23]. In the scenario where MOOC provides free open educational resources, informed consent and invasion of privacy needs to be protected [24].

The comments and views of learners were collected online from various forums and blogging web sites. Together, views and comments of 130 users were collected. This qualitative data were analysed using content analysis. The term Content Analysis was noticed in early 1940s academic literature, mainly in the field of mass communication [25]. Early Content Analysis was used as a quantitative based approach where content units were used for quantifications. In recent decades Content Analysis has been used as a qualitative approach in many fields e.g. Nursing, Education and Business [26].

The Content Analysis could be used as approach for manifest content where patterns and behaviours are directly evident from the data or the latent content where meanings and relations are not evident and involves interpretation of the data [26–28].

In this study the analysis will be based on the latent content as the focus of the research is not only to observe a particular behaviour of the users but to understand the underlying causes of the behaviour within specific scenario. For example, if a question about the importance of Privacy is asked to people nearly everyone will agree that Privacy is important for them, but it may not be clear to them why they show more anxiety towards invasion of Privacy in certain situation as compared to others.

The Content Analysis could be used in an inductively or deductively. The inductive approach moves from specific to general themes [29, 30] and deductive approach moves from general to specific [30, 31]. The inductive approach is used when enough knowledge is not available for a particular phenomenon or behaviour as compared to deductive approach where analysis is based on the existing body of knowledge. This study used the inductive approach as all of the underlying reasons of specific users' behaviour and emotional state due to certain changes in system and procedures were not clear in a specific case.

The Content Analysis is conducted in three stages based on the model presented by Elo and Kynga [30] leading to systematic approach for data collection, categorisation, themes generation and abstraction (Fig. 1).

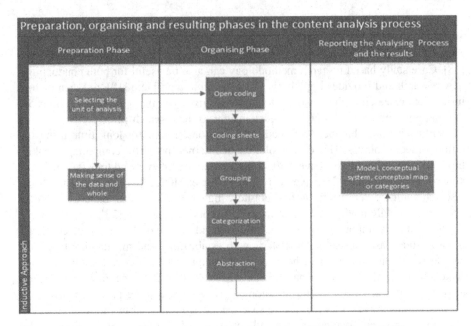

Fig. 1. Inductive content analysis (Adapted from Elo & Kynga, 2007)

The preparation phase starts with the selection of unit of analysis which could be a word or a theme [30, 32]. In our study the unit of analysis is the word leading to themes emerging from sentences starting from the specific instances to generalisation and category formation, resulting in abstraction and conceptual formation of the research topic [30, 32–34].

4 Data Analysis and Finding

The preparation phase starts with identifying unit of analysis and are derived from – key-words-in-context KWIC [35, 36]. The word count frequencies and tag cloud are used to identify the main areas to focus in addition to going over the data manually and generating notes for the main topics emerging. A sample tag cloud based on the word frequencies is provided below (Fig. 2).

The word tree maps are also used to probe main areas of interests emerging to see how they are related to other areas of interest for example Proctortrack key word shows links to spyware, privacy invasion etc. Similarly content analysis is carried out for other key words at initial stage. The instance count for key words was Privacy: 380, Proctortrack: 763, Software: 594, Student: 482, Video: 158, Webcam: 350 resulting in sufficiently large base for open coding. The open coding was used as the first stage and enabled categorization and grouping of related themes leading to abstraction of ideas and conceptual formation of the topic under investigation (Fig. 3).

The main point of discussion in the data was the concerns for privacy with the induction of new online verification tool Proctortrack by the university. The underlying

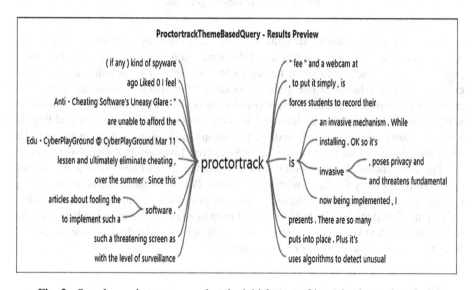

Word	Length	Count
you	3	819
proctortrack	12	763
ago	3	689
months	6	664
online	6	618
software	8	594
an	2	578
students	8	482
more	4	464
privacy	7	380
reply	5	354
webcam	6	350

Fig. 2. Sample tag cloud used at the initial stage of investigation and analysis

ProctortrackThemeBasedQuery - Results Preview

(if any) kind of spyware

ago Liked 0 I feel

Anti - Cheating Software's Uneasy Glare : "

are unable to afford the

Edu - CyberPlayGround @ CyberPlayGround Mar 11

lessen and ultimately eliminate cheating ,

over the summer . Since this

articles about fooling the

to implement such a

software .

such a threatening screen as

with the level of surveillance

proctortrack

" fee " and a webcam at

, to put it simply , is

forces students to record their

an invasive mechanism . While

installing . OK so it's

is

, poses privacy and

invasive

and threatens fundamental

now being implemented , I

presents . There are so many

puts into place . Plus it's

uses algorithms to detect unusual

Fig. 3. Sample word tree map used at the initial stage of investigation and analysis

causes for this privacy concern were not evident directly from the data as if a question is asked to a person whether privacy is important to them then their answer will overwhelmingly be yes, although if it is asked what do they mean by privacy then their answers will vary based on the context through which they will define the privacy. The latent thematic analysis tried to probe the underlying meaning and causes for certain phenomenon or behavior.

Our results suggest that users of Proctortrack showed anxiety for the use of webcam when it was used as the biometric scanning tool in users' personal space for example in the bed room or private place. The potential of misuse of this technology caused anxiety in the users and it was compounded by the fact that their biometric data coupled with their private spaces could be compromised. The perceive invasion of privacy was linked with the sense of insecurity and injustice when using such system, for example students feel being tracked and they perceive that if they make a mistake or someone else make a mistake whilst using this system, they will not have the chance to justify the events or actions and they will flagged as cheaters (Fig. 4).

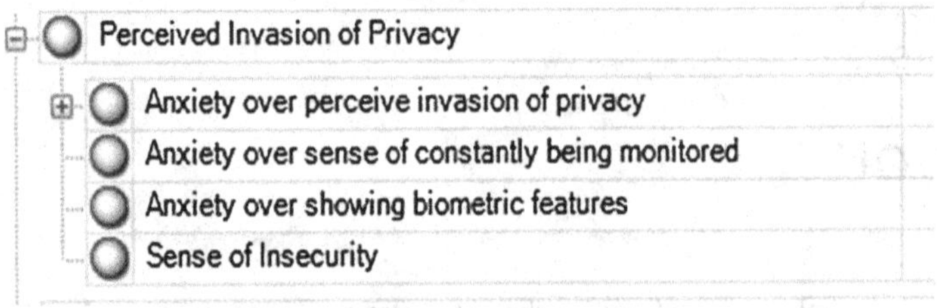

Fig. 4. Sample themes generated

The efficacy is defined by Bandura [37] as, "… it involves generative capability in which component cognitive, social and behavioral skills must be organized into integrated courses of action to serve innumerable purposes." The self-efficacy could be defined as, "one's belief in one's ability to succeed in specific situations" [38]. The users or intended users of the system showed anxiety with self-efficacy with new online verification technology (when inducted to their online University course) adding to sense of injustice and emotional anxiety. The sample codes are provided in Table 1. To show the process of theme 'Anxiety Over Perceived Invasion of Privacy' generation.

The users showed un-satisfaction over unexpected costs of additional software and hardware (potentially for those without webcam). The users wanted to be aware of the changes for the assessment of the online courses prior to registration. This observation point to the fact that all stake holders should have been consulted thoroughly before the induction of online verification tool resulting in better understanding of their needs and limitations of groups of users (Tables 2 and 3).

5 Discussion and Implications

The findings presented above suggest that privacy is a fundamental human right and people expect that their rights should be protected like previous generations no matter whether the environments are online or offline. Learners/users of online course environments were seriously concerned about the ill-timed launch and elusive tracking feature of the Proctortrack software as users were neither given adequate notice of its deployment nor the extent of data collection. Consequently, the annoyance and anxiety of users is not unjustified since notice/awareness is one of the fundamental principle of

Table 1. Theme from content analysis showing privacy concerns and underlying causes

Theme	Anxiety over perceived invasion of privacy			
Category	Anxiety based on potential technological misuse	Emotional anxiety		Anxiety over self-efficacy and technology comfort
Sub-category	Anxiety over Biometric Scanning	Sense of Insecurity and injustice	Anxiety over sense of constantly being monitored	Anxiety over interaction with unfamiliar technology
Codes	*"I'm signing because this is ridiculous - watching me out of my webcam, and knuckle scanning?!"* *"This is ridiculous! I shouldn't have to pay for extra software when I was not told beforehand. Also, I don't feel comfortable showing my face."*	*"This is absolutely creepy, and it probably means you also can't get up to get some water or go to the bathroom which is cruel and unusual."* *"The privacy of one's room and computer."* *"I am uncomfortable being "scanned" throughout my online course. I am not recorded during in-person classes, so I am against it online."* *"I am forced to use proctor track which can flag my rest if my parent walk into my room accidentally and start speaking to me in my native tongue about something unrelated."*	*"I signed up for an online course not knowing I'd have to purchase a program that stalks me. This is extremely creepy and I wish that I could drop the course now but it's too late. They didn't even tell me about this program until after the add/drop period was over. I have no choice but to be monitored in my own home, and as a victim of stalking this is a serious trigger for me."*	*"And merely because a person's eyes are not fixated on the screen during an examination does not mean that they are violating an academic integrity policy. Some people have ADD and have the tendency to stare off into space and the level of anxiety, on top of the atmosphere of the exam itself, is hardly conducive to a learning environment when one constantly has to remind him/herself to stare at a monitor for fear of being labeled a cheater."*

Table 2. Theme from content analysis showing user un-satisfaction and underlying causes

Theme	User un-satisfaction with perceive lack of change management and risk analysis	
Category	Anxiety over hardware and software cost and lack of awareness of risks	
Sub-category	Anxiety over extra cost for taking online test using specialised verification software	Anxiety over hardware costs and risks
Codes	*"It is not only an invasion of privacy, but an invasion of privacy we have to pay for. We already pay tons of money in tuition, pay extra course fees for online courses, now we have to pay to make their job easier for them."* *"Due to costs of the actual online course, adding this Proctortrack software at the cost of $32 is also unjust, while we, as students, are already paying tuition. This is not fair to any student who are already on financial debts."*	*"Not everyone who attends college and opts for online courses has the access to webcams."* *"I've taken online courses and have numerous friends that have gone to ▮▮▮▮, this should not be mandated at all. If the college wants to use this software fine, but offer in person options...what if you didn't have a personal computer? Not a fan of this"* *"With ▮▮▮▮ systems being hacked recently with quite ease, it would seem extremely foolish to have students give up their privacy. What if ProctorTrack too gets hacked?"*

privacy published with the Fair Information Practice principles (FIPPs) published by the United States Federal Trade Commission [39]. Ironically, the educational institution launch the tool is located in the U.S. The notice/awareness principle requires the companies to specifically notify consumers as to who will be collecting what data by using what means of data collection. Sadly, in this particular case study, users were neither given adequate notice nor made aware of what different means would be used to collect data on them. This indeed would have practical implications for the acceptability and credibility of the tool as well as the education institution as the users launch online petition which could tarnish company reputation.

So what could have been a successful innovation now have become a shambolic act for the institution launching it because the complex nature and form of privacy concerns within online learning environments was not understood.

It is vital, to establish a process, which can authenticate originality of student work and maintain academic integrity [40] with increased popularity of online courses and MOOCs among colleges and universities [41]. As more and more technology companies like Coursera and Udacity are collaborating with universities to offer coursers

Table 3. Theme from content analysis showing user un-satisfaction and underlying causes

Theme	User un-satisfaction with perceive lack of awareness handling		
Category	Awareness of the utility of the new system	Anxiety due to lack of awareness	
Sub-category	Lack of awareness for the new online verification tool.	Lack of awareness for the alternative solutions and procedures.	Lack of awareness for the change in assessment procedure for online courses.
Codes	*"I'm signing because the unexpected and forced cost is unfair, and it is invasive and ridiculous for me to pay for someone to access my personal webcam."* *"Now, there's more. Up to this point, I still didn't know exactly what Proctortrack was. My ▮▮▮ course tab, labeled "Proctortrack Notice", defines the software as "a remote proctoring service". What you do is you download the application and you launch it."*	*"I agree with the privacy issue. What does it take for ▮▮▮ to hear our voices?"* *"This point subject to change since ▮▮▮ states that there are alternatives to downloading Proctortrack and it is not mandatory, as said by ▮▮▮ spokesperson ▮▮▮. However, the alternative options have yet to be publicized on a large scale. Additionally, my attempts to register for in-person proctoring have been fruitless so far."*	*"This is ridiculous! I shouldn't have to pay for extra software when I was not told beforehand. Also, I don't feel comfortable showing my face."* *"Emails about officially mandating the use of Proctortrack were sent out during the THIRD WEEK of classes. It was already too late to drop classes and so, students essentially have NO choice but to pay the fee."* *"Countless students have been deceived simply because there was no public announcement about the implementation of Proctortrack."*

for credit, it has become a requirement to assess the validity of students taking exam through online automated ID validation method [9]. Although the traditional way of appearing in the examination centre is sufficiently fool proof for ID faking attempts, the online providers are increasingly showing interest in online proctoring to maintain the integrity of distance learning. The online proctoring service provide a mechanism of deterrence and is helping to minimize number of unfair means used [16].

Our study shows that the induction of online verification systems should be carefully planned with the involvement of all the stake holders minimizing the risk for the users – this could be due to lack of awareness of the tool, lack of understanding of configuration, lack of awareness for the significance of integration of tool and scope of tool's tracking ability. Our study also shows the need to fully understand the user needs and requirements in a meaning full way for their privacy concerns. Understanding of underlying potential causes of privacy anxiety and then devising strategies to minimize risks which compound the anxiety for privacy could potentially lead to smooth adoption of new online verification technology. Effectively handling the awareness of privacy when inducting new tools and services should not be just left to management and system designers but should include other bodies that could make significant contribution for this cause for example student union, social media marketing team, lecturers etc. The academic practitioners should incorporate the awareness of privacy as fundamental part of their online course provision especially in the environment of integrated services and tools.

6 Conclusion

This study investigated the underlying factors causing anxiety over privacy concern. The conceptual formation of the research topic could be used by the decision makers, planners, designers and academics when integrating online verification tools or similar services in their systems. The study shows that acutely understanding the users' privacy concern is extremely important and not doing so could lead to unsatisfied users and damage to the reputation of the institution. For example this study shows that just the use of webcam didn't trigger privacy concerns but the use of webcam as biometric scanning tool within private space of users and possibility of data breach caused the anxiety over privacy when Proctortrack was used for online courses by Universities.

References

1. Graneheim, U.H., Lundman, B.: Qualitative content analysis in nursing research: concepts, procedures and measures to achieve trustworthiness. Nurse Educ. Today **24**, 105–112 (2004)
2. Coursera Help Center: Honor Code & Plagiarism (2015). https://learner.coursera.help/hc/en-us/articles/201223999-Honor-Code-Plagiarism. Accessed 1 June 2015
3. Singer, N.: Online Test-Takers Feel Anti-Cheating Software's Uneasy Glare (2015). http://www.nytimes.com/2015/04/06/technology/online-test-takers-feel-anti-cheating-softwares-uneasy-glare.html. Accessed 15 May 2015
4. Change.org: The world's platform for change (2015). https://www.change.org/. Accessed 12 June 2015

5. Bertino, E., Paci, F., Ferrini, R.: Privacy-preserving digital identity management for cloud computing. IEEE Comput. Soc. Data Eng. Bull. 1–4 (2009)
6. Boyd, D.: Facebook's privacy train wreck: exposure, invasion, and social convergence. Convergence 14(1), 13–20 (2008)
7. Rotenberg, M.: Protecting human dignity in the digital age. In: Proceedings of the Third United Nations Educational, Scientific and Cultural Organization Congress on Ethical, Legal and Societal Challenges of Cyberspace (2000). http://webworld.unesco.org/infoethics2000/report_151100.html. Accessed 2 June 2015
8. Solove, J.D.: A taxonomy of privacy. Univ. Pa. L. Rev. 154(3), 477–564 (2006)
9. Briggs, L.: Assessment tools for MOOCs. Campus Technology (2013). http://campustechnology.com/Articles/2013/09/05/Assessment-Tools-for-MOOCs.aspx. Accessed 15 Apr 2015
10. Altbach, P.G.: MOOCs as neocolonialism: Who controls knowledge? [Blog post]. WorldWise (2013). http://chronicle.com/blogs/worldwise/moocs-as-neocolonialism-who-controls-knowledge/
11. De Waard, I., Abajian, S., Gallagher, M., Hogue, R., ÖzdamarKeskin, N., Koutropoulos, A., Rodriguez, O.: Using mLearning and MOOCs to understand chaos, emergence, and complexity in education. Int. Rev. Res. Open Distance Learn. 12(7), 94–115 (2011). http://www.irrodl.org/index.php/irrodl/article/view/1046/2026
12. Koet, M., Ahn, G.-J., Shehab, M.: Privacy-enhanced user-centric identity management. In: Proceedings of IEEE International Conference on Communications, pp. 998–1002. IEEE Press (2009)
13. Warren, S.D., Brandeis, L.D.: The right to privacy. 4 Harv. L. Rev. 193, 195–196 (1890)
14. Son, J.: Y., and Kim, S., S., (2008) Internet users' information privacy-protective responses: a taxonomy and a nomological model. MIS Q. 32(3), 503–529 (2008)
15. Carr, N.: The ethics of MOOC research [Blog post]. Rough Type (2012). http://www.roughtype.com/?p=2005. Accessed 10 Apr 2015
16. Verificient: Automated Remote Proctoring Solutions, Proctortrack (2015). http://www.proctortrack.com/
17. Schram, T.H.: Conceptualizing Qualitative In-quiry: Mindwork for Fieldwork in Education and the Social Sciences. Pearson, Upper Saddle River (2003)
18. Yin, R.K.: Applications of Case Study Research. Sage Publications Inc., Thousand Oaks (2012)
19. Taylor, B., Sinha, G., Ghoshal, T.: Research Methodology: (A Guide for Researchers in Management and Social Sciences). Asoke K. Ghosh, Prentice-Hall, New Delhi (2006)
20. Eisenhardt, K.M.: Building theories from case study research. Acad. Manag. Rev. 14, 532–550 (1989)
21. Liyanagunawardena, T.R., Adams, A.A., Williams, S.A.: MOOCs: A Systematic Study of the Published Literature 2008–2012. Int. Rev. Res. Open Distance Learn 14(3), 202–227 (2013). Irrodl
22. The New Media Consortium: The Horizon Report. USA: The New Media Consortium and EDUCAUSE Learning Initiative (2011)
23. Simons, H.: Cast study Research in Practice. Sage Publications Limited, London (2009)
24. Burges, R.G.: The Ethics of Educational Research. The Falmer Press, London (2005)
25. Franzosi, R.: Content analysis: Objective, systematic, and quantitative description of content. In: Franzosi, R. (ed.) Content Analysis. SAGE Benchmarks in Social Research Methods, pp. 2–43. Sage Publications, Thousand Oaks (2008)
26. Graneheim, U.H., Lundman, B.: Qualitative content analysis in nursing research: concepts, procedures and measures to achieve trustworthiness. Nurse Educ. Today 24, 105–112 (2004)

27. Downe-Wamboldt, B.: Content analysis: method, applica-tions, and issues. Health Care Women Int. **13**(3), 313–321 (1992)

28. Kondracki, N.L., Wellman, N.S., Amundson, D.R.: Content analysis: review of methods and their applications in nutri-tion education. J. Nutr. Educ. Behav. **34**(4), 224–230 (2002)

29. Chinn, P.L., Kramer, M.K.: Theory and Nursing a Systematic Approach. Mosby Year Book, St. Louis (1999)

30. Elo, S., Kynga, H.: The qualitative content analysis process. J. Adv. Nurs. **62**, 107–115 (2007)

31. Burns, N., Grove, S.K.: The Practice of Nursing Research: Conduct, Critique and Utilization. Elsevier Saunders, St. Louis (2005)

32. Polit, D.F., Beck, C.T.: Nursing Research: Principles and Methods. Lippincott Williams & Wilkins, Philadelphia (2004)

33. Robson, C.: Real World Research: A Resource for Social Scientists and Practitioner–Researchers. Blackwell Publishers, Oxford (1993)

34. Burnard, P.: Teaching the analysis of textual data: an experiential approach. Nurse Educ. Today **16**, 278–281 (1996)

35. Fielding, N.G., Lee, R.M.: Computer Analysis and Qualitative Research. Sage, Thousand Oaks (1998)

36. Leech, N.L., Onwuegbuzie, A.J.: Beyond constant comparison qualitative data analysis: using NVivo. School Psychol. Q. **26**(1), 70–84 (2011)

37. Bandura, A.: Self-efficacy mechanism in human agency. Am. Psychol. **37**, 122–147 (1982)

38. Wikipedia: Self-efficacy (2015). https://en.wikipedia.org/wiki/Self-efficacy. Accessed 12 June 2015

39. Ftc.gov: Federal Trade Commission | Protecting America's Consumers (2015). https://www.ftc.gov/. Accessed 12 June 2015

40. Hayes, F., Termini, V.: (2013). http://www.educause.edu/ero/article/ensuring-academic-integrity-distance-education-online-proctoring. Accessed 9 June 2015

41. Negrea, S.: (2014). http://www.universitybusiness.com/article/online-proctoring-gaining-popularity-moocs

Towards a Common Security and Privacy Requirements Elicitation Methodology

Eleni-Laskarina Makri[⊠] and Costas Lambrinoudakis

University of Piraeus, Piraeus, Greece
{elmak, clam}@unipi.gr

Abstract. There are many methodologies that have been proposed in the literature for identifying the security and privacy requirements that must be satisfied by an information system in order to protect its users. At the same time, there are several "privacy principles" that have been considered as equally important for the avoidance of privacy violation incidents. However, to the best of our knowledge, there is no methodology that can cover both the identification of the security and privacy requirements and at the same time to take into account the main privacy principles. The consequence is that the designers of an information system usually follow an ad hoc approach for the identification of security/privacy requirements, thus failing to protect users in an effective way. This paper introduces the main idea behind a methodology that integrates the basic steps of well-established risk analysis methodologies with those of methodologies used for the identification of privacy requirements, considering, at the same time, the most well-known privacy principles. The proposed methodology aims to assist information system designers to come up with a complete and accurate list of all security and privacy requirements that must be satisfied by the system.

Keywords: Security requirements · Privacy requirements · Privacy principles · Risk analysis

1 Introduction

Over the recent years there is a significant evolution in the way information and communication systems are utilized. Nowadays, personal data are available or/and can be collected at different sites around the world. Even though the utilization of personal information leads to several advantages, including improved customer services, increased revenues and lower business costs, it can be misused in several ways and may lead to security incidents or/and to privacy violation.

In the framework of e-commerce, several organizations, in order to identify the preferences of their customers and adapt their products accordingly, thus promoting their sales via Internet, develop new methods for collecting and processing personal data. This is often done during the initial stage (registration phase) of the connection of the client to the seller's web site. For instance, credit cards leave a trail to the places their holders' visit, in regard to where they shop and what they buy. Modern data mining techniques can then be utilized in order to further process the collected data,

H. Jahankhani et al. (Eds.): ICGS3 2015, CCIS 534, pp. 151–159, 2015.
DOI: 10.1007/978-3-319-23276-8_13

generating databases of the consumers' profiles through which each person's preferences can be uniquely identified.

Another example is that of Web sites providing users with medical information and advice. Anyone can address, through Internet, a specific request to the medical Web site and obtain the information she wants, provided that she has registered. The organization maintaining the medical Web site can easily generate "user profiles", by monitoring how often a specific user is visiting the site and furthermore the type of medical information she is interested on. Therefore, such information can be utilized for invading user's privacy and thus the 95/46 European Union directive on the protection of individuals with regard to the processing of personal and sensitive data.

Evidently, electronic transactions have raised the major problem of user's privacy protection. On top of that they have significantly increased the number of threats that they are vulnerable to. The probability that threats will materialize and lead to a security incident implies the existence of certain risks. In order to avoid confusion, it is important to stress the difference between privacy and security; a piece of information is secure when its content is protected, whereas it is private when the identity of its owner is protected. It is important for every Information System to achieve an adequate level of security for its data and also protect the privacy if its users. To this end, it is necessary to invoke the appropriate countermeasures. Considering that conventional security mechanisms, like encryption, cannot ensure privacy protection (encryption for instance, can only protect the message's confidentiality), new additional Privacy-Enhancing Technologies (PETs) have been developed.

Privacy and security should be considered as major issues in the process of designing an information system and should be taken into account from the very beginning [1, 6, 11, 12]. This can be done by identifying, through the appropriate methodologies, early enough in the design the security and privacy requirements that must be satisfied.

However, to the best of our knowledge, there is no methodology that can cover both the identification of the security and privacy requirements and at the same time to take into account the main privacy principles. The consequence is that the designers of an information system usually follow an ad hoc approach for the identification of security/privacy requirements, thus failing to protect users in an effective way. This paper introduces the main idea behind a methodology that integrates the basic steps of well-established risk analysis methodologies with those of methodologies used for the identification of privacy requirements, considering, at the same time, the most well-known privacy principles. The proposed methodology aims to assist information system designers to come up with a complete and accurate list of all security and privacy requirements that must be satisfied by the system.

The rest of the paper is organized as follows: Sect. 2 provides an overview of the security and privacy requirements as well as the privacy principles that are the most widely accepted by the scientific community. Based on them, Sect. 3 proposes a common security and privacy methodology that can be followed by an organization to ensure the protection of users' security and privacy. Section 4 draws the conclusions giving some pointers for future work.

2 Identification of Security and Privacy Requirements

2.1 Security Requirements

In order to select countermeasures one can choose between a rather uncomplicated baseline approach, based on checklists, and a more thorough custom-made approach, based on (qualitative) risk analysis [13, 14].

A qualitative risk analysis of an information system goes through the following phases (see Fig. 1):

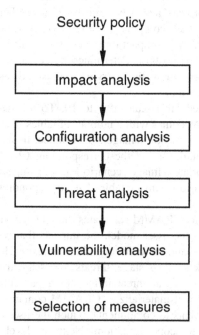

Fig. 1. Indicative phases of a risk analysis methodology

- Impact analysis to determine the security requirements imposed on the information system and its components, based on the potential damage on components and the potential damage in the business processes that use the information system.
- Configuration analysis to determine which components are present in the information system and which relations exist between those components.
- Threat analysis to determine which threats are relevant.
- Vulnerability analysis to determine the vulnerability of components with respect to the relevant threats.
- Selection of measures to determine a set of security measures that are capable of reducing the unacceptable risks.

An indicative risk analysis methodology is CRAMM (CCTA Risk Analysis and Management Method). It was originally developed by the UK Central Computer and

Telecommunications Agency (CCTA) for use by the UK government. Later, versions for commercial use and in other languages were developed. A CRAMM analysis (called review) consists of three stages:

Stage 1: The asset valuation stage
Stage 2: The risk analysis stage and
Stage 3: The risk management stage

Stage one, the asset valuation stage, starts with the definition of the scope of the review. Next, the value of the system that is subject of the review is determined by constructing an asset model which breaks down the system into its components (locations, equipment, software and data) and the relations between the components. The replacement costs of each component are determined (direct costs). The damage caused to the organization by an impact on the confidentiality, integrity or availability of the system (consequential costs) is determined by conducting interviews. For each impact on the system under review, the interviewee must indicate the damage caused to the organization.

Damages are expressed on a scale of 1 to 10. To translate actual damages into CRAMM values, CRAMM comes with a number of tables. Each of the tables contains ten descriptions of certain types of damage (for instance: financial damage, or damage to an organization's reputation), and the corresponding CRAMM values. The interviewee selects the appropriate damage scenario for each impact and selects the proper description from the scenario's damage table. The corresponding value is the CRAMM damage value.

At the end of stage one, CRAMM calculates the relevant impacts and damages for each component based on the asset model, the impacts that were considered relevant for the system as a whole, and the consequential damage each impact would cause.

In stage two, the risk analysis stage, threats are assigned to impacts and components, indicating that a particular threat influences a particular component and will cause a particular impact if it materializes. CRAMM contains a standard mapping of threats to impacts, and threats to components, which the user may edit for the current review, for example due to scope limitations. Next, the level of each threat is determined by conducting multiple choice interviews for each threat for each component. The answers to the interview determine the level of that threat for that particular component. Finally, the level of vulnerability of a component for a threat is determined by conducting vulnerability interviews. Threat and vulnerability interviews are usually conducted in one session, to limit the number of interviews. Similar components are grouped together at the start of stage two, to limit the number of threat-component relationships that need to be defined. Threat and vulnerability levels are defined for these groups as a whole, further limiting the number of interviews that need to be conducted.

After all this information has been entered, CRAMM calculates a Measure of Risk (MOR) value for each combination of asset group, threat and impact. The MOR indicates the level of risk, based on the chance that the threat will materialize, the chance that this will affect the asset group (based on that asset group's vulnerability for that threat) and cause the impact.

In stage three, the risk management stage, CRAMM automatically selects countermeasures from its database, based on the results from the previous stages, in particular the asset model and the MOR values. The selected countermeasures have to be compared with the existing measures. Consequently, the status of each selected countermeasure can be determined: already implemented (if there is an existing countermeasure that corresponds to the selected countermeasure), to be implemented, or accept risk (if the organization has chosen not to implement this countermeasure and accept the risk).

The most common security requirements that are derived from the risk analysis are:

- Confidentiality: Only authorized users can access the data
- Integrity: Only authorized users can modify/delete the data
- Availability: The provided service should be available whenever requested.
- Non-repudiation: Association of specific users to specific actions.

2.2 Privacy Requirements

In order for personal data of an information system to be protected, apart from the privacy laws and regulations which should be applied, many privacy requirement methodologies have been proposed in the literature [6, 16]. The existing privacy requirement methodologies adopt concepts from the field of IS security engineering and use them in order to explicitly represent security requirements (which also include privacy requirements) and they define the way that these requirements can be transformed in specific policies for the system under construction [6]. In other words, the privacy-oriented methodologies, presented next, aim to incorporate basic concepts for the clear representation of privacy requirements during system design.

The majority of these methodologies follow specific steps or/and phases in order to reach their goal and apply privacy. Indicatively, the steps of the PriS Method, a well-known example of such a methodology [2–6, 16], will be presented. It consists of three steps. In the **first step**, the privacy goals, related to an organization, are specified. During this step several stakeholders participate in order to identify the basic privacy concerns of the organization's information system. In the **second step**, firstly the impact of privacy goals on the organizational goals is identified and analyzed. Secondly, the privacy goals are examined and the processes that realize the privacy-related goals are identified and characterized as privacy-related processes. Then, it models them using privacy process patterns. In the **third step**, the methodology defines the system architecture and then identifies the proper implementation technique(s) that best support corresponding processes.

This type of methodologies achieves privacy protection through the satisfaction of the privacy requirements that the information system should adopt to be privacy-oriented. Indicatively, the most common privacy requirements are listed below:

- **Authentication:** Authentication is used more as a security requirement rather than a privacy requirement in an information system. However, it has significant contribution in privacy as well. Through the process of authentication the identity of the users is confirmed.

- **Authorization:** Through the process of authorization the users obtain rights and they have access in the services of an information system. In this way privacy is ensured.
- **Identification:** The process of identification does not allow unauthorized users to access personal data stored in the information system.
- **Data Protection:** Users' personal data should be protected according to the Directive 95/46/EC (Council 1995) that addresses the issue of the protection of individuals with regard to the processing of personal data and on the free movement of such data [7].
- **Anonymity/Pseudonymity:** The organization should be able to provide users with pseudonyms, anonymisers or anonymous data credentials, etc. in order for them to remain anonymous and thus protect their privacy.
- **Unlinkability:** The organization should exhibit mechanisms that do not allow any connection among users or among a user and an event.
- **Unobservability:** Unobservability prevents malicious users from finding traces of the users of an information system when they access information system' services or Internet services.

2.3 Privacy Principles

The Organization for Economic Co-operation and Development (OECD) proposed, back in 1980, eight privacy principles [15] that have had a great impact on privacy laws in many countries. From 1980, these principles have been used and analyzed from many public and private bodies while some of these bodies have proposed revised versions of them [8, 20]. The majority of existing privacy frameworks has been based on these eight OECD privacy principles:

- **Purpose Specification Principle:** Firstly, the organization should define a specific purpose for data collection. The personal data should be collected and used only for specified purposes.
- **Collection Limitation Principle:** Secondly, the organization should collect personal data with lawful and fair means based on specific purposes. The data collection should take place under the user's consent.
- **Data Quality Principle:** In addition, the organization should keep the personal data collected and used accurate, complete and updated.
- **Use Limitation Principle:** Also, the organization should limit the use of personal data without disclosing or making it available for any reason other than the purpose of the collection.
- **Openness Principle:** Throughout the implementation of the above privacy principles, the practices, policies, processes and procedures concerning the users' personal data should be easily accessible and transparency should be maintained in every stage of its collection and use.
- **Individual Participation Principle:** At the same time with the "Openness Principle", the organization should take into account the user's participation in the process of personal data collection and use.

- **Accountability Principle:** Furthermore, a data controller should be accountable for being in accordance with protection mechanisms which give effect to the above principles.
- **Security Safeguards:** When the organization has successfully satisfied all afore-mentioned principles, it should apply security safeguards in order to protect personal/sensitive data from potential security or/and privacy violation incidents [16].

3 Towards a Common Security and Privacy Methodology

The problem that IS designers are facing today is that there is no methodology that can cover simultaneously both the identification of the security and privacy requirements and at the same time to take into account the main privacy principles [9]. The existence of such a methodology would support information system designers to come up with a complete and accurate list of all security and privacy requirements that must be satisfied.

The methodology presented in Fig. 2 below, combines the results (security requirements) of a risk analysis process with the results (privacy requirements) of a privacy requirements' elicitation methodology and, furthermore, with the OECD privacy principles. The important thing is that the integration of these heterogeneous approaches is performed in independent well-specified discrete steps that follow a specific sequence.

More specifically, when an organization wishes to apply the proposed methodology in order to protect users' personal data and privacy, it should:

- **Satisfy first all Privacy Principles (middle column in Fig.** 2) according to several public and private bodies [10, 15, 17–19]. Each privacy principle should be addressed in the order appearing in the Figure below.
- **Identify security requirements (left column in Fig.** 2) through some risk analysis methodology.
- **Identify privacy requirements (right column in Fig.** 2) through some appropriate methodology.
- At this stage the organization should **select the appropriate security safeguards** for satisfying all security and privacy requirements and thus protecting users' personal data from potential security and privacy violation incidents [16]. These security safeguards will be implemented during the "Security Safeguards Privacy Principle".

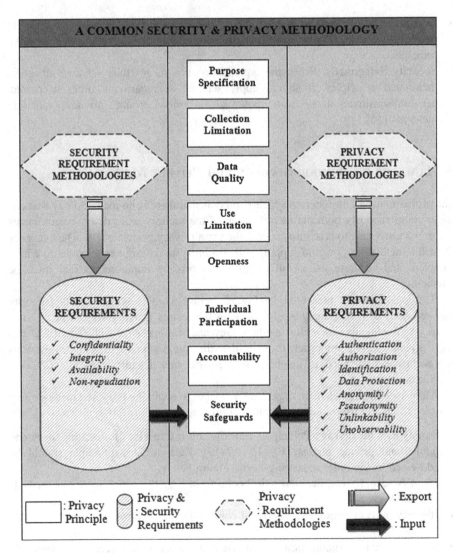

Fig. 2. A common security and privacy methodology

4   Conclusions and Further Work

Driven by the most widely used security and privacy requirements as well as privacy principles, which have been either introduced by countries or by public/private bodies, this paper presents a common security and privacy methodology that organizations can follow for protecting the security and privacy of their users.

Currently, we are in the stage of applying the proposed security and privacy methodology to a real environment in order to validate its correctness and effectiveness, as well as its importance for both organizations and users.

References

1. Cavoukian, A.: Privacy by design – the 7 foundational principles. Technical report, Information and Privacy Commissioner of Ontario, January 2011. (Revised version)
2. Kalloniatis, C., Kavakli, E., Kontellis, E.: PRIS tool: a case tool for privacy-oriented requirements engineering. J. Inf. Syst. Secur. 6(1), 3–19 (2010). AIS
3. Kalloniatis, C., Kavakli, E., Kontellis, E.: PriS tool: a case tool for privacy-oriented RE. In: Doukidis, G., et al. (eds.) Proceedings of the MCIS 2009 4th Mediterranean Conference on Information Systems, Athens, Greece, pp. 913–925 (e-version), September 2009
4. Kalloniatis, C., Kavakli, E., Gritzalis, S.: PriS methodology: incorporating privacy requirements into the system design process. In: Mylopoulos, J., Spafford, G. (eds.) Proceedings of the 13th IEEE International Requirements Engineering Conference – SREIS 2005 Symposium on Requirements Engineering for Information Security, Paris, France. IEEE CPS Conference Publishing Services, August 2005
5. Kalloniatis, C., Kavakli, E., Gritzalis, S.: Addressing privacy requirements in system design: the PriS method. Requirements Eng. (Indexed Thomson's ISI Web of Knowl.) 13(3), 241–255 (2008). Springer
6. Kalloniatis, C., Kavakli, E., Gritzalis, S.: Methods for designing privacy aware information systems: a review. In: PCI (2009)
7. Directive 95/46/EC of the European Parliament and of the Council, The European Parliament and the Council of the European Union, 24 October 1995. http://eur-lex.europa.eu/LexUriServ/LexUriServ.do?uri=CELEX:31995L0046:en:HTML
8. Directive of the European Parliament and of the Council, European Commission, Brussels, 25 January 2012. http://eur-lex.europa.eu/legal-content/EN/TXT/PDF/?uri=CELEX:52012PC0010&from=en
9. Generally Accepted Privacy Principles (GAPP). www.cica.ca/privacy, www.aicpa.org/privacy
10. Information technology — Security techniques — Privacy framework, International Standard, ISO/IEC 29100:2011(E) (2011)
11. Hoepman, J.-H.: Privacy design strategies, 7 May 2013
12. Hoepman, J.-H.: Privacy design strategies, 25 October 2012
13. Barnard, L., von Solms, R.: A formalized approach to the effective selection and evaluation of information security controls. Comput. Secur. 19(2), 185–194 (2000)
14. Eloff, M.M., von Solms, S.H.: Information security management: a hierarchical framework for various approaches. Comput. Secur. 19, 243–256 (2000)
15. OECD Privacy Principles (1980). http://oecdprivacy.org/
16. PriS Methodology: Incorporating Privacy Requirements into the System Design Process. In: 3rd Symposium on Requirements Engineering for Information Sequrity (SREIS 2005) In conjunction with RE 2005 - 13th IEEE International Requirements Engineering ConferenceParis, France, 29 August 2005. http://www.academia.edu/2845236/PriS_Methodology_Incorporating_Privacy_Requirements_into_the_System_Design_Process
17. Privacy, Accountability and Trust – Challenges and Opportunities, ENISA
18. PrivacySense.net, The 10 Privacy Principles of PIPEDA. http://www.privacysense.net/10-privacy-principles-of-pipeda/
19. Safe Harbor Privacy Principles, issued by the U.S. Department of Commerce, 21 July 2000. http://www.export.gov/safeharbor/eu/eg_main_018475.asp
20. The OECD Privacy Framework, OECD (2013)

Automated Security Testing Framework for Detecting SQL Injection Vulnerability in Web Application

Nor Fatimah Awang[1(✉)] and Azizah Abd Manaf[2]

[1] Faculty of Defence Science and Technology,
National Defence University of Malaysia, Kuala Lumpur, Malaysia
norfatimah@upnm.edu.my
[2] Advanced Informatics School (UTM AIS), UTM International Campus,
Kuala Lumpur, Malaysia
azizaham.kl@utm.my

Abstract. Today almost all organizations have changed their traditional systems and have improved their performance using web-based applications. This process will make more profit and at the same time will increase the efficiency of their activities through customer support services and data transactions. Usually, web application take inputs from users through web form and send this input to get the response from database. Modern web-based application use web database to store all critical information such as user credentials, financial and payment information, company statistics etc. However error in validation of user input can cause database vulnerable to Structured Query Language Injection (SQLI) attack. By using SQLI attack, the attackers might insert malicious code in the user input and trying to gain access to the confidential and sensitive data from database. Security tester need to identify the appropriate test cases before starting exploiting SQL vulnerability in web-based application during testing phase. Identifying the test cases of a web application and analyzing the test results of an attack are important parts and consider as critical issues that affects the effectiveness of security testing. Thus, this research focused on the developing a framework for testing and detecting SQL injection vulnerability in web application. In this research, test cases will be generated automatically based on SQLI attack pattern and then the results will be executed automatically based on generated test cases. The primary focus in this paper is to develop a framework to automate security testing based on input injection attack pattern. To test our framework, we install a vulnerable web application and test result shows that the proposed framework can detect SQLI vulnerability successfully.

Keywords: Security testing · Penetration testing · Test case generation

1 Introduction

Web application systems are one of the most ubiquitous software systems in use today. Since they appeared they have grown quickly and have evolved faster than other software systems. More than one billion people worldwide using the Internet and web

© Springer International Publishing Switzerland 2015
H. Jahankhani et al. (Eds.): ICGS3 2015, CCIS 534, pp. 160–171, 2015.
DOI: 10.1007/978-3-319-23276-8_14

applications as their daily routine activities for a variety of reasons, such as communicating with others, conduct research, shopping, banking and electronic commerce [1]. The web application is consider both, as a communication and a source of information [2]. It offers a collection of various services and resources such as customer support services, online banking and data transactions [2]. Most of the organizations use the web applications to make more profit and at the same time to increase the efficiency of their activities. The growth of these applications gave a high impact and business opportunity to the organization. As web applications become adopted by more and more organizations, they have become more complex and sophisticated. In many cases their success is crucial for the success of the organizations. Thus ensuring security of the Web application systems is a big concern for organizations.

Web application vulnerabilities represent huge problems for companies and organizations. These vulnerabilities leave organizations' web applications exposed to attack and majority of all security problems in web application is caused by string based injection through web form such as SQL injection and cross site scripting. SQL injection vulnerabilities have been described as one of the most serious attacks for Web applications [3, 4]. SQL injection vulnerabilities are based on injection strings input into database to construct SQL queries and may allow an attacker to extract data from database. A web application is consider vulnerable to an SQL injection attack if an attacker is able to insert SQL statements into an existing SQL query of the application and extract sensitive and confidential data from database. This SQL injection vulnerability usually occurs when web application does not properly sanitize the user input.

With the majority of vulnerability exists in web applications today, it is important to evaluate and detect the vulnerability of web application before it is sent to production [5]. Detecting and preventing vulnerabilities in web application has become an important concern for organizations. Many organizations are starting to take initiatives to prevent these types of attacks. To minimize the probability of vulnerabilities exist in web applications, organizations need some methodologies or approaches to increase efforts to protect against web-based application attack [5, 6]. Therefore, organizations have a big task to implement security testing methodologies into the software development life cycle. The purpose of security testing is to find any security weaknesses or vulnerabilities within an application and document all the vulnerabilities to help developer to fix them. In this paper we develop a framework for testing and detection SQL injection vulnerabilities in web applications. We automate the process of security testing based on input injection attack pattern. We separated the framework into three stages. (i) Develop Test Cases Generator which is used to generate test cases. In the first stage, we apply permutation technique in order to generate test cases automatically; (ii). Develop Attack Generator. This generator will be used to automate the injection attack process based on input generated in the first stage. (iii). Response Generator. The goal of response generator is to analyze and determine whether an attempted attack has been successful or not. Some manual work is still required before automating the testing process. The process of modeling test case generation may not be very time consuming if the tester has knowledge about the internal structure of the application and type of SQL injection vulnerabilities.

This idea is using penetration testing framework adapted from Open Web Application Security Project (OWASP) and security testing lifecycle as shown in Fig. 1 [6–8].

On the middle of Fig. 1, by selecting and combining some components in penetration testing framework and security testing lifecycle, we proposed the new framework to automate the security testing in web application. In this paper, we are focusing on SQLIA due to the common vulnerabilities that have evolved in the last decade. The rest of the paper, we follow the idea of developing our framework. Our framework closely related to [7, 9, 10].

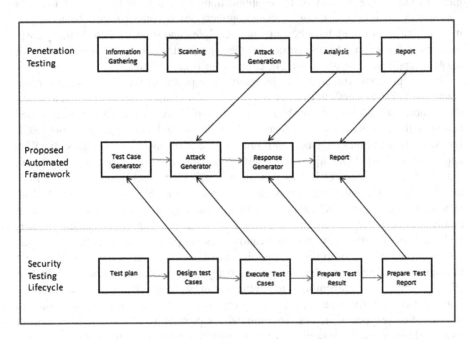

Fig. 1. Transition to new framework

The structure of this paper is as follows. Section 2 briefly describes the background of SQL injection attack. Section 3 discusses the proposed framework, Sect. 4 presents test result and Sect. 5 presents the conclusion.

2   Background of SQL Injection Attack (SQLIA)

SQL injection attacks are one of the topmost threats for applications written for the Web. In OWASP listing, SQLIA is always appear in top ten list. These attacks are launched through specially crafted user input on web applications that use input string operations to construct SQL queries [11]. These attacks used by attackers to steal data from back-end database of web application. It takes the advantage of dynamic input of web applications that allow users to insert data such as login form and registration page. This type of attack usually takes place when attackers insert some special code into web form. Online forms such as login prompts, search enquiries, guest book and registration forms are always the main target of SQL injection vulnerabilities.

The simple test to check for SQLIA is to append 'OR 1 = 1' [12] or just single quote (')
to any input of any form and wait for the data response returned. The response could be
error message or any information that may give some clue to the attackers to conducting next step of attack. In the rest of this section, we discuss three important
characteristics of SQLIAs that we use for describing SQLIA: how SQL works,
injection based on attack input, injection based on attack intend and injection based on
SQL types.

2.1 How SQL Works

SQL is stand for Structure Query Language and originally developed in the early
1970's by Edgar. SQL is used for accessing database servers including MySQL, Oracle
and SQL server. Web programming language such as Java, ASP.NET and PHP provide
various methods for constructing and executing SQL statements. In addition, SQL
language is a communication way between users and database in order to allow the user
to interact with database. SQL statement can modify the structure of databases and
manipulate the contents of databases [16].

2.2 SQL Injection Attack Based on Input Source

Malicious SQL statements can be introduced into a vulnerable application using many
different input mechanisms. In this section, we explain the most common mechanisms.
Table 1 explains the most common input that usually used by attackers [12–15].

Table 1. SQLIA based on input source

Classification	Description
Injection through user input	Injects malicious SQL commands into user input query in web form based on GET and POST parameter.
Injection through cookies	Injects malicious command and modified cookies variables containing SQLIA. Cookies are files used for an origin website and generated by website and send this state information to a user's browser or client machine. This state information can be used for authentication or identification of a user session. Cookie variables sometimes are not properly sanitized and can be used to bypass authentication or make any SQL query by injecting arbitrary SQL code.
Injection through server variables	Server variables are components of the message header that contain HTTP header, network header and environmental variable. They define the operating parameters for HTTP transaction such as request and response information. By using the request and response field, attackers can submit arbitrary input and exploit through HTTP header.
Second order injection	This injection occurs when data input stored in a place and then used in a different SQL query without correct filtering or without using parameterized queries

2.3   SQL Injection Attack Based on Attack Intend

SQLIA can also be characterized based on the goal, or intent, of the attacker. Attacks have been characterized by their intent are summarized in Table 2 [9, 12–14].

Table 2. SQLIA based on attack intend

Classification	Description
Identifying injectable parameter	The first step to identify SQLI vulnerabilities is to identify which input parameter values are likely to have vulnerabilities into SQL query statements. Attackers will use their knowledge to discover which parameters and user input fields are vulnerable to SQLIA
Extracting data	The goal of these types of attack is to extract data values from database. Attackers usually use GET and POST method to extract response from web server.
Adding or modifying	To add or change information in database
Performing denial of Service	To shutdown, locking or dropping database. Attackers can extract or dump the complete database by using "UNION" and "SELECT" commands.
Bypassing authentication	Attackers occurs use these types of attacks to inject some malicious code such as 'OR 1 = 1' into login form and try to bypass database and application authentication mechanism
Executing remote commands	To execute arbitrary commands on the database including stored procedure or functions
Determine database schema	Attackers use these types of attacks to obtain information about table names, column names, column type, etc.

2.4   SQL Injection Attack Based on Attack Techniques

There are a variety of techniques that attackers can use to perform these attacks [9, 12–14]. The most common SQLIA based on the attack type are summarized in Table 3. The different techniques of attacks are generally not performed in isolation. Attackers may use and combine these techniques in order to achieve several attack types based on attackers' goal. In this paper, we just summarize all possible attack without writing detail. These types of attacks will be used in the next section to generate test case generation.

3   Our Proposed Framework

As shown in Fig. 1, our proposed framework adapted from penetration model and security testing lifecycle model. In our framework, we develop three main components and Fig. 2 shows our proposed framework.

1. Input Generator - input generator component is used to generate test cases based on injection attack pattern. We apply permutation technique in order to generate test cases automatically [17].

Table 3. SQLIA based on attack technique

Classification	Description
Tautologies	Inject code to one or more SQL query and these query will always evaluates to true. For example: query = "SELECT * FROM users WHERE username = 'name' AND password = 'pwd'"; Attackers can use tautologies to exploit this peace of code by inserting this value 'OR 1 = 1' to the text box of login page in WHERE username clause. This make the system will always evaluates the result to be true and bypass the authentication system. In addition, tautology method can inject string type, numerical type and comment type. Once the user has got the access, he can modify the data in the database and this can cause a major loss for the organization. Injection Attack = SELECT * FROM users WHERE username =" OR 1 = 1– AND password = "
Illegal/Logical	When faced with invalid queries, databases will provide an error message that can give detailed information about the type of database that is running and further information about the query. Using error messages rejected by the database, the attacker will use to find useful data. A number of different approaches can be used to generate invalid queries. For example single quote string, double quote or other logical errors can all be used to help identify information about the database. Injection Attack = SELECT * FROM users WHERE name = '/*! – */' AND password = "
Piggy-backed	Piggy-Backed queries are used when the attacker would like to alter the developer statement and potentially run an entirely separate statement of their own. Insert additional queries to be executed. The secondary queries will be used to alter, delete or disable the application. Using the same example as before, the syntax of SQL defines the semicolon as a delimiter and executes the two separate statements. As a result, DROP syntax will remove the logs table from database. Injection Attack = SELECT * FROM users WHERE username = 'name' and password = ";DROP TABLE logs –
Union	Injected query is joined with a safe query using the keyword UNION. UNION statement in SQL allows an attacker to combine two separate SELECT statements into one result. By Unioning on extra data from other tables, or the same table in the system the attacker is able to recover additional information. Assuming the number and types of the columns in both the users and Email Addresses tables match, and there is no user with the username `, the database will union together the two sets. One containing all the Email Addresses in the database, the other containing all zero users with the username ". The ending result is the display of all Email Addresses in the system to the user. Injection Attack = SELECT * FROM users WHERE username ='UNION SELECT * from EmailAddresses – AND password = "

2. Attack Generator - this generator will be used to automate the injection attack process based on input or test cases generated in the first phase.

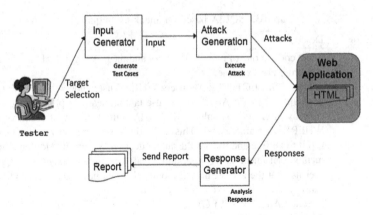

Fig. 2. Overview of proposed framework

3. Response Generator - The goal of response generator is to analyze and determine the response and output send by web server in order to detect vulnerabilities.

3.1 Input Generator

In this section, we discuss our approach in generating test cases automatically based on attack techniques. Based on input string in attack technique as shown in Fig. 3, we formulate and design the attack grammar and divide into six different patterns templates as listed below:

- #numeric = all numeric characters [0-9]
- #alphabet = all alphabet characters [A-z]

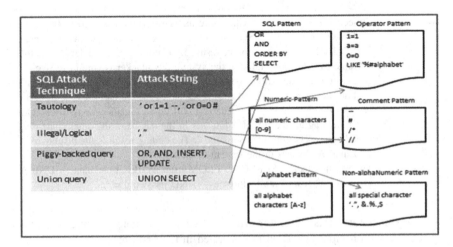

Fig. 3. Formulation of attack file to generate test cases

- #non_alphanumeric = not alphanumeric but printable (e.g.: punctuation)
- #sql = sql syntax (sql.txt)
- #operator = the operators used in various programming language (operators.txt)
- #inline_comment = various type of comments (inline_comments.txt)

Using permutation algorithm [17] this pattern generates different variations of test cases based on SQL injection attack as shown in Fig. 4. For example, from the tautology technique, the simple input string to inject to input field is 'OR 1 = 1. There are a lot of combination of tautology's input string in order to detect vulnerability such as 'OR 1 = 1–, 'OR 1 = 1#, etc. Testers are allowed to modify and insert new data in pattern template.

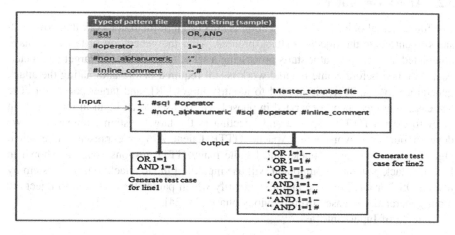

Fig. 4. Input generator component

In this section, we follow closely related paper for test case generation. [18–20]. The main important in this phase is master_template file. Master_template file will be executed after tester run the generator. The master template contains list of template for the application to perform permutation to generate more test cases. To form the template we introduce a syntax which started with '#' symbol to represent the data that needs to be replaced. The generator then generate the dictionary files that contains all pattern files (sql.txt, operators.txt, inline_comments.txt, etc.) to form list of string tokens for test cases. Each test case is generated automatically by using permutation algorithm based on the input line in the master_template file. Refer to Fig. 4.

Based on a sample in Fig. 4, we can see in master_template file, there are two lines listed and attack generator will generate the test cases separated and saved in a different file. By applying the permutation technique algorithm, we shall get the following results as stated in Table 4.

Table 4. Test Case Generation

Test cases for line 1:	Test cases for line 2:
OR 1 = 1	'OR 1 = 1 –
	'OR 1 = 1 #
	"OR 1 = 1 –
	"OR 1 = 1 #
AND 1 = 1	'AND 1 = 1 –
	'AND 1 = 1 #
	"AND 1 = 1 –
	"AND 1 = 1 #

3.2   Attack Generator

The fundamental objective of this section is the design of the framework that covers all steps to automate the injection attack process. After the generation of test cases have completed, Attack generator starts processing a set of target URL and target parameter. As mentioned before, some manual work is still required before automating the attack generator process. Tester is needed to identify target URL and target parameter. The test cases that have been generated in phase1 will be used as an input in this phase. In order to extract HTTP response and injecting to the target system automatically, we develop our framework with Apache HTTP Client API. We present an efficient algorithm to send many attacks and handle many HTTP response page as shown in Fig. 5. Attack generator component will use input.xml file to attack to target system by using POST or GET method and also identify which parameter is chosen to inject the input generated test cases from previous phase [21–24].

Sample of Input.xml file

```
<?xml version="1.0" encoding="UTF-8"?>
<client>
  <url>http://WackoPicko/users/login.php</url>
  <method>post</method>
  <parameters-group>
      <parameters>
      <param>username</param>
      <file>D:\\input.txt</file>
      </parameters>
        <parameters>
        <param>password</param>
        </parameters>
  </parameters-group>
</client>
```

3.3   Response Generator

After an attack has been launched, the analysis of response page will be send to the response generator. The response generator component uses attack specific response

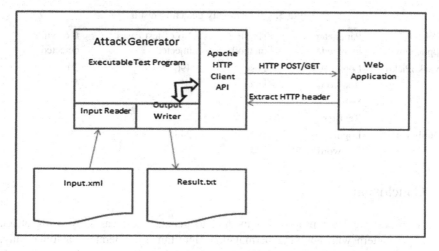

Fig. 5. Attack generator component

criteria to decide if the attack was successful. If the web application does not handle exceptions or server errors, the result for SQL error description will be included in the response page.

4 Result

This section presents the testing results that we have carried out to assess our framework. For the testing of our framework, two different vulnerable web applications were deployed locally and tested against SQLIA. This testing applications are namely as Mutillidae and WackoPicko website. Mutillidae website has an authentication bypass vulnerability, which allows the attacker to directly access the administrative functionalities. WackoPicko is an online photo sharing website that allows users to upload, comment and purchase pictures It is designed with a number of vulnerabilities, such as cross-site scripting and SQL injection [11]. Our framework was deployed by setting up Eclipse development environment with Java Program. Apache HTTP Client API library has been installed in our machine to extract HTTP header from response page. In test case generation phase, we generate 124 attack injection for SQL injection attack. Each parameter will be tested with 124 test cases. In this paper, we focus on the SQL injection vulnerability through input field such as login, search and registration field.

We test the framework with injecting attack test cases, and the results are summarized in Table 5. The response results will consider vulnerable if error messages and bypass authentication result are appeared in HTML document header. Based on testing results, we can conclude that all input forms are vulnerable to website. Response generator will analyze which input test cases have been generated to produce vulnerabilities.

Table 5. Vulnerability detection result

Web application	Parameter involved	HTTP method	No of test cases injected	# of vuln. detected
WackoPicko	Login	Post	496	20
	Password	Get		
	Search			
	Register			
Mutillidae	Login	Post	248	9
	Password	Get		

5   Conclusion

In this paper, we have proposed a method to generate test cases by using attack technique pattern with applying permutation algorithm to generate it automatically. This framework has been successfully tested and including several type of SQL injection vulnerabilities. Our framework is able to addresses the vulnerabilities based on results in Table 5. Future work will also be focused on extending our approach to cover other types of vulnerabilities such as Cross Site Scripting vulnerabilities.

Acknowledgment. This work was supported by the Advanced Informatics School (AIS), University Technology of Malaysia and National Defence University of Malaysia

References

1. Vermatt, S.: Discovering Computers 2009, Complete. Cengage Learning Course Technology (2009)
2. Anastacio, M., Blanco, J.A., Villalba, L., Dahoud, A.: E-Government: benefits, risks and a proposal to assessment including cloud computing and critical infrastructure. In: International Conference on Information Technology (2013)
3. Internet World Stats, Usage and Population Statistics (2013). http://www.internetworldstats.com/stats.htm
4. Symantec Corp.: Web Based Attacks (2013). http://www.symantec.com/content/en/us/enterprise/media/security_response/whitepapers/web_based_attacks_02-2009.pdf
5. Software Security Testing, Software Assurance Pocket Guide Series: Development, vol. III, Version 1.0, 21 May 2012
6. Gu, T.-Y., Shi, Y.-S., Fang, Y.-U.: Research on software security testing. World Academy of Science, Engineering and Technology **69**, 647–651 (2010)
7. Halfond, W.G.J., Choudhary, S.R., Orso, A.: Improving penetration testing through static and dynamic analysis. In: ICST 2009, the Second IEEE International Conference on Software Testing, Verification and Validation, vol. 21, pp. 195–214 (2011). doi:10.1002/stvr
8. Khan, S.A., Khan, R.A.: Software security testing process: phased approach. In: Agrawal, A., Tripathi, R.C., Do, E.Y.-L., Tiwari, M.D. (eds.) IITM 2013. CCIS, vol. 276, pp. 211–217. Springer, Heidelberg (2013)

9. Djuric, Z.: A black-box testing tool for detecting SQL injection vulnerabilities. In: 2013 2nd International Conference on Informatics and Applications, ICIA 2013, pp. 216–221 (2013). doi:10.1109/ICoIA.2013.6650259

10. Akrout, R., Alata, E., Kaaniche, M., Nicomette, V.: An automated black box approach for web vulnerability identification and attack scenario generation. J. Braz. Comput. Soc. **20**, 4 (2014). doi:10.1186/1678-4804-20-4

11. Awang, N.F., Manaf, A.A., Zainudin, W.S.: A survey on conducting vulnerability assessment in web-based application. In: Hassanien, A.E., Tolba, M.F., Taher Azar, A. (eds.) AMLTA 2014. CCIS, vol. 488, pp. 459–471. Springer, Heidelberg (2014)

12. Halfond, W.G.J., Halfond, W.G.J., Viegas, J., Viegas, J., Orso, A., Orso, A.: A classification of SQL injection attacks and countermeasures (2006)

13. Stuttard, D., Pinto, M.: The web application hacker's handbook: discovering and exploiting security flaws. Wiley Publishing, Inc., Indianapolis (2007)

14. Bisht, P., Madhusudan, P., Venkatarish-nan, V.N.: CANDID: dynamic candidate evaluations for automatic prevention of SQL injection attacks. ACM Trans. Inf. Syst. Secur. **13**(2), 1–39 (2010). Article 14

15. Ezumalai, R., Aghila, G.: Combinatorial approach for preventing SQL injection attacks. IEEE International Advance Computing Conference, IACC (2009)

16. Kindy, D.A., Pathan, A.S.K.: A detailed survey on various aspects of SQL injection in web applications: Vulnerabilities, innovative attacks and remedies. Int. J. Commun. Netw. Inf. Secur. **5**, 80–92 (2013)

17. Wodarz, P.N.: Algorithms for Generating Permutations and Combinations, pp. 1–7 (2008)

18. He, K., Feng, Z., Li, X.: An attack scenario based approach for software security testing at design stage. In: 2008 International Symposium on Computer Science and Computational Technology, pp. 782–787. IEEE Computer Society (2008)

19. Wassermann, G., Yu, D., Chander, A., Dhurjati, D., Inamura, H., Su, Z.: Dynamic test input generation for web applications. In: International Symposium on Software Testing and Analysis (ISSTA), pp. 249–259 (2008)

20. Alata, E., Kaaniche, M., Nicomette, V., Akrout, R.: An automated approach to generate web applications attack scenarios. In: Proceedings - 6th Latin-American Symposium on Dependable Computing, LADC 2013, pp. 78–85 (2013). doi:10.1109/LADC.2013.22

21. Bozic, J., Wotawa, F.: XSS pattern for attack modeling in testing. In: 2013 8th International Workshop on Automation of Software Test, AST 2013 - Proceedings, pp. 71–74 (2013). doi:10.1109/IWAST.2013.6595794

22. Bozic, J., Wotawa, F.: Security testing based on attack patterns. In: Proceedings - IEEE 7th International Conference on Software Testing, Verification and Validation Workshops, ICSTW 2014, pp. 4–11 (2014). doi:10.1109/ICSTW.2014.58

23. Chen, J.M., Wu, C.L.: An automated vulnerability scanner for injection attack based on injection point. In: ICS 2010 - International Computer Symposium, pp. 113–118 (2010). doi:10.1109/COMPSYM.2010.5685537

24. Duchene, F., Richier, J., Groz, R.: KameleonFuzz: Evolutionary Fuzzing for Black-Box XSS Detection. In: CODASPY (2014)

A Survey on Financial Botnets Threat

Giovanni Bottazzi[1(✉)] and Gianluigi Me[2(✉)]

[1] Department of Civil Engineering and Computer Science,
University of Rome – "Tor Vergata", Via Del Politecnico 1, Roma 00133, Italy
giovanni.bottazzi@students.uniroma2.eu
[2] CeRSI - Research Center in Information Systems,
LUISS Guido Carli University, Via T. Salvini, 2, Roma 00197, Italy
gme@luiss.it

Abstract. Botnets, although technically based on long lasting well established attacking models, currently represent an increasing threat, moving huge amounts of capitals from legal system to criminals. This is mainly due to its adaptability, based on Crime-as-a-Service model, where different, transnational, actors are located in the different rings of the crime supply chain. Moreover, botnet success has been enabled by two main factors: the weak countermeasures adoption, reinforced by the well-known dominance of software attacker versus defender and the revenue model, which considers the target of the attack out of the victim (ICT users) control. Finally, the losses are typically in charge of silent financial/ insurance organizations. These botnet pillars are available for renting at low-cost by criminal organizations, exploiting the dark side of the success factor of the Internet business players, the network externality, where targets, e.g. Internet two sided markets, can be easily predicted but not yet adequately protected. In this paper, the authors will describe, by Zeus and other botnet examples, the revenue model and its related costs as cybercrime, focusing on the concerning evolution of this threat and proposing some strategies to cope with it.

Keywords: Botnet · Economics · Revenue · Supply-chain · Financial services

1 Introduction

Cybercrime is a growth industry. The revenues are great, considering that the Internet economy is capable of generating **2 to 3 trillion dollars per year**. It has been estimated (June 2014) that the likely annual cost to the global economy from cybercrime is more than $400 billion. A conservative estimate would be $375 billion in losses, while the maximum could be as much as $575 billion [1].

The cost of cybercrime includes the effect of hundreds of millions of people having their personal information stolen—incidents in the last year include more than 40 million people in the US, 54 million in Turkey, 20 million in Korea, 16 million in Germany, and more than 20 million in China. Criminals still have difficulty turning stolen data into financial gain, probably due to some difficulties in money mules management, but the constant stream of news contributes to a growing sense that cybercrime is out of control.

© Springer International Publishing Switzerland 2015
H. Jahankhani et al. (Eds.): ICGS3 2015, CCIS 534, pp. 172–181, 2015.
DOI: 10.1007/978-3-319-23276-8_15

Moreover, the current trends suggest considerable increases in the scope, sophistication, number and types of attacks, number of victims and economic damage [2]. There are some important factors worth highlighting in this context: the widespread of unsecured targets and the low cost barriers for "Crime as a service" rental model. This has facilitated a move by traditional organized crime groups (OCGs) into cybercrime areas. The financial gain that cybercrime experts have from offering these services stimulates the commercialization of cybercrime as well as its innovation and further sophistication.

The best data on cybercrime, unsurprisingly, comes from the financial sector, which is regulated, pays serious attention to cybersecurity, and can easily measure loss. E.g., in Mexico, banks lose up to $93 million annually just to online fraud. The National Police Agency estimates that Japanese banks lose about $110 million annually. The 2013 hack against the US retailer target, alone cost banks more than $200 million, and this does not count associated costs for the retailer and its customers. High profile cyber heists that garner tens of millions of dollars from banks, get a lot of attention and are a global phenomenon. Financial crime usually involves fraud, but this can take many forms to exploit financial accounts. In fact, even if the most damaging financial crimes should seek to penetrate bank networks, with cybercriminals gaining access to accounts and siphoning money, analytics on the phenomenon seem to highlight that attacking the weakest link of the Internet value chain (phishing users or exploiting client software vulnerabilities) is one of the most used technique by attackers.

One of the best ways to cheat the largest number of Internet users is through the spread of malicious software agent that could subsequently be managed by a remote attacker to perpetrate a myriad of criminal actions such cyber-extortion, click-fraud, information stealing, etc. These architectures are called botnets.

Botnets are just the leading actors of modern financial-oriented cybercrime (perhaps can be considered as the common framework for all on-line financial crimes), allowing, e.g., to steal more than 36 million euros from European banks [3] with peaks of €500,000 in just one week [4].

The exact incidence of botnet economy on cybercrime economy is hard to estimate, due to a strong data incompleteness, but if we consider that the European Central Bank reported in 2014 a value at around €800 million only in the euro areas [5], for the on-line transaction frauds, carried out by botnets, we can easily argue that the threat posed by botnets should not to be undervalued.

As stated by the FBI in a recent Senate statement, "Botnets have caused over $9 billion in losses to US victims and over $110 billion in losses globally. Approximately 500 million computers are infected globally each year, translating into 18 victims per second" [6]. One botnet of one million hosts could conservatively generate enough traffic to take most Fortune 500 companies collectively offline. A botnet of 10 million hosts (like Conficker) could paralyze the network infrastructure of a major Western nation. With the present work we will describe the state of the art of financial botnets together with their possible future developments.

2 Botnet Architectures and Capabilities

One of the most insidious cyber threats for the IT community is currently represented by a diffusion of networks containing infected computers (called bots or zombies), which are managed by attackers and are called botnets [6]. The use of botnets is very common in various IT contexts, from cybercrime to cyber warfare. They are able to provide a very efficient distributed IT platform that could be used for several illegal activities such as launching Distributed Denial of Service (DDoS), attacks against critical targets or starting with a "sample" attack followed up with an email or other communication threatening a larger DDoS attack (if a certain amount of money is not paid—cyber extortion), malware dissemination, phishing and frauds (e.g., banking information gathering) or to conduct cyber-espionage campaigns to steal sensitive information. In these scenarios, the controller of a botnet, also known as botmaster, controls the activities of the entire structure giving orders to every single zombie through various communication channels. The infected machines receive commands from the Command & Control (C&C) servers that instruct the overall architecture how to operate to achieve the purpose for which it has been composed. The diffusion of botnets has recently increased due to various factors such as:

- increased availability of powerful internet connectivity and hosts, providing a larger attack surface. 50 to 100 billion things are expected to be connected to the Internet by 2020. This paradigm is usually referred as "Internet of Things";
- high level of malware customization (introduced by Zeus botnet and its Software Development Kit);
- presence in the underground/black market of cyber criminals that rent services and structures that compose the malicious systems.

There are various classifications of botnets based on the overall topology and the command and control channels used, through which they can be updated and directed, the developing technology used and the scope of the services implemented. Emerging trends show that newer architectures are migrating toward completely distributed topologies (P2P networks) instead of centralized structures, mobile implementations of malware and the use of TOR networks and social platforms as hiding techniques. The high sophistication and spread of botnets has led to the emergence of a new criminal business model that can be synthesized with "Cybercrime-as-a-Service" (CaaS).

In fact, cybercriminals radically changed the way they target revenues of their activities; they don't need to have great technical expertise to operate; they just have to buy or rent all they need (tools, infrastructures and services) with more and more complete and efficient approaches. The supply chain management already could be completely outsourced to partners for illegal services: e.g. hacking services, hosting services, software development, distribution of malicious agents, and, of course, customer support (in many cases post-sales services and bug tracking has been observed). They are real for-profit organizations, some of which clearly devoted to crime (black market), while others have a not easily identifiable market, that may be labeled as unethical at the most (gray market).

The malware that both have introduced the concept of victim machine connected to a communication channel to listen for malicious commands, beginning with the socalled botnet-era, were "Sub7" and "Pretty Park"— a Trojan and worm, respectively. These two pieces of malware first emerged in 1999 and botnet innovation has been steady since then.

Steadily botnets migrated away from the original IRC Command & Control channel and began to communicate over HTTP, ICMP and SSL ports, often using custom protocols.

The spread of today botnets involves the production and availability of software architectures highly structured, aimed at their efficient dissemination and, especially, monetization.

From a technical point of view it is possible to identify two major milestones in the development and spread of botnets.

In 2005, a Russian group of five developers known as UpLevel started developing Zeus, the first "Point-and-Click" program for creating and controlling a network of compromised computer systems [7]. The next version of this software became, five years of development later, one of the most popular botnet platforms for spammers, fraudsters, and people who deal in stolen personal information. Its construction kit contained a program for building the bot software and Web scripts for creating and hosting a central Command and Control server.

Just as Zeus was the cornerstone of the next generation botnets, Blackhole is definitely the cornerstone of the next generation exploit kits. In fact, in late 2010, the Blackhole exploit kit became one of the most notorious exploit kit ever encountered [8].

From that point, the world of botnets has seen a constant evolution towards a more structured approach; a clear symptom of the maturity of the underground market which has become a complete enterprise very lucrative for its members.

3 Financial Botnets Roadmap

The world of financial Trojans is a thriving and profitable one for the cybercriminals. The financial fraud marketplace is a well-organized service industry where a wide variety of trojans, web injects, and distribution channels are traded. These offerings help to improve the effectiveness of established attack techniques. Location-aware distribution services deliver payloads with precision, while web injects which are remotely updated by third parties (e.g. blackhole) are available to help circumvent security countermeasures. The tools are offered on a software-as-a-service basis and allow anyone to conduct a large array of intelligent attacks against different financial institutions.

Malware targeting financial institutions have become one of the most prevalent threats on the Internet today. A successful compromise of an online bank account can be very profitable for the attacker.

Nearly every flavor of financial institution is targeted, from commercial banks to credit unions. Traditional banking websites are still the focus of most of the campaigns, but attackers are also exploring different institutions that provide online transactions.

Institutions that facilitate high value transactions have been targeted as well as platforms shared by a number of banks and even payroll systems [9].

Some financial threat families are constantly being updated and adapted to thwart newer protection methods, and enjoy great popularity among cybercriminals.

In fact, the king of financial malware (ZeuS), existed at least since 2007, has evolved over time – including a mobile variant called ZitMo designed for TAN code stealing – allowing the most novice hackers to easily steal online banking credentials and other online credentials for financial gain [11]. Since 2007, Zeus, in its many variants (Fig. 1), despite the many takedowns, is still considered one of the most dangerous malware (Fig. 2) targeting almost any financial sector (Fig. 3). In particular Fig. 2 shows that the top three most common botnets in 2013 are different variants of the same malware (Zeus).

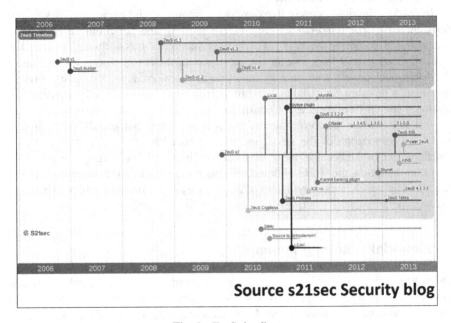

Fig. 1. ZeuS timeline.

By mixing various strategies and techniques, attackers will continue to streamline their campaigns to maximize return on their efforts. During the 2014, we did not see much innovation in fraud techniques. Most attackers relied heavily on man-in-the-browser attacks through web injects. They perfected and automated proven techniques, expanded to newer regions like Asia, and went after specialties in local markets like the Boleto Bancário payment system in Brazil. Recently, many attacks with banking Trojans are used against non-financial services, in order to steal master passwords for password safes.

Attackers can use the broad strokes approach trying to infect as many users as possible. The malware used in this approach involves the use of attack scripts aimed at

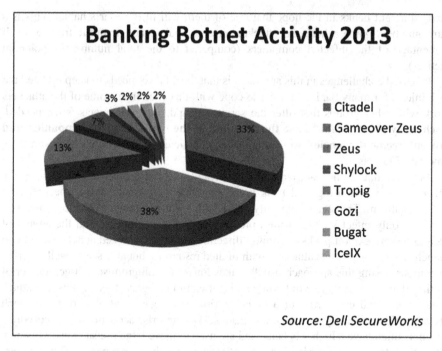

Fig. 2. Botnet activity in 2013.

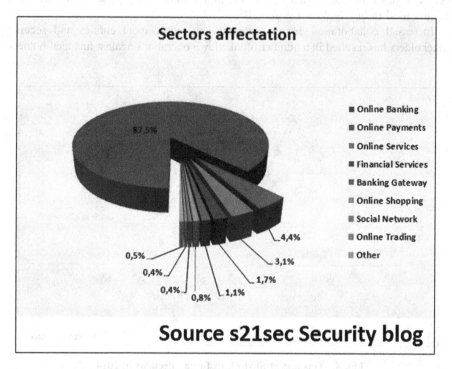

Fig. 3. Sectors targeted by botnets.

many different banks in the hope that one of them will fit the user's habits. This is a pure numbers game where the attacker aims to make enough profit from a small percentage of the infected computers (compared to the total number of potential victims).

One of the challenges in this approach is that the attacker needs to keep updated the web injects for many banks. In order to cope with this challenge, some of the attackers work with other groups that offer the service of updating web injects when needed. **Such noisy attacks could raise the attention of the bank, security companies, and law enforcement agencies**, so they are often conducted in short bursts against a large amount of targets.

Focused attacks, instead, target a smaller and well-defined set of users, such as a specific area where a regional bank brand might be very popular or a specific technology platform. The attacks typically begin with spear-phishing or drive-by download sites that only infect victims from a predefined IP address range. With the advent of location-aware exploit packs and traffic-direction services, localized attacks are easy to launch. This strategy suits attackers with limited resources, but also scales well to larger operations. Using this approach usually takes longer to compromise a large number of victims, but the success rate of finding an ideal victim is higher. Besides this, the attack is less noisy and could run for a longer period of time without attracting too much attention. One special type of focused attack seeks enterprise accounts. These corporate accounts often have a higher balance and are used to make large transactions. This may allow the attacker to steal high volumes of money in a short time period. For example, recently Ryanair has fallen victim to €4.6 million hacking scam made through the bank account used to buy fuel for the aircrafts.

Increased collaboration among different law enforcement entities and security stakeholders has resulted in a number of takedown operations against financial botnets.

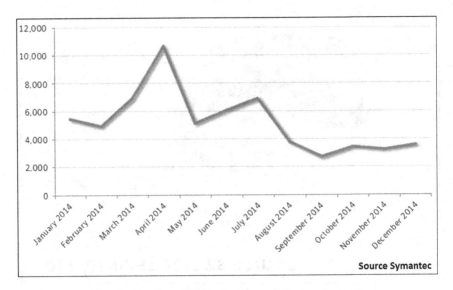

Fig. 4. Timeline of Shylock malware infections in 2014.

For instance, in July 2014, a joint takedown operation, led by the UK National Crime Agency (NCA) and European Cybercrime Centre (EC3) at Europol, resulted in the seizure of C&C servers and domains used for Trojan.Shylock's communications between infected computers. This banking Trojan mainly targeted financial institutions in the UK and US. The damage caused by Shylock is estimated to cost several million US dollars. The financial Trojan was distributed by at least five exploit kits (Blackhole included). As we can see in Fig. 4, after the takedown, the number of Shylock infections fell by more than half.

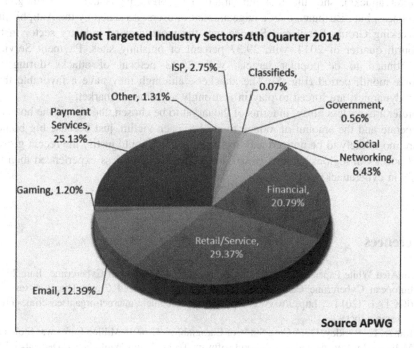

Fig. 5. The industry sectors most targeted by phishing in 4th quarter of 2014.

4   Conclusion

The data available seem to show unequivocally that the world of botnets is almost completely oriented to financial gain. In addition it is possible to highlight also how the high sophistication of malware and architectures poses a serious obstacle to the term "botnet disruption". In fact ZeuS is not the only case of malware longevity. We are currently witnessing to a possible revival of ZeroAccess, a very famous click-fraud botnet [12].

Instead, although there is no particular technological evolution in the infection vectors (the mail is still the most popular technique), in a mix of broad strokes and focused attacks, attackers will continue to streamline their campaigns to maximize return on their efforts [10]. For example the entrepreneurial-minded cybercriminals, have recently developed TOX, a quite common ransomware, TOR-Bitcoin dependent, but with an innovative business feature: the malware is customizable and downloadable for free, but the botmaster will held the 20 % of the ransom [13].

This leads to the hypothesis, using the "Game Theory" terminology, that the rational choice common to all attackers, is to:

- direct attacks toward platforms widely used (hardware and software). This should justify both the increase of malware for Android platforms and the latest exploits of the "Magento" platform (over 100,000 e-commerce sites and relative users may suffer attacks), showing that the target to be preferred is the one with greater richness, but distributed over a huge amount of users. As stated by the Antiphishing Working Group, Retail and Service was the most-targeted industry sector in the fourth quarter of 2014, with 29.37 percent of phishing sites. Payment Services continued to be popular targets, with 25.13 percent of attacks during the three-month period (Fig. 5). The attackers, although they have a favorable thermodynamics, are forced to play in a strongly asymmetric market;
- prefer attacks less noisy, in terms of the target to be chosen, the size of the botnet to operate and the amount of money to steal to each victim, just because big botnets are more likely to be noticed and dismantled. This should justify the recent growth of attacks in regions such as Brazil and Japan, certainly less experienced than the US in cyberattacks [14].

References

1. McAfee White Paper, Net Losses: Estimating the Global Cost of Cybercrime, June 2014
2. European Cybercrime Center (EC3), The Internet Organized Crime Threat Assessment (iOCTA) (2014). https://www.europol.europa.eu/content/internet-organised-crime-threat-assesment-iocta
3. Kalige, E., Burkley, D.: A Case Study of Eurograbber: How 36 Million Euros was Stolen via Malware. In: Versafe and Check Point software Technologies White Paper, December 2012
4. Kaspersky Security Bulletin (2014)
5. European Central Bank, Third Report on card fraud, February 2014. www.ecb.europa.eu/pub/pdf/other/cardfraudreport201402en.pdf
6. Statement before the Senate Judiciary Committee, Subcommittee on Crime and Terrorism, Washington, D.C., July, 15 (2014). http://www.fbi.gov/news/testimony/taking-down-botnets
7. Bottazzi, G., Me, G.: Responding to cybercrime and cyber terrorism — botnets an insidious threat. In: Cyber Crime and Cyber Terrorism Investigator's Handbook, pp. 231–257. Elsevier's Syngress (2014)
8. Lemos, R.: Rise of the point-and-click botnet. In: MIT Technology Review – Computing, 23 February 2010
9. Howard, F.: Exploring the Blackhole Exploit Kit, Sophos White Paper, March 2012
10. Wueest, C.: The state of financial Trojans 2014, In: Symantec White Paper, March 2015
11. Falliere, N., Chien, E.: Zeus: king of the bots. In: Symantec White Paper, November 2009
12. Greenberg, A.: ZeroAccess botnet reactivates, click fraud activity resumes, January 2015. http://www.scmagazine.com/zeroaccess-botnet-reactivates-click-fraud-activity-resumes/printarticle/395553/

13. Walter, J.: Meet 'Tox': Ransomware for the Rest of Us. McAfee Blog, May 2015. https://blogs.mcafee.com/mcafee-labs/meet-tox-ransomware-for-the-rest-of-us

14. Li, Z., Liao, Q.: Toward a Monopoly Botnet Market. Inf. Secur. J.: Global Perspect. - Cybercrimes, Secure Emerg. Web Environ., Digit. Forensics **23**(4–6), 159–171 (2014). Taylor & Francis

Wavelet Based Image Enlargement Technique

Akbar Sheikh Akbari[1(✉)] and Pooneh Bagheri Zadeh[2]

[1] Faculty of Arts, Environment and Technology, School of Computing,
Creative Technology and Engineering, Leeds Beckett University, Leeds, UK
a.sheikh-akbari@leedsbeckett.ac.uk
[2] School of Computer Science and Informatics, De Montfort University, Leicester, UK
Pooneh.bagherizadeh@dmu.ac.uk

Abstract. This paper presents an image enlargement technique using a wavelet transform. The proposed technique considers the low resolution input image as the wavelet baseband and estimates the information in high-frequency sub-bands from the wavelet high-frequency sub-bands of the input image using wavelet filters. The super-resolution image is finally generated by applying an inverse wavelet transform on the high resolution sub-bands. To evaluate the performance of the proposed image enlargement technique, five standard test images with a variety of frequency components were chosen and enlarged using the proposed technique and six state of the art algorithms. Experimental results show the proposed technique significantly outperforms the classical and non-classical super-resolution methods, both subjectively and objectively.

Keywords: Super-resolution · Image enlargement · Wavelet transform

1 Introduction

With rapid advances in digital technology and communication, cybercrime activities have dramatically increased. Surveillance cameras and mobile device embedded cameras have been a major source of information for forensic/criminal investigations. Digital image/video footage of the crime or cybercrime activity can be used to reconstruct the sequence of events, identify the criminal/s, confirm the time and location of the crime and other types of evidence in the legal proceedings. Hence, the quality of the recorded image/video footage, is crucial for any forensic/criminal investigation and subsequently legal proceedings. However, the quality of the recoded image/video footage is sometimes insufficient for the investigation purpose due to the distance and angle of the camera from the scene. This causes the object of interest for example the face of a person in the scene to be of low resolution which increases the difficulty of the recognition process. Therefore, the application of the image/video resolution enhancement technique to improve the quality of the footages is necessary.

Traditional image interpolation methods such as Bilinear, Bicubic, Bspline and nearest neighbourhood, do not provide sufficient visual quality particularly around sharp edges due to use of local smoothness filters [1]. Wavelet based super-resolution techniques in some extents could mitigate the over smoothing problem of the traditional

© Springer International Publishing Switzerland 2015
H. Jahankhani et al. (Eds.): ICGS3 2015, CCIS 534, pp. 182–188, 2015.
DOI: 10.1007/978-3-319-23276-8_16

image resolution enhancement techniques by using a set of filter banks. A wavelet-based interpolation method was proposed by Carey et al. in [1]. The proposed method estimates the wavelet high frequency coefficients of the input image by exploiting the regularity of the edges across the scales. Authors reported significant improvements over the traditional interpolation methods. However, this method may not be able to estimate the wavelet high-frequency coefficients with small values, which could reduce the effectiveness of this technique.

Demirel and Anbarjafari [2] reported a Complex Wavelet Transform (CWT) based image resolution enhancement technique. The proposed algorithm applies a dual-tree CWT (DT-CWT) to the input image, decomposing the input image into its frequency subbands. The resolution enhancement is achieved by using directional selectivity provided by the CWT, where the high-frequency subbands in six different directions contribute to the sharpness of the high-frequency details. An inverse DT-CWT is then applied to the coefficients in the high-frequency subbands to generate the high-resolution image. A Dual-Tree Complex Wavelet Transform (DT-CWT) and a Non-Local Means (NLM) based image resolution enhanced technique were reported in [3]. In this technique, the high frequency subbands are first generated using a DT-CWT. Windowed form of the Sinc filter are then employed to interpolate the high-frequency subbands and the low resolution input image. The NLM filter is then applied to the high frequency subbands to reduce artefacts generated by the DT-CWT. Finally, an inverse DT-CWT combines the resulting high frequency subbands and the low resolution input image, generating the super-resolution image. They reported significant improvements over the state of the art techniques, both subjectively and objectively.

A wavelet based image resolution enhancement technique was proposed in [4]. The proposed algorithm uses a Discrete Wavelet Transform (DWT) to decompose the input image into its frequency subbands. The resulting frequency subbands are then interpolated using the Bicubic algorithm. The difference between the input low resolution image and the interpolated low frequency subband is then used to refine the interpolated high frequency subbands. An inverse DWT is finally used to generate the super-resolution image. Authors reported superior results compared to the traditional and state-of-art image resolution enhancement techniques. Temizel and Vlachos proposed another wavelet based image resolution enhancement technique using Cycle Spinning (CS) [5], which outperformed other state of the art techniques, at the time. The authors of this paper reported another wavelet based image resolution enhancement algorithm, which operates in a quad-tree wavelet decomposition framework and exploits wavelet coefficient correlation in a local neighbourhood sense [6]. This method employed linear least-squares regression algorithm to estimate the wavelet high-frequency coefficients and generates superior results compared to the conventional methods for a wide range of test images.

However, the application of wavelet filters in estimating super resolution subbands, which have the potential in improving the quality of the enlarged image, have not been reported in literature. In this paper, wavelet filters are used to estimate coefficients in high frequency subbands of the super resolution image, from the detail subbands of the input low resolution image. Results demonstrate the merit of the proposed technique. The rest of the paper is organized as follows: the proposed technique will be explained in Sect. 2, experimental results are given in Sect. 3 and finally paper will be concluded in Sect. 4.

2   Wavelet Based Image Enlargement Technique

Figure 1 shows a block diagram of the proposed Wavelet based Image Enlargement (WIE) technique. A low resolution image is input to the system.

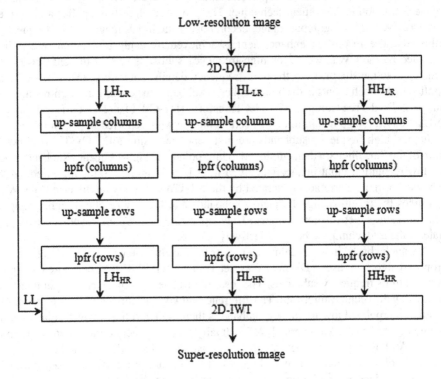

Fig. 1. Block diagram of the proposed image enlargement technique.

A two dimensional wavelet transform is applied on the input image, transforming it into its frequency subbands called: baseband (LL_{LR}), and LH_{LR}, HL_{LR} and HH_{LR} high-frequency subbands. Estimating edge information is essential in generating a high quality super resolution image. In the proposed WIE algorithm, information in high frequency subbands of the input image are used to estimate the edge information, within the high frequency subbands' of the super resolution image. To achieve this, the high frequency subbands of the low resolution image are processed as follows:

Each column of the LH_{LR} subband is first up-sampled by a factor of two, to double its height. Each resulting column of the LH_{LR} is then filtered using the wavelet transform high-pass reconstruction filter, named hpfr. Each row of the resulting filtered up-sampled LH_{LR} subband is then up-sampled by a factor of two, doubling the width of the LHLR subband. Each resulting row is then filtered using the wavelet transform lowpass reconstruction filter, called lpfr, generating an estimation of the coefficients in the LH subband of the super-resolution image. The other two low-resolution subbands, HLLR and HHLR, are processed using a similar method. However, the lpfr and hpfr filters are used for filtering information in each column of the HLLR and HHLR subbands, respectively and the hpfr filter is used for filtering coefficients in each row of the HLLR and HHLR subbands. The above processes generate estimations for coefficients in high frequency subbands' of the super resolution image, called: LHLR, HLLR and HHLR.

The resulting subbands and input low resolution image, which is assumed to be an estimation of the super resolution baseband image called LL, are then used to create the super resolution image by applying a two dimensional inverse wavelet transform on the subbands.

3   Experimental Results

To generate experimental results, five standard test images which contain a wide range of frequency components, called: Lena, Elaine, Peppers, Mandrill, and Barbara were taken. Each of these five images, were first lowpass filtered using a 2D Blackman lowpass filter with a cutoff frequency of Fs/2 to mitigate the aliasing artefact of the down sampling. The filtered images were then down sampled by a factor of 2 in both horizontal and vertical directions, generating a replica low resolution image for each of the input images. Hence, the input images could be treated as the ground truth for comparing the performance of the image enlargement techniques. The Blackman 2D FIR filter coefficients are tabulated in Table 1 [7].

Table 1. The Blackman 2D FIR filter coefficients [7].

0.0381	0.1051	0.0381
0.1051	0.4273	0.1051
0.0381	0.1051	0.0381

To evaluate the performance of the proposed Wavelet based Image Enlargement (WIE) technique, the resulting low resolution Lena, Elaine, Peppers, Mandrill, and Barbara test images were enlarged using the proposed WIE method, Nearest-neighbourhood, Bilinear, Bicubic, Sinc, Cycle Spinning (CS) [5], Directional Cycle Spinning (DSC) [2] techniques. Bi-orthogonal Daubechies 9/7 wavelet filters were used for generating experimental results. These filters were chosen because they are commonly used in image processing and image coding applications; but the proposed WIE algorithm works with most other wavelet and subband filters as well, providing that the filters are of sufficient length to yield basis functions that are more regular than the signals being analyzed.

The Peak Signal to Noise Ratio (PSNR) measurement and the Structural SIMilarity (SSIM) index, which has proven to be inconsistent with human eye perception, were chosen to assess the quality of the enlarged images against their corresponding ground-truth images (the original test images were assumed to be the ground truth images). The PSNR measurements and the SSIM indexes for the enlarged images were calculated and tabulated in Tables 2 and 3, respectively. From Tables 2–3 it can be seen that the proposed WIE technique provides the most improvement over the state of the art methods, both subjectively and objectively. From Table 2, it can be seen that the proposed technique generates a slightly lower PSNR when enlarging Lena and Mandrill images in comparison to the Sinc technique. However, it is well known that the PSNR is not a reliable metric to judge the visual quality of the enlarged images and the human eyes are the final judges for assessing the quality of the images. Hence, the SSIM index, which is more inconsistent with the perception of the human eyes, is a more reliable metric to be used for evaluating the quality of the enlarged images and this index shows that the proposed technique outperforms the state of the art techniques.

Table 2. The PSNR comparison of different methods.

Technique	PSNR (dB)				
	Lena	Elaine	Peppers	Mandrill	Barbara
Nearest	29.15	30.15	29.20	25.30	23.85
Bilinear	29.90	30.45	29.69	26.28	23.85
Bicubic	30.25	30.59	29.90	26.91	23.91
Sinc	**34.49**	32.89	33.26	**31.55**	24.74
CS	33.75	32.50	32.79	30.17	24.86
DCS	34.31	32.92	33.22	31.16	25.09
Proposed	34.32	33.06	33.32	31.40	25.48

Table 3. The SSIM comparison of different methods.

Technique	SSIM				
	Lena	Elaine	Peppers	Mandrill	Barbara
Nearest	0.9607	0.9610	0.9662	0.9323	0.9079
Bilinear	0.9519	0.9532	0.9592	0.9002	0.8851
Bicubic	0.9584	0.9564	0.9626	0.9228	0.9003
Sinc	**0.9822**	0.9673	0.9774	**0.9787**	0.8993
CS	0.9816	0.9681	0.9780	0.9703	0.8951
DCS	0.9831	0.9700	0.9797	0.9769	0.9014
Proposed	0.9832	0.9712	0.9797	0.9808	0.9142

To give a visual perception of the resulting enlarged images, a section of the original Barbara test image, its generated low resolution image, and its enlarged image using the Sinc, Cycle Spinning (CS), Directional Cycle Spinning (DSC) and the proposed technique were shown in Fig. 2. From Fig. 2, it can be seen that the enlarged image using the proposed technique is the closest to the original image. It is also clear that the enlarged image using CS and DSC suffer from general blurriness and the Sinc image has less blur with superior contrasts, however it suffers from pixilation within the smooth areas. At the same time, the proposed technique produces an image with high contras and less pixilation in smooth areas while preserving precise edges.

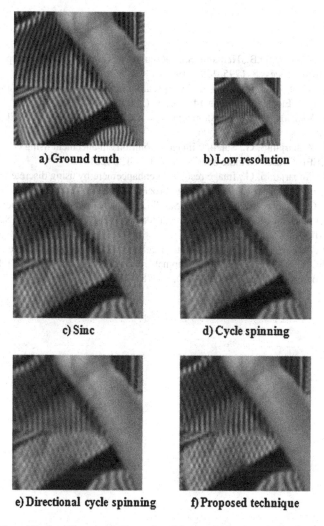

a) Ground truth   b) Low resolution

c) Sinc   d) Cycle spinning

e) Directional cycle spinning   f) Proposed technique

Fig. 2. A section of Barbara image: (a) Ground truth image (b) low resolution image and enlarged image using (c) Sinc, (d) cycle spinning, (e) directional cycle spinning and (f) proposed techniques.

4 Conclusions

In this paper, a new image resolution enhancement technique was proposed. The proposed technique estimated the wavelet coefficients of the high frequency subbands of the super resolution image from the wavelet subbands of the low resolution image by up-sample and then filtering the low resolution detail subbands using inverse wavelet filters. Results showed that the enlarged images using the proposed technique exhibit significantly higher visual quality to that of the state of the arts techniques, subjectively and objectively.

References

1. Carey, W.K., Chuang, D.B., Hemami, S.S.: Regularity preserving image interpolation. IEEE Trans. on Image Process **8**, 1295–1297 (1999)
2. Temizel, A., Vlachos, T.: Image resolution upscaling in the wavelet domain using directional cycle spinning. J. Electron. Imaging **14**, 040501 (2005)
3. Temizel, A., Vlachos, T.: Wavelet domain image resolution enhancement. IEEE Proc. Vision Image Sig. Process. **153**, 25–30 (2006)
4. Demirel, H., Anbarjafari, G.: Satellite image resolution enhancement using complex wavelet transform. IEEE Geosci. Remote Sens. Lett. **7**, 123–126 (2010)
5. Demirel, H., Anbarjafari, G.: Image resolution enhancement by using discrete and stationary wavelet decomposition. IEEE Trans. Image Process. **20**, 1458–1460 (2011)
6. Iqbal, M.Z., Ghafoor, A., Siddiqui, A.M.: Satellite image resolution enhancement using dual-tree complex wavelet transform and nonlocal means. IEEE Geosci. Remote Sens. Lett. **10**, 451–455 (2013)
7. Zadeh, P.B., Akbari, A.S.: Image resolution enhancement using multi-wavelet and cycle-spinning. In: The United Kingdom Automatic Control Council (UKACC) International Conference on Control (CONTROL 2012), pp. 789–792 (2012)

Understanding Android Security

Gregor Robinson and George R.S. Weir[⊠]

Department of Computer and Information Sciences, University of Strathclyde,
Glasgow, G1 1XH, UK
gregor.robinson.2013@uni.strath.ac.uk, george.weir@strath.ac.uk

Abstract. This paper details a survey of Android users in an attempt to shed
light on how users perceive the risks associated with app permissions and in-built
adware. A series of questions was presented in a Web survey, with results
suggesting interesting differences between males and females in installation
behaviour and attitudes toward security.

Keywords: Mobile security · Android OS - user awareness

1 Introduction

Android is currently developed and maintained as an open source mobile operating
system (OS), by Google. In August 2005, two years after the OS's creation, Google
purchased the company behind Android, as a strategic move into the mobile operating
system market place. With the subsequent rise in smartphone adoption, along with other
handheld devices such as tablets, Android has grown to become the leading mobile
operating system in terms of global smartphone market share [1]. Android currently has
the largest market share in terms of users and devices, accounting for 84.4 % of the
smartphone market in 2014 Q3 [2], and over 1 billion active users worldwide across all
their device platforms [3]. Android applications have been downloaded and installed
over 50 billion cumulative times since its creation in 2003 [4].

Key to Android success is the fact that it is open source, which allows for hardware
developers to augment the OS to meet the requirements for their particular device. In
turn, this leads to cheaper handsets [5]. In the market to date only Apple is a close
competitor in terms of devices and market share [1].

While Apple devices can install a variety of applications from the Appstore, much
in the same way as Android devices from Google's play store, Apple takes a more rigid
approach to app integrity. This includes sending code to third parties for analysis before
being published in the Appstore. In contrast, Google has traditionally relied upon the
principle of least privilege [6]. On this principle, a user is only allowed access to what
they require in order to complete the task but no more than that. When creating applications, Google entrusts the developers of the application to only code relevant permissions that the application needs to run and no more. However, recent research found that
33 % of applications ask for permissions beyond what they require [6]. Results reported
by [6] showed that only 3 % of Internet survey respondents could answer permission

© Springer International Publishing Switzerland 2015
H. Jahankhani et al. (Eds.): ICGS3 2015, CCIS 534, pp. 189–199, 2015.
DOI: 10.1007/978-3-319-23276-8_17

comprehension questions and only 17 % of participants paid attention to permissions during installation.

2   Security Risks

The primary security risks associated with the Android operation system are the misuse of permissions, which may allow developers to install certain types of software onto a device or acquire data from a user. Such risk is primarily associated with Android because there is no relevant party to check comprehensively what applications are released into the Google Play Store.

Previous attempts to create systems to check for irrelevant or malicious permissions include DroidRanger [7], which looked at how to detect malicious software in applications. DroidRanger did this by looking for permission-based footprints in order to detect malware families hidden within an application. Despite such attempts at creating an application check, the everyday consumer of Android applications has no reliable way to detect such malicious types of applications. In 2012, Google introduced a security service (codenamed 'Bouncer') that is credited with a 40 % drop in the number of malicious apps in its app store, but risks continue both through the Play Store and via third-party app sites.

Many software apps are termed 'grayware'. Such software treads a fine line between legitimate application and malware. Adware is one variety of grayware that automatically displays or downloads adverts within an application [8]. Researchers from antivirus software firm Avast recently discovered three popular applications within the play store that contained Adware [9]. The game Durak, for example, which has between 5–10 million installations, contained Adware that suggested your phone was at risk and that you should protect it by downloading another application. This is a clear threat to user personal information as they were informed that they have to download more applications with different permissions, despite the fact their application and device could have been perfectly fine.

Another security risk associated with Android permissions is that of Spyware, wherein the permissions granted to an application give the ability to spy upon and record private conversations by accessing the device's microphone/camera. The user's recent location and texts could also be vulnerable. This permission group exists because some legitimate applications (such as Skype and Snapchat) need these permissions to function correctly. Recent misuse of this permission recently came to light through the use of voice commands on a range of Samsung smart TVs. The misuse arose in regard to voice recording, when the user issued a voice command, it was then sent across the Internet for analysis without the user knowing [10].

One further serious and sinister use of spyware within Android applications is the ability of spyware to track users. This can be achieved through the location permission enabling the app developer to monitor user locations. Such spyware has been used in the past by suspicious partners and to stalk domestic abuse victims.

Another security and personal information risk that can arise from extraneous permissions in applications is that developers can harvest large amounts of personal data. If handled correctly by the developers, this would fall under the Data Protection Act, requiring that all data given to a third party must be managed in accordance with legally sanctioned data protection principles.

Apps that deploy malicious permissions are able to flout this law, and most users will not realise that data has been taken from them when using the application. With permission granted, the developer can access contact numbers, location, messages, call logs, calendars and other personal information on phones. Such data can be used by the developer or sold to third parties.

3   Survey

In designing an Android user survey, we sought to evaluate the level of user understanding and recognition with regard to permissions. For this purpose, the survey had to shed light on the users' recognition of both permissions and their groups, while looking at how this may affect phone usage. An online survey was implemented using the free survey hosting facility provided by Survey Monkey (www.surveymonkey.com). This allowed us to reach a wide demographic and focus on respondents who had considerable experience of using an Android.

The survey comprised several types of question. For example when asking about the respondents' awareness of current issues, this was asked using an open question in order to find out what they knew and what they did not. Closed questions were also used, where a user was presented with a variety of options to choose from as well as 'none of the above' as a response, if they were not inclined to select any of the other answers.

The survey received 52 responses in the two days that it was open. Three of these responses have been filtered out as the individuals concerned had never owned an Android device. The total of responses that were collected and evaluated was 49.

The first question that was asked in the survey, was to find out what sex the respondents where. The main purpose of this was just to find out who was responding, and be able to consider whether different attitudes towards the permission group existed between the genders.

The second question asked the respondents' age. The only age group that is not represented within this survey, is the under 18 age group. Respondents were then asked if they had ever owned an Android device.

Question 4 was the first to specifically address Android permissions and security and asked whether the user recognised any permissions from five permission groups: Location, SMS, Phone, Contact and Photo/Media/File. This was an important question, as one our goals was to gauge the degree to which users recognise permissions and the associated permission groups.

Question 5 was a follow up to question 4 that asked the respondents what exactly they knew about the listed permission groups. This question was designed to find out how much they knew about the permissions and to compare their understanding about permissions and their groups.

Question 6 addressed how users respond when installing applications. This was a key issue since installing an application, is the point in the process where individual permissions are shown to the user.

Question 7 looked into recent news stories discussing Android security problems. In order to understand how wide spread these stories are and how much effect these stories could have on the future of Android popularity with it users and market share. The researcher used an open text box allowing respondents to enter what they knew, instead of discussing a story and seeing if they had any recognition of it.

Question 8 in the survey, was designed to look at how many of the respondents were aware of security issues associated with Android permissions. Question 9 explored what types of Grayware attacks users have been exposed to when using Android applications. The purpose of this question was to gauge what varieties of attack are more prominent among Android applications and draw conclusion on what attacks are the most common and what types of personal information could be lost. In order to gauge what type of attack was more common, respondents were presented with four options: Adware, Spyware, Malware and Other. The user could also specify that they had not seen any attacks or if it was different in nature to those stated.

The final question was included to consider the type of proactive measures that a user can take to protect their Android device. This question asked how many of the respondents had downloaded anti-virus software onto their device.

4   Results

The gender distribution of the respondents shows a slightly larger group of males than females, with 57 % male compared to 43 % female (Fig. 1).

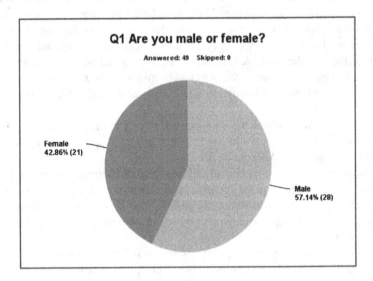

Fig. 1. Gender distribution

Table 1 (below) shows the age range response derived from Question 2.

Table 1. Age range

Age Range	Number	%
18–30	22	44.90
31–45	7	14.29
45–55	8	16.33
55–65	8	16.33
65+	4	8.16

Question 3 determined how many of the respondents, owned or had owned an Android device, with only 3 of the 52 respondents never owning a device.

The fourth question looked at respondents' understanding and recognition of permission groups. Results show that users have a high level of recognition when it comes to permission groups, with only 10 % of respondents not recognizing any of the permission groups. The breakdown of permission recognition is shown in Fig. 2.

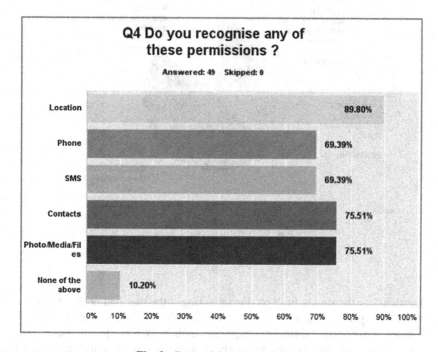

Fig. 2. Recognition of permissions

Question 5 allowed the user to input what they thought the permission groups, actually did. This was important to ascertain as it went to show how much the user understood about permissions and their groups. The responses ranged from people understanding the permission exactly to people thinking of various permissions in terms of physical attributes that are contained within a device. For example, one response when discussing the Photo/Media/File permission mentioned how they personally stored the media and other files on a their PC: "Having an Android Mobile I already frequently use SMS for messaging, and the contacts folder for address and phone numbers. For my location and destination for weekend car journeys I use Google Maps for information along with a TomTom Satellite Navigation Unit, and in my hobbies of music and photography I keep files in several different formats on my desktop PC at home".

Question 6 of the survey looked at how a user interacts with permission when installing an application to their device. The results for this question are shown in Fig. 3 and Table 2 (below).

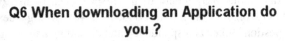

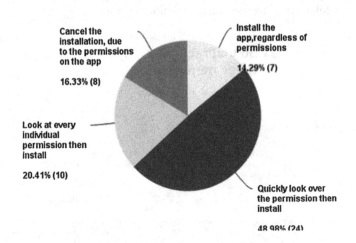

Fig. 3. Installation responses

Question 7 of the survey built on this by asking if the user had heard of any recent news stories regarding Android security issues. The responses varied, with some respondents mentioning particular programs, such as WhatsApp, to more generic responses related to news stories, but without detailing the particular story they had heard. The more common response, was n/a which meant they either had not heard of any stories, or they had heard of the stories but the story did not change their mind about Android device ownership.

Table 2. Installation responses (detail)

Response	Number	%
Install the app, regardless of permissions	7	14.29
Quickly look over the permission then install	24	48.98
Look at every individual permission then install	10	20.41
Cancel the installation, due to the permissions on the app	8	16.33

Question 8 determined how many of the respondents knew about the security risk associated with the permission within an application, with just under 75 % of user stating that they were aware of the security risk, the results from this question are shown in Fig. 4 (below).

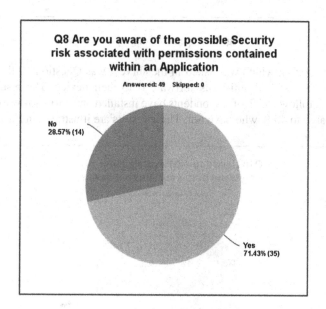

Fig. 4. Permissions risk awareness

Results for Question 9 show that the most prominent type of attack was Adware, with over 28 % of respondents suffering from this type of Grayware compared to 8 % for Spyware and 4.08 % for Malware (Fig. 5, below).

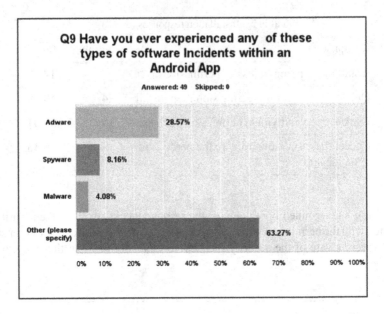

Fig. 5. Experience of grayware

The final question which was asked in the survey, was Question 10 this looked at how many users installed anti-virus software onto their device. The results for this question are as follows 55 % of respondents have installed anti-virus software onto their device compared to 45 % who have not. These results are illustrated in Fig. 6 (below).

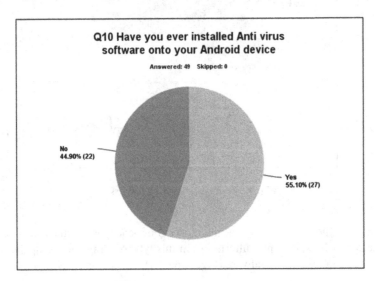

Fig. 6. Android antivirus use

5 Conclusions

In analysing the results, we compared our responses to the figures reported by Felt et al. [6]. They looked into how many users paid attention when installing an application onto their device and reported 83 % [11]. Our survey shows a marginal increase in this to 86 % (see Fig. 2).

An interesting aspect of attitudes to permission and the installation process was the apparent difference in the way that male and females approach this issue. The survey shows that males tend to be more cautious when installing applications on their devices than females. In the survey results, only 9.52 % of female respondents would look at every permission before installing, whereas for males, 20.41 % of respondents would look closely at every permission before installing. This suggests that gender has an effect of just under 11 % in the approach when installing applications.

More evidence to show that male respondents tended to be more cautious and wary when downloading applications is seen in the fact that 16 % of the male respondents would cancel the installation of the application if they were unhappy with the permissions requested by the application. In comparison, only 14.29 % of female users would behave in this way.

One final piece of evidence that was observed through this survey would suggest male respondents tend to err on the side of caution compared to females. We see that 57 % of females quickly look over the permissions then install, compared to only 49 % of male respondents. This was an interesting insight on how users interact with their device, as it shows that males, were more likely to be cautious and alert when installing and protecting their own device from malicious permission, as compared to females. Of course, the survey population was 43 % female and 57 % male so not equally comprised of males and females and this may slightly skew the gender results.

The next result that was important to compare and contrast was the fact that when Felt et al. ran their survey they found that 97 % of users could not fully identify every permission that was contained within an application [11]. Following changes in the way that Android implements and displays permissions when installing an application (showing the permission group and not the detailed permissions), it would have been difficult to recreate this exact experiment. To explore this issue we first looked into how many of the respondents recognised the permission and then contrasted this information from Question 5 (in which respondents were asked to give long-hand accounts of permissions). This gave insight into the degree of understanding for permissions against each respondent.

The first permission group evaluated in this fashion was the location permission group. This was the most commonly recognised permission group when the sample was taken as a whole or split by gender. With 89 % of respondents recognizing the permission, or 80.95 % for females compared to 96.43 % for male respondents. Although the recognition of this permission was almost 90 % when looking into the responses, we found that only 16 % of respondents understood what the permission actually did and could provide a relevant explanation.

The next permission groups to be evaluated were the Phone and SMS permission groups. The reason behind the grouping of these two permissions was that both achieved the same recognition rate of 69 % for the combined sample (despite different rates on the split sample with 66 % female and 71 % male, respectively). Although it contained a relatively high recognition rate amongst permissions groups, the phone and SMS permission groups actually had one of the lowest level of understanding amongst respondents with only 10 % for the phone permission group compared to 12 % for SMS. These results show that although the majority of users can recognise the permission group, the majority struggle to comprehend what is contained within the group and this is why a malicious permission within applications can be so damaging.

The final permission groups to be evaluated were Photo/Media/File and Contacts permission groups. Again, the reason behind the grouping of these two permission was that both achieved the same recognition rate of 75 % of the combined sample, unlike the SMS and phone permission group that shared both the same recognition until split between male and female. The contacts permission was recognised by females with a rate of 71 % and 78 % for males. Whereas the Photo/Media/Files permission had a split of 75 % for males and 76 % for females, which was the first permission that female respondents recognised more than their male counterparts.

Although these permissions consisted of a relatively high recognition rate amongst the permissions groups, the Contact group and Photo/Media/Files had some of the lowest scores in terms of understanding what an application actually does with only 10 % of respondents understanding what the Photo/Media/Files permission group can do. This compared to 12 % for the Contacts permission group. Again, this demonstrates that although people recognise that these permissions are in most applications, when it comes to understanding how they actually work, the functionality of these permissions and what effect these can have on your device, the gap in knowledge is significant and should be considered in more depth by Android and its developers. This may allow Android to protect their customers against malicious applications that can cause security issues and personal information loss.

One conclusion apparent in this survey is that Android users have a relatively poor understanding of what permissions allow within an application. This can be seen from the fact that although just under 90 % of respondents could recognise the location permission group, only 16 % of those respondents could give a coherent response to what that the permissions actually could do.

The final area of research that was examined through this survey was the difference between how males and females approach Android permissions and the risk associated with this. Many of our results suggest that males are more cautious and knowledgeable Android users compared to their female counterparts.

One interesting aspect of the results was how different attacks affect the different sexes. This is seen from Question 9 of the survey where the data shows that 32 % of males were subjected to some form of Adware attack, compared to 23 % of females. This difference could arise from different downloading habits, with males more inclined to download less 'worthy' applications than their female counterparts. In comparison when it comes to spyware attacks, females are more likely to be the victim, with 9 % respondents informing that they had experienced this type of attack. In comparison, only 7 % of males respondents had experience this type of attack. In terms of malware attacks, the trend for women to be the victim continues with only 3 % of males experiencing this issue compared to 5 % of females who have experienced this issue.

When looking at these trends it is easy to suppose that because women are seen to be less cautious about their device, when installing any applications, this is why they would experience more security issues than men. But the survey shows that the majority of female Android users actually have installed Anti-virus software onto their device (Question 10). At 57 %, this is 4 % higher than males. In addition, the majority (66 %) of female respondents understood the risk associated with Android permissions (Question 8). Since the male figure for this question was 75 %, we can see that both genders are knowledgeable and proactive in securing their phone against threats. However each gender seems more prone to certain types of attacks than the opposite sex.

References

1. Hahn, J.: Android claims 81.5 % of the global smartphone OS market in 2014, IOS DIPS to 14.8 % (2015). http://www.digitaltrends.com/mobile/worldwide-domination-android-and-ios-claim-96-of-the-smartphone-os-market-in-2014/. Accessed 10th March 2015
2. IDC: Smartphone OS market share Q4 2014 (2015). http://www.idc.com/prodserv/smartphone-os-market-share.jsp. Accessed 12th February 2015
3. Trout, C.: Android still the dominant mobile OS with 1 billion active users (2014). http://www.engadget.com/2014/06/25/google-io-2014-by-the-numbers/. Accessed 15th March 2015
4. Statista: Global smartphone operating system market share of Android from 2009–2015 (2015). http://www.statista.com/statistics/216420/global-market-share-forecast-of-smartphone-operating-systems/. Accessed 20th March 2015
5. Lee, B.T.: Android poised to dominate developing world (2011). http://www.forbes.com/sites/timothylee/2011/08/16/android-poised-to-dominate-the-developing-world/. Accessed 28th March 2015
6. Felt, P.A., et al.: Android permission demystified (2010). http://hibou.cs.wpi.edu/~kven/courses/CS4401-C15/papers/Android-App-Permissions.pdf. Accessed 26th January 2015
7. Zhou, Y., et al.: Hey, you get, of my market: detecting malicious apps in official and alternative Android markets (2011). http://www4.ncsu.edu/~zwang15/files/NDSS12_DroidRanger.pdf. Accessed 2nd February 2015
8. TechTerms: Adware (2015). http://techterms.com/definition/adware. Accessed 14th March 2015
9. Dredge, S.: Several Android apps removed from Google Play Store after 'adware' claim. The Guardian (2015). http://www.theguardian.com/technology/2015/feb/04/android-apps-google-play-adware. Accessed 5th March 2015
10. BBC News: Not in front of the telly: warning over 'listening' TV. (2015) http://www.bbc.co.uk/news/technology-31296188. Accessed 20th February 2015
11. Felt, P.A., et al.: Android permission: user attention, comprehension and behavior (2011). https://blues.cs.berkeley.edu/wp-content/uploads/2014/07/a3-felt.pdf. Accessed 15th January 2015

Gender Impact on Information Security in the Arab World

Fathiya Al Izki and George R.S. Weir[✉]

Department of Computer and Information Sciences, University of Strathclyde,
Glasgow, G1 1XH, UK
{fathiya.al-izki,george.weir}@strath.ac.uk

Abstract. Access to technology and the benefits derived from its use are not available on equal terms to men and women. In this paper, we review research that sheds light on the relationship between the Digital Divide and Gender in the context of Arab countries and suggest that the extent of gender digital divide is influenced by cultural attitudes and consider how this divide may affect information security.

Keywords: Information security · Gender impact · Digital divide · Arab society

1   Introduction

In recent decades, the spread of Information and Communication Technology (ICT) has accelerated the process of economic and social change to the extent that the new environment in which we live and work has come to be described as the Information Society (IS). In such a society, access to technology and the benefits people derive from its use are not available on equal terms to men and women. This raises the issue of the relationship between the Digital Divide and Gender.

The United Nations Gender Inequality Index [1] shows that no country in the world has achieved gender equality. According to [2], most women tend to be poorer than men and in many countries they are less educated. The majority of the world's illiterates are women.

In general, women tend to earn less, hold fewer positions of power and make fewer decisions in the family, in business and political and public life. These inequalities impact women's ability to benefit equally from the opportunities offered by ICT and to contribute fully to shaping the developing global knowledge economy and society. Beyond the obvious significance of correlation between gender and digital divide, it is important to explore whether such a divide may have a direct impact upon information security and how it operates in this regard. The present paper explores the gender/digital divide relationship through a survey of relevant publications and focuses on the related prospective impact of gender on information security.

© Springer International Publishing Switzerland 2015
H. Jahankhani et al. (Eds.): ICGS3 2015, CCIS 534, pp. 200–207, 2015.
DOI: 10.1007/978-3-319-23276-8_18

2   Women and Information Security Related Practices

According to Leyden, based upon a survey conducted by the security software company PC Tools, women are shown to be more cautious than men with regard to common information security – related practices [3]. According to the survey, 47 % of men use the same password for every website they visit, compared to 26 % of women who use the same insecure practice. Further, nearly two-thirds of men polled said they would open a link or attachment from a friend without first checking its provenance, compared to a more cautious 48 % of women.

2.1   Women and Social Engineering

Insight on gender differences in the context of online risks if offered by Elyan, who describes a game carried out during the DefCon gathering in 2010, in which contestants telephoned company employees and convinced them to voluntarily reveal information they probably should have kept secret [4]. In that game, 135 employees from 17 large companies, including Google, Wal-Mart, Symantec, Cisco and Microsoft, were contacted to measure their ability to resist social engineering attacks.

When conducting the game, contestants were not allowed to ask for really sensitive information like passwords or social security numbers. However, they tried to get information, such as the locally deployed operating system or the preferred types of antivirus software or Internet browser, which could be misused later by potential attackers. They also tried to push company employees to connect to unauthorized web pages.

Of the 135 employees contacted, only five refused to deliver any information about their business. These five were women employees. With male employees, the success rate of the contestants was 100 %, which underpins the view that women are more cautious and generally less vulnerable to social engineering attacks. On the other hand, according to Jagatic et al., the attack was more effective when it appeared as though the email was sent by a person of the opposite gender: 'this was true for both males and females but the effect was more marked for males'. The response rate for males increased from 53 % - when the message was from a male - to 68 % when sent by a female [5].

2.2   Women and Facebook

In 2011, Bitdefender conducted a study to assess how social networks users respond to friend requests from a stranger [6]. The study, which targeted 1,649 individuals in the UK and USA, concluded that men are more likely than women to be victims on social networks such as Facebook and Twitter. Results from the Bitdefender survey show that 64.2 % of women always reject friend requests from strangers on social networks, while only 55.4 % of men would do so. Evidently, men are more likely to accept such requests, especially when presented with an associated picture of an attractive woman.

3   Gender Divide in the Arab World

According to the United Nations Human Development Report of 2013, there is no society in which women have the same opportunities as men [7]. The extent of discrimination can be measured through the Gender Inequality Index (GII), which captures the loss of achievement due to Gender Inequality in three dimensions: reproductive health, education and labour market participation. This represents the percentage loss of human development due to shortcomings across these dimensions. The value of GII ranges between 0–1, with 0 being 0 % inequality, indicating women fare equally in comparison to men, and 1 being 100 % inequality, indicating women fare poorly in comparison to men.

The GII ranks 186 countries on a global scale. Higher GII values signify greater discrimination. The UNDP report shows that the GII has large variation across countries, ranging from 0.045 (in Netherlands) to 0.747 (in Yemen), with an average of 0.463. When we pass the 32 top ranked countries, the value of the GII reaches 0.171 (with a further 153 countries below this level). This shows that it will take a long time for women across the world to achieve the equality, even in countries that seem to do better in this regard.

Regarding the Arab World and according to the report, high gender disparities persist in the Arab States (where the GII value is 0.555). In addition, the report shows that Arab states suffer from the widest education gender gap in the world (as depicted in Fig. 1).

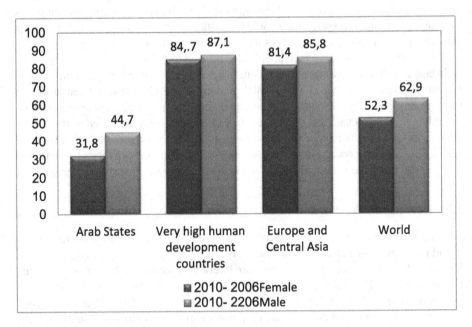

Fig. 1. Percentage of the population ages 25 and older that have reached secondary education

The Arab Social Media Report from 2013, showed that the percentages of young women graduating from schools and attending universities in some regions of the Arab World are much higher than that of young men, but women still face multifaceted barriers to enrolment in schools and universities in other regions of the Arab World (such as some countries within the Gulf Cooperation Council) [8].

Further insights from the Arab Social Media Report indicate that of the 20 countries with the largest increases in mean years of schooling over 1980–2010, 8 were in the Arab States. In most of these countries, employment opportunities failed to keep pace with educational attainment, as shown by below-median employment to population ratios. In line with this finding, the UN fact sheet from 2011, concludes that young Arab women are confronted with a double burden: their age and their gender [9]. In Arab countries, the conflation of these two factors has resulted in the highest regional gender gap in terms of unemployment, due to profound cultural, social and economic gender divisions. According to the aforementioned UN Fact Sheet, 'studies indicate that only 30 % of women of working age participate in the labour market, and those who do find work are limited to low–paying jobs in the private sector, whether formal or informal' [9, p. 3].

3.1 Gender Digital Divide in the Arab World

The Gender Divide has induced a Gender Digital Divide whose existence, according to the literature, is due to two types of cause: the position of women in the labour market and cultural/institutional issues. Men and Women show differences in Internet access and use according to the different availability of free time. Women are less incorporated into employment than men and a greater percentage of their time is spent in housework, while men spend more time in work where they embrace the use of the Internet in the workplace. Additionally, in countries with high Digital Divide, like many Arab countries, the Internet reproduces and amplifies gender stereotypes that identify women with the private sphere of household chores and men with the public sphere of paid work.

According to Asgari, 'the Arab World is a strictly male-dominated culture, where male supremacy is the norm. In such a patriarchal society, the dominant discourse is based on a power relationship in which women's interest is subordinate to men' [10]. In clarification, Fairclough notes that the term discourse is 'used in general sense for language as an element of social life which is dialectically related to other elements' [11].

These gender-based stereotypes also dominate media discourse, video games and even computer based educational material. Across the Middle East and North Africa (MENA), analysing the status of mainstream ICT from a gender perspective reveals the profile of the Gender Digital gap and highlights differences between men and women in terms of access and use of ICT. Thus, according to a World Bank briefing document, 'in MENA, the gender gap in mobile phone ownership is twice the global average, with women 24 % less likely to own a mobile phone, and only 37 % of Facebook users are female compared with 56 % in the USA. Twice as many men in MENA use Twitter than women contrary to global trends of 55 % female users' [12].

A key aspect of Internet accessibility is the cost of installation and availability of quality connections (such as ADSL). This is a significant factor that impacts households, and particularly affects rural women with specific economic difficulties due to the high rate of unemployment and low wages.

There is another barrier from the perception of the symbolic space, a space of life-styles within which each person is identified in function of gender. Internet cafes, for example, have been spaces used mostly by young people and men. At home, the priority of use is for husbands and sons. Another important aspect that may alienate some women from using ICT is their lack of technology friendliness which reflects the level of ICT-based training.

Lack of high technological skills is a further aspect of the Gender Digital Divide, a new divide related to women who lack the adequate skills that make them achieve technological fluency, i.e., have the qualifications that are required to work with information technology, knowing the conceptual foundations of how technologies work, solving problems, managing complex systems and implementing solutions. Such an aspect mainly affects the younger generation and calls into question the possibility that the Gender Digital Divide is self-correcting over time.

According to the ITU report of 2013, 'data show that there is a gender gap in the use of computers, mobile phones and Internet, and that the gap is more prevalent in developing than developed countries' [13, p. 12]. Further, according to this report, available data suggest that men in developing countries, among which are Arab countries, tend to use the Internet more than women in commercial Internet access locations (such as cybercafés); and that men tend to be online more frequently than women (Fig. 2).

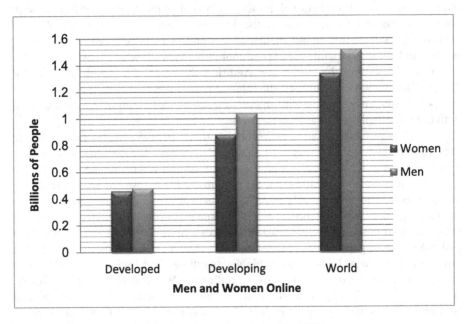

Fig. 2. Men and women online [13]

With regard to the gender distribution of social network use in the Arab World, the Arab Social Media Report [8], which discusses the outlook and trends of Social Networks in the Arab World, states that Social Networks are central to the digital experience of Arab World users, reaching an audience of millions of people and generating a very high level of engagement. Among 54,552,875 Facebook users in the Arab world, the percentage of female users has remained constant at 33.4 % (in May 2013), having fluctuated slightly between 33.4 % and 34 % in the previous two years. This is still significantly lower than the global average of roughly 50 %. Presently, no further reliable data on the Gender Digital Divide landscape in the Arab world is available.

Boujemi [14] indicates that 'the main challenge, with regard to gender Digital Divide landscape in the Arab world, is that ITU depends entirely on the data submitted by each government to set up ICT indicators. This data submitted by Arab countries rarely includes any gender specification which makes it difficult to define gender access discrepancies in the Arab region and therefore one has to rely on the socio-economic and socio-cultural facts to assess the state of the art of ICT access by Arab women' (op. cit.).

Despite this limitation on available data, we can shed more light on the Gender Digital Divide in the Arab world by examining the available information about the Digital Divide. The Arab World, in a global perspective, according to the ITU report [13], has a significant Digital Divide in many of its countries in comparison to the developed world. According to this report, Arab States international ranking, with regard to IDI access and use sub-indexes that reflect the diffusion of ICT, closely reflects income disparities in the region. Thus, Gulf countries have high ranking while other Arab countries have relatively low ranking.

In the ITU report, skills indicators (adult literacy, gross secondary enrolment and gross tertiary enrolment) provide a good indication of the overall level of human capacity in a country [13]. This is important because, in addition to ICT infrastructure, education and skills are necessary for making effective use of ICTs and building a competitive and inclusive information society (op. cit.). The report highlights that the skills ranking is considerably low in all Arab countries, even in Gulf countries that have a high degree of penetration of ICT and the Internet and a good ranking in ICT use and access.

Considering the findings from the ITU report and the noted education gender gap in Arab states, we suppose that this gap correlates to the Gender Digital Divide in Arab states. This is in line with the disparity of men and women on-line (as depicted in Fig. 2). Given that each Arab country has its own aspect of gender divide, reflecting the socio-economic context in that country, we suggest that the different size of Gender Digital Divide of each Arab country reflects the prevailing gender attitudes.

4   Conclusions

As a result of what has been addressed in the previously noted reports, we can say that, due to the wide education gender gap in the Arab world, indicated by the GII value, there is a corresponding Gender Digital Divide and, accordingly, a higher Information Security risk among women. This means that while men, who represent half of the society, are at high Information Security risk due to the Digital Divide measured by the lack of adequate education, women (the other half of the society) are at even higher Information Security risk because this lack of adequate education is amplified due to the Gender Divide. In consequence, the society as a whole has higher Information Security risk due to the Gender Divide.

Additionally, social engineering attacks exploit the principles of ordinary human behaviour, and target vulnerability in an organization's workforce. In the Arab World, only 30 % of working-age women participate in the labour market. When correlating this with the results of the DefCon test, we can conclude that men employees, who represent a high proportion of the labour market, place organizations at high Information Security risk because they are less cautious with regard to social engineering attacks, while women, who represent a low proportion in the labour market, are more cautious and less likely to be victims in such attacks.

Women are also, according to the PC Tools survey [3], more cautious with regard to some Information Security-related practices, such as opening attachments and changing passwords. This means that Gender Divide serves to deprive organizations of the cautious behaviour of women with regard to social engineering attacks and with such Information Security related practices, with an associated increase Information Security risk.

To this context, we may add the insight from the Bitdefender study [6], that women exhibit lower risk behaviour than men on social networks. Consequently, decreasing the extent of the digital gender divide on the diffusion of social networks in the Arab world would induce lower Information Security risk in the society.

On the other hand, Arab countries of low-income economy remain on the other side of the Digital Divide and have, accordingly, another context related to Information Security. The only feature keeping millions of people in such countries from being victims of cybercriminals is the Digital Divide and lack of web penetration. The number of victims and offenders will be standing together on the rise. This means that while men, who represent half of the society, are at low Information Security risk due to lack of web penetration in Arab countries of low income, women (the other half of the society) are at lower Information Security risk because this lack of web penetration is emphasised due to the gender divide. So, the society as a whole in Arab countries of low-income economy attains lower Information Security risk due to the gender divide.

Of course, this does not mean that we should keep such societies undeveloped in order to reduce the negative side effects of ICT, among which are the accompanied Information Security risks. On the contrary, we should encourage ICT-based development in order to improve all aspects of life in those societies and extend the benefits of the Information Society to all, regardless of gender. The primary means to address the negative side effects of ICT are education and training.

From a global perspective, Information Security affects, and has been affected by, the Digital Divide in many ways. Due to digital illiteracy, which is a significant component of the Digital Divide, many people in the Arab World have not taken adequate measures to ensure Information Security. In its turn, the Gender Digital Divide, which represents an aspect of the multifaceted Digital Divide, has increased Information Security risks in the Arab World since it impacts upon women, who represent half of the society, more than men. With the effect that more of this (female) half of the society becomes less worried about Information Security risks.

Achieving equality between men and women in the Information Society is not only a matter of making efforts to increase access and use of ICT for residents of areas on the other side of the Digital Divide. Further endeavours should be dedicated to promote inclusion of women in the Information Society in order to reduce the Digital Divide in terms of Gender. And it is essential for such endeavours, to be successful, that we accommodate the different expectations and different uses of ICT in men and women.

The challenge has two aspects. On the one hand, there is the need to ensure equal opportunities for women in the information society - which is a social objective. On the other hand, more incorporation of women in the workforce could mean an increase in cautious Information Security behaviour as well as different capabilities, beside those that are characterized by men.

References

1. UNDP HDR: Gender inequality index (2012). http://hdr.undp.org/en/statistics/gii/
2. WTIS: In: 11th world Telecommunication/ICT Indicators Symposium (WTIS-13) (2013). http://www.itu.int/en/ITUD/Statistics/Documents/events/wtis2013/001_E_doc.pdf
3. Leyden, J.: http://www.theregister.co.uk/2009/09/02/password_security_survey. Accessed 2 September 2009
4. Elyan, J.: Defcon 2010: women more resistant to social engineering hackers (in French). http://intrapole.com/spip.php?article852
5. Jagatic, T.N., Johnson, N.A., Jakobsson, M., Menczer, F.: Social phishing. Commun. ACM **50**(10), 94–100 (2007)
6. Bitdefender: (2011). http://www.generation-nt.com/bitdefender-homme-femme-reseaux-sociaux-facebook-securite-scam-spam-actualite-1502781.html
7. UNDP HDR: Human development report 2013, the rise of the south: human progress in a diverse world. http://hdr.undp.org/en/content/human-development-report-2013
8. ASMR: Arab social media report. Dubai school of Government (2013). http://www.dsg.ae/En/News/ASMR_5_Report_Final.pdf
9. UN fact sheet, youth year, fact sheet prepared by the United Nations Economic and Social Commission for Western Asia and the United Nations Programme on youth. http://social.un.org/youthyear/docs/Regional%20Overview%20Youth%20in%20the%20Arab%20Region-Western%20Asia.pdf
10. Asgari, H.: Documentaries and women's voice in Arab uprising (2013). http://www.academia.edu/6475035/documentaries_and_womens_voice_in_Arab_uprising
11. Fairclough, N.: Analyzing Discourse: Textual Analysis for Social Research. Routledge, London (2003)
12. Brief 11. In: Mena: Policies to Promote Employment Opportunities. http://siteresources.worldbank.org/INTKNOLEA/Resources/AWB-1.pdf
13. ITU: Measuring the information society. International Telecommunication Union (2013). www.itu.int/en/ITU-D/Statistics/.../MIS2013_without_Annex_4.pdf
14. Boujemi, H.: The role of ICT in empowering Arab women. http://www.diplointernetgovernance.org/profiles/blogs/the-role-of-information-and-communication-technologies-in

Systems Security, Safety and Sustainability

Some Security Perils of Smart Living

(A Day in the Life of John Q Smith, a Citizen of Utopia, and His Twin Brother, Who Isn't)

David Lilburn Watson[(✉)]

Business Compliance and Recovery Management Ltd, London, UK
dlwatson@bcrm.co.uk

Abstract. We live in a world that continuously wants to live in a smarter manner, from the invention of fire and the wheel through the Industrial Revolution to today. Modern home automation started in the Victorian era with labour saving devices and the motor car facilitated transport, as did trains. The onset of electricity allowed more labour saving devices to be developed, again in the home and at work. These were typically 'standalone' devices that needed localised control. In the 1940s industrial control systems were making their presence felt in industry. In 1978 the X10 protocol was patented and allowed remote control of electrical appliances. In the last twenty years there has been a thrust towards 'smart everything', including cities, transport, health, home and work. Without understanding the risks of the 'smart approach' to life and addressing them at the outset, the world risks disaster.

Keywords: Smart technology · Smart homes · Smart grid · Smart cities · Smart meters · Smart utilities · Smart health · Smart travel · Smart living · SCADA · X10 · Security · Vulnerability · Risk

1 Introduction

Smart technology is an everyday fact of life and is pervasive and growing silently with few people realising its impact and where the future will take us.

Whilst this move to smart living and 'e'-everything has its benefits, these have to be carefully weighed against the risks that this approach brings.

This paper examines aspects of the some areas of everyday life that are impacted by Smart Living and considers some of the inhibitors to its success and some risks and impacts of the adoption of this smart way of living. This paper was written from a practitioner's view point who happens to be a consumer of Smart Life, whether he want to be or not.

2 Overview

In the not too distant future almost every object in your life will be 'Smart', online and able to 'talk' to each other and also to you. This will revolutionise the way that we live.

© Springer International Publishing Switzerland 2015
H. Jahankhani et al. (Eds.): ICGS3 2015, CCIS 534, pp. 211–227, 2015.
DOI: 10.1007/978-3-319-23276-8_19

Every device will, in the future, be a possible Smart Component on the Internet. Many everyday devices already have a computer chip in them that people do not realise, which if connected to the Internet can start broadcasting or receiving information, either to each other (Machine to Machine or M2M) or to various collection or aggregation points.

It is estimated that by 2020 between 25 Bn and 75 Bn devices will be connected to the Internet (depending on whom you believe). These will include sensors and actuators, streetlamps, industrial components, utility services, CCTV, cars and domestic appliances, a list that is forever growing.

This growth of devices being able to communicate and share data is known as the 'Internet of Things' (IoT). This term was coined in 1999 by Kevin Ashton, but in those days the technology did not exist to make the IoT a reality – today it does, where miniature computing devices that can claim that they consume minute amounts of electricity and run off a solar cell or miniature battery.

In essence, the IoT will allow people and Smart Devices to be connected anyhow, in any location, using any network at any time of their choosing.

3   How They Work

Smart Devices will receive data from a near infinite range of sensors that can monitor and measure anything that can be recorded and using that data will activate switches, servos, valves, flow control devices and communicate over wireless connections as well as the wired internet to each other or one or more centralised collection or aggregation points.

It will be possible to give any item or component an unique identity (an UID) and be able to trace its movement around the world. The ability to trace it will also be available for its whole lifecycle, should that be the item or device owner's wishes.

3.1   Utopia

These devices can exist in almost all areas of our lives, some examples of their benefits are given below in a scenario of John Q Smith's working day from waking up in Centreville, Utopia.

3.2   Smart Homes

It is early in the morning and John's alarm clock is connected to the internet and his daily planner. It knows when his first appointment of the day is and knows his route to the office from his GPRS and engine management system. From the traffic news, it knows if there are any holdups and so will wake him up in time to make it in good time to the office.

The smoke alarm will no longer just beep if it detects smoke but will call the fire brigade, alert John with loud noises (Heavy Rock music of his choice), turn off the gas to the house and optionally alert the neighbours.

As he (or any of his family) get out of bed, the burglar alarm, that was automatically set when the last of the family went to bed, is automatically deactivated. His towel will be warming on the towel rail if it is winter time and the home lighting system provides the required lighting level throughout the house whilst the air humidity system ensures that the home climate is optimised.

His breakfast is waiting for him and he has some quality time with his family before everyone sets off for the day. Actually they won't speak much as John will be catching up on email, his wife will be reading an on-line magazine and the kids will either be texting, Twittering, Facebooking or playing on line games.

The Smart Fridge can tell if the door has been opened or not, whether the temperature is too high and adjust the thermostat as well as summon help if it suffers a technical malfunction. It can scan all of the food put in it, work out what is past its 'use by date' and advise the family as well as define the shopping list of used items and place an order online to the cheapest purveyor of those items (the first internet enabled fridge was produced by LG in 2000). It can do this on the display panel on the front of the fridge (and also have audible alarms) or on a Smart Phone, tablet, PC, laptop or via an Intranet.

Before John leaves for work, a message to his Smart Communicator (Sorry Star Trek!) tells him that his children have brushed their teeth, combed their hair, completed their homework, put on all of their uniform and are ready to leave for school. Another message tells him that Bonzo has used the pet door, done what he needed to and is safely back inside.

As everyone leaves the house for the day, he can remotely set the alarm on the house, locking all the doors and windows whilst unlocking his car and being authenticated as a valid driver against the insurance policy (also on line).

If it is really smart it will restrict his driving to the criteria in the insurance policy and check to see that he is not over the drink drive limit – whilst also checking that if his children are allowed to use the car they cannot travel at more than 50 mph, travel further than 20 miles from home and be home by 22:00, carrying no passengers.

After the family leave for the day, the Smart Home Robot does its domestic chores and the appropriate household devices are programmed to do their tasks whilst the family is out, so that when they come home the dishes are clean, clean clothes are in the dryer, the garden has been watered and the plants fed, the pool topped up, Bonzo has been fed and been out and dinner is waiting for the family in the oven with their favourite music playing and mood lighting on.

After dinner, the family use their Smart TVs, with a selection of programs it 'knows' the watcher likes, as well as the ones that have been recorded and also those that were missed on 'catch-up'. As well as watching the TV on a Smart TV, they can be used as a computer, to access the internet, use social media, and play games. Additionally, any of the pay per view services available can be watched, if the appropriate fee is paid.

3.3 Health, Sport and Fitness

John is concerned about his health and does some early morning calisthenics. His wife is always nagging him how little exercise he gets and about the horror stories she reads about health in her on line magazines.

So John now regularly undertakes a morning exercise routine, after getting up and before his bath, his toothbrush manages how he brushes his teeth. After brushing them he puts on his Smart Glasses which overcome his visual impairment and interpret what he sees.

His Smart Gym monitors his sports health as he exercises, optionally sending the information to his personal trainer, who may either just record the information or set up a tailored exercise programme for him.

As he wife is convinced he has a health weakness, he wears a smart vest that continuously monitors his vital signs and movement. The vest monitors his blood pressure, heart rate, temperature, sweat and even conducts an electrocardiogram (ECG), sending the data wirelessly to a collection point where it can be analysed for anomalies of indications that something may be wrong. This may be to a subscription services or to his own family doctor. As the vest has a Global Positioning System (GPS) inbuilt, it can alert the emergency services to his exact position in case of medical emergency.

Alternatively, a sensor to perform similar (or different) functions can be implanted in his body.

When his elderly mother or family member with a baby come to stay, then there are a range of smart medical devices that can monitor their state of health and provide alerts should an anomaly be detected or a health threshold be breached.

The former can be adapted to manage such events as medication taking, eating, and sleeping habits and alert careers, neighbours or family if needed. The latter may assist in preventing cot deaths.

Of course, more sophisticated smart medical devices exist in hospitals.

Once he has finished his exercise, the bath will be run for him to the right temperature. He then shaves using a Smart Shaver that reports on the state of his skin and finally combs his hair with a Smart Comb that reports on the state of his hair (follicle loss – baldness), scans for lice, fungus and dandruff.

He then dresses and makes his way downstairs where a skinny latte will be waiting for him in the kitchen.

3.4 Smart Utilities

His house, like almost every other one in the country, has utilities servicing it, including gas, electricity and water (as appropriate).

Almost all homes have Smart Meters for controlling and managing utility supply, very few now are still read on a regular basis by an army of meter readers.

A smart meter is a meter that can be remotely accessed, controlled and read eliminating the need for a meter reader or any estimated meter readings if you are out. Smart meters use Radio Frequency (RF) technology to send meter readings and also to receive instructions for controlling the Smart Meter from the energy supplier.

This approach allows John to monitor energy usage costs using an in-house display device that will show exactly how his energy is used down to individual devices using Waveform Analytics, improve efficiency and reduce costs.

He is able to manage his utility consumption by using appropriate tariffs that match his needs and the local environment (weather, time of day, time of year etc.) rather than be stuck with a 'one size fits all' approach that used to be the only one available (called Demand Response (DR)).

He is investigating generating his own power, so as to be more eco-friendly and his Smart Meter will allow him to sell any surplus power back to the grid and integrate this exported power to reduce his energy bill.

Smart Metering allows the energy suppliers to accurately forecast demand, reduce energy theft, detect faults earlier, generally improve service and reduce the cost to the consumer as well as reduce carbon emissions.

The smart meters will be connected to the Smart Grid.

3.5 Smart Grid

Historically, the electric power grid was used for simply powering electric lights. Today the uses of electrical power has expanded dramatically and beyond all recognition from the early days of electricity. More than ever, John and his family rely on electricity for every facet of their life, including transportation, communication, food, health, environment, and most other basic needs.

If power is lost, then civilisation is quickly paralysed with no method of charging a phone, using a computer or the internet (let alone Facebook), heating or cooling food, managing health or running a business or household.

There are many variations on the definition of 'Smart Grid' (and none universally accepted) but in essence it is an electricity supply network that uses digital communications technology to detect, monitor, react to local changes in and control usage of the electricity supply in a given area (typically a city, county, state or country).

In a number of cases, there are regulations mandating the use of smart metering/grids and other legislation that, whilst not mandating it, positively encourages it.

The Smart Grid can integrate everything from the end user (private or industrial consumer), through distribution and transmission systems to solar wind farms, power generation plant of any type. This is integrating and connecting using a variety of communications systems from satellites through mobile communications to the Plain Old Telephone System (POTS). Monitoring is carried out using remote sensing (e.g. sensors, monitoring devices, smart appliances etc.), viewing (e.g. satellite, CCTV, etc.) and monitoring and control systems (e.g. Supervisory Control and Data Acquisition - SCADA).

It is possible to undertake real time analytics on 'Big Data' combined with spatial or geographic mapping and produce trending information to allow optimised energy supply.

In the future this will all run over Next Generation Architectures (NGEs) or use the some form of Cloud Service Platform (CSP), though in some cases it must still be partially run over legacy networks.

The Smart Grid is a basic building block of our Smart Cities of the future.

3.6 Smart Personal Travel

After unlocking his car, John disconnects it from the electricity supply as it is a Smart Hybrid Car.

There has been a gradual move away from oil-dependent transport to hybrid technology, not only for efficiency but environmental considerations and to reduce reliance on oil based technology and also countries that are relied on to provide it. John's car knows its way to work and it has already received information from sensors in the road as to traffic conditions and navigates to work using the optimum route.

The roads are also smart with sensors embedded in them to detect traffic flow as well as road conditions. This can be used for traffic or weather bulletins to be displayed on John's Smart Communicator, on roadway signage or even be used as part of the road's planned maintenance program.

Streetlamps collect solar power to run them, returning any spare power to the national grid, whilst the Passive Infra-Red (PIR) detector determines exactly when sunrise and sunset occur to turn them on or off for maximum use efficiency. They are programmed to turn off if there is no traffic or pedestrians present and turn back on when they are present and alert when the bulb is blown or there is some other malfunction. This means that anyone with malicious intent will have no place to 'lurk' as lighting will always be on to deter them and linked to Close Circuit Television (CCTV) will be able to assist Law Enforcement to trace and prosecute offenders.

However, using Automatic Number Plate Recognition (ANPR) technology linked to the CCTV, it can identify any car that passes a streetlamp or other device and automatically detect if it is stolen, is on a 'watch list' or is being driven without insurance and take appropriate action. This makes the roads safer, reduces the cost of insurance and assists in apprehending offenders.

In the not too distant future, driverless cars will appear that will take John to work so he can use the car as an extension of the office and work all the way to the office.

On the way to the office, John gets a message to say that his children have arrived safely at school from the detector that has identified them from their RFID tag secreted into their clothes.

Following that message, John gets a call on his Smart Communicator that tells him that his eldest child, who has just graduated, has an interview for the job he really wants that afternoon and is off to it. John wishes him well and orders a present to be delivered to him to celebrate the (hopefully forthcoming) job.

On arrival at work, John needs to find somewhere to park, and a significant amount of congestion on the roads is caused by people like John looking for parking spaces. Smart car parks show the availability of parking spaces today, and office car parks will be access card controlled in most cases, leaving car parking in the street the problem area. Sensors in the street will detect where there are spaces available and this information will be available through a service provider who will also provide details of charges, duration permitted for parking and pay for the privilege. By simply entering a post code or tapping a map, this information will be available in real time.

After leaving his car and locking it, John walks to his office, on the way he ensures that he has his car remote that interfaces with the diagnostic port built into any car manufactured after 1996. This allows him to monitor the health of his car, according to what the manufacturer has made available (e.g. fuel, oil, temperature, tyre pressure, time to service or need for it if running badly). The GPS will allow him to find it if he cannot remember where he left it but also show all past journeys undertaken. One of his friends has told him of an excellent App for his Smart Communicator that will eliminate the need to carry his car remote as his Smart Communicator can do this for him.

3.7 Smart Office Buildings

On arrival at the office, he is scanned by a biometric reader that is connected to the access control system, which recognises him and permits him access to the areas of the office he is authorised to access.

The office has a full Smart Building Management system that controls the temperature and humidity of the office, and uses Smart Metering to optimise the energy use in the building whilst minimising costs.

All of the building sensing equipment, flood, fire, smoke and burglar alarms are all linked to a central Security Operations Control centre which oversees the building and is in constant touch with the Concierges that patrol each floor.

As Centreville is in a earthquake zone, sensors have been implemented to detect building movement, speed of seismic waves travelling through the building, changes in structural integrity etc. allowing decisions to evacuate or not.

His Smart Office has 'hot desking' and when he chooses an empty location, his physical desk with paperwork is brought to him, his computer already has access to all of his electronic files, email and his phone number is diverted to his current desk location.

Asset tracking enables the staff to quickly locate 'his' desk, but all assets owned by 'Big Co' are asset tagged. This allows them to be traced so that all can be properly maintained, managed and reported against as required. It has also eliminated the past problems of authorised 'borrowing' of corporate equipment that is never returned. John, as a Big Co asset, is also traced in the building using the access control system so that when he is working late on his own, he can be checked to ensure that he is medically healthy and not at risk.

3.8 Smart Shopping

At lunchtime John has the option of shopping on line and paying for it by a number of different methods including credit cards or PayPal.

When he wants he can go to the nearest mall and physically walk around a shop. The goods that he purchases are all RFID tagged so that the Smart Point of Sale terminal reduces error and ensures the up to date price is charged. Goods can also be checked to ensure that they are not counterfeit by detecting products with invalid, cloned or otherwise counterfeit labels.

At the same time, if appropriate, the till prompts him for his details. Having captured his details and that of his purchases, this is sent to the manufacturer who is building a profile of his shopping so they can send him targeted advertising of their products and remind him of the expiry of any warranty. The retail outlet also keeps this so they can invite John to events which are promoting goods that he has previously purchased.

In real time, the store management and the manufacturers are able to track sales as they happen and profitability, update stock control and ordering and plan where to move stock so that it gets maximum exposure and therefore optimise sales opportunities.

At the same time, this reduces merchandise theft and increases management control.

3.9 Smart City Travel

After shopping, John hops on a shuttle bus or train, probably driverless, and pays with his Smart Card which will know where he alights and where he exits so it can charge him the correct amount for the journey.

To help John's journey, based on traffic flow and other possible disruptions, the traffic lights ensure a smooth and optimised journey back to the office.

The shuttle bus or train has on-board sensors to detect events like engine temperature, driving efficiency, speed, braking, oil pressure, loading etc. This allows better predictive analysis for scheduling of services and maintenance and indicates possible requirements for additional driver training.

What John may realise as he crosses the bridge over the Wide River by the office is that this is actually a Smart Bridge. It contains numerous sensors that are constantly monitoring the bridge's temperature, vibration, pressure and humidity etc. and passing these back, with data from all other smart bridges in the city to the City Engineers. This allows them to diagnose any possible threats to the structural health of any Smart Bridge in real time and take appropriate action.

3.10 Smart Industrialisation

In the afternoon, John has to visit the Big Co factory, and uses the Smart Shuttle Bus to get there. The factory is on the outskirts of the city, where the rents are cheaper and this is just one factory unit amongst many on the industrial park.

The same access control system is used in the factory as in the office to authenticate him. On walking into the factory, John is immediately required to wash his hands to cut down on infection and contamination of the workforce or the product. The Smart Hand Washer records that John has washed his hands and a number of work stations around the factory require everyone to wash their hands within a specific period of time before touching the product. The hand washing system recognises John when he is at a station that requires him to have washed his hands and when he last performed this task, providing management with a record of his hand washing activity.

Inside the factory, all components can be tracked using RFID tags containing an UID. This allows better stock and production control as well as determining which components fail.

It allows total traceability of the product from the component parts to the sale to the wholesaler or distributer. The cleverer companies ensure that this filters down to the point of sale, so that they know where every single product they have produced has ended up allowing targeted marketing of similar or upgraded products, extended warranties, market research and actual sales figures from sales outlets.

This allows better management control as these are in real time as the sale is rung up on the till, and identifies slow movers as well as products not moving quickly enough through the distribution chain.

Once the products are ready to be shipped, route control can be plotted and optimised based on weather and road conditions so that collections (returns) and deliveries (drop) are optimised.

On collection or delivery, the collection or delivery can be automatically scanned and systems back at headquarters updated as the event occur. Deliveries can be planned based on usage, optimising cash and stock flow.

An added advantage of this is that every delivery vehicle can be tracked in real time, journey statistics recorded (speed, distance, duration, vehicle health and driver health (fatigue, compliance with local legislation regarding driving regulations).

3.11 Smart Cities

A significant amount of the world's electricity is used by cities, so it makes eminently sense to ensure that it is used in a 'smart' manner in cities. Gothenburg was the first city in the world to cover an entire city with a ZigBee network for gas. Electricity and district heating grids.

Smart use of utilities within Centreville has led to a smaller carbon footprint, reduced energy consumption and been environmentally friendly,

By using Smart Monitoring and Sensing Devices, it can control the City environment for the benefit of its citizens.

3.12 Smart Government

Both local and national government now have all of their service offerings on line so that John can manage all of his government interactions on line at times to suit him. This is backed up by a real person in a call centre if he needs to access a human being, but almost all the time, this is irrelevant as he can do all of his interactions over the internet.

3.13 Utopia?

John is content with his life, and looks forward to the next Smart Initiative that he sees as improving the quality of his life and that of his family and protecting him in his job and workplace.

A bit far-fetched?

Most of this is here today or within the next 5 years.

3.14 Inhibitors to John's Idea of Utopia

Whilst much of John's Utopia is available today, there are still a number of issues to overcome to create a sustainable and secure Utopia. Some of these are very briefly described below from the consumer view as well as from a technical viewpoint and are in no particular order apart from alphabetic.

4 User and Non-technical Concerns

- **Ability to use Smart Technology** – Whilst John is happy with his dream of Utopia, there are large sectors of society that may easily become excluded, included in this are those with no ability to use Smart Devices, no internet connections, geographic exclusions, the socially disadvantaged, medically incapable, elderly and those unable for some reason to adopt Smart Technology.

- **Communication between Devices and Back End Databases** – Integral to Smart Living there needs to be seamless and secure interaction between devices and databases so that intelligence and full reporting can be produced. Databases will be in a variety of different formats and this exacerbates the problem, as does different identifiers for the same person in multiple different database systems.
- **Consumer Confidence** – Consumers have to be confident in the accuracy and efficiency of any Smart Devices or Technology that they use. Experiences from other countries indicate that there is some serious backlash against the implementation of Smart Meters and the tripling of some bills in the USA. Consumer confidence also links to consumer uptake, and some countries have had to relax their requirements for this.
- **Cost** – There is no such thing as a free lunch, and the consumer will end up paying for the upgrades to make the world 'Smart', whether this is direct (e.g. through utility bills for utility consumption) or indirectly via taxes for government initiatives.
- **Data Breaches** – What will happen to the data collected and how safe is it? Just like the data breaches that exist today, there will be even bigger breaches in the future as information security will always be playing catch-up. As we cannot secure the much of the data that is already held, how will there be a sea change with the massive amounts of data (much of it personal data) that is to be collected and processed in the future We have to be excellent and best of breed every day, a hacker only has to be lucky once. Don't forget that general data breaches are just as likely caused by poorly trained and incompetent employees as they are by a hacker.
- **Data Protection Legislation** – Linked to privacy concerns is the ability of the Data Protection Legislation in each country (and for cross border transfers) to handle the IoT. Currently, the purpose for which the data is to be used has to be declared at the point of collection and agreed to by the Data Subject. In the future, new uses for the data, (cross matching, blending, automated decision taking, co-joining and other data manipulations) will emerge on a daily basis in different countries with differing interpretations of data privacy. It would be impossible to gain consent from all Data Subjects to new uses of their personal data on a daily basis. It would also not be possible to have opt in/out fields for each possible differing purpose to which that data could be put. The fear is that governments and 'big business' will drive through legislation to weaken the Data Subject's rights relating to their personal data (Now called Personally Identifiable Information (PII) – which is any data that could potentially identify a specific individual).
- **End User Smart Device Security** – Many Smart Devices have a low level of security for accessing them (e.g. PIN numbers or a 9 point pattern on a current mobile phone). With the increasing ability to affect lives, a better process of authentication for all Smart Devices must be devised.
- **Health and Safety Issues** – A number of concerns have been raised relating to Smart Devices catching fire or emanating harmful radiation – much like the issues relating to mobile phones in the late 1990s and 2000s.
- **Identity Theft** – It is simple these days, and even reasonably simple with Smart Technology, to steal someone else's identity. Searching the internet identifies a number of devices that can do this or even subvert Smart Devices such as Smart Meters.

- **Increased Risk of Burglary** – Where it is possible to determine activity (or lack of it) in a house, it is possible to determine occupancy trends. These could be used to determine when the house is unoccupied and therefore a target for burglary.
- **Legislation** – Whilst it possible to devise and implement legislation to protect the Citizen, this is usually too little, too late, not fit for purpose as it is not maintained, and has few resources to actively enforce it. It is of interest that only about 75 prosecutions have been brought after 25 years of the Computer Misuse Act 1990 and until recently the maximum fine under the Data Protection Act 1998 was £5000 (it is now £500,000 and may go up to 2 % of turnover)
- **Privacy Concerns** – The opening up of the IoT, the use of so many Smart Devices and the adoption of a joined up world will lead to the 'real world' morphing into the 'cyber world'. Our every move will be trackable, recorded and processed. The results being matched against other collated information and monetised and sold to the highest bidder. An unique insight into our private lives, much of which we have no desire to share, will be available, literally at the press of a key. This can be used by legitimate companies or stolen by unauthorised parties. Who will be liable for breaches and how will recompense be decided is yet to be established.
- **Remote Disconnection** – Whilst Smart Meters make it easier for utility suppliers to remotely disconnect a supplier (e.g. moved house, failure to pay bills, etc.), there has been fears that that this can be done by hackers as well as the utility company. Whilst disconnection is a simple matter, it may well prove more difficult to get reconnected.
- **Smart Device Makers** – there is a fear that the manufacturers could leave 'kill switches', back door or similar in a Smart Device. In devices that can be automatically triggered (e.g. the infamous 'Star of David Packet'). In the extreme this could paralyse a whole country by attacking its utility supply chain.
- **Smart Devices** – there is the need to replace current 'dumb' devices and have interoperable Smart Devices so device 'plug and play' will work seamlessly. Smart Device Controllers will have to have internationally accepted standards and will have to cope with a multiplicity of Smart Devices from a variety of manufacturers and countries;
- **The Law of Unintended Consequences** – The potential benefits of the IoT and Smart Devices is huge, but the possible downsides are colossal. Think of 50 Bn devices interacting with each other, which is 25×10^{25} potential network to network interactions if they can all interact with each other. With the lack of connectivity standards currently in place and legacy devices, it is possible that by indicating to turn right in a car in Centreville, John may just switch off a life support system in Omaha, Nebraska!
- **Total Dependence** – Once locked into Smart Devices and the IoT, there is no return to the days before the IoT. The toothpaste is out of the tube, and there is no putting it back.
- **Training and Awareness** – Not only will consumers need to understand how to use their Smart Devices for optimum efficiency, there will be the increased need for competent designers, manufacturers, installers and maintainers of Smart Devices.
- **Utility Supply Failure** – Recent inclement weather in a number of countries (e.g. US – Hurricane Sandy, UK – Floods at Christmas /New Year 2014, etc.) left a large

number of homes without power, sometimes for up to weeks, in fact the New York Stock Exchange was shut for 2 days because of Hurricane Sandy. Time after time, the same vulnerable and legacy systems were reinstalled or simply patched in order to restore power as soon as possible. Lack of utility supply can severely impact home and work environments.

5   Technical

- **Availability of the Smart Grid** – The uptake of some Smart Services will be restricted by the number of charging points on the Smart Grid and the capacity of the Smart Grid to support a rapidly growing number of Smart Devices that want to use the Smart Grid
- **Battery Life/Recharging** – Some Smart Devices require batteries and these will run out eventually, battery life has to be factored into maintenance.
- **Complexity** – There are massive size and logistical deployment considerations whilst maintaining customer service levels to be resolved. The architecture of the IoT will be complex with a very high number of endpoints, participants, interfaces and communication channels and with different levels of protection in the underlying systems. In general, it is always a challenge and requires effort to achieve an adequate level of protection for such a complex system.
- **Configuration Failures** – In today's IT departments there are failures to design, plan, implement and maintain appropriate configurations for networks, network components (e.g. firewalls) and other 'smart' components. This will only grow exponentially with the rapid growth of Smart Devices being added to the IoT. Configuration is also vulnerable to external attack.
- **Identification and Authentication** – all entry points must ensure strong authentication, however, this has a massive overhead. If it is not carried out, then access control is weakened. The use of free hotspots must also be secured as this allows anonymous access to the internet, secure private and encrypted channels must be used. This will also assist parents in restricted theirs children's access to inappropriate content.
- **Increased Endpoints** – The introduction of the IoT and its supporting processes and systems will increase the number of endpoints dramatically and will move them to private property. Physical security is hard to achieve in these scenarios and time and motivation to penetrate the IoT are in plentiful supply.
- **Increased Vulnerabilities** – By definition, vulnerabilities increase when systems become integrated and interconnected and endpoints increase. This is also exacerbated where Big Data is suddenly introduced into the equation. Inadequate patching is a current problem in many IT departments today, this will only grow exponentially as more Smart Devices are added to the IoT.
- **Legacy Systems** – Many components of the IoT can be characterized as legacy where security has never been an important requirement. Bolt on security to these systems is neither effective nor efficient.

- **RFID Tags** – The size, cost, read range, read rate and security of passive RFID tags is an issue.
- **Risks to Firmware** – The smarter hacker does not attempt to attempt to hack the application to access data, but attacks the physical components of the device. This means subverting the physical elements of the device by attacking its firmware, which is present on every electronic device that is the foundation of our 'smart lives'.
- **Specific Device and network Attacks** – Attacks can be launched against specific Smart Devices, makes or classes of Smart Device or even specific Smart Devices in a given location. These attacks could include Denial of Service (DoS) or Distributed Denial of Service (DDoS), scrambling, manipulation, eavesdropping, jamming and physical attacks. These are evident today and will only grow with more attractive targets on offer. Whilst the use of optic fibre, which is often regarded as providing an acceptable level of security, is subject to software tapping, micro-bending, light injection and splicing – which is easily detectable but can be used to disruption/denial of service. However, attacks against fibre optic cable require physical presence at the cable.
- **Threat and Intelligence information** – This must be shared amongst all of the interested parties in the IoT so that common threats and vulnerabilities can be addressed. This is in sharp contrast to the situation today where any incident that may affect an organisation is protected and not shared.
- **Various Attacks that Already Exist** – There are a number of information security attacks that already exist before the implementation of any Smart Devices or the IoT. All of these are possible for the future, and given the level of failure to protect systems and information against them historically, these are of increased importance with the onset of a fully populated IoT containing increasing numbers of Smart Devices. These include and are not limited to (excluding those mentioned in detail above):
  - Botnets;
  - Business logic and design vulnerabilities;
  - Cross site scripting,
  - Default settings not reset on promotion to 'live';
  - Deficiencies in Log and Audit Trail Management;
  - External unrealistic pressures to deliver;
  - Failure to adequately screen staff, and especially third parties, by employers;
  - Failure to consider information security at all stages of every project;
  - Failure to define necessary rules and protocols;
  - Failure to ensure individual accountability;
  - Failure to implement segregation of duties and environments;
  - Failure to manage risks appropriately;
  - Failure to properly test application code;
  - Failure to properly manage third parties and suppliers;
  - Failure to undertake appropriate risk assessments;
  - Failures in cryptographic implementation;
  - Inadequate change management;
  - Inadequate configuration management;
  - Inadequate incident management;

- Inappropriate error handling;
- Inappropriate system access;
- Incompetent Auditors;
- Ineffective auditing;
- Lack of competent First Responders and forensics skills;
- Lack of joined up security;
- Lack of management commitment;
- Lack of management oversight and control;
- Lack of training for employees and users;
- Logic bombs;
- Non-standard coding and poor code quality;
- Passive wiretapping;
- Password and authentication vulnerabilities;
- Phishing and Spear Phishing;
- Poor physical security;
- Reliance on insecure third party software;
- Spam;
- Trojan Horses;
- Untested or inadequate Business Continuity Plans;
- Viral infection;
- War Driving;
- Worms;
- Zero Day exploits;
- **Volumes of Data** – Data management is going to be a key issue, especially when interactions with other service providers are required with different UIDs and data structures/format. Data collection is moving for Smart Utilities from once every three months to continuous.

6 Dystopia

John's brother, Kevin, lives in the next city along called Dystopia, he lives in a house the same as Johns, has the same family makeup, his wife is John's wife's sister, drives the same car and works for the same employer. He has also embraced a smarter way of life. He has some different experiences to share.

Kevin gets up in the morning and starts his exercise regime as his wife has nagged him about his health also.

His smart exercise and health equipment (including his toothbrush, comb and vest) are all linked to his personal trainer, who unknown to him, has sold this information to a data aggregation company, who in turn have resold it to an insurance company. What Kevin does not know is that his next health insurance premium is in for a massive rise, if indeed they will even insure him as his health and exercise regime have identified a number of unacceptable and uninsurable risks. What he also does not know is that insurance company shares insurance information with all other insurance companies in a bid to substantially reduce insurance fraud. All insurance companies will know his health details and will charge massive premiums if they even accept the risk.

After getting dressed he comes down to breakfast with the family. He logs into his computer and logs into his email system. His inbox is flooded with spam offering all sorts of deals. What he does no know is that all of the purchases that he made on line yesterday were monitored using some spyware on his Smart Communicator – he had forgotten to renew his subscription to his malware provider who turned off the service for non-payment, leaving him vulnerable to all types of malware. This tracked all of his internet searches and all of his past purchases on eBay, Amazon and numerous other sites. This was sold to a broker who contacted the suppliers of similar goods to those he had purchased who spammed him. He had fifty seven thousand emails in his inbox and somewhere amongst it were the twenty or so important ones that he was used to getting on a daily basis.

His wife asks him if he has checked the settings on their new Smart Mater as it needs to be customised for their patterns of usage, she has been asking him about this since it was installed some three months ago. He says he will get round to it, but his mind is on the spam outbreak and trying to restart his malware protection.

He goes to the fridge to get his packed lunch, and is bombarded as he opens the door, with advertising on the fridge display, this has been subverted as well as his email.

He walks out of the house with the household refuse and throws it absentmindedly in the bin.

In a bad mood he gets into his car and starts the drive to work. There has been an accident on the way to work causing a holdup, but his Smart Hybrid Car gives him the optimal route to the office.

On the drive in, as his mind is elsewhere, he does not notice all of the CCTV cameras on the street lighting with their ANPR enabled facility. He clocks up speeding ticket after ticket, one of them for exceeding the speed limit by just 1mph.

Oblivious to this, Kevin gets a very distressed call from his son Adam, who has just graduated and was at a job interview for a job he really wanted. Adam was on a number of databases as a child, in common with all other children, from their time of birth onwards.

His school records, including academic results and attendance records were in one database, his health records containing childhood illnesses and operations in another, as is all interaction with any government department.

A trial scheme has just been started to try to detect and prevent crime by using a series of criteria including family traits.

As Adam is a child of known offender (his Grandfather was caught shoplifting and when his house was searched, inappropriate material was found on his computer), the system flags Adam as a possible offender in the future. This has been matched with his less than clean driving record and being photographed on demonstrations as a student.

He has been turned down for the job because of his 'criminal past' and the opinion that he may become an offender, his poor attendance at school (he lacks 'application') and his health records show he was treated for a range of childhood illnesses that the marking scheme indicates may affect his future working life.

This information has been shared with other employers and Adam is now effectively unemployable.

Kevin parks his car and in a very despondent mood, walks to the office. The biometric scanner lets him access the building and his office, his 'hot desk' is brought to him and he starts work.

His Smart Communicator bleeps and he sees it is a call from his wife, who advises this that all of the utilities have been remotely disconnected for non-payment. He calls the utility company who confirm this and say that they have sent him the bill by email, but he claims not to have received it. The Utility Company Call Centre Operator says 'we sent you the email so you must have received it'. She goes further to say that they tried to request payment for the bill from his bank, but they refused payment. When Kevin asked the amount he was horrified, it was five times the previous pre-Smart Meter bill and he had not budgeted for this. The Call Centre Operator stated that they did advise the new users to read the instructions and select an appropriate tariff. Kevin remembered his wife telling him to do this but he had other things on his mind.

Playing 'keeping up with the Joneses' with his successful twin, John, left him on the edge financially and he could not extend his overdraft at the bank, so he had to get a 'pay day' loan at an usurious interest rate to get the utilities restored.

Kevin does not go to the Mall at lunch but for a walk to try to clear his head. On return to the office, he discovers he has dropped his wallet and logging into his PC to report it he notices an urgent email from his boss who wants to see him in the HR department.

Kevin arrives and is told this is a formal disciplinary meeting. Company records show that his timekeeping is not acceptable, he is frequently late. Records also show how much time he spent working whilst in the office, from a sensor in his chair and proximity devices in the bathroom and in the coffee queue showed how much time he spent in the office but not at work. Additionally, it was noticed that his personal cleanliness whilst in the factory (i.e. washing his hands) was also unacceptable. He was put on a final warning.

He leaves at the end of the day, wondering how he will afford the repayments on his payday loan and how he will tell his wife about the predicament they are in.

He gets home and she is not home yet, so he starts to try to clear the remainder of his email spam backlog, when he notices and email from the City Finance Department advising him that the sensors in his refuse bins indicate that he did not segregate the rubbish he put in the bins and that a statutory fine for each incorrectly loaded bin was being issued.

Just after that, he received an email from his life insurer for life and health insurance saying that they were not offering him a renewal on his policy due to adverse health risk. This was quickly followed up by a series of speeding ticket fines and an email from his motor insurance company who were terminating his motor insurance. The reasons given were the number of speeding fines and his driving pattern was erratic as determined by his engine management system, which is also automatically uploaded to them as part of his insurance agreement.

He got a drink and sat down to watch his Smart TV whilst waiting for his wife and children, little realising that it had been hacked and was recording his every actions and beaming them to a remote database.

A knock on the front door shows two Policemen who want to interview him about a crime in downtown Centreville. The suspect had been apprehended, who gave Kevin's name and address and produced his credentials from his wallet and was then released. Would Kevin accompany them to the Police Station?

Could it get worse for Kevin?

7   Summary

With the inexorable march of the IoT, there will be no option to 'opt out' of using these devices or services provided by governments/corporations as to do so will effectively exclude you from society as a whole.

Best Value Performance Indicator (BVPI) 157 for all local authorities in the UK is a key objective of the Office of the Deputy Prime Minister (ODPM) Public Service Agreement, provides a focus for priority working within the Government's target to reach 100 % e-enablement of services. This can effectively exclude those with no internet access or mobile device. With more counties adopting a similar approach, there will be a 'cyber-world underclass' of those unable (for whatever reason) to interact with the 'brave new cyber-world'.

For those who are part of this brave new world, with numerous seemingly innocuous devices reporting their measurements and findings. Once these are processed and correlated, a frightening picture emerges and this not just if the information is leaked, but used by legitimate users.

Whilst the IoT and smart devices have dramatically increased the range of services that can be provided to enhance our lives, the downside is that we have colossally increased the threats to that lifestyle. This is being ever extended by corporations and governments who want to benefit from the joined up IoT world, but without actually addressing the security threats created. Well, perhaps paying lip service to them.

What we will have will not be an Internet of Things, it will be an Internet of Things that I can go and hack, my own worldwide toyshop of hackable toys.

8   A Final Thought

A Foreign Intelligence Service (FIS) that wants to take over a country does not need an army, it can just cut off the utility supply, after three days or so of no water supply the population will have died or left the country with not a shot fired and all of the infrastructure intact.

An Analysis of Honeypot Programs and the Attack Data Collected

Chris Moore[1](✉) and Ameer Al-Nemrat[2]

[1] University of St Mark & St John, Plymouth, England, UK
cmoore@marjon.ac.uk
[2] University of East London, London, England, UK
a.al-nemrat@uel.ac.uk

Abstract. Honeypots are computers specifically deployed to be a resource that is expected to be attacked or compromised. While the attacker is distracted with the decoy computer system we learn about the attacker and their methods of attack. From the information gained about the attacks we can then review and harden out security systems. Compared to an Intrusion Detection System (IDS) which may trigger false positives, we take the standpoint that nobody ought to be interacting with the decoy computer; therefore we regard all interactions to be of value and worth investigation. A sample of honeypots are evaluated and one selected to collect attacks. The captured attacks reveal the source IP address of the attacker and the service port under attack. Attacks where the exploit attempts to deploy a binary can capture the code, and automatically submit it for analysis to sandboxes such as VirusTotal.

Keywords: Honeypots · Security · Intrusion detection

1 Introduction

As a security monitor, Spitzner [1] gives the definition "a honeypot is an information system resource whose value lies in unauthorized or illicit use of that resource". A honeypot is a tool that does not have any authorised use, so any interaction is deemed to be of malicious intent.

We are familiar with firewalls and Intrusion Detection and Prevention Systems (IDPS) as methods of network defence; however a honeypot offers a different approach. Kaur, Malhotra and Singh [2] argue that firewalls logging all traffic would collect an overwhelming amount of information that an administrator would find prohibitive to analyse; a honeypot however would only log attacks to a host, Joshi & Sardana [3] state that the small data sets are easier to manage and analyse.

Their work also argues that Intrusion Detection is not a definitive security solution, as IDPS have high occurrences of false positive alerts requiring extensive tuning of the IDPS. Similarly undetected intrusions (false negatives) also occur when malicious activity is not detected as a signature of the malware available to identify yet unknown or novel threats. From the viewpoint that a honeypot does not advertise any resources for regular use, any interaction with the honeypot is assumed to be an intrusion and

© Springer International Publishing Switzerland 2015
H. Jahankhani et al. (Eds.): ICGS3 2015, CCIS 534, pp. 228–238, 2015.
DOI: 10.1007/978-3-319-23276-8_20

worthy of further investigation. A honeypot can be used to check if intruders are rattling your door locks to test your home security, and the logging is analogous to the use of wet cement for detecting footprints.

2 Background

The concept of deceiving an attacker as a network security method has origins with the work documented of Cliff Stoll in 1986 [4] where he discovered an attacker had infiltrated the systems at Lawrence Berkeley Lab where Stoll was an astronomer. Rather than locking the attacker out of the system, Stoll decided to allow the attacker to stay on the system enabling Stoll to covertly learn more about the attacker and his techniques.

Where Stoll looked to track a specific user, in 1990, Bill Cheswick [5] intentionally built a system to be attacked. Cheswick created a 'Jail' that presented a contained environment to the attacker and appeared to include vulnerabilities that allowed him to study threats and how they were compromised. With his system in place, Cheswick's work describes how it was possible to monitor a user's techniques as they infiltrated system vulnerabilities and gained control.

The idea of emulating system vulnerabilities was developed in 1997 by Fred Cohen with his Deception Toolkit (DTK) [6], regarded as the first publically available honeypot that could be downloaded and deployed on one's own systems. As well as logging the attacker's interactions, the DTK was designed to deceive and psychologically confuse them. One method was actually to use port 365 as a deception port; suggesting attackers recognise this port was in use, and therefore avoid attacking that system, or utilised as a double-bluff and advertise this port on a production system.

The term honeypot was first used by Lance Spitzner in 1999 [7] in the series of papers for the Honeynet project, 'Know your Enemy' asserted that based on the knowledge you gain discovering what attackers are looking for and their tools, this knowledge can be used to secure and protect your systems. The work of the Honeynet project established awareness and value of honeypot systems. Spitzner distinguished different interaction types of honeypots, High-interaction and Low-interaction. High-interaction honeypots offer a vulnerable real operating system allowing an attacker or worm to interact with the system, however all interactions are captured for analysis and can be used to detect zero-day attacks [8]. However high-interaction honeypots need a lot of monitoring and carry the risk that they can be compromised. Low-interaction honeypots simply look to emulate some of the services to be attacked. This is a simpler system to create, requiring less code to create the honeypot. However as a subset of services are emulated some responses or lack of them may help the attacker determine that a fake system is being attacked rather than a full system. This absence of a full operating system however reduces the risk that that honeypot system can be compromised. Spitzner also characterises different ways to deploy a honeypot, research and production. In a research environment; typically operated by anti-malware research and government organisations, methods of unauthorised access being employed by the hacker community can be gathered to gain knowledge of new attacks, leading to developments to defend against those attacks. Production honeypots are located alongside other servers on a production network to increase the security monitoring within the network. Generally production honeypots are low-interaction, accordingly capturing limited information compared to a research honeypot.

In the 2000s, network worms such as Code Red began to proliferate across the Internet, honeypots were an effective mechanism to capture the works and allow their attack to be analysed. By the mid-2000s the value of honeypots is becoming recognised, Provos & Holz [9] advocate virtual honeypots, allowing multiple honeypots to be deployed on a single system. This virtual strategy provides a more efficient method to deploy a collection of honeypot systems. If a virtual honeypot were compromised it could be restored efficiently.

Many different honeypot tools and services have been listed by the Honeynet project [10], the research aims to evaluate a range of honeypot solutions and to determine the most suitable candidate to perform attack monitoring.

3   Methodology

There are two themes to the collection of data about honeypots in this study, first is an evaluation of available honeypot systems to identify an appropriate product to perform the data collection for the second theme where we analyse the information collected by a suitable honeypot system.

3.1   Production Honeypot Products

Over the research period a variety of honeypot programs have been evaluated, some are Microsoft Windows based, while others run on a Linux distribution. Where a Linux distribution is used, the common base is Ubuntu 12.04. The Honeypot systems were given an appraisal on several criteria, such as the simplicity deploy, and the information from attacks reported.

BackOfficer Friendly. (BOF) is a simple Windows program dating from 1999, available from http://www.guardiansofjustice.com/diablo/Frames/Fileutil.htm. BOF was one of the first programs to give alerts when the system was probed for open ports. Basic replies to connections are returned, however it does provide a simple demonstration to determine how often a system is probed for intrusion.

While the live output of BOF alerts are displayed (Fig. 1) this would require the operator to constantly monitor the display, more beneficial is the log output Fig. 2 which can be used to review attacks made onto the system.

HoneyBOT. (HoneyBOT) is a commercial Windows product; however an academic version is available for the evaluation period. Simple to deploy and initially detects at lot of background noise traffic, however the ports commonly seen on a network can be turned off, leaving just the unusual ports to be monitored for unusual activity. Figure 3 demonstrates the information captured by HoneyBOT.

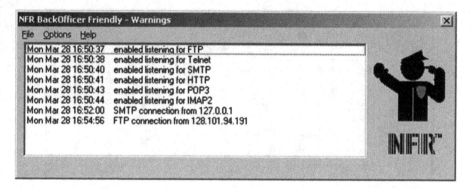

Fig. 1. Screen display from BackOfficer Friendly

```
Mon May 18 20:13:17   Telnet connection from 115.75.209.123
Mon May 18 20:13:21   Telnet login attempted from 115.75.209.123: user: root, password: admin
Mon May 18 20:13:25   Telnet connection from 115.75.209.123
Mon May 18 20:13:29   Telnet login attempted from 115.75.209.123: user: root, password: Admin
Mon May 18 20:13:33   Telnet connection from 115.75.209.123
Mon May 18 20:14:09   HTTP request from 115.75.209.123: POST /cgi-bin/firmwarecfg
Mon May 18 23:48:41   SMTP connection from 118.165.71.122
Tue May 19 06:17:31   SMTP connection from 205.209.161.229
Tue May 19 08:04:51   HTTP bogus request from 79.110.133.215: OPTIONS / HTTP/1.1
Tue May 19 09:11:58   IMAP2 connection from e17.10.140.196
Tue May 19 09:22:18   HTTP bogus request from 189.16.81.166: OPTIONS / HTTP/1.1
Tue May 19 11:16:26   SMTP connection from 118.165.86.53
Tue May 19 13:57:27   SMTP connection from 61.247.233.92
Tue May 19 14:19:55   SMTP connection from 205.209.161.229
Tue May 19 15:41:31   HTTP bogus request from 79.26.13.74: OPTIONS / HTTP/1.1
Tue May 19 16:59:59   SMTP connection from 205.209.161.229
Tue May 19 20:11:01   HTTP request from 194.177.98.221: GET //appserv/main.php?appserv_root=http://ematrimoniale.go.ro/a.txt??
Tue May 19 20:11:29   HTTP request from 194.177.98.221: GET //appserv/main.php?appserv_root=http://ematrimoniale.go.ro/a.txt??
Tue May 19 22:16:39   HTTP bogus request from 95.s19.233.38: OPTIONS / HTTP/1.1
Tue May 19 22:16:53   HTTP bogus request from 219.167.137.187: OPTIONS / HTTP/1.1
Wed May 20 01:11:57   Telnet connection from 59.184.28.85
Wed May 20 01:12:00   Telnet login attempted from 59.184.28.85: user: root, password: admin
Wed May 20 01:12:03   Telnet connection from 59.184.28.85
Wed May 20 01:12:07   Telnet login attempted from 59.184.28.85: user: root, password: Admin
Wed May 20 01:12:10   Telnet connection from 59.184.28.85
Wed May 20 01:12:13   Telnet login attempted from 59.184.28.85: user: root, password: password
Wed May 20 01:12:16   Telnet connection from 59.184.28.85
Wed May 20 01:12:39   Telnet login attempted from 59.184.28.85: user: admin, password: admin
Wed May 20 01:12:42   HTTP request from 59.184.28.85: POST /cgi-bin/firmwarecfg
Wed May 20 04:47:20   SMTP connection from 205.209.161.236
Wed May 20 10:11:44   HTTP request from 87.208.35.87: GET /w00tw00t.at.ISC.SANS.DfindD
```

Fig. 2. Log obtained from BackOfficer Friendly

Nepenthes. Turning to Linux distributions for honeypots, Provos & Holz [9], suggest Nepenthes as a system to install as a virtual honeypot. Installation is possible by down-loading and compiling the source code, however deployment packages are available to acquire the software. Unlike the previous Windows example, there is no graphical output to monitor attacks made onto the honeypot. Attack data is collected in a series of log files, Fig. 4 shows an example from *nepenthes.log*; of significance are events where a TCP connection is accepted. These lines can be parsed at the command line and used to analyse the attack, better reports require the data to be exported into a spreadsheet for manipulation.

Nepenthes, however does more than just log the attempts to connect to the honeypot, it is able to imitate some of the operating system commands, and in the occurrence of an intrusion attempting to deploy malware, the executable code is captured. Captured code can be submitted to a sandbox service to analyse the malware.

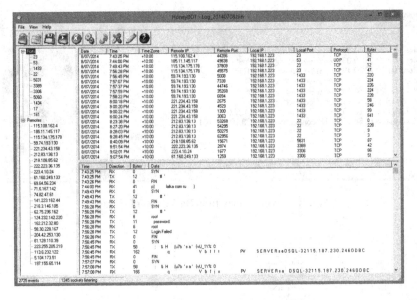

Fig. 3. Screen display from HoneyBOT

```
[09102009 15:45:40 spam net handler] <in virtual int32_t nepenthes::TCPSocket::doRecv()>
[09102009 15:45:40 spam mgr event] <in virtual uint32_t nepenthes::EventManager::handleEvent
(nepenthes::Event*)>
[09102009 15:45:40 spam net handler] doRecv() 5
[09102009 15:45:50 debug net mgr] Socket TCP  (bind) 0.0.0.0:0 -> i1.i2.i3.i4:25
    DialogueFactory Watch Factory create Watch Dialogues could Accept a Connection
[09102009 15:45:50 spam net handler] <in virtual nepenthes::Socket*
nepenthes::TCPSocket::acceptConnection()>
[09102009 15:45:50 spam net handler] Socket TCP  (accept) e1.e2.e3.e4:53781 -> i1.i2.i3.i4:25
[09102009 15:45:50 spam net handler] Adding Dialogue Watch Factory
[09102009 15:45:50 spam mgr event] <in virtual uint32_t nepenthes::EventManager::handleEvent
(nepenthes::Event*)>
[09102009 15:45:50 debug net mgr] Accepted Connection Socket TCP  (accept) e1.e2.e3.e4:53781 ->
i1.i2.i3.i4:25
32 Sockets in list
[09102009 15:45:51 spam net handler] <in virtual int32_t nepenthes::TCPSocket::doRecv()>
[09102009 15:45:51 spam mgr event] <in virtual uint32_t nepenthes::EventManager::handleEvent
(nepenthes::Event*)>
[09102009 15:45:51 spam net handler] doRecv() 2
[09102009 15:45:51 spam net handler] <in virtual int32_t nepenthes::TCPSocket::doRecv()>
[09102009 15:45:51 spam mgr event] <in virtual uint32_t nepenthes::EventManager::handleEvent
(nepenthes::Event*)>
[09102009 15:45:51 spam net handler] doRecv() 1 |
```

Fig. 4. Output from Nepenthes.Log file

Dionaea. Released as the successor to Nepenthes, however the author's experience of
the download, compilation and installation cycle has found this Dionaea to be less
straightforward and ultimately less successful than the previously tested honeypot solutions. Work by Andy Smith [11] on automating this process made getting a Dionaea
honeypot working much more efficiently. Once running, Dionaea collects attack information into logfiles and a SQLite database that requires further inspection to understand
the attacks collected by the system.

Python scripts have been developed to gain graphical representations of the data
from the command line, however additional extensions to Dionaea have provided a
graphical front end to enable an operator to get an overview of attacks on the system,

Fig. 5 illustrates some of information available. Recently a project from ThreatStream, has introduced Modern Honey Network [12] as a honeypot management system to assist in the deployment of honeypots. Dionaea is just one of several honeypots that MHN allows a user to deploy.

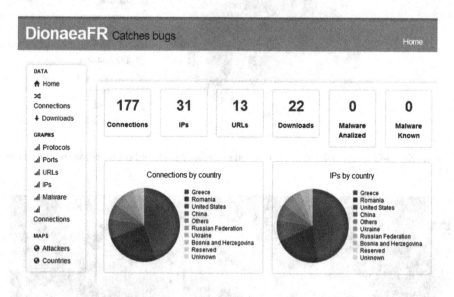

Fig. 5. DionaeaFR graphical interface (Color figure online)

Kippo. Many intrusions look to take remote control of the attacked system via the Secure Shell command interface. Kippo is a medium interaction honeypot and concentrates on emulating the SSH interface to a higher level of sophistication than Dionaea offers. Kippo is included as part of the HoneyDrive virtual appliance, that also includes Kippo-Graph [13] scripts allow the visual display of the data collected by Kippo. For example Fig. 6 shows the attempted username/password combinations are captured, and Fig. 7 utilises a Geographical mapping of source IP address to locate the origin of an attack.

During the trial, the majority of attacks are reported as originating from China and Japan.

Evaluation. The HoneyDrive distribution gives a rapid method to begin collecting attack data and easy to understand graphical display, however for this study, the MHN deployment of Dionaea was selected to collect attack data as this offered simpler access to the attack data.

3.2 Attack Data Collection

The honeypot experimental system was created on a virtual installation of Ubuntu 12.04 under VMware Workstation with a bridged network configuration allowing the virtual machine to be addressed on the network. After installation of Ubuntu, the Modern Honey

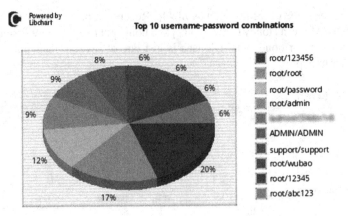

Fig. 6. Kippo-Graph visualisation of collected username / password combinations (Color figure online)

Fig. 7. Kippo-Graph Geo IP representation of source address of attacks

Network −11− platform was installed and configured following default settings. The honeypot system was then connected to a DMZ arm of the firewall and configured with a public address. Once the MHN platform was running, it offers a choice of scripts to deploy under the MHN platform. A Dionaea honeypot [14] was selected and the command generated was executed on the Ubuntu command line.

This initiates the installation of a Dionaea honeypot. Once a honeypot is deployed, there is a wait to see when an attack is detected, although an interaction can be forced with an nmap [15] scan against the IP address of the MHN system. When connected to a public IP address the first attack can come in minutes after deployment.

MHN offers a map representation of live attacks, see Fig. 8 for an example, an interesting graphical overview of the attacks being logged by the honeypot, however the database of the attack information can be extracted for deeper analysis. Additionally if you have a VirusTotal account, the Dionaea configuration can be updated with a suitable API Key and captured malware can be automatically directed to VirusTotal for analysis.

For the data analysis, the R statistical programing language [16] with the R-Studio [17] interface was installed. R is a free system allowing the user to write scripts to analyse the data. The data from MHN was exported via FTP to the R workstation for analysis.

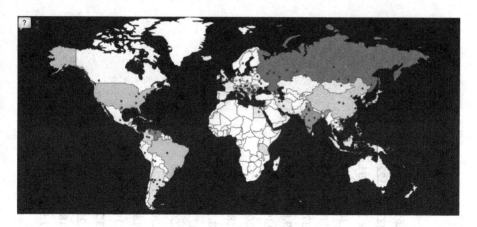

Fig. 8. Live map of attacks

Scripts were written to remove unrequired information, and manipulate the timestamp fields by reformatting strings to date-time objects.

Among the fields available for analysis were: timestamp, source IP address and destination port. R scripts were developed to summarise the data and display bar charts.

4   Data Results

4.1   Source IP Address

Figure 9 shows that over the period of the experiment, the IP Address 188.165.238.186 attacked the DMZ honeypot 13708 times. This is noteworthy as the next most frequent source IP addresses generated around 500 attacks. The count of attacks was almost 30 times greater than the average number of attacks for a typical address in the remaining 19 of the top 20.

4.2   Destination Port

Figure 10 shows the destination port of attacks over the period of the experiment, notably Session Initiation Protocol (SIP) port 5060 attracted a relatively large number of attacks compared against other attacks looking for vulnerabilities in Microsoft Directory Services (445) SSH Remote Login Protocol (22) and Telnet (23).

4.3   Timestamp

Figure 11 shows an average of around 500 attacks per day, however there is a distinct peak around 18th and 19th November 2014.

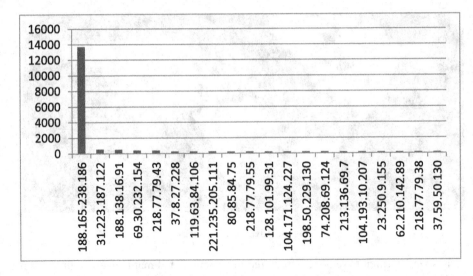

Fig. 9. Analysis of source address

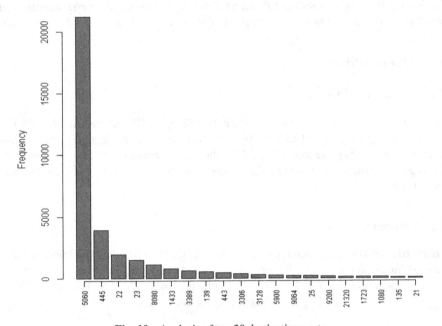

Fig. 10. Analysis of top 20 destination ports

5 Data Analysis

The honeypot was connected to a public facing IP address and gathered a lot of unsolicited interest from remote devices. Regarding the number of attacks per day, we can establish a baseline of the number of expected attacks, and therefore be aware when this

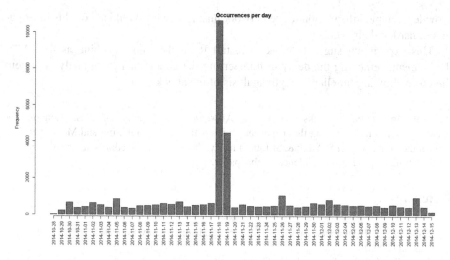

Fig. 11. Analysis data timestamp

threshold is exceeded would statistically indicate a more persistent stream of attacks. For this honeypot experiment number of attacks per day (n = 49) averaged 484 (σ157) in the experiment period 28th October to 15 December 2014. This implies that the mean of the population of attacks onto experimental honeypot, with 95 % confidence, is in the interval of 484 ±(1.96 × 157), which is from 176 to 792. This would suggest a exceeding a threshold of around 800 attacks per day would indicate extraordinary activity and merit further investigation.

The graphs indicate where peaks in the data occur, when regarding the results of timestamp, source and destination together we can establish that between the 18th and 19th November 2014, IP address 188.165.238.186 generated over 14,000 attacks on port 5060. This suggests a sustained attack against Session Initiation Protocol (SIP), a protocol for handling telephone calls over an IP network. Our organisation currently does not use SIP, so this traffic would be denied at the firewall, however the awareness that SIP vulnerabilities are actively sought [18] would inform the network manager to harden any SIP services that may be installed in future.

6   Summary and Conclusion

There are many varieties of honeypot deployments, and we have established that an implementation of Dionaea allowed the collection of a rich set of attack data. Other well established honeypots from the Honeynet projects page need to be examined for comparison, during the period of the study extra honeypot features became available, such as Splunk in MHN and Kibana for Kippo.

The honeypot deployment only offers limited vision of attacks to its IP address rather than the whole sub-network. Nevertheless the honeypot indicated the number of attacks a public facing IP address attracts, and emphasises the need for security on these systems. Evidence specifying the source of threats and how they attempt to infiltrate the system provide valuable information to the network manager, who should act on this information to harden their security.

This experiment suggests work to install R on the same machine as the MHN deployment, removing the delay in transferring the attack data to an analysis system therefore allowing timelier in depth analysis of the attack data.

Acknowledgements. Thanks to Ameer Al-Nemrat, University of East London for encouragement on developing this paper and support from the Computing and Media Services team at the University of St Mark & St John. Finally, thank you to the editors and peer reviewers for their time, expertise and guidance on this paper.

References

1. Spitzner, L.: Honeypots: Tracking Hackers. Addison-Wesley Educational Publishers Inc., Boston (2003)
2. Kaur, T., Malhotra, V., Singh, D.: Comparison of network security tools - firewall, intrusion detection system and Honeypot. Int. J. Enhanced Res. Sci. Technol. Eng. 200–204 (2014)
3. Joshi, R., Sardana, A.: Honeypots: A New Paradigm to Information Security. Science Publishers, Enfield (2011)
4. Stoll, C.: The Cuckoo's Egg: Tracking a Spy Through the Maze of Computer Espionage. Pocket Books, New York (2007)
5. Cheswick, B.: An evening with Berferd. In: Denning, D., Denning, P. (eds.) Internet besieged, pp. 103–116. ACM Press/Addison-Wesley Publishing Co., New York (1998)
6. Cohen, F.: The Deception toolkit home page and mailing list. In: All.Net. http://www.all.net/dtk/. Accessed 30 Mar 2015
7. Honeynet Project: Know your enemy: III. In: Honeynet Project. http://old.honeynet.org/papers/enemy3/. 30 Accessed Mar 2015
8. Göbel, J., Dewald, A.: Client-Honeypots: Exploring Malicious Websites. Oldenbourg Verlag, München (2011)
9. Provos, N., Holz, T.: Virtual Honeypots: From Botnet Tracking to Intrusion Detection. Pearson Education, Boston (2007)
10. Honeynet Project: Projects. http://www.honeynet.org/project. Accessed June 2015
11. Quick install of Dionaea on Ubuntu. In: Andy Smith's Blog. http://andrewmichaelsmith.com/2012/02/quick-install-of-dionaea-on-ubuntu/. Accessed May 2015
12. Trost, J.: Modern honey network. In: ThreatStream. https://www.threatstream.com/blog/mhn-modern-honey-network. Accessed May 2015
13. Kippo-Graph. In: BruteForce. https://bruteforce.gr/kippo-graph. Accessed May 2015
14. Dionaea - Catches bugs. In: Carnivore. http://dionaea.carnivore.it/. Accessed March 2015
15. Insecure.org: Nmap security scanner. In: Nmap.org. http://nmap.org/. Accessed March 2015
16. R Project: Getting started. In: The R Project for Statistical Computing. http://www.r-project.org/. Accessed March 2015
17. RStudio: Take control of your R code. In: RStudio. http://www.rstudio.com/products/rstudio/. Accessed March 2015
18. Popeskic: Attack on SIP protocol – VoIP vulnerability. In: How does Internet work. http://howdoesinternetwork.com/2012/voip-sip-attack. Accessed 1 June 2012

An Immunity Based Configuration for Multilayer Single Featured Biometric Authentication Algorithms

Henrique Santos[1], Sérgio Tenreiro de Magalhães[1,2(✉)], and Maria José Magalhães[2]

[1] Algoritmi Research Center, University of Minho, Guimarães, Portugal
{hsantos,psmagalhaes}@dsi.uminho.pt
[2] Faculty of Philosophy and Social Sciences, Catholic University of Portugal, Braga, Portugal
{stmagalhaes,mjmagalhaes}@braga.ucp.pt

Abstract. Immune systems have been used in the last years to inspire approaches for several computational problems. This paper focus on behavioural biometric authentication algorithms' accuracy enhancement by using them more than once and with different thresholds in order to first simulate the protection provided by the skin and then look for known outside entities, like lymphocytes do. The paper describes the principles that support the application of this approach to Keystroke Dynamics, an authentication biometric technology that decides on the legitimacy of a user based on his typing pattern captured on he enters the username and/or the password and, as a proof of concept, the accuracy levels of one keystroke dynamics algorithm when applied to five legitimate users of a system both in the traditional and in the immune inspired approaches are calculated and the obtained results are compared.

Keywords: Authentication · Biometrics · Bio inspired systems

1 Introduction

The way that the living creatures fight intrusions in their systems, by virus or any other intruders, have inspired many approaches in the Computer Sciences. What this paper presents is an approach that can help to increase the accuracy levels of biometric authentication systems, by imitating the way immunity systems distinguish a cell that is friendly and in the correct place, from an external cell (like a bacteria) or an internal cell placed incorrectly (like a liver cell reproducing itself in the heart).

2 The Immunity System

Complex living beings have several layers of protection. In the human case, the first of them all are the external barriers like the skin, a membrane that surrounds the body protecting it from external arming elements, this is, elements that are very distinct from what is supposed to be inside the body are kept out of it. This process is made without any implications in the comfort of the user but, unfortunately for us, some non-desirable elements can make their way through the external barriers, causing diseases.

© Springer International Publishing Switzerland 2015
H. Jahankhani et al. (Eds.): ICGS3 2015, CCIS 534, pp. 239–243, 2015.
DOI: 10.1007/978-3-319-23276-8_21

The second layer of protection is constituted by the leucocytes, cell that have some kind of chemical memory that allows them to identify an intruder's cell and to know how to react to them. This memory bank is updated whenever a new infection is fought with success, or when new information is introduced externally in the form of vaccines.

3   Biometric Technologies

In the Computer Science context, biometric technologies refer to the use of specific measures of person's physical or behavioural characteristics to authenticate him (process of confirming an alleged identity) or identify him (process of establishing an identity towards an information System. This use of personal data has become a widely discussed subject. While governments and corporations are pressing for a deeper integration of these technologies with common security systems (like passports or identity cards), human rights associations are concerned with the ethical and social implications of its use. This situation creates a challenge to find biometric algorithms that are less intrusive, easier to use and more accurate [1].

The precision of a biometric technology is usually measured by its False Acceptance Rate (FAR), the permeability of the algorithm to attacks, by its False Rejection Rate (FRR), the resistance of the algorithm to accept a legitimate user, and by its Crossover Error Rate (CER), the interception point of the FAR curve with the FRR curve, that indicates the level of usability of the technology (see Fig. 1). Typically, when an algorithm is forced to be more restrictive, its FAR gets lower but its FRR gets higher; usually the FAR and FRR values are defined by the system administrator, according to the security requirements – normally an outcome of the risk evaluation. The threshold can also be, in theory, dynamic and defined with the help of an Intrusion Detection System [1].

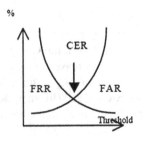

Fig. 1. CER – Crossover Error Rate

Establishing the error rates of a biometric technology is a complex issue. Studies have been made to normalize that evaluation, but the results are strongly dependent of the number of individuals involved in the process and, what is worst, of their characteristics. This means that, even with a large amount of data collected, the results can be very different if the evaluated group is changed. This happens because it is very difficult to obtain a sample representative of the population, since we do not know how to characterize the population. A good example of this disparity are the results of the Fingerprint

Verification Competition (FVC) 2004, where the best CER achieved was 2,07 % [2], compared with the results of the FVC 2002, where the best CER achieved was 0,19 % [3]. Some international companies were present in both contests and the only justification for the disparity of the results is the difference in the sample data used to test the algorithms. This means two algorithms are only comparable using the same test data. The results also vary according to the final use: a system used to identify an individual is less accurate that a system used to just authenticate him/her.

4 The Immunity Approach to Biometric Authentication

Until now, biometric authentication algorithms are implemented by establishing a threshold that defines the level of tolerance used to accept a pattern that is presented to the system as belonging to a specific user. This means that every time a user tries to enter the system, the algorithm is used only once: to compare the proposed pattern with the one from the supposedly legitimate user that is trying to enter. In order to keep the comfort levels, the system's administrator is forced to decrease the security levels. What it is now proposed is a two stages authentication process that imitates the immunity systems. The next sections explain those two stages and present the results obtained when testing this methodology in a small group of five users. For this proof of concept, an algorithm of keystroke dynamics, a behavioural biometric technology that can be used with the collaboration of the user or in stealth mode and that allows a high precision level, both in authentication and in identification, was used. Furthermore it does not require any special device since it works by analysing the user keystroke patterns, as he types (a password, a passphrase or general text) on a keyboard. Due to the possible integration level, these algorithms can also adjust their parameters to adapt themselves to evolutions of the user typing patterns. It is important to notice that all the error rates here presented and related to this technology are calculated after the secret code is made public. For instance, a False Acceptance Rate of 10 % means that, if one makes its secret password public (e.g. by losing a paper where he has written it) 10 % of the attackers will have access to my account, while 90 % of the user's will be rejected despite having the correct password. This biometric is now well know and quite mature [4–6] and has also been used as the base algorithms for some for initial developments of pointer dynamics, a behaviour biometric technologies that uses the user's patterns created when using a pointing device or the finger (in touchscreens) [7, 8].

4.1 Stage 1 – The External Barrier

Imitating the immunity systems, the first run of the algorithm uses a threshold that can provide a low False Rejection Rate, despite the resulting high False Acceptance Rate. What it is aimed at this stage is to reject all those patterns that are clearly too distinct from the user's, without reducing the comfort of the user. In many biometric technologies it is possible to obtain in this stage a False Rejection Rate equal to zero, while rejecting more than 50 % of the attackers.

4.2 Stage 2 – The Leucocytes Barrier

The second stage aims to use the existing knowledge on other patterns to verify if the proposed one is very similar to one know by the systems as belonging to someone that is not the alleged legitimate user. This is done by comparing the proposed pattern with all the other patterns in the database (from other legitimate users and from unsuccessful attempts that were never associated to any user) using the some authentication algorithm but with a threshold that can provide a very low False Acceptance Rate. So this will establish a high level of certainty if a pattern belongs to someone else, if so the proposed pattern is rejected, like leucocytes establish if a cell is a virus or bacteria. Patterns belonging to know hackers can be fed to the system, providing vaccines against known attacks.

4.3 The Algorithm

In order to verify if this methodology has implementation potential, instead of being only a theoretical approach, a test was done using existing biometric records resultant from a previous experience with keystroke dynamics. The used algorithm has two distinct phases: the enrolment and the authentication attempt. In the enrolment phase, the user types his secret key twelve times and the systems records the times spent between the several strokes, calculating the average, the median and the standard deviation for those twelve times. The authentication attempt phase consists on, for each two keys stroked, collect the Proposed (once the alleged user is proposing that time as a legitimate one) Time Spent – PTS – and compare it with the corresponding value stored during the enrolment stage through the acceptance criteria presented in Eq. (1), where alpha is a definable parameter that was set in 0,05 [1]. This correct use of this variable in this particular setting requires further studies.

$$Lowest(Average, median) * [1 - \alpha - Sdeviation/Average]$$
$$\leq PTS \leq Higher(Average, median) * [1 + \alpha + Sdeviation/Average]$$

Once all the times corresponding to the sequence of keys constituting the secret password were classified, they received the value of 0 (zero) if they didn't satisfy the criteria, 1 (one) if the time satisfies the criteria and the time before didn't (or if it is the first time evaluated) and 1.5 (one point five) if it satisfies the criteria and so did the time before. Those values were added together and the final sum A corresponded to the level of trust in the presented pattern. If the value A is not smaller than the defined threshold (a defined parameter) then the user is accepted as legitimate and the algorithm replaces the oldest stored time sequence by this one, therefore allowing some evolution in a user's pattern.

5 Empiric Results

The simulation included 70 login attempts to establish the FAR, from four users belonging to a system with nine legitimate users and many attacking patterns from hundreds of illegitimate users. A simulation with 65528 illegitimate attacks was done to establish the FRR. For the some data two runs were made. The first used the traditional approach in the average CER threshold and the second used the immunity approach with the skin's threshold set at seven and the leucocytes' threshold set at nineteen. The results were better, despite the fact that the algorithm was not specifically designed for this approach, with the FAR falling from 3,28 % to 2,96 % (after the secret password is made public) and the FRR falling from 16,87 % to 13,89 %.

6 Conclusions

In conclusion, this paper has presented a new approach, based on the immunity systems, which can be applied to any existing authentication biometric technology. Further studies are required to verify, for each technology, if there are advantages in adapting the algorithms and if this work both with small systems (with limited number of users) and with big systems (like those web based). Nevertheless, the existing tests seem to indicate that this is an approach that can improve in a significant way the accuracy of the biometric authentication processes.

Acknowledgements. This work has been supported by FCT – Fundação para a Ciência e Tecnologia within the Project Scope UID/CEC/00319/2013.

References

1. Magalhães, S.T., Revett, K., Santos, H.: Password secured sites - stepping forward with keystroke dynamics. In: Proceedings of the IEEE International Conference on Next Generation Web Services Practices. IEEE CS Press (2005)
2. Maio, D., Maltoni, D., Cappelli, R., Wayman, J.L., Jain, A.K.: FVC2004: third fingerprint verification competition. In: Zhang, D., Jain, A.K. (eds.) ICBA 2004. LNCS, vol. 3072, pp. 1–7. Springer, Heidelberg (2004)
3. Maltoni, D., Maio, D., Jain, A.K., Prabhakar, S.: Handbook of Fingerprint Recognition. Springer, New York (2003)
4. Revett, K.R., Tenreiro de Magalhães, S., Santos, H.M.D.: On the use of rough sets for user authentication via keystroke dynamics. In: Neves, J., Santos, M.F., Machado, J.M. (eds.) EPIA 2007. LNCS (LNAI), vol. 4874, pp. 145–159. Springer, Heidelberg (2007)
5. Revett, K., et al.: A machine learning approach to keystroke dynamics based user authentication. Int. J. Electron. Secur. Digit. Forensics 1(1), 55–70 (2007)
6. Stefan, D., Shu, X., Yao, D.D.: Robustness of keystroke-dynamics based biometrics against synthetic forgeries. Comput. Secur. 31(1), 109–121 (2012)
7. Revett, K., de Magalhães, S.T.: Cognitive biometrics: challenges for the future. In: Tenreiro de Magalhães, S., Jahankhani, H., Hessami, A.G. (eds.) ICGS3 2010. CCIS, vol. 92, pp. 79–86. Springer, Heidelberg (2010)
8. Revett, K., Jahankhani, H., de Magalhães, S.T., Santos, H.M.: User dynamics in graphical authentication systems. In: Jahankhani, H., Revett, K., Palmer-Brown, D. (eds.) Global E-Security, pp. 173–181. Springer, Berlin (2008)

Security and Feasibility of Power Line Communication System

Ali Hosseinpour[1], Amin Hosseinian-Far[2(⊠)], Hamid Jahankhani[3],
and Alireza Ghadrdanizadi[4]

[1] School of Architecture, Computing and Engineering,
University of East London, London, UK
Najarkolaei@ieee.org
[2] School of Computing, Creative Technologies and Engineering,
Leeds Beckett University, Leeds, UK
A.Hosseinian-Far@leedsbeckett.ac.uk
[3] GSM London, London, UK
Hamid.Jahankhani@gsm.org.uk
[4] Azad University, Tehran Central, Iran
Alirezaizi@yahoo.com

Abstract. Power Line Communication (PLC) has the potential to become the preferred connectivity technique for providing broadband to homes and offices with advantage of eliminating the need for new wiring infrastructure and reducing the cost. The PLC channel, its characterization, standardization and applications has been well studied. However, the security of PLC has not been investigated sufficiently, and such assessments are required for prospective implementation of successful PLC communication systems. Since PLC uses power line as the medium, it has similar characteristics with wireless communications from the security perspective. This paper provides discussion of security issues and feasibility for PLC networks. The authentication and cryptographic scheme used in PLC standard is also discussed.

Keywords: Authentication · Cryptography · Integrity control · Power Line Communication · Security

1 Introduction

Today the Internet technology has become an important phenomenon in business, academia, and daily life. Wired internet network (such as XDSL and cable networks) and wireless internet networks (e.g. Wireless Local Area Network) are readily available in urban areas rather than rural areas for commercial reasons. A PLC system therefore becomes an attractive option for high speed data transfer for communication in such regions. Broadband over power line can provide Internet access over the power line system. A laptop or any other device can theoretically be plugged into any power outlet (by use of PLC modem) in building to get access to high-speed internet [1]. The main advantage of using the existing infrastructure of power line grid would result in economising the infrastructure cost and providing Internet to customers in areas with

© Springer International Publishing Switzerland 2015
H. Jahankhani et al. (Eds.): ICGS3 2015, CCIS 534, pp. 244–251, 2015.
DOI: 10.1007/978-3-319-23276-8_22

limited access to internet infrastructural service - e.g. in rural areas and for the customers who do not have access to cable modems. Conversely, power line cables are not designed for transfer of data; therefore there are limiting factors such as electromagnetic interference, degrading the system such as from noise loads and other devices connected to the power line grid. While, several approaches have previously been attempted to avoid these issues, such gaps still exist in security aspect of providing high bit-rate transmission through power lines. The aim of this paper is to investigate suitable techniques for securing PLC systems. Such techniques will facilitate defensive approach against any security threat that such systems may face. The following section provides a brief overview of the basic concept of PLC channel and securing options and then it is then followed by a discussion on PLC feasibility study.

2 Power Line Distribution Systems

A power plant generates the electric power then transports it through High Voltage (HV) cables to Medium Voltage (MV) substations. The substation transforms the Medium Voltage into Lower Voltage (LV) and then distributes it to a large number of LV grids. Typical voltage values for HV, MV and LV transmission lines respectively are 425 kV, 33 kV and 11 kV [2].

PLC works through electrical signals. These signals carry information over the power line. A communication channel can be explained as a physical path that exists between two communicating nodes [3].

The type of communication that takes place through the power line channels determines the quality of the channel [4]. The channel quality is generally a factor of the level of the noise at the receiver and the attenuation of the electrical signal at different frequencies [5]. The noise on the power line is generated by every load (electrical devices), which is linked to the grid. The power line is considered as a very harsh environment due to the time variant attributes of the noise and the attenuation [5]. However, this also prevails in most communication systems and limits the performance that can be achieved.

PLC systems comprise different components which function together to provide Internet connectivity services to consumers in their houses, offices or buildings. The data is carried by either fibre optic or telephone lines to avoid HV transmission power lines [6]. As illustrated in Fig. 1, the data is injected into the MV power distribution grid and special electronic devices, known as repeaters, re-amplify and re-transmit the signal because the signal loses strength as it travels along the MV power line. Other technologies are used to detour the signal around transformers [7].

3 Power Line Communication (PLC) and Its Applications

Due to the increasing importance of communication networking, the power line channel has been considered as a good candidate for the communication medium. PLC is using an existing power line system, i.e., this is great saving in cost and time. The general idea of PLC system is to modulate a radio signal with data and transmit it

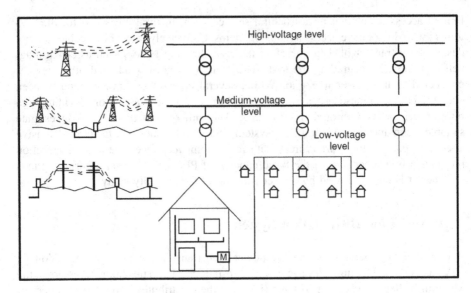

Fig. 1. Structure of electrical supply

through power line channels in a different band of frequencies that are not used for supplying electricity. PLC technology can be divided into two categories; the narrowband and Broadband communication. The frequency range of up to 150 kHz is for narrowband with the theoretical bit rate of kilobits (up to 2 Mbit/s). The frequency range for Broadband technology is between 1.61–30 MHz with theoretical bit rate up to 200 Mbit/s. Remote switching of public lights (single- directional communication), gas/electric meter reading and home automation application such as fire detection and intruder alarm (bidirectional application) are some of the narrowband application for PLC. Nowadays due to increase in demand for high speed data broadband, PLC technology provides a wide range of application such as video, voice, multimedia and networking to customers at their houses [8].

The narrowband PLC are normally used in automation systems. The automation systems based on PLC technology are implemented with no any additional insulation of communication networks which results substantially reduction in costs for the installation and realisation of the new network within the existing buildings. The automation system in this system can be used in [9]:

(i)   Central control of various home system such as controlling doors/windows
(ii) Controlling connected devices to the internal wiring such as lighting, air conditions
(iii) The Security function, sensor control

Another application for narrowband technology is called smart metering. The smart meter system includes meters at the consumer site, communication medium between a service provider and consumer, such as a gas, an electric, or water, and data management systems in service provider site that make the information available. The smart meter transmits the collected data through PLC to a Meter Data Management System for data analysis and billing (Fig. 2).

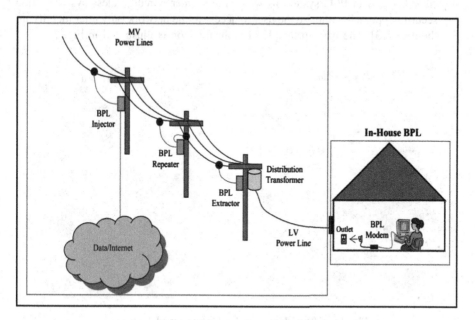

Fig. 2. Overview of End to End PLC system [17]

4 Security of Power Line Communication Systems

One of the major issues in any telecommunication system is a Security. This is even bigger issue in the case of using a shared medium/channel such as a power line channel. However, in theory the PLC system is more secure compare to the wireless system due to the fact that the physical medium of power line channel is not easy to get accessed [10]. For instance, with suitable tools, the Wi-Fi system which uses a shared channel with its accessibility for people in the coverage area the network traffic can possibly be intercepted and even any electronic device connected to the network can also be reconfigured [11].

Another advantage of security aspect for PLC is its potential for involved danger due to the presence of the AC electrical signal [12].

Although in theory the power line systems are more resistant to attacks, but they are not fully protected and need some software security to reach to the acceptable security levels against possible attacks such as an [11];

- attacks for damaging the available working network
- attack to prevent the system operation
- attack that aims to access to the devices connected to the network

These possible treat can possibly be countered by use of:

(a) Authentication is one of the possible software security approaches that can possibly be used in PLC system as well as any other wired/wireless systems. This security approach authorise the user to access to the network only after identifying the user [13]. The basic principle of authentication is illustrated in Fig. 3.

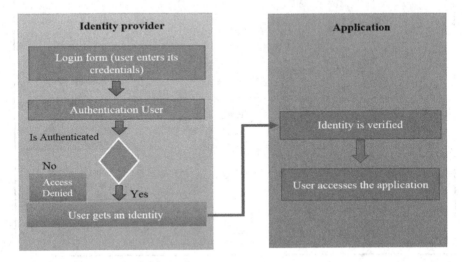

Fig. 3. A flow chart of authentication for PLC system

(b) Cryptography is an approach that can be used in PLC network to deny hackers access to the information in the network. An encryption key is used to encode the information before transmission through the channel. The encoded information makes the signals incomprehensible to the hackers. A decoding key then required to retrieve the coded information carried in the signal at the receiver side. The basic principle of cryptography is illustrated in Fig. 4 an encryption key is used to encode a plain text. At any time during the transmission, somebody can recover the encrypted text, called a cryptogram, and try to decipher it using various methods.

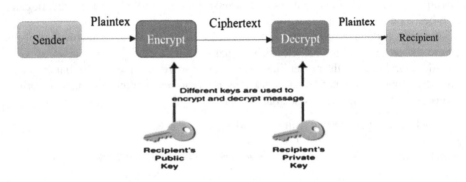

Fig. 4. Generic schematic of cryptography

There are three different types of Cryptography:

1. Shared key cryptography: When the same/common key is used to encrypt or decrypt the data [14].
2. Public key cryptography: different keys can be used to encrypt and decrypt the data. As there are two keys, the encryption key can be shared to anyone i.e. it is a public key, so that anyone can use this public key to encrypt the data. But only the owner of the decryption key can decrypt the message. This key is called as private key [15].
3. Modern Cryptography: these algorithms (such as RSA-public key algorithm and AES-symmetric algorithm) are widely used in many domains such as WEP, HTTP, SSL [16].

(c) Integrity control is used to identify if the sent information through the power line network has been modified during transmission. Electronic signatures can be used to check if the received information has been any changed or modified during the transmission over the power line networks [18]. Therefore it stops any unauthorised change to information passing through the transmission channel.

5 Feasibility of Power Line Communication

The feasibility of PLC system has been investigated in [19]. Due to importance of energy for living, electricity are ever-present in most of the residential (urban and rural) areas compared to telephone systems. Therefore, it would be rationale to provide high speed data to consumers at their homes as it comes cheaper compared to providing high speed data with the coaxial or telephone cables. Especially in areas where a DSL or a cable is not available, power line grid can be a cost effective connectivity solution.

Evidently, using an existing infrastructure for high speed data transmission would be a great reduction in the network deployment cost. The feasibility of such a system has been investigated for a few countries. In rural areas the provision of the PLC system for data transmission in place of the current alternative technologies (wireless/satellite), such as a backhaul and last mile, has been considered.

From the technological perspective, the basic idea of PLC system is just to modulate a radio signal with data and send it through the power lines in a range of frequencies which are not used for supplying electricity. As it was mentioned earlier, the frequencies used and the encoding approach have a significant influence on the efficiency and the speed of PLC technology. From the customer's perspective, the equipment needed to set up PLC in the building (home/office) is cheaper compared to other broadband solutions such as cable and DSL modems due to the need for additional wiring or installation.

Although the PLC system does not appear to represent the major distribution technology in competitive markets, it is very suitable for rural areas and can be considered as the major strategy for future policy. In addition any progress in the PLC system with high speed data transmission can be a great aid for the transmission of narrow band system such as those used in smart meter technologies (gas and electricity) [19].

6 Conclusions

There is an increase interest in the PLC technology as an alternative for data transmission over power lines. However, the security aspects of PLC have not been well explored. This paper presents a brief overview of PLC systems, some of its applications and its security issues with possible solutions. An authentication procedure, cryptography and Integrity control for security of the PLC networks were discussed. However these security schemes are just in theory and may not eliminate the vulnerability perfectly. More researches are required for security standards for PLC to protect critical private information.

References

1. Agrawal, D.G., Paliwal, R.K., Subramanium, P.: Effect of turbo coding on OFDM transmission to improve BER. Int. J. Comput. Technol. Electron. Eng. (IJCTEE) 2(1), 94–102 (2011)
2. Al Mawali, K.S.: Techniques for broadband power line communications: impulsive noise mitigation and adaptive modulation. School of Electrical and Computer Engineering College of Science, Engineering and Health College of Science, RMIT University, Melbourne, Victoria (2011)
3. Apoorva, A., Singla, P.: A review of information sharing through shared key cryptography. Int. J. Res. Eng. Technol. Manag. 1–6 (2014)
4. Cacciaguerra, F.: Introduction to power line communication (November 2003). http://en.kioskea.net/contents/cpl/cpl-intro.php3. Accessed June 2011
5. Carcelle, X.: Power Line Communications in Practice. Artech house, London (2006)
6. Celebi, H.B.: Noise and multipath characteristics of power line communication channels. Doctoral Thesis, University of South Florida, Florida (2010)
7. Consumer Focus UK GOV: Smart meters – what are they and how can I find out more? (Consumer Focus) (2013). http://www.consumerfocus.org.uk/get-advice/energy/smart-meters-what-are-they-and-how-can-i-find-out-more/benefits-and-disadvantages-of-smart-meters. Accessed 29 August 2013
8. Diffie, W.: The first ten years of public key cryptography. Proc. IEEE 76(5), 560–577 (1998)
9. Dostert, K.: Telecommunications over the power distribution grid; possibilities and limitations. In: International Symposium on Power Line Communications and its Applications, Essen, Germany (1997)
10. Fernandes, A.D., Dave, P.: Power Line Communication in Energy Markets. CYPRESS, San Jose (2011)
11. Fink, D., Jeung, R.J.: Connectivity Solutions Based on Power Line Communication to Rural and Remote Areas. Information and Communication University, Korea (2008)
12. Grosse, E., Upandhyay, M.: Authentication at scale. IEEE Comput. Reliab. Soc. 11, 15–22 (2013)
13. Haldankar, C., Kuwelkar, S.: Implementation of AES and blowfish algorithm. IJRET: Int. J. Res. Eng. Technol. 3(3), 143–146 (2014)
14. Hosseinpournajarkolaei, A., Hosseinian-Far, A.: Channel characterization for broadband power line communication system. In: 6th SASTech International Symposium. Sastech, Kuala Lampur (2012)

15. Hosseinpournajarkolaei, A., Jahankhani, H., Hosseinian-Far, A.: Vulnerability considerations for power line communication's (PLC) supervisory control and data acquisition. Int. J. Electron. Secur. Digit. Forensics 6(2), 104–114 (2014)
16. Hosseinpournajarkolaei, A., Lota, J., Hosny, W.: Data transfer over low-voltage european power distribution. In: 47th Power Engineering Conference. IEEE, UPEC, London (2012)
17. Industry Canada: Consultation Paper on Broadband over Power Line Communication Systems (2005). https://www.ic.gc.ca/eic/site/smt-gst.nsf/vwapj/bpl-e.pdf/$FILE/bpl-e.pdf. Accessed August 2015
18. Lu, X., Wang, W., Ma, J.: Authentication and integrity in the smart grid: an empirical study in substation automation systems. Int. J. Distrib. Sens. Netw. 2012, 1–13 (2012)
19. Selander, L.: Load profile and communication channel characteristics of the low voltage grid. DistribuTech DA/DSM Europe 98, London (1998)

A Comparison Study for Different Wireless Sensor Network Protocols

Faris Al-Baadani and Sufian Yousef[✉]

Anglia Ruskin University, Chelmsford, UK
sufian.yousef@anglia.ac.uk

Abstract. In Wireless Sensor Network (WSN) nodes are usually communicate with each other through wireless channels with no need for any network infrastructure. Multiple hops are used by the nodes to exchange data, therefore a routing protocol is needed to communicate in such a network for efficient, short time delivery of the data and prolong the network life. There are different types of protocols can be used in these networks based on what is used for. In this study, AODV, DSDV, DSR were explained and compared as they are some of the main protocols used in WSN. We also highlight the Throughput and Average End to End delay which been used to compare these protocols with variations of the number of nodes.

Keywords: AODV · DSDV · DSR · MANET · WSN throughput · Average delay

1 Introduction

The growing interest in wireless network creates new challenges requiring the adoption of application specific deployment. Mobile adhoc networks (MANET) addresses the use of wireless network in applications where nodes communicate with each other without any existing infrastructure and wirelessly. MANET allows multihop transport to destination and has the advantage of flexibility, rapid deployment, robustness, and inherent support for mobility [1]. The flexibility of MANET enable self-configuration and self-administration, effectively making it attractive for various applications in military operations, wireless mesh networks, and wireless sensor networks (WSN). Due to the requirement for a prolonged network life in WSN, the routing protocol deployed should be efficient in power consumption. This way, the availability, reliability, and efficiency of the WSN can be guaranteed. Routing protocols WSN networks can be classified into two main categories: Proactive or table Driven routing protocols and on-demand routing protocols [2].

The former maintains a routing table for a source-destination pair and a path computation process is triggered each time a change is detected in the network. Example of table driven protocol is Destination Sequenced Distance Vector (DSDV). On-demand, on the other hand, does not require route entries in a table and the routes are created at the time of request. It can be fully on demand in which all creation of paths and advertisements are purely on request basis. Partial on-demand allows the protocol to send

© Springer International Publishing Switzerland 2015
H. Jahankhani et al. (Eds.): ICGS3 2015, CCIS 534, pp. 252–259, 2015.
DOI: 10.1007/978-3-319-23276-8_23

periodic information on the network. Example of on-demand protocol is Ad hoc On-Demand Distance Vector Routing (AODV) and Dynamic Source Routing (DSR). Various research works have attempted to present comparisons between the various routing protocols based on packet delivery fraction (Pdf), Average End to End Delay and Routing Load [3, 4]. This paper aims to provide a step by step comparative analysis of the three WSN routing protocols: AODV, DSR and DSDV based on Throughput and Average End to End Delay.

The rest of the paper is organized as follows: Sect. 2 presents an overview of the Wireless routing protocol that is analysed and compared. Section 3 gives a brief description of the Simulation parameters, assumptions hold and description of the step by step comparing methodology used in the paper. Section 4 provides the simulation results and discusses it. Finally the conclusion is provided in Sect. 5.

2 Wireless Routing Protocols

Mobile Ad Hoc Networks can be divided into Table-Driven and On-Demand Routing protocol where Table Driven protocols are proactive and maintain a routing table and On-Demand are active and do not maintain a routing table. The following routing protocols are analyzed in the research:

2.1 Ad hoc On-Demand Distance Vector Routing (AODV)

AODV [5] is a wireless routing protocol which uses the traditional routing table mechanism where the routes are calculated on-demand. It employs periodic message advertisement by node to other neighbouring nodes in the network. The table maintains one entry per destination, it uses the destinations sequence numbers associated with each entry or routing packet to prevent routing loops and establish the routing information updates. Enforcing sequence number preference, a requesting node is required to choose the route with highest sequence number. The sequence numbers are changed every time a node identify itself as the destination node, a link break or expiration update is received from neighbouring nodes, or an AODV message with new information is received.

In AODV, only active entries in the communication path are maintained in the routing table, effectively eliminating the "infinite path" issue and the expensive Bellman-Ford Algorithm. Routing tables are updated at both the end and intermediate nodes using information in the route request (RREQ) and route reply (RREP) respectively. Error trace mechanism is implemented to check link failures on a per neighbourhood update. The error message is in form of a route error (RERR). RERR consist of fields to indicate the failure type, the unreachable destination IP, and the number of unreachable destination count [5]. On receiving the failure update each router on the path erases unreachable entries in its routing table. All messages are exchanged using the UDP or traditional IP based protocol. Another feature of this protocol is the capability to switch traffic using least congested path as routes are computed at the time of forwarding (on-demand).

A fundamental requirement of AODV is the need to deploy the protocol in a network where there is significant level of trust among the nodes. This trust can be achieved by, for example, using preconfigured keys or ensuring the absence of malicious users. To define a bidirectional physical link, the field "Type" in the RREQ is set to Gratuitous RREP flag (G).

2.2 Dynamic Source Routing (DSR)

This wireless routing protocol operates a truly on-demand source-routing mechanism where routes are calculated at the point of request from a sender and, unlike AODV, no periodic message update are sent by nodes to other nodes (Table 1). This reduces the power consumption, the size of routing updates, and the need for large bandwidth. DSR is a source-based protocol where the sending node is aware of the hop-by-hop information to the destination. Route discovery is used by the sending node to obtain information about the destination prior to the actual transmission. DSR relies on router discovery (at the time of transmission) and route maintenance (every time a sending node detects a change in topology) of the network. Information about the destination host, and the path to the destination, are attached to header by the sender (also called the initiator in case of new routes) to facilitate route discovery. The discovery process is in form of broadcast packet which is received by some or all the nodes in the network area. To avoid unnecessary discovery process, each sending node searches its cache for any previous learnt route to the destination. This way, expensive discovery is avoided and bandwidth usage reduced. Packets awaiting route discovery are stored in a buffer and marked with a timeout to avoid overflow.

For the maintenance, each node is responsible for ensuring the reachability of the next hop in the route and the information about the next hop is communicated using a simple acknowledgment message. In most wireless networks, this acknowledgement is provided as MAC layer message. In case of a broken link, the node communicating the failure search its cache for any alternate route to the destination and then replace (if available) the route field in the header in a process called "Salvage" [6].

DSR is also stateless where only the current statuses of the nodes are maintained in the routing table. A phenomenon referred to as "soft-state" allows any failed node to rejoin the network immediately on reboot, and without causing any disruption to the network topology. Bidirectional physical link is established by excluding the route in the blacklist. The blacklist is indexed by neighbouring nodes and every node which intends to use the requested path should remove the path from the black list.

An important feature of DSR is the capability to handle traffic as flows effectively eliminating the need to explicitly specify the source field of the traffic. This feature allows the protocol to enforce specific flow-by-flow policy on the traffic.

In DSR, each caching node maintains a stability table which indicates the perceived stability of the node. Each time a route is reported as broken, the stability factor of the two end points connected the route is multiplied by a factor, F, such that $F < 1$.

2.3 Destination Sequenced Distance Vector (DSDV)

DSDV is, like AODV, a distance-based and table driven protocol where information about source destination traffic are maintained in a routing table [7]. DSDV maintains a sequence number to prevent any routing loop. Each node increments the sequence number by two every time there is a change in the network topology. A node cannot change the sequence number of other nodes except where the node reports the break of a node to the neighbouring nodes. In which case, it increments the sequence number by one. On receiving the updates, each node examines the sequence number, if the number is odd then it removes the entry from its routing table.

Furthermore, each node sends the received updates to all neighbouring nodes in the area. A broken link is assigned ∞ metric and an updated sequence number [7]. To address frequent movement of the mobile devices in a network, the broadcast and the incremental update is adjusted. Similar to AODV, the route information with the most current (higher) sequence is used in case of immediate routing. Conversely, routes with oldest (smaller) sequence are discarded. Another strategy adopted to reduce the size of routing update is to maintain two tables - one for routing and the other for advertisement. This way the advertisement of new route may be delayed where new better route is expected.

The updates, in addition to normal fields such as hardware and network address, include the destination address, the number of hops to reach the destination, and finally the sequence number for the last update. To operate at lower layers of the interconnect stack, DSDV encapsulate the information of an upper layer (e.g. layer 3) into the lower layer (e.g. layer 2) information.

Table 1. Comparison of the three protocols

	AODV	DSR	DSDV
On-demand	Partial	Full	ANone
Update Advertisement	Periodic	None	Periodic
Loop Prevention	Sequence number	Explicit source routing	Sequence number
Route Discovery	RREQ Broadcast	Broadcast Packet	Broadcast and Multicast
Flows Handling	Not Available	Flow State	Not Available
Handling Bidirectional Link	Flag ("G")	Blacklist	Default
Path Computation	None, Uses active state	Bellman-Ford	Distributed Bellman-Ford
Route Break Update	Using RERR Message	Multiply stability metric by F<1	Seq. No = 1, Metric=∞

In DSDV, links are assumed to be bidirectional [8] although this is not true for all wireless networks where unidirectional links are also available. DSDV proposed two strategies to address this possibility using knowledge asymmetry and link unreachability.

Table 1 shows the compression of the three main protocols (ADOV, DSR and DSDV) in summary.

3   Research Methodology

The popular simulation software NS2 was used to perform the simulation experiments in this study. CBR (continuous bit-rate) are used as traffic sources and there was a random spread of source-destination pairs over the network.

A 'Random Waypoint Model' was used in for the mobility model, in a rectangular space of 500 × 500 metres containing 16/50/100 nodes. For this simulation, it was important that both the starting point and end destination of each node were randomly located. On reaching its final destination, the node of interest is able to then rest and following the pause time, the next random end point is selected. Over the course of the simulation, this is repeated, resulting in the topology of the network having continuous variation. The experiments that were undertaken are shown in Table 2.

Table 2. Simulation parameters

Parameter name	Value
Routing protocols	AODV, DSR, DSDV
Mobility model	Random Waypoint
Simulation time	500 s
Number of nodes	16/50/100 nodes
Simulation area	500 × 500
Transmission range	250 m
Traffic type	CBR
Packet size	512 bytes
Bandwidth	2 Mbps
Simulator	NS2

3.1   Performance Metrics

To fully understand and appreciate the overall performance of a network, it is important to understand the several parameters involved in routing protocol evaluation. Here, we use a comparative analysis to study performance metrics of the following [3, 4].

3.2 Average End-to-End Delay (AED)

This represents the speed at which data packets reach their planned termini. In this speed, is included any delays due to processing, queues or propagation, and suchlike.

3.3 Throughput

This denotes the success in communication of the intended message or its delivery via a communication channel. The message or data delivered may have been through logical or physical links. Often, they pass via particular nodes in the network and is measured in data packets per second or data packets per time slot. It can also be measures in bits per second. More recently, it has been calculated as throughput and is often described as maximum, minimum, maximum theoretical, maximum sustained, peak or normal throughput.

4   Results

Figures 1 and 2 shows two graphs displaying data obtained in simulation experiments.

Figure 1 shows the relationship between the numbers of nodes in the simulation against the number of packets used per second. This was considered in three different variables; AODV, DSDV and DSR.

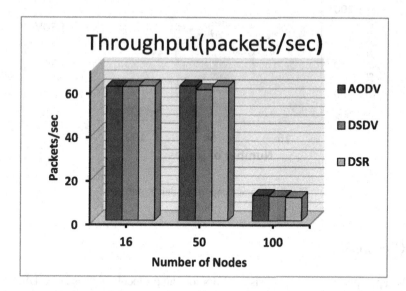

Fig. 1. Throughput (packets/sec)

The general result shown here is that with an increase of nodes, the number of packets used per second decreases drastically. At 16 nodes, there appears to be 60 packets per second for all three variables, and a slight change is observed on increasing the number of nodes to 50, with only a slight decrease observed in DSDV. The decrease is small, approximately 2 % but the fact that this decrease occurs only in DSDV is for consideration. On increasing the number of nodes to 100, a very large decrease in packets per second is observed; an average decrease of approximately 75 %. The decrease is consistent between the three variables; AODV, DSDV and DSR. It is clear that the number of packets per second is directly affected by the number of nodes.

Figure 2 shows the number of nodes compared against time in milliseconds. This was also considered using the previous variables; AODV, DSDV and DSR.

It is clear that there is more discrepancy here between the three variables used. At 16 nodes, the fastest variable appears to be DSDV, at approximately 205 ms, followed by AODV and DSR at approximately 155 and 100 ms, respectively. On increasing the number of nodes to 50, there is little observable difference in time for AODV; however there appears to be a clear decrease in time for DSDV and an increase for DSR. Finally, on increasing the number of nodes to 100, a clear decrease in time is observable for all three variables, where they lie close to zero in time, appearing to have lost all function in time.

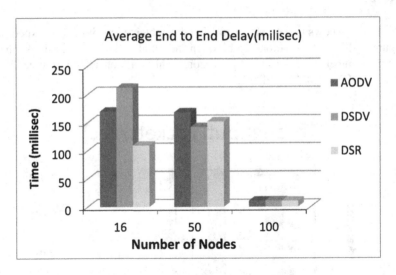

Fig. 2. Average end to end delay (millisec)

5   Conclusion

In this paper, performance analysis on WSN routing protocols such as DSR, DSDV and AODV has been performed focusing on scalability of the nodes. The analysis is performed based on Throughput and Delay parameters.

Our simulation results show that there is an impact on the performance of WSN network based on scalability. For our study, 16, 50 and 100 nodes were used to analyse the impact on the network performance based on WSN protocols.

In case of throughput, it was observed that up to 50 nodes, performance of AODV, DSDV and DSR is similar. However, further increase of nodes to 100 reduces the throughput drastically. This is owing to the fact that by increasing the nodes, network traffic increases. In addition, delivery of packets per second reduces drastically because of collision.

In case of packet delay, it was observed that DSDV down performs than AODV and DSR protocols at smaller nodes. Interestingly, by increasing nodes to 50, AODV and DSR protocols down performs than DSDV protocols. However, at the large nodes such as 100, the delay is much less. At larger nodes, throughput is less that means number of packets per second is less. Consequently, packet delay is also less.

Finally, simulation results shows that the performance of the network depend on the scalability of nodes and can be confirmed increase scalability reduces number of packets delivered by second. Due to this fact, delay of packet delivery is also much reduced irrespective of the routing protocol used in WSN network.

In future, various other parameters such as impact of pause times, multi speed network, power capacity of nodes, mobility model, and defective nodes will be studied for WSN network. By doing this, there will be an insight on overall protocols perform-ance and to standardize routing protocols for different network conditions.

References

1. Vijaya, I., Mishra, P.B., Dash, A.R., Rath, A.K.: In: 2nd International Conference on Emerging Applications of Information Technology, IEEE (2011)
2. Zhang/RFID and Sensor Networks AU7777_C012 Page Proof Page 323 2009-6-24
3. Yaday, N.S., Yadav, R.P.: Performance comparison and analysis of table-driven and on-demand routing protocols for mobile ad-hoc networks. Int. J. Inf. Commun. Eng. (2008)
4. Nishiyama, H., Abdulla, A.-E.A.A., Ansari, N., Nemoto, Y., Kato, N. (2010) HYMN to improve the longevity of wireless sensor networks. In: Proceedings of IEEE GLOBECOM. Miami, Florida, USA, Dec 2010
5. Kassim, M., Rahman, R.A., Ismail, M., Yahaya, C.K.H.C.K.: Performance analysis of routing protocol in WiMAX network. In: IEEE International Conference on System Engineering and Technology (ICSET) (2011)
6. Das, S.R., Belding-Royer, E.M., Perkins, C.E.: Ad hoc on-demand distance vector (AODV) routing (2003)
7. Johnson, D., Hu, Y., Maltz, D.: The dynamic source routing protocol (DSR) for mobile ad hoc networks for IPv4. RFC 4728, Feb 2007
8. Perkins, C.E., Bhagwat, P.: Highly dynamic destination-sequenced distance-vector routing (DSDV) for mobile computers. In: ACM SIGCOMM Computer Communication Review, vol. 24, no. 4. ACM (1994)
9. He, G.: Destination-sequenced distance vector (DSDV) protocol. Networking Laboratory, Helsinki University of Technology (2002)

Security Audit, Risk and Governance

Responsive Cyber-Physical Risk Management (RECYPHR)

A Systems Framework

A.G. Hessami[1(✉)], H. Jahankhani[2], and M. Nkhoma[3]

[1] Vega Systems, London, UK
hessami@vegaglobalsystems.com
[2] GSM-London, London, UK
hamid.jahankhani@gsm.org.uk
[3] RMIT International University, Ho Chi Minh City, Vietnam
mathews.nkhoma@rmit.edu.vn

Abstract. Organizations are highly exposed to the vulnerabilities inherent in Internet connectivity, and the exposure increases every day as cyber-attacks become more lethal. Competitiveness demands an ever-increasing presence, and therefore reliance, on all things electronic. Over the past generation, businesses, consumers and governments around the globe have moved in to cyberspace and cloud environment in order to conduct their businesses. However, criminals have identified rewards from cyberspace frauds therefore, the risks and threats have increased too which indicate that the current risk management methodologies are inefficient and fast becoming obsolete in order to assess, manage, reduce, mitigate and accept risk in real time to effectively reduce cyber incidents. For our societies to function, securing the cyber space is essential and will be an enabler with result in better use of the digital environment. In this paper a new Responsive Cyber-Physical Risk Management Framework (RECYPHR) is proposed in order to tackle the traditional shortfalls and provide a Near Real-Time (NERT) response to managing risks.

1 Introduction

Risk Management is a multi-disciplinary approach that combines a number of diverse technical, regulatory, business and societal concerns to arrive at a judgment about the existence of threats/risks in a given context and a prudent course of action given the scale or immediacy of the threat.

This discipline suffers from all dysfunctions of a typical management regime in that it is often planned and provisioned at the start of a project or undertaking and remains largely static throughout its life with iterative review and audit cycles at predetermined intervals or when undesirable consequences surface. In this spirit, the identification, evaluation, assessment and management of risks has remained unresponsive to the challenges of the modern world in which news and information travels at web speed, reaction to undesirable events causing harm and loss is almost at the same pace and in some sectors such as online services, the damage can be instantaneous and extensive.

© Springer International Publishing Switzerland 2015
H. Jahankhani et al. (Eds.): ICGS3 2015, CCIS 534, pp. 263–274, 2015.
DOI: 10.1007/978-3-319-23276-8_24

This calls for a whole new approach that by its very nature needs to tackle the traditional shortfalls and provide a Near Real-Time (NERT) response to risks as opposed to waiting for review and audit cycles to highlight non-conformities. The new responsive approach needs to intelligently identify changes in the threat/vulnerability/risk profile of a product, process, undertaking or organisation and provide the infrastructure and supporting tools for timely awareness and response. To this end we propose the following as initial systemic requirements for the concept solution to the problem statement cited above:

1. The Responsive Cyber-Physical Risk Management Framework (RECYPHR) shall be founded on the advanced systems thinking and systems engineering best practice and beyond;
2. The architecture and implementation of RECYPHR shall be scalable and adaptive to the requirements of Cyber-physical risks;
3. The framework shall incorporate and respond to the requirements from a multiplicity of stakeholder community each with specific security profile;
4. The framework shall provide the foundation for the development of a suite of advanced tools and supporting processes to a responsive approach to risk management;
5. The framework shall provide a suite of performance KPIs and metrics to enable principal stakeholders to determine the nature of threats/risks and the adequacy of response measures;
6. The framework shall be capable of modularised and continual enhancement taking lessons learnt into the enhanced architecture for improved responsiveness and resilience.

The generic requirements constitute a robust framework for the conceptual development of a responsive risk management framework that will transcend the current practice and withstand the demands of the rapidly evolving and developing information technologies.

2 Current Practice

2.1 Current Advantages and Strengths

The current cyber-physical risk management approach focuses on business needs with clear and distinguished steps in operation. Therefore, it helps keep the business objectives on track as the enterprises take steps to ensure a controlled information systems environment.

It provides tools to communicate with managers of the business and in case, problems occur, it is rather simple to pinpoint related people or institutions.

Rigorous cycle of risk identification and management: The risk management approach together with audit cycles are standardized, hence, the response time to incidents is shortened, and information is delivered in a professional manner.

Single point of entry to report, acknowledge and process claims in a timely fashion.

2.2 Current Shortfalls and Dysfunctions

Organizations tend to overinvest in protecting IT assets while underinvesting in a full and strategic understanding of the nature of the threats; therefore, cyber-physical risk management approach is not effective:

- Cyber-security is misaligned within organizational priorities.
- Response frameworks are out-dated or incomplete and remain too focused on IT.
- Solutions have traditionally relied on a multitude of heterogeneous security software products.
- Lines of accountability within organizations are unclear.
- Analytics are underutilized

Organizations typically include cyber risks in enterprise risk-management programs but do not regularly assess threats. According to a recent survey conducted by PwC of more than 500 executives of business in the US in 2014, only 47 % perform periodic risk assessments and 24 % have an objective third party assess their security program.

It seems clear cut that cyber-security spending would be most productive when the allocation of resources is based on specific business risks. However, only 38 % of survey respondents said they have a methodology to prioritize security investments based on greatest risk and impact to the organization's business strategy.

Cyber-security incidents carried out by employees have serious impact, but these incidents are not addressed with the same rigor as external threats like hackers.

Cyber-security programs also should be designed with flexibility and agility in the short run to enable the organization to quickly address cyber threats as they multiply and evolve. In reality, nevertheless, the scope and duration of cyber-security initiatives are often designed and funded for the typical three- to five-year business plans.

3 Outline Research Concepts

Given the ubiquitous and critical role of the information technology in the research, industry, commerce and governance of modern societies, matters of security of information resources are high on most private, public and third sector enterprises' agenda. A plethora of international standards have emerged to provide a systems backbone to the security assurance efforts. This offer codified methods and approaches that in principle attempt to prevent or remedy vulnerabilities in the information technology services and infrastructure [1–5]. However, majority of these are hinged around conventional, and slow paced risk management processes and techniques that generally prove inadequate in the dynamic and fast paced environment of internet and cyber attacks. To this end, we have undertaken this research with a view to arrive at initial concept solution to the problem statement namely:

1. Extensive review of the best practice risk management approaches, solutions and frameworks from industrial and academic sources;
2. Stakeholder identification and Requirements Capture for a Responsive Cyber-Physical Risk Management Framework (RECYPHR);

3. Establishing the principal dysfunctions associated with the existing framework versus the functional, operational and specific stakeholder requirements;
4. Developing a conceptual framework for RECYPHR and evaluation for conformity against principal requirements;
5. Developing the requirements for the essential set of supporting tools and procedures to implement RECYPHR;
6. Piloting the framework within the context of a Critical Infrastructure or stakeholder chosen case for demonstration of compliance with principal requirements and identify major shortfalls;

4 RECYPHR Concept and Approach

The research into a responsive risk management framework commensurate with the requirements of the Information Technologies and global cyber space is a multi-disciplinary and multi-stakeholder task.

We employ a fusion and integration of best practice from existing research and information technology frameworks to devise advanced responsive risk management architecture for the modern cyber space applications. This by necessity embodies three orthogonal architectures comprising:

1. An advanced systemic Risk Management framework [17];
2. An advanced Information Management framework;
3. A responsive expert driven detection and response framework.

The three dimensional RECHYPHR framework is depicted in Fig. 1.

The three orthogonal dimensions of the Responsive IS Risk Management framework are outline as follows.

4.1 Advanced Risk Management Framework

The code of practice for the implementation of the ISO31000 standard on risk management highlights a number of principles that any risk management system shall ideally follow and embed. The key principles relevant to RECYPHR are:

1. **Risk management should be systematic and structured,** the approach to risk management should, where practicable, be consistently applied within the organisation.
2. **Risk management should take into account organizational culture, human factors and behavior**
3. **Risk management should create and protect value,** the organization should optimize risk management to contribute to the demonstrable achievement of objectives and maximize overall business and commercial benefits
4. **Risk management should be transparent and inclusive,** Management and stakeholders should be actively involved in risk identification, assessment and response
5. **Risk management should be dynamic, iterative and responsive to change,** The organization should ensure its risk management continually identifies and responds to changes affecting its operating environment

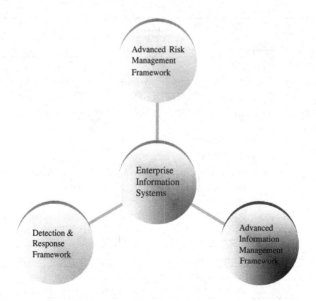

Fig. 1. The three dimensional responsive RECYPHR architecture

A risk management framework developed in response to the SafeRelNet [24] European Network of Excellence (FP5 & FP6 Framework) complies with the above broad principles and the main ISO standard. This is adopted as an advanced and comprehensive framework in RECYPHR. The systematic risk management framework depicted in Fig. 2 comprises seven principles namely:

I.   Prediction and Proactivity;
II.   Prevention;
III.   Protection and Containment;
IV.   Preparedness and Response;
V.   Recovery and Restoration;
VI.   Organisation and Learning;
VII.   Continual Enhancement.

The quantitative risk management framework is dynamic and orthogonal to the Information System Architecture. The principle I is applied at the outset and II and III are run continuously for every tier of the ISA. Upon detection and activation at any tier, principles III, IV and V are triggered to provide expert driven immediate protection, response and recovery policies whilst also triggering system wide alerts and limitation of services. Principles V and VI are triggered upon cessation of threats to capture the key learning and enhancements of the prevention and protection systems.

In principle, all three orthogonal facets of the responsive risk management in RECYPHR are dynamic and concurrent processes.

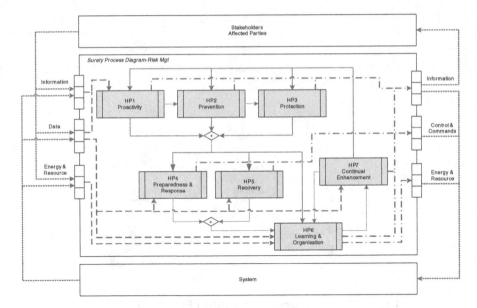

Fig. 2. Advanced risk management framework in RECYPHR

4.2 Advanced Information Management Framework

The enterprise Information System provides one of the three dimensions of RECYPHR. This is illustrated by the Service Oriented Architecture (SOA) in Fig. 3. The nature of

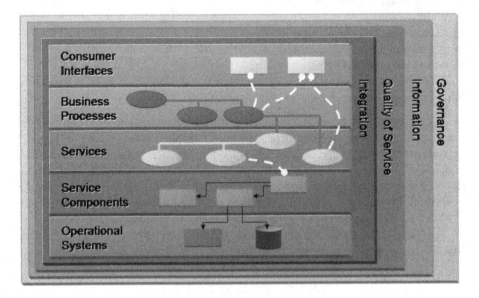

Fig. 3. Illustrative SOA reference architecture for information management

the IS architecture can be chosen or determined by the nature and preferences of the enterprise.

The enterprise Information System Architecture and tiering is fully customizable and can accommodate bespoke or a many public domain templates from OSI, WOA to SOA etc.

4.3 Advanced Detection and Response Framework

This constitutes an algorithmic expert driven hear of RECYPHR that provides a near real time detection of anomalous states of the IS and triggers the risk management policies and phases aligned with the specific layer in which detection has been made and validated.

A different and bespoke detection and response algorithm is developed and implemented at every tier of the ISA. The schema in Fig. 4 illustrates a typical detection and verification agent.

Note that the three orthogonal frameworks within RECYPHR are not all IT biased or derived and they work systemically to generate an advanced and responsive defence in depth strategy that is highly desirable in the cyber domain given the challenges that we've already highlighted.

There's an implementation and execution model that governs the interaction of the three frameworks in RECYPHR. In view of the complexity and adaptability for a given IS architecture and environment, a full description of the execution model is beyond the scope of the current paper.

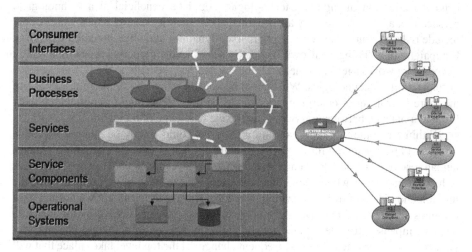

Fig. 4. The violation detection architecture in RECYPHR

5 Emerging Challenges

Understanding the implications and challenges faced in risk management with respect to the proposed framework (RECYPHR), "what is new" in risk management is a topic that's multi-dimensional. Emerging technologies, best practices (industry or otherwise) and even risks themselves are counter parts of the standardization of organizational dynamics. Anything we may think is likely to become increasingly important towards managing risk. It is not yet common knowledge today for senior executives and corporates in the next decade to mitigate risks with minimal exposure to technology.

A number of academics, consultants, analysts and business managers are signalling (or influencing) the incorporation of risk awareness and management into the everyday procedures of an organization's goals, vision and mission statements. It is conventional to witness that an organization's human resources are functionally inclined with the strategy(s) of the organization. What these eyewitnesses and experts are trying to convey is that there needs to be alignment with the risks to that of the strategy(s) set in place, and that those risks need to be identified, known, and tracked across the company. Our perception on creating this research framework would be based on the following questions on this point: to what degree or extent is this happening right now? What companies are incorporating with success? How substantial will this development be in the next year or two?

So the world is in the dilemma of having on one hand high-end cost benefits which if they discard through private or dedicated ICT infrastructure and embrace the cloud (public offering) like Microsoft Office 365 or the Adobe creative cloud. On the other hand the adoption of high-end technologies could be beneficial at a technological perspective, as individuals they are sceptical about security related issues which could include risks of stolen data, competing market dynamics and other potential risk areas. Campaigns like "Bring your own device to work" in the corporate world is a reality today. More work is getting done at 'Home' by people especially in the ICT sectors due virtualization of technologies. What could be consider now and in the future as one of the more prevailing or emerging risks would be the safekeeping of confidential data. Finding a balance between the two would be the challenge of tomorrow.

Within the context of an organisation(s), a risk could simply be ignored while the same could be a potential for execution as a great threat in the ever changing stream of human resources namely the senior management or executives under them. The Focus is lost momentarily while numerous activities are executed in alignments with the mission and vision of the organization. Once the impetus drops all known normal risks becomes an internal threat within the context of best practices upheld by top management. Companies struggle to place high enough emphasis on what seems to be taken for granted especially when too many frequent changes at the top level takes place that will without doubt try to build risk layers leading to complexity in everyday activities.

Security threats to business operations become increasingly complex, as traditional and digital worlds converge. Emerging technologies, user mobility and the sheer volume of data exchanged daily all represent opportunities for hackers to target the digital assets that drive modern enterprise. One attack is all it takes to jeopardize an organization's stability, if not its existence.

Recent contractor data leaks and payment card heists have proved that adversaries can and will infiltrate systems via third parties, but most organizations do not address third-party security. For instance, flow of data to supply chain partners continues to surge, yet they are not required to comply with privacy and security policies.

Mobile technologies and risks are proliferating but security efforts are not keeping up. The growth in scale and scope of cybercrime since the mid-2000s has been mainly due to proliferation of "botnets" as mass tools for computer misuse. Transnational characteristics of cybercriminals, both individual and organized crime group

In recent years there has been much discussion concerning the nature of computer crime and how to tackle it. There is confusion over the scope of computer crime, debate over its extent and severity, and concern over where our power to defeat it lies, Jahankhani and Al Nemrat [25]. There are many available policy documents and studies that address how the nature of war is changing with the advent of widespread computer technology.

Unlike traditional crime, which is committed in one geographical location, cybercrime is committed online and it is often not clearly linked to any geographical location.

In 2014 a world-leading unit to counter online criminals was established in UK in order for police to deal with cybercrime effectively, with following fivefold aims:

1. To bring more fraudsters and cyber-criminals to justice;
2. To improve the service to their victims;
3. To step up prevention help and advice to individuals and businesses;
4. To dedicate more organised crime teams to stemming the harm caused by the most prolific cyber-criminals;
5. To invite business and industry to match the Metropolitan police determination and work with together to combat fraud and cybercrime.

Clearly, the traditional way of policing cybercrime has not been working despite, plethora of internet-related legislation. This is because of the high volume online nature of the crimes, Jahankhani and Al Nemrat [26].

As we move into proliferation of Internet of Things (IoT), cybersecurity risks will inevitably increase again due to the inherent risks associated with mobile health, smart cities, etc., therefore, it is envisaged that the vulnerabilities would be greater, if policies and standards such as IPV6, that drive the adoption and implementation of IoT is not put in place soon.

5.1   The European Perspective

Since the Horizon 2020 call DS-6-2014 on risk management and assurance models, statements from the Member States and EU institutions have emerged that further acknowledge the need to protect their networks and critical infrastructure and respond effectively to cyber-threats. They have also adopted both national and EU-level cyber-security strategies and regulation. The adoption of the Network and Information Security Directive, currently in the legislative process, should mark an important step forward in this context. One of the key priorities of the European Cybersecurity Strategy is to develop industrial and technological resources for cybersecurity. However, it is acknowledged that specific gaps still exist in the fast moving area of technologies and solutions for online network security. A more joined-up approach is therefore is sought to step up the supply of more secure solutions by EU industry and to stimulate their take-up by enterprises, public authorities, and citizens. In addition, an effective law enforcement response to online criminal activity is found necessary. The EU Commission has set out proposals for this issue in its European Agenda on Security.

It is instructive to note that only 22 % of Europeans have full trust in companies such as search engines, social networking sites and e-mail services whilst 72 % of European Internet users worry that they are being asked for too much personal data online.

The EU is committed to the highest standards of protection on personal data and privacy, guaranteed by Articles 7 and 8 of the Charter of Fundamental Rights. The General Data Protection Regulation is anticipated to increase trust in digital services, as it should protect individuals with respect to processing of personal data by all companies that offer their services on the European market. Special rules apply to electronic communications services (e-Privacy Directive) which may need to be reassessed once the general EU rules on data protection are agreed, particularly since most of the articles of the current e-Privacy Directive apply only to providers of electronic communications services, i.e. traditional telecoms companies.

6 Future Research and Way Forward

In the future, risk management will spread even further away from the traditional venues of corporate and financial domains with respect to safety and security as a risk factor. What this will mean is that a formal integration of risk would possibly take place within the context of other disciplinary domains. Initially, this will support the status quo of "risk managers/analysts" with the supplementary vanity and the banquet of over-paid professionals who eventually add no value to the growth of the product line or organization's goals. As the trend progresses, there will be a shift in pathways from "compliance to practices" and a back to the basics integration that focusses on whether the risk was mitigated or not.

Best practice manuals such as the ISO31000 standard or its practitioners may talk about various approaches to risk mitigation and management, another domain area to lookout for would primarily be the rise of the 'fuzzy' approaches to risk management. This will recognise and acknowledge the fact that the associated risks and risk management processes are not completely a linear practice. Initially, the time variable will be added for both length and frequency of exposure. Soon there will be the development of the multivariate leading to "fuzzy risk". This may arise, not from risk managers, but from the application of new information technology processes, possibly utilising the latest in social media tracking, Big-Data analytics and tracking and linking with Google maps GPS enabled systems. This will lead to real-time monitoring of risk through the linking of data from smartphones, tablets, remote monitoring and production equipment, environmental monitoring etc. Of course, good risk managers will process massive quantities of subtle data subconsciously and make decisions based on their instinctive feelings, just like they always did in the past.

Risk will be the defining criteria for Regulators and it will help us all to understand the world around us better. Our perceptions on risk will have the focus of risk management in regulated organisations with an incremental effect on the customer. An example of this would be the Financial Conduct Authority (FCA) having been the major driver of this in the UK by ensuring that organisations put good consumer results at the heart of the business, from the Board down to senior and operational management engraving consumer behaviour and anticipations as the core DNA of the organization.

Risk Management in the nearest future will be any corporate board's top agenda wherein risk managers from different sectors will be able to speak one language like financial analysts and IT managers. Real-time monitoring of risk is another example: GE's vision of the "Internet of Everything" is one such example. Another example is the numbers of online and e-tail stores hit with larceny of customer information are the frightening trends of today's businesses. Awareness of companies implementing this today or signs that companies are going to invest in it in the near future are definitely the current and future trends we can perceive in the near future. Integration and cross functionality with Human Resources due to recent legislative changes, advancement in technological superiority and globalization as well as localization are examples of true risk management in the future.

References

1. Information technology –Security techniques –Information security management systems – Requirements (ISO/IEC27001:2005), English version of DIN ISO/IEC 27001:2008-09
2. Information technology — Security techniques —Information security management system implementation guidance IEC 27003-2010
3. Information technology — Security techniques —Information security management system implementation guidance, ISO/IEC 27005:2011
4. Risk Management – Principles and guidelines, ISO 31000:2009
5. Risk Management – Risk assessment techniques, IEC 31010:2009
6. Developing a Risk Prevention Culture in Europe, Annual Report 2002, European Agency for Safety and Health at Work, ISBN 92-9191-024-4
7. Railway Safety Management System Guide, Railway Safety-Transport Canada, Ottawa-Ontario, February 2001
8. Hessami, A.G.: Risk, a missed opportunity, risk and continuity. Int. J. Best Pract. Manag. 2(2), 17–26 (1999)
9. Hunter, A., Hessami, A.G.: Formalisation of weighted factors analysis. Knowl. Based Syst. 15, 377–390 (2002)
10. Hessami, A.G.: A systems framework for safety and security—the holistic paradigm. Syst. Eng. J. USA 7(2), 99–112 (2004)
11. Palmer, C.: Using IT for competitive advantage at Thomson Holidays. Long Range Plann. 21(6), 26–29 (Institute of Strategic Studies Journal. Pergamon Press, London, December 1988)
12. Hessami, A.: Safety assurance, a systems paradigm. Hazard Prev. J. Syst. Saf. Soc. 35(3), 8–13 (1999)
13. Hessami, A.: Risk management a systems paradigm. Syst. Eng. J. Int. Counc. Syst. Eng. 2(3), 156–167 (1999)
14. ISO/IEC15288, System Life Cycle Processes - ISO/IEC October 2002

15. Skyttner, L.: General Systems Theory, Ideas and Applications. World Scientific Publishing Co., Singapore (2001). ISBN 981-02-4176-3:88-89
16. Waring, A.E., Glendon, A.I.: Managing Risk-Critical Issues for Survival and Success into the 21st Century, pp. 70–86. International Thompson Business Press, (1998). ISBN 1-86152-167-7
17. Hessami, A.G.: Framework for safety, security and sustainability risk management. In: Soares, C.G. (ed.) Safety and Reliability of Industrial Products, Systems and Structures, pp. 21–31. CRC Press, Boca Raton (2010). ISBN 978-415-66392-2
18. Broadhurst, R., Grabosky, P.: Crime in Cyberspace: Offenders and the Role of Organized Crime Groups, Working Paper. http://ssrn.com/abstract=2211842 (2013)
19. EY, Cyber program management – Identifying ways to get ahead of cybercrime, Insights on governance, risk and compliance, October 2014
20. Johnson, J., Sung, M.C., Ma, T.: Toward Future Cyber-Security Risk Management, Lecture note, University of Southampton. http://www.southampton.ac.uk/assets/imported/transforms/peripheral-block/UsefulDownloads_Download/D90CE65EDA3747B4A8259B30E94290BD/8%20johnson-ma-sung.pdf (2012)
21. NCSC, Cyber Security and Risk Management – An Executive level responsibility (2013)
22. PwC, CSO magazine, CIO magazine, The Global State of Information Security® Survey 2014, September 2013
23. BS 31100, Risk Management – Code of Practice and Guidance for the Implementation of BS ISO 31000
24. SafeRelNet: http://maikbrehm.com/project-saferelnet.html
25. Jahankhani, H., Al Nemrat, A.: Cybercrime classification and characteristics. In: Cybercrime and Cyber Terrorism Investigators' Handbook, Chap. 4. Elsevier, Amsterdam, July 2014. ISBN 978-0-12-800743-3
26. Jahankhani, H, Al Nemrat, A.: Cybercrime profiling and trend analysis. In: Intelligence Management: Knowledge Driven Frameworks for Combating Terrorism and Organised Crime, Chap. 12, pp. 181–195. Springer, Berlin (2011). ISBN 978-1-4471-2139-8

Risk and Privacy Issues of Digital Oil Fields in the Cloud

Hamid Jahankhani[1(✉)], Najib Altawell[1], and Ali G. Hessami[2]

[1] GSM-London, London, UK
{hamid.jahankhani,Najib.Altawell}@gsm.org.uk
[2] Vega Systems, London, UK
hessami@vegaglobalsystems.com

Abstract. Considering the complexities of digital oil fields in the cloud, oil and gas industry is still geared to migrate to the cloud because of the various advantages in exploration and production information delivery, collaboration and decision-support. However, for an effective migration to cloud environment, it is paramount that a set of clear metrics based on business analytics objectives are defined. Once a comprehensive and systematic identification, evaluation and assessment of risks to the enterprise cloud operations is conducted, a responsive risk management framework is called for. The research into a responsive risk management framework commensurate with the requirements of the modern internet and Information Technologies and global cyber space is a multi-disciplinary and multi-stakeholder task. This paper aims to review risk and privacy issues of digital oil fields in the cloud and introduce advanced responsive risk management architecture for the modern cyber space applications such as digital oil fields.

Keywords: Digital oil · Cloud computing · Risk

1 Introduction

As technology improve and become commercially available and viable, many industries begin to adapt to it, such as what is taking place presently in the form of cloud technology. The inclusion of the above technology is for the purpose of improving businesses output and profit, such as in the form of search for raw materials, to improve drilling techniques/distribution and the output of the final product, while at the same time reducing their overall costs.

The oil and gas companies, with their various sectors, such as upstream (also named exploration and production "E&P" sector), a stage mostly related to the finding and drilling for oil & gas, while midstream deals with the shipping and storing of the oil and gas, and the last stage, downstream, is mainly covers the refining and distribution of the processed oil-based products, all of them are using this technology to further improve and speed-up the process in relation to the above three sectors.

The oil and gas industry, as any other industry, is following steps by adapting itself to this form of technology, i.e. what has been termed as "digital oil & gas" or "digital oilfield (DOF)" by employing approaches such as smart drilling. This technology is changing the

© Springer International Publishing Switzerland 2015
H. Jahankhani et al. (Eds.): ICGS3 2015, CCIS 534, pp. 275–284, 2015.
DOI: 10.1007/978-3-319-23276-8_25

old costly approach (two-dimensional "2D" seismic map) at various levels within the sectors of the oil and gas industry. The new "Cloud Technology" or as some refer to it "to the Cloud" is the technology that will structure oil and gas companies in the form of managing their information infrastructure and their overall products in much efficient way than at any other time. The cloud computing have been with us for some time now, and therefore, is not a new technology. However, new approaches and new designs related to computing hardware and mobility have generated viable commercial aspects to all businesses, including oil and gas industry to employ this kind of technology.

Cloud computing has generated significant interest in both academia and industry, but it is still an evolving paradigm. Confusion exists in IT communities about how a cloud differs from existing models and how these characteristics affect its adoption. Some see cloud as a novel technical revolution, when people consider it a natural evolution of technology, economy, and culture, [1]. Nevertheless, cloud computing is an important concept, with strong ability to considerably reduce costs through optimization and increased operating and economic efficiencies. Furthermore, cloud computing could significantly enhance collaboration, agility, and scale, thus enabling a truly global computing model over the Internet infrastructure. However, without appropriate security and privacy solutions designed for clouds, this potentially revolutionizing computing paradigm could become a huge failure. Several surveys of potential cloud adopters indicate that security and privacy is the primary concern hindering its adoption.

Cloud computing is a system to enable suitable, on demand network access to a shared pool of adjustable computing resources like the network, server, storages, applications, and services that might be quickly arranged and distributed with negligible management attempt or service provider communication. Cloud models promote accessibility and are composed of five necessary uniqueness, three delivery models, and four deployment models.

To understand the importance of cloud computing and its adoption, we must understand its principal characteristics, its delivery and deployment models, how customers use these services, and how to safeguard them. The main five key uniqueness of cloud computing consist of on-demand self-service, ubiquitous network access, location-independent resource pooling, rapid elasticity, and measured service for all of which are geared towards using cloud seamlessly and transparently. Rapid elasticity let us quickly scale up (or down) resources. Measured services are primarily derived from business model properties and indicate that cloud service providers control and optimize the use of computing resources through automated resource allocation, load balancing, and metering tools.

Cloud computing provides several benefits to an organization including, cost, investment on physical or software infrastructure, users can access their data anywhere and finally, easier and faster data sharing.

The cloud computing concept arises from the notion of "software as a service" (SaaS). A set of services is provided on a set of platforms at various locations.

The benefits obtained from cloud computing are huge for the oil and gas companies, some are listed below:

1. Cloud computing help in oil and gas companies in managing far more efficiently environmental impact

2. Monitoring remotely variety of equipment in real time
3. Oil and gas companies (for business and retail customers) will have the ability to deal and implement new approaches and better offers rapidly to their customers and offset rival competition
4. Oil and gas companies will be able to manage their costs more effectively
5. The technology can make it much easier in opening a new market
6. Cloud computing can provide the oil and gas companies a global integrated access to information on regular basis
7. Low costs video conferences
8. Access in real-time to data and analytical capabilities. However, oil and gas companies may have some concerns/issues when it comes to cloud computing, some of these issues have been listed below:

    1. *Security*: General concern about security, in particular important data and information access, storage and how secure it is
    2. Data and how big it can be: The speed of obtaining the geographic information in order to meet the business needs and on time
    3. Valuable Trade Secrets: The security related to personal and financial information and possible theft.

The five key characteristics and benefits of cloud computing can pose downside risks that require identification, evaluation, assessment and mitigation. For example, unavailability of on-demand self-service, sensitivities to location-independent resource pooling such as security concerns, unresponsive elasticity/scalability are illustrative downside risks that a fully cloud dependent/migrated enterprise may need to be aware of and provide requisite solutions for. A comprehensive risk register, identifying, characterizing, assessing and mitigating all risks need to be devised to ensure business continuity should any of the promised key benefits be interrupted due to local or global disruptions or threats.

These days, sensors and actuators are increasingly embedded in various physical objects, i.e. in a way that link them through wired and wireless networks with a connection to the Internet. The volume of data provided from such a system is considerable. The speed of development in this field using the above approach has been born out from new designs in wireless and networking hardware coupled with closer co-ordinations in communications (e.g. standardization). At the same time, the cost itself has been rapidly declining which make these kinds of data network communication systems possible to implement anywhere in the world, and, consequently, the vast amount of data obtained can be always in real time, i.e. the user can view the status and location of mobile resources from anywhere over the internet.

Therefore, the embedded systems have evolved recently for the following reasons:

1. Standard run-time platforms (e.g. java)
2. Embedded systems connected to the Internet
3. Advance integrated software applications

In relation to application related to energy in general, the sensors are parts of various applications, such as smart metering, smart grid, off-shore renewable energy installations, high temperature energy devices, corrosion monitoring and nuclear systems, to mention but few.

When it comes to oil and gas industry, the use of embedded sensors are there in order to monitor a variety of conditions, such as fluid pumps, monitoring gas content of the process fluid, cavitation within the pump, corrosion measurement and many more other related functions.

According to Photonic Sensor Consortium, [2] *"..the distributed fiber optic sensor market stood at $585 million in 2013. The market was projected to approach $1.5 billion in 2018 with 70 % associated with the oil and gas segments. The sudden and unexpected drop in oil prices will negatively impact the market with the overall forecast falling short of the $1.5 billion forecast".*

2   Cloud Storage Models

The goal of cloud storage system is an effective organizational system node to store data. Following are the common four types of services:

2.1   Elastic Compute Clusters

A compute cluster includes a set of virtual instances that run a customer's application code. Each virtual instance can be a bare-metal VM (in an infrastructure-as-a-service provider, such as AWS and Cloud Servers) or a sandbox environment (in a platform-as-a-service provider, such as AppEngine). Clusters are elastic in that the number of instances can scale dynamically with the application's workload. For instance, in a cloud-based Web application, the number of front-end server instances can scale according to the incoming request rate, so that each server instance won't be overwhelmed by too many simultaneous requests.

2.2   Persistent Storage Services

These services store application data in a non-ephemeral state; all instances in the cluster can access them. They're different from the local storage (for example, the local hard drive) in each virtual instance, which is temporary and can't be directly accessed by other instances. They're also different from block storage services that some providers offer (for example, Amazon's Elastic Block Storage). The latter can't be accessed by multiple instances simultaneously and serves primarily as backup. There are several common types of storage services. Table storage (SimpleDB, Google's DataStore, and Azure's Table Storage) is similar to a traditional database. Blob storage (S3, Rackspace's Cloud Files, and Azure's Blob Storage) keeps binary objects such as user photos and videos. Queue storage (SQS and Azure's Queue Storage) is a special type of storage service.

Persistent storage services are usually implemented as RESTful Web services (REST stands for Representational State Transfer) and are highly available and scalable compared to their non-cloud siblings.

2.3   Intracloud Networks

These networks connect virtual instances with each other and with storage services. All clouds promise high-bandwidth and low-latency networks in a data centre. This is because network performance is critical to the performance of distributed applications such as multitier Web services and MapReduce jobs.

2.4   Wide-Area Networks

Unlike intra cloud networks, which connect an application's components, wide-area networks (WANs) connect the cloud data centres, where the application is hosted, with end hosts on the Internet. For consumer applications such as websites, WAN performance can affect a client's response time significantly. All cloud providers operate multiple data centres at different geographical regions so that a nearby data centre to reduce WAN latency can serve a user's request.

2.5   Putting It All Together

These four types of services are fundamental in building a generic online computation platform. Imagine a typical online cloud application, such as a social network website. Its servers can run in the compute cluster, leveraging the scaling feature to absorb flash-crowd events. Its user data can be stored in the various storage services and accessed through the intracloud network. Its Web content can be delivered to users with just a short delay, with a WAN's help. Other important cloud services, such as MapReduce (Hadoop) services and backup services, aren't as common, probably because they aren't essential to most cloud applications.

Considering the complexities of digital oil fields in the cloud, oil and gas industry still is geared to migrate to the cloud because of the various advantages in exploration and production information deliver, collaboration and decision-support. However, for an effective migration to cloud environment, it is paramount that a set of clear metrics based on business analytics objectives are defined. Of course, the choice of appropriate deployment model is based on the security, compliance, cost, integration and quality of service.

3   Cloud Storage Challenges

Cloud services are applications running in the Cloud Computing infrastructures through internal network or Internet. Cloud computing environments are multi domain environments in which each domain can use any security, privacy, and trust needs and potentially employ various mechanisms, interfaces, and semantics, [3]. Such domains could signify individual enabled services or other infrastructural or application components. Service-oriented architectures are naturally relevant technology to facilitate such multi domain formation through service composition and orchestration.

3.1 Authentication and Identity Management

By using cloud services, users can easily access their personal information and make it available to various services across the Internet. An identity management (IDM) mechanism can help authenticate users and services based on credentials and characteristics. The key to the issue concerning IDM in clouds is interoperability drawbacks that could result from using different identity tokens and identity negotiation protocols. Existing password-based authentication has an inherited limitation and poses significant risks. An IDM system should be able to protect private and sensitive information related to users and processes. How multi-tenant cloud environments can affect the privacy of identity information isn't yet well understood. In addition, the multi-jurisdiction issue can complicate protection measures. While users interact with a front-end service, this service might need to ensure that their identity is protected from other services with which it interacts. In multi-tenant cloud environments, providers must segregate customer identity and authentication information. Authentication and IDM components should also be easily integrated with other security components.

3.2 Access Control and Accounting

Heterogeneity and diversity of services, as well as the domains' diverse access requirements in cloud computing environments, demand fine-grained access control policies particularly, access control services should be flexible enough to capture dynamic, context, or attribute- or credential-based access requirements and to enforce the principle of least privilege. Such access control services might need to integrate privacy-protection requirements expressed through complex rules.

It's important that the access control system employed in clouds is easily managed and its privilege distribution is administered efficiently. We must also ensure that cloud delivery models provide generic access control interfaces for proper interoperability, which demands a policy-neutral access control specification and enforcement framework that can be used to address cross-domain access issues. The access control models should also be able to capture relevant aspects of SLAs. The utility model of clouds demands proper accounting of user and service activities that generates privacy issues because customers might not want to let a provider maintain such detailed accounting records other than for billing purposes. The outsourcing and multi-tenancy aspects of clouds could accelerate customers' fears about accounting logs.

3.3 Trust Management and Policy Integration

Even though the multiple service providers coexist in the cloud and collaborate to provide various services, they might have different security approaches and privacy mechanisms, so it is important that we must address them heterogeneity among their policies. Cloud service providers might need to compose multiple services to enable bigger application services. So mechanisms are placed to ensure that such a dynamic collaboration is handled securely and that security breaches are effectively monitored during the interoperation process. Now, even though individual domain policies are verified, security violations can easily occur during integration and providers should carefully manage access control policies to ensure that policy integration doesn't lead to any security breaches.

In cloud computing environments, the interactions between different service domains, which are driven by service requirements, can also be dynamic, transient, and intensive and a trust framework should be developed to allow for capturing a generic set of parameters required for establishing trust and to manage evolving trust and interaction/sharing requirements. The cloud's policy integration tasks should be able to address challenges such as semantic heterogeneity, secure interoperability, and policy-evolution management. Furthermore, customers' behaviors can evolve rapidly, thereby affecting established trust values. This suggests a need for an integrated, trust-based, secure interoperation framework that helps establish, negotiate, and maintain trust to adaptively support policy integration.

3.4 Privacy and Data Protection

Privacy is a core issue here, including the need to protect identity information, policy components during integration, and transaction histories. This helps to store their data and applications on systems that reside outside of their on-premise data centers. This might be the single greatest fear of cloud clients. By migrating workloads to a shared infrastructure, customers' private information faces increased risk of potential unauthorized access and exposure, [4]. Cloud service providers must assure their customers and provide a high degree of transparency into their operations and privacy assurance. Privacy-protection mechanisms must be embedded in all security solutions. In a related issue, it's becoming important to know who created a piece of data, who modified it and how, and so on. Provenance information could be used for various purposes such as trace back, auditing, and history-based access control. Balancing between data provenance and privacy is a significant challenge in clouds where physical perimeters are abandoned, [5].

4 Responsive Risk Management

Once a comprehensive and systematic identification, evaluation and assessment of risks to the enterprise cloud operations is conducted, a responsive risk management framework is called for. The principal categories of risks that may require systematic mitigation range from the cyber security related issues to business continuity, short-term service disruptions to some major global strategic issues. The research into a responsive risk management framework commensurate with the requirements of the modern internet and Information Technologies and global cyber space is a multi-disciplinary and multi-stakeholder task.

We employ a fusion and integration of best practice from existing research and information technology frameworks to devise an advanced responsive risk management architecture for the modern cyber space applications. This by necessity embodies three orthogonal architectures comprising:

1. An advanced systemic Risk Management framework;
2. An advanced Information Management framework;
3. A responsive expert driven detection and response framework.

The code of practice for the implementation of the ISO31000 standard [6] on risk management highlights a number of principles that any risk management system shall ideally follow and embed. The key principles relevant to cyber risk management are:

- Risk management should be systematic and structured, the approach to risk management should, where practicable, be consistently applied within the organisation
- Risk management should take into account organizational culture, human factors and behaviour
- Risk management should create and protect value, the organization should optimize risk management to contribute to the demonstrable achievement of objectives and maximize overall business and commercial benefits
- Risk management should be transparent and inclusive, Management and stakeholders should be actively involved in risk identification, assessment and response
- Risk management should be dynamic, iterative and responsive to change, The organization should ensure its risk management continually identifies and responds to changes affecting its operating environment.

A risk management framework developed in response to the SafeRelNet [7, 8] European Network of Excellence (FP5 & FP6 Framework) and earlier research [9, 10] complies with the above broad principles and the main ISO standard. This is adopted as an advanced and comprehensive framework that comprises seven principles namely:

I.   Prediction and Proactivity;
II.   Prevention;
III. Protection & Containment;
IV.   Preparedness & Response;
V.   Recovery & Restoration;
VI.   Organisation and Learning;
VII. Continual Enhancement.

The quantitative risk management framework is dynamic and orthogonal to the Information System Architecture. The principle I in the above framework is applied at the outset and principles II & III are run continuously for every tier of the ISA. Upon detection and activation at any tier, principles III, IV and V are triggered to provide immediate protection, response and recovery policies as devised through expert knowledge elicitation and customization whilst also triggering system wide alerts and limitation of services. Principles V & VI are triggered upon cessation of threats to capture the key learning and enhancements of the prevention and protection systems. In principle, all three orthogonal facets of the responsive risk management are dynamic and concurrent processes.

5   Conclusions

Security threats to digital oil fields operation have become increasingly complex, as traditional and digital worlds converge. One of the Oil and gas industry priorities has continuously been security, since it plays an important part in the nations critical infrastructures due to highly interconnected and mutually dependent in complex ways, both physically and through a host of information and communications technologies. An incident in one infrastructure may directly and indirectly affect other infrastructures through cascading and escalating failures.

These days, sensors and actuators are increasingly embedded in various physical objects, in a way that link them through wired and wireless networks with a connection to the Internet. The volume of data provided from such a system is considerable.

Considering the complexities of digital oil fields in the cloud, the industry still is geared to migrate to the cloud because of the various advantages in exploration and production information delivery, collaboration and decision-support.

Therefore, a comprehensive risk register, identifying, characterizing, assessing and mitigating all risks need to be devised to ensure business continuity should any of the promised key benefits be interrupted due to local or global disruptions or threats.

Understanding the implications and challenges faced in risk management in this paper a new Responsive Cyber-Physical Risk Management Framework (RECYPHR) is proposed in order to tackle the traditional shortfalls and provide a Near Real-Time (NERT) response to managing risks.

References

1. Takabi, H., Joshi, J.B.D., Ahn, G.: Security and privacy challenges in cloud computing environments. IEEE Secur. Priv. 8(6), 24–31 (2010)
2. Information Gatekeepers. Photonic Sensor Consortium. http://www.igigroup.com/ (2015). Accessed 2 Jun 2015
3. Zhou, M., Zhang, R., Xie, W., Qian, W., Zhou, A.: Security and privacy in cloud computing: a survey. In: 2010 Sixth International Conference on Semantics, Knowledge and Grids, pp. 105–112 (2010)
4. Tianfield, H.: Security issues in cloud computing. In: IEEE International Conference on Systems, Man, and Cybernetics. COEX, Seoul, Korea, 14–17 Oct 2012
5. Carroll, N., Helfert, M., Lynn, T.: Towards the development of a cloud service capability assessment framework. In: Mahmood, Z. (ed.) Continued Rise of the Cloud: Advances and Trends in Cloud Computing, Chap. 12, pp. 289–336. Springer, London (2014)
6. BS 31100, Risk Management – Code of Practice and Guidance for the Implementation of BS ISO 31000
7. Hessami, A.G.: Framework for safety, security and sustainability risk management. In: Soares, C.G. (ed) Safety and Reliability of Industrial Products, Systems and Structures, pp. 21–31. CRC Press, Boca Raton (2010). ISBN 978-415-66392-2
8. SafeRelNet: http://www.mar.ist.utl.pt/saferelnet/overview.asp

9. Hessami, A.G.: A systems framework for safety & security - the holistic paradigm. Syst. Eng. J. USA **7**(2), 99–112 (2004)
10. Hessami, A.: Risk Management a Systems Paradigm. Syst. Eng. J. Int. Counc. Syst. Eng. **2**(3), 156–167 (1999)

Simulation of Cloud Data Security Processes and Performance

Krishan Chand[⊠], Muthu Ramachandran, and Ah-Lian Kor

School of Computing, Creative Technologies and Engineering,
Leeds Beckett University, Leeds, UK
k.chand7596@student.leedsbeckett.ac.uk,
{M.Ramachandran,A.Kor}@LeedsBeckett.ac.uk

Abstract. In the world of cloud computing, millions of people are using cloud computing for the purpose of business, education and socialization. Examples of cloud applications are: Google Drive for storage, Facebook for social networks, etc. Cloud users use the cloud computing infrastructure thinking that these services are easy and safe to use. However, there are security and performance issues to be addressed. This paper discusses how cloud users and cloud providers address performance and security issues. In this research, we have used business process modelling and simulation to explore the performance characteristics and security concerns in the service development life cycle. The results show that Business Process Modelling Notations (BPMN) simulation is effective for the study of cloud security process in detail before actual implementation. The total simulation duration time was 51 days and 9 h 40 min but the results are displayed in 7 s only.

Keywords: Cloud computing · Performance · Security · Bonnita soft

1 Introduction

Cloud computing has increased impact on business and and other sectors. Cloud computing encompasses services which are provided by a company or third party provider on the internet and these services are accessible from anywhere over the internet. Increased demand for cloud computing services provides so many benefits over the web connected devices. Such web services use the cloud server to store massive amount of data.

As per the definition given by CSA [1] cloud computing also provides a platform where applications, infrastructure, and information sources are separated. According to techtarget.com, cloud computing has given the opportunity to businesses to use the computer resources as a utility rather than investing too much money on building a computing infrastructure. Companies can use the cloud servers to store data or use the infrastructure in the cloud instead of building one locally. That will also help to reduce the cost of maintenance [2].

Due to the growing popularity of cloud computing and the massive data available in the cloud, security are the biggest issue and challenge faced by cloud users. Khanghahi and Ravanmehr [3] have stated that for better performance, cloud computing resources

© Springer International Publishing Switzerland 2015
H. Jahankhani et al. (Eds.): ICGS3 2015, CCIS 534, pp. 285–295, 2015.
DOI: 10.1007/978-3-319-23276-8_26

should be efficiently managed. A structured security framework is necessary for securing data in the cloud. Cloud data security is very important, it should be secure, authenticated and encrypted. According to an article on computerweekly.com, many small organizations are willing to take advantages of cloud computing yet they are also wary of the performance, privacy of the data and the reliability of the services. In addition, FSB (Federation of Small Business) also states that the use of cloud computing for small business would be a challenge because they are not sure who will be responsible if something went wrong [4].

Security and performance concerns provide the ground for this research. A framework has been designed to provide better services with security to the cloud users. The paper is divided into five sections. Section 2 describes the literature, security and performance concerns. Section 3 explains how a simulation and questionnaire have been used as an approach. Section 4 shows the results of simulation and questionnaire. Finally, Sect. 5 presents the conclusion of the report.

2   Background

Cloud computing is the fastest growing sector of the information technology field. According to Munir et al. [5], data security and reliability is also a major concern for the cloud users. These security issues can be divided into two different classes: first is the security concern for cloud providers and the second is the security for the cloud user. Moreover, Khanghahi and Ravanmehr [3] also state that higher performance of services and whatever is connected to the cloud has a direct impact on cloud users and providers. Therefore, performance evaluation is also an important consideration for cloud users and providers.

Harauz et al. [6] highlight security related regulatory and legal anxieties. Cloud providers should propose the encryption of data scheme at the time of data storage on the cloud so that consumers can avoid unapproved access and can also be assured of data integrity, confidentiality and availability. Strict access control tools and scheduled data backups mechanism should be proposed. According to NIST [7], it is also stated that three-level security should be applied in cyber security so as to ensure data confidentiality, integrity and availability.

Security and privacy issues are the main barriers in the acceptance of cloud computing. On the grounds of the discussed issues relating to security, data should be secured at the time when data is processed in the cloud. Additionally, data privacy should also be respected in order to win customers' confidence. A customer's privacy manager tool should be proposed so as to mitigate security issues and also to provide additional privacy features [8].

2.1   Security Issues in Cloud

Sarwar et al. [9] suggest security threat is biggest when data in cloud are stored by a third party vendor at some remote location. Consequently, consumers will either have limited or less control on the data which is hosted in the cloud. Additionally, trust between the service provider and the client is extremely important in the context of cloud security. In this paper, some security related aspects of a Cloud Computing system will be discussed.

Mahmood [10] has listed data-related issues in a cloud environment:

- **Data Location and Data Transmission:** The variation in policies, regulation, environment, and legislation between client's country and service provider's country might lead to a potential risk.
- **Data Availability:** The unavailability of data when required might lead to service outage.
- **Data Security:** When data travels between two different territories with high speed internet technology, the likelihood of security breach increases.

Behl and Mahmood [11] states that security-related issues in the Cloud has emphasized on various aspects of data usage, treatment, and disbursal. Those issues are:

- **Availability and Performance:** Service Level Agreement forms an essential part in cloud data security because it helps with real time data monitoring.
- **Service Disruptions:** If the connections come from known IP tools and Domain Name Server then problems concerning non-availability of resources at the service provider's end would not exist.

In order to overcome the above challenges, it is significantly important to draft and design a security model which provides data security in cloud environment (ibid).

2.2 Performance Issues in Cloud

Due to increasing demand of cloud computing, many factors can affect its performance. According to Khanghahi and Ravanmehr [3], some of the factors are as follows:

- **Recovery:** At the time of errors and failures, data can be lost without reasons, and thus the volume of recoverable data can impact performance.
- **Network bandwidth:** This could be a major factor for the performance, if the bandwidth of a network of service provider is low then by default the performance will be low.
- **Number of users:** Overload of users can also reduce performance, as service providers have a limit on the number of concurrent users.
- **Unavailability:** Unavailability of the services and restricted access can reduce performance.

3 Approaches

Modelling and quantitative method have been used in this research. The modelling method is related to the simulation which will provide some graphical results and through these graphical analysis, the performance of the services provided will be evaluated. The quantitative aspect of the research involves a survey using a questionnaire.

According to De Leeuw [12] use of a range of approaches can provide particular advantages to the researcher because they are complementary.

3.1 Simulation

According to Naim [13] simulation involves a series of processes for building a computerised model so that particular results can be achieved through the observation of the model. Simulation process includes assumption making and parameterization. An experimenter is the user or modeller who conducts experiments using the model.

In this research, the Business Process Modeling Notation (BPMN) with Bonita soft is used. Running the BPMN model will help to provide inghts into the performance and cloud business security process.

The BPMN process includes the different cyclic phases shown in Fig. 1. The process always starts with a green round notation that is called the client or user. The user sends a message which contains a task to a particular process. According to the particular processes defined by the experimenter, the process ends with the finishing red end circle. (Creation of BPMN process with green and red round notations are shown in Fig. 2). After the creation of the whole process, the next task for the experimenter is to provide appropriate notation and assign variable to each process. Subsequently, the next task is to manage resources and load profiles. And then finally, run the simulation. The experimenter can run the simulation multiple times according to the requirement of the process. The experimenter can change the variables and resources accordingly in order to enhance the performance.

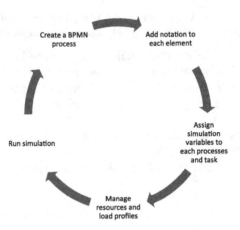

Fig. 1. BPMN simulation process cycle

Simulation Framework. Many simulation tools are available in the field of computers but this research has used the BPMN with Bonita Soft for particular reasons. The main reason for using Bonnita Soft is that no waiting time is required to obtain the simulation results because it could generate the report within a minute. Simulation process has been used to optimize a cloud business security process to check the performance of the cloud. The researcher has used the BPMN simulation tool to check performance of the cloud servers before deploying the services for the benefit of cloud providers. Cloud users are not aware of these processes because these are part of the cloud internal framework which is used by every cloud provider. Through this BPMN model, cloud providers can check the performance of the cloud by experimenting with different parameters. This model can be used to check the performance of the cloud before deploying it. Before deploying the cloud, simulation process will provide the opportunity to diagnose faults, blockage in a system, resource management and how to manipulate the different varia- bles in order to make optimize the process. The manipulation of resources and variables will enable cloud providers to uncover how performance can be improved to provide quality services with security. The following simulation design (Fig. 2) has been made to check the performance of the cloud services with security. This is the internal frame- work for cloud providers, which includes the different processes and task to provide better and optimized services with security. The different results of running the simu- lation will be discussed in the next section.

The above Fig. 2 shows a design which includes all the different processes which cloud computing uses. Process starts with the log in authentication where Customers ID and passwords are required. If the id or password is wrong, it will not allow the user to proceed further. If id and password are valid then the user can go ahead with the data uploading process. In this state, a customer can upload the data through his account and the rest of the part is operated by the cloud providers. After the user has finished, the cloud provider checks the data status then the data will go through the security Centre,

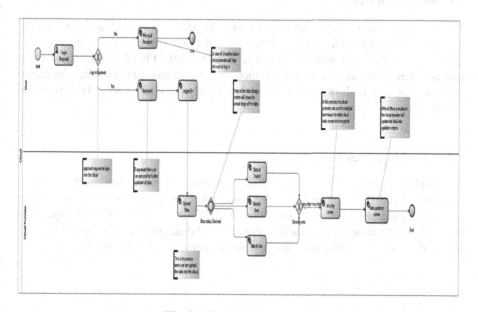

Fig. 2. Simulation framework

where the data encryption techniques will be employed to encrypt the data in different codes. After encryption the data, the Centre stores the data in the cloud server.

3.2 Questionnaire

A questionnaire approach has been used to collect the quantitative data which will help to support the simulation data. Questionnaire is the most popular research method used in academic research [14]. Additionally, Bryan [15] has illustrated that questionnaire removes the distance factor between researcher and participant. Also the questionnaire is a tool used by the researcher to collect data in a limited time period [16].

The questionnaire includes questions relating to security concern of the cloud users and the performance availability. The questionnaire consists of four parts: (a) awareness about cloud computing in cloud users; (b) how the cloud user feels about data security; (c) data execution time while uploading the data on the cloud; (d) awareness of security settings of the cloud provider.

According to Cohen et al. [14], there are so many ways to distribute the questionnaire to the respondents. For example: email, via online or can be delivered by hand. By distributing the questionnaire by hand will take less time but researcher needs to find the respondents in order to get the responses. Therefore, the method selected in the research is online, as the researcher has better access to a wider range of respondents.

4 Result and Analyses

4.1 Simulation Results

This section will describe the simulation results that the researcher obtained by running the simulation. To go to a starting point, the simulation has been set with the start date 11/04/2015 at 02:42:04 with the end date of 01/06/2015 till 12:22:04. Bonnita soft process gives results almost instantly without waiting till end date. The total simulation duration time was 51 days and 9 h 40 min but, results came in 7 s only. The results are as follows.

4.2 Cloud Instances Execution Time

As it can be seen in Fig. 3, there is a direct proportional relationship between the instances time and execution time. This means that the resources which has been provided in this process will not be able to cope the increase in the number of cloud users beyond its breaking point. Consequently, the case cloud user should consider this point in order to reduce the cloud execution time and increase the performance level of services.

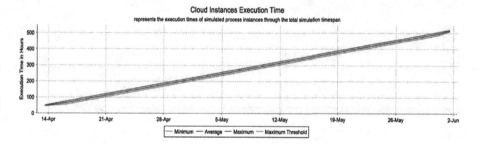

Fig. 3. Cloud instances execution time

4.3   Variation in Approved Instances Waiting Time

Undoubtedly, increase in execution time will increase the waiting time as well (see Fig. 4). This graph shows the variation in waiting time. It means that during busy times, the waiting time is high and vice versa. Consequently, a cloud user can increase the resources during peak hours so as to reduce the waiting time and they will be able to provide optimized services to the end-users.

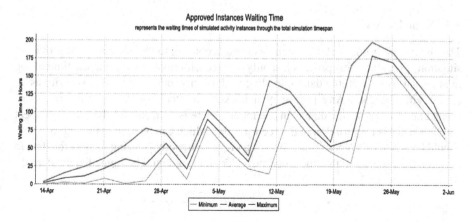

Fig. 4. Approved instances waiting time

4.4   Upload Data Instances Execution Time

Figure 5 shows the average, minimum and maximum execution time to upload data. The uploading time increases with the increase of user instances. In this scenario, a cloud user can put more resources to decrease the execution time, which results in the end-user getting better services.

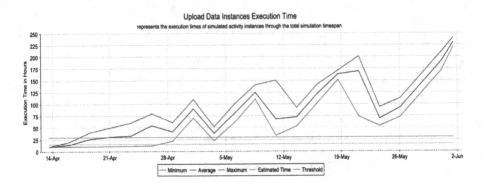

Fig. 5. Upload data instances execution time

This graph is almost same like as upload data execution time graph. Because there is a direct relation between the approved waiting time and upload data execution time. If the waiting time will increase then it will also impact the time of uploading the data. As the cloud server is busy at the time of the approval so it will impact the whole cloud services as well. So if the cloud user will manage the resources in the first instance then this time will automatically decrease and the cloud performance will be optimized.

4.5 Security Area

The simulation framework has been designed according to the current cloud providers situation. Therefore, this process has only one security pool, which is at the time of log in approval. But, from the data uploading to data encryption there is no security associated with the data. Any professional hacker can steal the data in the process of uploading the data, as the data is in use mode. There is no result for the security aspect and thus there is no variation in the security part, which can be seen in the Fig. 6. There should be alarm or trigger or any kind of alert, if somebody is trying to steal the data in between the process so that the cloud provider and user could be immediately alerted.

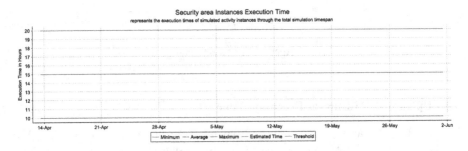

Fig. 6. Security area execution time

4.6 Questionnaire

This part of the paper explains the data collected through the questionnaire. This data is quantitative and provides insights into the respondents' views on cloud performance and security. The questionnaire was been sent out to 50 participants (30 via facebook messaging boxes and 20 via google mail). However, the researcher only received responses from 39 respondents. Through the analysis of these responses, the researcher has drawn the following conclusions specific to this sample (note: these findings may not be representative of the entire population):

How safe is data on cloud? The question was asked to obtain the views of cloud users with respect to cloud data security. The most popular cloud-based services is data storage in the cloud server. It can be seen in Fig. 7, that out of 39 responses, 48.7 % of the participants felt that the data is not secure on the cloud. And 48.7 % had no clue about data security. From the pie chart below, it can be concluded that almost 50 % of the users were not aware of security concerns and the rest 50 % had no idea about security.

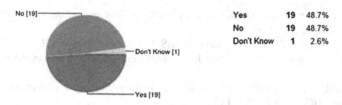

Yes	19	48.7%
No	19	48.7%
Don't Know	1	2.6%

Fig. 7. How safe is data on cloud server?

Data Uploading in the Cloud. To check the performance of the services provided by the cloud users, a question asked was about data uploading. As Fig. 8 shows, a big proportion of users (i.e. 64 %) had faced some kind of problem relating to data uploading. This could be ratified through proper resource management which could cope with users overload.

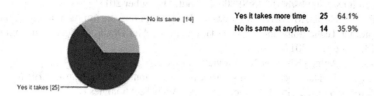

Yes it takes more time	25	64.1%
No its same at anytime.	14	35.9%

Fig. 8. Data uploading problem

5   Conclusion

The paper has proposed a design to check the performance and security before deploying the services to end users. Through the review of selected literature, it is found that the security and performance is affecting the cloud computing business. With the help of simulation processes, the research reveals that the execution time increases with the increase in instances. Consequently, the available resources will not be able to cope with the increased user load at a certain point in time. The proposed design in Bonnita soft can help cloud users to manage their business resources in order to provide better services to the end users. It has also been found that, in the current situation, no security aspect has been addressed at the time of data usage. Cloud providers can incorporate some alarm or trigger, when a data theft occurs. The Bonnita soft tool can be a useful guide for cloud providers. Additionally, outcomes of the questionnaire analysis reveals that cloud users are using the services everyday without being aware of the cloud security level. In the world of computers and cloud computing, cloud users ought to be made aware of such type of security and it is imperative for cloud providers to better manage the resources in order to provide better services with security.

References

1. CSA: Security guidance for critical areas of focus in cloud computing v2.1. Cloud Security Alliance, December 2009
2. Techtarget: What is Platform as a Service (PaaS)? - Definition from WhatIs.com (2015). http://searchcloudcomputing.techtarget.com/definition/Platform-as-a-Service-PaaS. Accessed 29 May 2015
3. Khanghahi, N., Ravanmehr, R.: Cloud computing performance evaluation: issues and challenges. IJCCSA **3**(5), 29–41 (2013)
4. ComputerWeekly.com: Security fears stop small firms using cloud computing (2015). http://www.computerweekly.com/news/2240240940/Security-fears-stopping-small-firms-using-cloud-computing. Accessed 20 April 2015
5. Munir, K., Palaniappan, S.: Secure Cloud Architecture. Adv. Comput. Int. J. (ACIJ) **4**(1), 9–22 (2013)
6. Harauz, J., Kauifman, L., Potter, B.: Data security in the world of cloud computing. IEEE Secur. Priv. Mag. **7**(4), 61–64 (2009)
7. NIST: Guidelines on security and privacy in public cloud computing. http://csrc.nist.gov/publications/nistpubs/800-145/SP800-145.pdf. December 2011
8. Siani, P., Miranda, M.: Security threats in cloud computing. In: 6th International Conference on Internet Technology and Secured Transactions, Abu Dhabi, United Arab Emirates, pp. 11–14, December 2011
9. Sarwar, A., Ahmed Khan, M.N.: A review of trust aspects in cloud computing security (2013)
10. Mahmood, Z.: Data location and security issues in cloud computing. In: IEEE International Conference on Emerging Intelligent Data and Web Technologies (2011)
11. Behl, A.: Emerging security challenges in cloud computing. In: IEEE international Conference Information and Communication Technologies (WICT) (2011)
12. De Leeuw, E.: To mix or not to mix data collection modes in surveys. J. Official Stat. **21**(2), 233–255 (2005)
13. Kheir, N.A.: System Modelling and Computer Simulation, 2nd edn. Marcell Dekker, New York (1996)

14. Cohen, L., Manion, L., Morrison, K.: Research Methods in Education, 6th edn. Routledge, Abingdon (2007)
15. Bryman, A.: The debate about quantitative and qualitative research: a question of method or epistemology? Br. J. Sociol. **35**(1), 75–92 (1984)
16. Best, J., Kahn, J.: Research in Education. Pearson Education Inc., Upper Saddle River (2006)

A Framework for Cloud Security Audit

Umar Mukhtar Ismail[1(✉)], Shareeful Islam[1],
and Haralambus Mouratidis[2]

[1] School of Architecture, Computing and Engineering,
University of East London, London, UK
{U0852138,shareeful}@uel.ac.uk
[2] School of Computing, Engineering and Mathematics,
University of Brighton, Brighton, UK
H.Mouratidis@brighton.ac.uk

Abstract. More and more individual users and businesses are earnestly considering cloud adoption for achieving mission objectives. However, concerns being raised include the ability of users to ascertain the security posture of cloud service providers to adequately safeguard data and applications. We present a cloud security audit framework that entails a set of concepts such as goals, constraint, plan and evidence to enable prospective cloud users to identify their migration goals and introduce constraints that must be satisfied by a potential cloud provider before migration. The concepts are considered as a language for describing the properties necessary for cloud security audit through a metamodel. An example is given to demonstrate the applicability of the approach.

Keywords: Cloud computing · Security · Audit · Evidence · Control · Constraint · Secure plan

1 Introduction

The emergence of cloud computing (CC) as an information technology (IT) phenomenon is transforming the way services are delivered and managed. It has brought a fundamental shift in how services are developed, deployed, scaled, and maintained using a pay-per-use model. It is changing the contemporary landscape of IT service delivery models for both businesses and individuals. Despite the many benefits, various concerns are associated with CC services including security, auditability, management and control, compliance, transparency, etc. These issues and many others have limited the aspiration of corporate organizations, businesses and individuals to adopt the services. We therefore, attempt to approach this obstacle from a cloud migration security audit perspective as an evaluation and assessment method that facilitates decision making process. Security audit involves a systematic evaluation and assessment of controls in determining conformance to established set of criteria [1, 17, 19].

Existing researches have approached cloud migration security audit from varying understandings and approaches. For instance, [2] proposed an approach to quantify the impact of cloud migration for existing organizational architecture and applications. Also, [3] proposed a cryptographic technique for verifying integrity as a method for

© Springer International Publishing Switzerland 2015
H. Jahankhani et al. (Eds): ICGS3 2015, CCIS 534, pp. 296–309, 2015.
DOI: 10.1007/978-3-319-23276-8_27

realising audit services in the cloud. However, a systematic auditing framework that uses a set of concepts relevant to the goals and risk appetite of a cloud computing customers (CSC) is lacking. The standpoint of our approach presumes that in order to minimize the impact of issues and concerns ingrained in CC services, it is imperative for CSCs, prior to cloud adoption, identify their goals and the risks associated to those goals, as well as ensuring that strategies that sufficiently protect and safeguard their data and applications are adequately implemented in the cloud environment. This paper contributes in this direction. We follow a set of concepts, such as actors, constraints, and goals based on the existing software engineering methodology, i.e., Secure Tropos, and extend it with new concepts such as evidence, risk, and audit report in an attempt to develop an audit framework [5]. The reason for choosing Secure Tropos is that it provides in-depth analysis of security issues within an organization and its social setting. The concepts of Secure Tropos and those proposed in our approach are integrated to enable the identification of CSC goals, imposing constraints based on the goals, and assessing CSP generated evidence, which could potentially fulfill the formulated goals. A use case scenario is used to exemplify the validity of the proposed framework.

The paper is structured as follows. Section 2 discusses the existing works covered under cloud auditing, and Sect. 3 covers the challenges of performing audit in cloud context. Section 4 introduces the concepts necessary for developing the framework. Section 5 demonstrates the implementation of the various concepts within the framework using a use case. Section 6 provides a discussion and concludes the paper.

2 Security Audit in Cloud

2.1 Cloud Auditing Approaches

This sub-section covers the related works that have been performed in CC audit domain. [6] introduced the current trends in cloud audit and assurance initiatives and evaluated the feasibility of accessing different security documentations provided by CSPs to determine whether they provide adequate information to meet customers' risk assessment and be compliant with legislative requirements. [4] developed an assessment methodology as a standardized way for CSPs to provide and share detailed information about their service performance and security with prospective CSCs. Such approaches provide a systematic method of data collection, while others proposed applications that assist CSCs in assessing the impact of migrating IT architecture to cloud based environment. [7] proposed the Complete-Auditable-Reportable (C.A.RE) approach to help prospective cloud customers' measure the sufficiency of security services offered by CSPs and map those offerings with their internal operational requirements through an assessment process that identifies risks, security and privacy handling, internal and external audit and how information on security issues could be transparently shared with cloud customer. [8] presented Security-Audit-as-a-Service architecture that uses the concept of utilizing autonomous agents for monitoring a cloud infrastructure. The SaaS architecture is considered as a possible audit infrastructure that could be used in the audit of cloud systems from the context of both cloud provider and consumers. [9] framework attempted to address audit and compliance in cloud services by developing an automated and standardised way to facilitate information gathering regarding the performance and security of cloud services.

In summary, all the above mentioned efforts introduce valuable contributions to the realm of CC auditing. However, some efforts require the inter-collaboration between CSPs, which is difficult in real context. There have been little efforts made towards building an auditing framework that could support organizations in analyzing security needs while migrating to the cloud platform. Therefore, a comprehensive auditing framework that is applicable to all cloud service and deployment model is needful. Such framework needs to be able to support organizations in identifying business goals, security requirements, and sufficient assessment of cloud offerings for a well-founded decision making.

3   Challenges to Cloud Auditing

The emergence of CC has brought a significant effect to the practices and approaches used in performing an audit particularly in the assessment of controls, checks and balances. This is because the various security concerns and issues associated with cloud technology cannot be addressed by traditional measures, and it requires a different approach to evaluate the information systems, practices and operations in the cloud [10]. The major challenges to cloud audit are identified below:

Difficulty in Identifying Control Objectives. The challenge in this regard as identified by [11] deals with auditors' competence and knowledge to identify what control objectives to audit in order to address cloud-specific security concerns. This means that for a cloud security audit to be effective, ultimate familiarity and knowledge of the cloud system is required to enable an auditor to focus on those security factors that may require more attention.

Scale and Scope of Cloud Audit. The scale of cloud audit also raises a serious challenge because a single physical machine is configured to host multiple virtual machines, which indeed becomes overwhelmingly difficult to perform considering substantially number of machines and identical elements to be audited. The audit scope also results to a challenge due to the types, extent and boundary of cloud technologies to audit in the cloud environment such as virtual switches, virtual firewalls, and virtual machines etc. Furthermore, an escalation of the audit scope and scale, added with the multiple geographical locations of cloud systems, tremendously provoke the complexity of the audit process.

A notable problem identified in our paper is the shortage of audit approaches for the verification of CSP offerings while placing focus on specific user goals from the inception of migration. Evaluating CSP at early stages prove to be cost-effective strategy in mitigating risks and unforeseeable losses that may transpire due to unsubstantiated migration decisions. Therefore, our framework addresses these problem through a language that defines concepts and modelled activities necessary for enabling CSCs to audit CSP offerings. It uses a goal-driven approach to help provide stakeholders with an insight of identifying the crucial requisites to fulfilling formulated goals. The framework also assists in managing the risks associated with user goals and CSP offerings. Small and large organizations and businesses are the beneficiaries of this work. The work is novel in approach and makes an important contribution in making cloud migration more transparent, systematic and user-centric.

4 Modelling Concept

As stated before, we follow Secure Tropos methodology to define the language and extend the methodology with new concepts that are necessary for cloud security audit [5]. Secure Troops adopts the i* modelling by [12] that focuses on the elicitation and analysis of security requirements. It uses the concepts of actors, goals, constraints, and uses social dependencies for defining the obligations of actors (dependees) to other actors (dependers) in-terms of security. An overview of the concepts used by the proposed framework is given below:

Actor. An actor represents an entity that has strategic goals within its organisational setting [5, 17]. Based on the layers of CC services model, actors are identified as CSPs and CSCs. A CSP develops and operates services that offer value to the CSC. They develop applications that are offered and deployed on the CC platform, and also supply infrastructure, network facilities and other computing and storage services needed to run applications within the cloud. A CSC requires the services provided by a CSP to attain their business goals, hence resort to patronising computing services from CSPs.

Goals: A goal represents the overall aims and objectives of an actor that support its business requirements and strategic interests. The CSC is the main actor with four strategic goals:

- *Technical.* Deals with ensuring that technology adequately provides for technical requirements in terms of data, application, and management interoperability/ portability.
- *Security & Privacy.* Involves ensuring the integrity and confidentiality of migrated data and applications.
- *Business Goals.* Involves services and operations that support the CSC in attaining business objectives and transforming their business models such as cost reduction, flexibility, and increased efficiency.
- *Auditability Goal.* Represents an assessment process of ensuring that adopted technology support goals. It defines the scope and criteria of an assessment.

Constraints. Constraints are defined as a set of conditions, rules or restrictions imposed to an actor that prevent specific goals from being achieved unless the constraints are otherwise fulfilled [5, 14, 18]. In our case, the security control and compliance action imposed by CSC are treated as constraints to the CSP in order to support their goals. Security control constraints require considerable implementation of technical and nontechnical measures to safeguard and protect CSC entities. Compliance action constraints require the delivery of CSP services to be in accordance with established standards, best practices, law and regulations. CSA's CCM [13] control objectives are taken to formulate the security constraints, while compliance to standards and industry best practice that are relevant to a CSC's domain of operations are introduced as the compliance constraints.

Plan. Plan is a way by which an actor uses resources to execute tasks so as to fulfil goals or constraints. The fulfilment of a plan can be a means for satisfying or contributing towards the satisfaction of a goal [15]. A CSP's plan of meeting constraints is by generating evidence on the implementation of security controls in its environment, and compliance actions to prove that those controls have been verified, certified, and accredited by relevant third-party authorities.

Evidence. Evidence represents affirmations in various forms by a CSP to disclose how constraints are addressed. The CSP is required to produce evidence(s) as a means of demonstrating how they implement their plans to satisfy the constraints. This is based on a well justified verification that desired processes, controls and technologies are sufficiently implemented and practiced in accordance to established principles. Evidence is generated on the basis of scope and sources. Scope is the operational area of cloud for which evidence is provided; and evidence source implies the source of information through which evidences are generated.

- *Scope.* The evidence scope is characterised by (i) Security controls dealing with the aspects of technical, human, physical, and operational safeguards in CSP environment to avoid or minimise loss of integrity, availability and confidentiality of CSC entities. (ii) Compliance actions meet the requirements of prescribed rules and regulations, accepted practices, legislations, or specified standards.
- *Source.* The available information documenting CSP service provisions are validated through such sources as: audit reports, SLA, benchmarks (e.g. CSA CloudAudit), observations, third-party asserted certifications, etc.

Audit Report. The audit report is defined as a written opinion or decision about the evidences based on findings. The findings are compared against audit criteria in order to determine how evidences satisfy goals. Audit criteria is a reference what procedures, policies, specifications, or requirements evidences are compared against [16]. In evaluating the audit result, the CSC's internal auditors and other stakeholders are involved to define the criteria requirements or select the procedures and policies that should be used as a criteria, as well as determining how such evaluation result satisfy the goals. For example, an objective checklist may be developed for which the audit findings are compared against and the outputs assigned a ranking of how they satisfy goal.

The metamodel illustrated in Fig. 1 shows an overall view of the framework. An actor has a single or multiple goals such as business and security. These goals need to be fulfilled by meeting constraints.

CSC is an actor that has interest in the CC service and deployment models offered by another actor, the CSP, hence planning to adopt their services. The CSC may have different categories of goals such as security & privacy, and auditability goals. The goals are general ambitions of what a CSC aims to achieve by migrating to the cloud. While concerns are raised regarding how these goals can be fulfilled by a potential

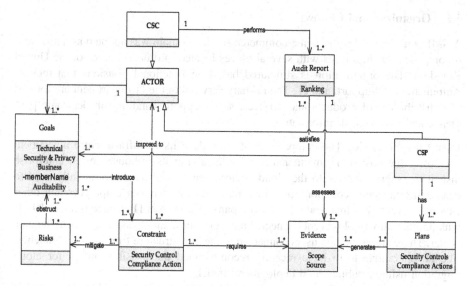

Fig. 1. Meta model

CSP, constraints for migration are introduced. A constraint represents a description of a set of actions that need to be fulfilled for certain occurrences to take place [14]. Security and compliance are defined as two separate indispensable attributes that support the CSC goals. Therefore, they are introduced as two constraints to the CSP so that evidences that fulfil those constraints are provided. When a constraint is introduced, further analysis is required to establish how they can be satisfied [5]. A plan represents a way of doing something and how constraints are approached [15], it is therefore provided by the CSP to show how it incorporates a set of security control mechanisms that sufficiently safeguard its environment. It also shows compliance actions that demonstrate how general operations are performed according to best practices. However, the plan does not independently substantiate CSP claims, they need to be validated. Evidences on the implementation of the plans are provided by the CSP, particularly in relation to the areas specified in the constraint (security controls and compliance) to prove validation. An audit report process is then applied to evaluate the evidences by comparing them against established criteria (such as policies, procedures, or CSP defined requirements) and determining how the evidences satisfy goals.

5   Example

This section presents an example to demonstrate the applicability of the proposed approach.

5.1 Organizational Context

A SME with line of business in e-commerce service domain was adopted as a use case. It comprises 80 employees with several offices located in different cities of the United Kingdom. The organization is structured based on functional divisions that include Administration, Support, and IT. The primary services of the IT department are formed of e-distribution of products and services, sales support, handling of electronic payments, and exchange of information.

User Case Scenario. The company wants to reduce its IT infrastructure investment and lower the cost of IT maintenance by outsourcing its in-house hosted enterprise instant messaging service to the cloud environment, which is predominantly used to enable instantaneous collaboration and communication between employees and other external stakeholders that deal with the company. The current IT storage is about 10 TB with 35 internal virtual servers connected through four main physical servers in the data center. There are in total 65 users connected to the infrastructure from various branches. The IT operations team have recently recommended the possible option for cloud migration using a public cloud deployment model.

A brief description of a scenario allows us to exemplify how the SME could exploit the benefits of our framework to achieve the security and compliance of its instant communication platform. We will focus on the key steps and activities of the framework, while disregarding the general formalities in cloud migration process. The result of the case study scenario can be extended and applied to any organization regardless of the migration type, deployment and service model.

5.2 Implementation of Cloud Security Audit Framework

In implementing our framework and its concepts through the use scenario, the following outputs are consolidated

Actor. The SME is identified as the CSC while the CSP implies the entity that provides CC services.

Goals. The SME has a list of goals they want to achieve by migrating to the cloud. The goals are classified according to three categories that contain sub-goals. However, due to space limitations, we are not considering all the identified goals for further illustrations. Our focus is particularly placed on confidentiality, integrity, and availability goals.

- *Technical Goals.* (i) The compatibility, interoperability and portability of the CSP environment to support the messaging service.
- *Security and Privacy.* (i) The confidentiality and integrity of information; (ii) high availability to support significant number of employees to share and exchange information; (iii) the handling of communication instances in accordance with security standards and data protection laws of the United Kingdom.
- *Business Goal.* (i) Realising cost reduction and business sustainability.

- *Auditability Goal.* (i) Ensuring the realization of goals through high efficiency, effectiveness by adopting CC; (ii) ensuring compliance with standards, laws, regulations, policies, procedures and agreements in the cloud environment.

Risks. The issues and concerns that could prevent the SME from attaining their goals include:

- The unavailability of services as a result of intentional or accidental service disruptions.
- The violation of information confidentiality and integrity arising from unauthorised access, modification, alteration or theft of information.
- Non-conformance of operating environment to data protection acts and security standards.
- The failure of adopted CSP to provide secure services.

Constraints. From the identification of goals, constraints are imposed to the CSP, which require the demonstration of evidences on how to fulfill them. The CCM's security objectives that are relevant to ensuring the confidentiality, integrity, and availability of cloud services were interpreted to form the security control constraints. The company's area of business is within banking and finance domain and for that reason, it ought to comply with basic relevant security standards such as PCI DSS and ISO27001, as well as Data Protection Act of the United Kingdom. Table 1 shows the constraints necessary for satisfying the goals.

Table 1. Goals and Constraints

Goals	Constraint ID (C)	Constraint (security & compliance)
Confidentiality & integrity	C1	Protect data in transit and at rest.
	C2	Strong access control measures that incorporate identity and access management.
	C3	Compliance to PCI-DSS, and ISO 27001.
	C4	Conformance to data protection act of the United Kingdom.
Availability	C5	BCP, DRP and backup plans that ensure optimum availability of service.
	C6	System availability monitoring for service continuity.
	C7	A validated customer support strategy that support users for technical, operational, and management issues.

Plans. In relation to the constraints introduced by the SME, existing and reputable CSPs that specialize in the delivery of SaaS provided details into their plans of supporting such constraints. The plans have indicated the implementation of comprehensive control environment that comprises all the necessary control, activities, processes and procedures for the delivery of offerings. They also provide a highly secure and controlled platform that support a wide range of security features to safeguard customer entities. Furthermore, compliance programs are in place to validate their control environments through accreditations, certifications, and independent third-party audit reports. The CSP has manifested the implementation and credibility of their plans by providing evidences. The existing action plans to support the constraints include;

- Data protection for both data in transit and at rest.
- Control and management of access to customer entities and the entire operational environment.
- Compliance programs with industry security standards.
- Compliance programs with law, legal, and data protection acts.
- Service recovery, protection, and continuity architectures.
- Continuous monitoring of operational systems and architectures.
- Continuous support to customers.

Evidence. Two cloud providers, CSP 'A' and CSP 'B', provided a wide range of information as evidences to establish the application and functionality of their plans. The evidences are operationalized by evidence scope and source. The evidence source on the one hand explored CSP web-portals, Request for Information (ROI), and audit reports for relevant information. The evidence scope on the other hand, is the focus area of investigation into the domains of (i) information security controls from technical and operational perspectives; and (ii) operational procedures in accordance to security standards and data protection acts. All the evidences specifically aim at protecting customer data against loss, destruction, unauthorized access and unlawful destruction. Many evidences were generated, however, in order to minimize space usage, we selected a few worthy of evaluation. The collected evidences were evaluated and assessed in an attempt to measure their relevance, effectiveness and how they satisfy the SME's goals. The extent of the audit scope focuses on security controls and compliance programs as maintained in the CSP plans. Table 2 shows the audit observation after a rigorous assessment. Evidences are drawn in line with constraints.

Audit Report. The audit report constitutes an evaluation on the outcome of observations performed on the evidences. Evidences are compared against defined criteria in order to determine the degree to which each of the evidences potentially satisfy goals. The criteria could be requirements, policies, procedure, or specification, however, we defined requirements criteria for this comparison in consideration of the essential goals of the SME. The criteria are represented according to a ranking of 'High – Medium – Low' as below:

- *High.* The sufficient controls, technologies and practices that ensure the confidentiality, integrity, and availability of data and applications are significantly implemented. Compliance programs are certified to be useful and relevant to the organisation, and diligently practiced in accordance to internationally recognized standards and frameworks. CSP services are certified to be trustworthy, reliable, and secure for adoption.

Table 2. Audit Observation

Constraint	CSP 'A'	CSP 'B'
C1	• An integrated encryption technique is used to store and transmit data in encrypted form. • Users are also supported to use a third-party encryption technique as an optional choice. • Unique encryption keys are created per tenant and key stored in separate locations from the data for enhanced key management.	• Support both user-side and server-side encryption techniques for data confidentiality and integrity. • Industry cryptographic standards such as SSL/TLS are used to protect data integrity. • For further data protection, an encryption mechanism using AED is deployed on servers that hold messaging data including emails and IM conversations.
C2	• Access to systems and data is subjected to monitoring and accessibility is based on user privilege. Logical isolation is ensured for customer data. • Access controls are provided so that user accounts are added, modified, and deleted in a timely manner. The controls are periodically reviewed to ensure security. • Multi-factor authentication is provided to support an extra level of security for sign-in credentials. Users are required to use a combination of username and password for access to resources.	• Data and services are secured using identity & access control management tools at the data centre, network, logical, storage and transit levels. • Azure active directory is used as the underlying identity platform. Federated identity management and single sign-on security provided. • Users have the flexibility to enforce client-based access control that allow them to define and control how users access information.
C3	• Independent auditors and external certification and attestation bodies are engaged to validate information regarding processes and controls in the operating environment. • Control environment certified by ISO27001, PCI DSS Level 1, FedRAMP, ISO9001, FISMA and HIPAA, and ITAR,	• Undergoes an annual third-party audits for an independent validation of compliance to policies and procedures for security, privacy, continuity and compliance. • Compliance program is designed to help customers meet compliance requirements. • Industry certifications: ISO27001, PCI DSS Level One, HIPAA, EU model clauses, SAS 70/SSAE17 agreements, EU Safe Harbor.
C4	• Compliance with EU data protection act. • Customers choose the region in which their entities will be located. This allows customers to operate	• Compliance with EU data protection. • Steps are taken to help customers with regulatory requirements related to EU data protection acts.

(Continued)

Table 2. (*Continued*)

Constraint	CSP 'A'	CSP 'B'
	within a geographical location that meets their privacy laws. • Customers are responsible for ensuring the usage of services are in compliance to applicable laws and regulations.	• Customers are responsible to make sure that it is legal to send personal data over the services being hosted.
C5	• BCP & DRP services, architectures, and policies for fast recovery of critical IT systems. • There is the flexibility for customers store data within multiple geographical regions and availability zones for enhanced availability. • Automated backup methods. • Redundancy on multiple devices across multiple locations. • An uptime service guarantee of 99.99 %.	• BCP & DRP services and policies across all data centres located in multiple locations. • A service maintenance and continuity process is supported, which contains a strategy for the recovery of essential assets and the resumption of business processes that guarantees service availability of 99.9 %. • A dedicated development and operations support team is provided to complement the provision of business continuity. • Entities stored in a redundant environment with robust backup, restore, and failover capabilities for ensuring availability
C6	• Hardware & software monitoring tools for acceptable service performance & availability	• Dedicated monitoring systems that monitor services for failure. • Automatic service availability and recovery systems in case of system failure.
C7	• Web service support for technical or account issues. • Additional support features provided using voice calls, user guide, and knowledge centres.	• Customer support services provided to users through online help, community forums, online requests, and voice call supports,

- *Medium.* Security controls, technologies and practices are rather moderately implemented and practiced to an acceptable level. Compliance programs are partially useful and relevant to the CSC, but practiced in accordance to internationally recognised standards and frameworks. The CSP services are considered to be moderately trustworthy, reliable and secure for adoption.
- *Low.* The security controls, technologies and practices are not adequately implemented. Compliance programs are irrelevant to the CSC and evidence of practice in accordance to internationally recognised standards not provided. The CSP services are untrustworthy, unreliable and insecure for adoption.

We provide an example of the comparison and ranking process. Assuming C1 (constraint) requires encryption mechanisms for ensuring confidentiality and integrity of data. To demonstrate the fulfillment of this constraint, CSP 'A' generated evidences that disclose the implementation of an encryption technique and the support provided to users allowing them to use a desirable encryption mechanism for their entities. Based on the comparison result, we assess this evidence with a ranking of 'High' because data is encrypted and a supplementary capability is provided to support users deploy what technique is considered relevant to their requirements.

Audit report Table 3 illustrates different ranking assigned to the two CSPs that provided evidences. Significant and sufficient implementation is achieved in most areas of the constraints by both CSPs. This may be attributable to the fact that two market-leading CSPs were selected for the analysis and evaluation process. In such a situation where both CSPs meet all constraints, the decision on which CSP to go for is left to the stakeholders to consider the depth for which evidences are provided for the constraints. We therefore, assume that CSP 'B' is more suitable for adoption.

Table 3. Audit report ranking

Constraint ID	CSP 'A' assurance ranking	CSP 'B' assurance ranking
C1	High	High
C2	High	High
C3	High	High
C4	Medium	Medium
C5	High	High
C6	Medium	High
C7	High	High

6 Discussion

The relevance of our framework is shown using the example of a use case scenario. The main novelty of this approach is to allow a CSC have an in-depth analysis of CSP offerings based on specific goals prior to cloud migration, which is achieved through a systematic audit framework that uses the introduction of constraints and collection of evidences in relation to the goals. The outputs produced from the concepts have indicated the relevance of the framework in cloud security auditing. The case study results also revealed that the selected CPSs provide convincing evidences to support the goals and constraints of the SME, hence a ranking of 'High' for most constraints. However, CSP 'B' provided a more in-depth and elaborate description of evidences as well as providing additional features that add quality to cloud services, such as helping customers to achieve user-side compliance requirements. This result was passed to the top management and upon evaluation, they decided to migrate to CSP 'B'.

7 Conclusion

More companies are now thinking to move their data from corporate data center to the cloud environment in an attempt to utilize the numerous benefits offered by the cloud. These benefits come with associated risks, uncertainties and concerns as a result of relinquishing total control of entities to a third party. It has therefore become increasingly important to demand evidences relating to the proper operations of a CSP in protecting migrated data and applications. There is a shortage of systematic processes and concepts of cloud security audit that is adequately pertinent to migration instances from existing works. We contributed to this area by presenting a framework that is significant to cloud users in analyzing the services of a potential cloud provider based on their security requirements. The objective of the framework is to provide practitioners with a coherent approach of tasks and activities that can be easily executed to achieve successful security analysis of cloud offerings. The concepts of the framework were modelled following the approach of Secure Tropos Methodology which enabled us to provide structured approach that facilitates the consideration of security requirements. An example on the applicability of the framework was provided with the use of an organization. The case study results demonstrates that using the concepts, it is feasible to assess CSP offerings in a comprehensive way that focuses on user requirements, and also determining CSP trustworthiness and capabilities.

Acknowledgement. This work was partly supported by the Austrian Science Fund (FWF) project no. P26289-N23.

References

1. Moeller, R.: IT Audit, Control, and Security. Wiley, Hoboken (2010)
2. Mateescu, G., Vlădescu, M., Sgârciu, V.: Auditing cloud computing migration. In: 9th IEEE International Symposium on Applied Computational Intelligence and Informatics, Timişoara, Romania (2014)
3. Vidya Marshal, S.: Secure audit service by using TPA for data integrity in cloud system: Int. J. Innovative Technol. Exploring Eng. (IJITEE) 3(4) (2013). ISSN: 2278-3075
4. Cloud Security Alliance CloudAudit: Automated, Audit, Assertion, Assessment and Assurance (2011). http://cloudaudit.org-Accessed. Accessed 29 Mar 2015
5. Mouratidis, H., Giorgini, P.: Secure tropos: a security – oriented extension of the tropos methodology. J. Auton. Agents Multi-Agent Syst. 17, 285–309 (2007)
6. National IT and Telecoms Agency: Cloud Audit and Assurance Initiatives. The National IT and Telecoms Agency, Denmark (2011). http://www.digst.dk/~/media/Files/English/Cloud%20Audit%20and%20Assurance%20EN_cagr.pdf. Accessed 12 Apr 15
7. Ouedraogo, M., Mouratidius, H.: Selecting a Cloud Service Provider in the age of cybercrime. J. Comput. Secur. 38, 3–13 (2013)
8. Pearson, S., Yee, G.: Privacy and Security for Cloud Computing. Computer Communication and Network. Springer, London (2013)
9. Cloud Security Alliance CloudAudit: Automated, Audit, Assertion, Assessment and Assurance, (2010). http://cloudaudit.org-Accessed. Accessed 29 Jan 2015
10. Nicolaou, C.A.: Auditing in the cloud: challenges and opportunities. CPA J. 82, 66 (2012)

11. Ryoo, J., Rizvi, S., Aiken, W., Kissell, J.: Cloud security auditing: challenges and emerging approaches. IEEE Secur. Priv. 12(6), 68–74 (2014)
12. Yu, E.: Modelling strategic relationships for process reengineering. Ph.D. thesis, Department of Computer Science, University of Toronto, Canada (1995)
13. Cloud Security Alliance: Cloud Control Matrix (2011). https://cloudsecurityalliance.org/research/ccm/. Accessed 29 Mar 2015
14. Mouratidis, H.. Giorgini, P., Manson, G., Philp, I.: A Natural Extension of Tropos Methodology for Modelling Security
15. Giunchiglia, F., Mylopoulos, J., Perini, A.: The tropos software development methodology: processes, models and diagrams. In: Giunchiglia, F., Odell, J.J., Weiss, G. (eds.) AOSE 2002. LNCS, vol. 2585, pp. 162–173. Springer, Heidelberg (2003)
16. ISO 19011: Auditing Definitions Translated into Plain English. http://www.praxiom.com/iso-19011-definitions.htm. Accessed 13 Apr 15
17. Kalloniatis, C., Mouratidis, H., Islam, S.: Evaluating cloud deployment scenarios based on security and privacy requirements. Requirements Eng. J. (REJ) 18(4), 299–319 (2013). Springer
18. Mouratidis, H., Islam, S., Kalloniatis, C., Gritzalis, S.: A framework to support selection of cloud providers based on security and privacy requirements. J. Syst. Softw. 86(9), 2276–2293 (2013). Elsevier
19. Islam, S., Mouratidis, H., Weippl, E.: An empirical study on the implementation and evaluation of a goal-driven software development risk management model. J. Inf. Softw. Technol. 56(2), 117–133 (2014). Elsevier

Secure Software Engineering

Software Security Requirements Engineering:
State of the Art

Muthu Ramachandran[✉]

School of Computing, Creative Technologies and Engineering,
Leeds Beckett University, Leeds LS6 3QS, UK
M.Ramachandran@leedsbeckett.ac.uk

Abstract. Software Engineering has established techniques, methods and technology over two decades. However, due to the lack of understanding of software security vulnerabilities, we have not been so successful in applying software engineering principles that have been established for the past at least 25 years, when developing secure software systems. Therefore, software security can not be just added after a system has been built and delivered to customers as seen in today's software applications. This keynote paper provides concise methods, techniques, and best practice requirements guidelines on software security and also discusses an Integrated-Secure SDLC model (IS-SDLC), which will benefit practitioners, researchers, learners, and educators.

Keywords: Software security engineering · Software security requirements engineering · Secured software development · SQUARE method · BSI · Touchpoint · SDL

1   Introduction

There is no doubt that the internet technology has revolutionised human lives, communications, digital economy, socialisation, and entertainment. At the same time demands for internet enabled applications grows rapidly. Almost all businesses, applications, entertainment devices, mobile devices, robots, large scale systems (aircrafts, mission control systems), safety-critical systems, medical systems, internet of things devices are internet enabled for various reasons such as online upgrade, distributed applications, team projects, and server connectivity. Therefore, there is ever growing demand for secured applications and trust. Cyber attacks are increasing continuously from spam, phishing, identify theft, and others in much larger scale attacks such as money laundering and cyber terrorism. Fortify report (2009) says that there is a real possibility that a cyber attack could disable command systems, bring down power grids, open dam floodgates, paralyse communications and transport systems, creating mass hysteria: Any or all of which could be the precursor to terrorist or military attack. These are some of the threats since we (personal, govt. organisations, companies, and business) mostly depend on computers and mobiles for communications and management.

This keynote paper aims to outline the importance of developing secured software systems using a disciplined approach known as software security engineering and it is

H. Jahankhani et al. (Eds.): ICGS3 2015, CCIS 534, pp. 313–322, 2015.
DOI: 10.1007/978-3-319-23276-8_28

also known as secure software development. In particular, this paper identifies key methods and techniques on software security requirements engineering as it is the heart of developing secure software systems. This paper discusses clear best practice guidelines on software security and discusses our Integrated-Secure SDLC (IS-SDLC) model which overcomes current difficulties in identifying and visually representing security process which have been elaborated from security requirements.

2 Why Software Security Engineering?

Software Engineering has established techniques, methods, and technology over two decades. However, security issues are direct attributes of various software such as applications, user interface, networking, distribution, data-intensive transactions, and communication tools, etc. Current applications are being developed and delivered where security has been patched as aftermath. Early commercial developers have tackled security problems using firewalls (at the application level), penetration testing, and patch management.

We are also faced with tackling fast growing information warfare, cybercrime, cyber-terrorism, identify theft, spam, and other various threats. Therefore, it is important to understand the security concerns starting from requirements, design, and testing to help us Build-In Security (BSI) instead of batching security afterwards. McGraw [1] says *a central and critical aspect of the computer security problem is a software problem.* This paper defines *software security engineering as a discipline which considers capturing and modelling for security, design for security, adopting best practices, testing for security, managing, and educating software security to all stakeholders.*

Software engineering has well established framework of methods, techniques, rich processes that can address small to very large scale products and organisations (CMM, CMMi, SPICE, etc.), and technology [modelling (UML), CASE tools, and CAST tools, and others]. Software Engineering has also been well established quality models and methods, reuse models and methods, reliability models and methods, and numerous lists of other techniques. The so called –lities of software engineering long has been contributed as part of quality attributes (Quality, Testability, Maintainability, Security, Reliability, Reusability). These attributes can't be just added on to the system as they have to be built in from early part of the life cycle stages (a typical software development lifecycle include starting from requirements engineering (RE), software specification, software and architectural design, software development (coding), software testing, and maintenance. Security has become highly important attribute since the development of online based applications. Software project management has well established techniques and breadth of knowledge including global development (due to emergence of internet revolution and people skills across the globe), cost reduction techniques, risk management techniques, and others. Nowadays, most of the current systems and devices are web enabled and hence security needs to be achieved right from beginning: need to be identified, captured, designed, developed and tested. Ashford [2] reports UK business spends 75 % of the software development budget on fixing security flaws after delivering the product. This is a huge expenditure and it also creates untrustworthiness amongst customers.

Allen et al. [3] state that the one of the main goals of Software Security Engineering is to address software security best practices, process, techniques, and tools in every phases and activities of any standard software development life cycle (SDLC). The main goal of building secured software which is defect free and better built with:

- Continue to operate normally in any event of attacks and to tolerate any failure
- Limiting damages emerging as an outcome of any attacks triggered
- Build Trust and Resiliency In (BTRI)
- Data and asset protection.

In other words, secured software should operate normally in the event of any attacks. In addition, it involves the process of extracting security requirements from overall system requirements (includes hardware, software, business, marketing, and environmental requirements) and then also further refined and extracted security and software security requirements from software and business requirements. Then the refined software security requirements can be embedded and traced across the software development life cycle (SDLC) phases such as requirements, design, development, and testing. This has not explained well in security related literatures so far. This provides a clear definition of eliciting software security requirements.

3   Software Security Requirements Engineering

Requirements are the starting point, responsible for any system, legal and contractual issues, governance, and provide full functional perspective of the system being developed. Requirements Engineering is a discipline in its own right, which provides process, tools, techniques, modelling, cost estimation, project planning, and contractual agreements. There are wealth of requirements engineering methods, techniques, best practice guidelines, and tools [4–7]. However, due to the nature of increased demands for security-driven applications, current techniques are inadequate for capturing security related requirements effectively. Firesmith [8, 9] reports that poor requirements are the main reasons for cost and schedule overruns, poor functionality and delivered systems that are never used. Requirements are classified into two major parts such as functional requirements which deal with the functionality of the system and non-functional requirements which deal with constraints, quality, data, standards, regulations, interfaces, performance, reliability, and other implementation requirements. Studies [4–7] have shown that requirements engineering defects cost 10–200 times to correct the system after implementation. Therefore, it is paramount to get the requirements correct, concise, and unambiguous.

Capturing business security requirements is a collaborative effort involves many stakeholders such as business analysts, software requirements engineer, software architect, and test managers. Security requirements should provide a clear set of security specific needs and expected behavior of a system. The main aim is to protect systems assets (data and files) and unauthorised access to the system from intentional attacks to the application software systems and other forms of internet based security attacks such as spam, denial of service, identity theft, viruses, and many other forms of intentional attacks that emerges every day. Security remains a software problem as the number of threats and vulnerabilities reported to CERT (Computer Emergency Response team) [10, 11] of 2493 % increase between 1997 (311 cases reported), 2006 (8064 cases reported), and as of 30th April 2015 (3192 cases reported).

In traditional RE, security requirements are considered to be a part of non-function properties and are considered an aspect of implementation strategies such as password protection, authentication, firewalls, virus detection, denial-of-service attacks, etc. Therefore, security needs to be considered as highly specific set of requirements for every functional requirements that has been identified, and has to be applied throughout the life cycle so that we can achieve build in security (BSI). *In addition current RE methods have considered mostly what the system must do, but what the system must not do.* This is the key issue that will be considered when selecting RE methods for software security. Moreover, in Software security RE methods, there are more stake-holders than traditional RE methods have considered such as social engineers, security specialist, business process modeling experts, service computing specialists, and users. Often attackers look for defects in the system, not the system features and function-alities. A number of techniques have emerged to address RE from an attacker's perspective:

- Attack patterns are similar to design patterns which has been designed to study attacks from destructive mode, Allen et al. [3] and BSI [12].
- Misuse and abuse cases are a set of use cases from an attackers perspective, McGraw [1]
- Attack trees provide a formal mechanism for analysing and describing various ways in which attacks can happen from an attacker's perspective. Simply represent attacks against a system in a tree structure, with the goal as the root node and different ways of achieving that goal as leaf nodes, Schneier [13, 14] and Ellison and Moore [15]
- Microsoft SDL provides support on threat modelling which describes a set of security aspects by defining a set of possible security attacks. This has an integral part of Microsoft's SDL method, Howard and LeBlanc [16]
- Building Security In (BSI) method [12], process, design principles, and techniques provided by McGraw [1] and others which is now officially supported by the US department of Homeland security. Some of the design principles include:
  - Correctness by Construction (CbyC)
  - Securing the Weakest Link
  - Defense in Depth
  - Failing Securely
  - Least Privilege
  - Separation of Privilege
  - Economy of Mechanism
  - Least Common Mechanism
  - Reluctance to Trust
  - Never Assuming that your Secrets are Safe
  - Complete Mediation

- Psychological Acceptability
- Promoting Privacy
- The SEI's (Software Engineering Institute) has identified a method known as SQUARE (Secure Quality Requirements Engineering) [17] which is to elicit and prioritise requirements and its consists of nine steps as follow:
  - Agree on definition
  - Identify security goals
  - Develop artefacts
  - Perform risk assessments
  - Select an elicitation technique
  - Elicit security requirements
  - Categorise security requirements
  - Prioritise security requirements
  - Inspect security requirements
  - Clear identification of requirements of the whole applications system and extract security requirements. Interact with stakeholders to clarify security requirements and the technology they want to use, and cost implications.
- OCTAVE method by Caralli et al. [18], Alberts and Dorofee [19] and Woody and Alberts [20] provides clear activities on security requirements:
  - Identify critical assets
  - Define security goals
  - Identify threats
  - Analyze risks
  - Define security requirements
- Other methods include CLASP [21] and S-SDLC [22] and have given detailed descriptions by Ramachandran [23]

Chen [24] distinguishes the key difference between software security engineering with that of robustness for software safety engineering. Software security engineering deals with engineering approach to software development with an aim to engineer and implement security features whereas robustness deals with engineering software for safety critical systems. Therefore, we need to identify, analyse, and incorporate security requirements as part of the functional requirements process. Belapurkar et al. [25] have identified a list of some high-level areas for each security specific functional requirements as follows:

- Identification should address how a system recognises the actors/entities (humans or systems) interacting with the system.
- Authentication should address how a system validates the identity of entities
- Authorisation should address what privileges are to be set to an entity interacting with a system
- Non-repudiation should address how a system prevents entities from repudiating their interactions with the system functionality
- Integrity should address how a system protects information from any intentional or unintentional modifications and tampering
- Auditing should address how a system allows auditors to see the status of the security controls in place

- Privacy should address how a system prevents the unauthorised disclosure of sensitive information
- Availability should address how a system protects itself from intentional disruptions to service so that it is available to users when they need it.

Software security requirements are not only a set of constraints on the software systems but they satisfy required governance and provides protection and trust. This means that we need far more newer techniques such as attack patterns, misuse and abuse cases as part any requirements process.

4 Integrated Security Software Development Lifecycle Process

The above discussed drawbacks and requirements for a concise method, lead us to develop a model that integrates various activities of identifying and analysing software security engineering into software development process, and this new process and its activities is shown in Fig. 1. However, this paper focuses on only software security requirements specific activities. According to this model, SSRE (software security requirements engineering) consists of identifying standards and strategies of the organisation with regards to requirements elicitation (including analysis, validation, verification), conducting risk management and mitigation, and identifying software security requirements consists of a further sub-processes of defining security, identifying security strategies, conducting areas and domain scope analysis, business process modeling and simulation, identifying security issues, applying use cases and misuse cases, attack patterns.

Likewise, this model also provides security-specific processes for identifying security threats during design, development, testing, deployment, and maintenance. There are a numerous number of good design principles that can be found in a vast majority of software design literatures. However, the following is a list of some of the key design principles that are highly relevant to software security design and are part of our IS-SDLC model:

- Principles of least privilege states to allow only a minimal set of rights (privileges) to a subject that requests access to a resource. This helps to avoid intentional or intentional damage that can be caused to a resource in case of an attack.
- Principles of separation of privilege states that a system should not allow access to resources based on a single condition rather it should be based on multiple conditions which has to be abstracted into independent components.
- Design by incorporating known CVE
- Design for resilience for which we have team up with IBM [26] to develop a resilience model which supports system sustainability along side with Building Trust and Security In (BTSI)
- Select software security requirements after performance simulation using BPMN (Business Process Modeling Notation) and is described in detail by Ramachandran [27].

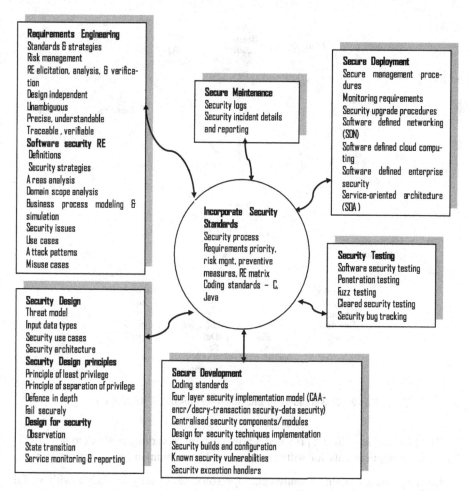

Fig. 1. Integrated secure software development engineering life cycle (IS-SDLC)

SSRE activities in our IS-SDLC supports security in software defined networking (SDN), Cloud computing services (Software as a service (SaaS), Platform as a Service (PaaS), and Infrastructure as a Service (IaaS)), Enterprise security includes cloud service providers and service consumers, and design for security principles and techniques. This the unique contribution of this model and for the body of knowledge in software security research.

5 Software Security Requirements Engineering Method as Part of IS-SDLC

Software development and secure software development involve many stakeholders and business leaders and their coordination is critical for delivering secure software systems. The various stakeholders is shown in the Fig. 2.

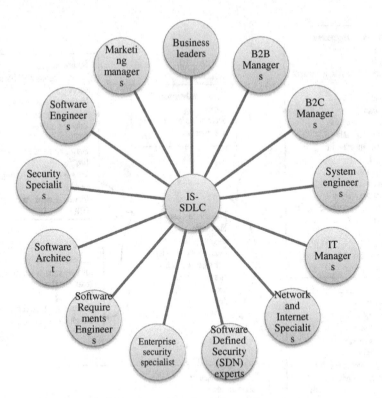

Fig. 2. Stakeholders in integrated secure-SDLC (IS-SDLC)

The previous section has provided a brief account of various methodologies [1–27] for eliciting requirements for software security. Most common best practices are:

1. Eliciting and extracting requirements for software security explicitly with visual notations
2. Prioritising software security requirements
3. Risk assessment and mitigation for software security requirements
4. Design and implement software security requirements
5. Providing SDLC life-cycle support.

Existing methods lack heavily on incorporating social engineering to study software security requirements (learning from real experiences), security-specific business process modeling, performance simulations of the security-specific business processes, service computing, current and emerging technologies such as cloud computing, software-defined networking architecture, and software-defined enterprise security, and emerging vulnerabilities, and cyber attacks. This leads us to develop an integrated-secure software development model supporting software security requirements to be assessed and implemented explicitly in our method as presented in Fig. 1. Ramachandran [23] provides a comparative analysis of various SSRE methods based on our evaluation criteria used and this will help organization and engineers to choose appropriate method that is suitable for the system being developed. Based on the experience with IS-SDLC model in various projects, this paper has identified a set of best practice guidelines and recommendations on SSRE and SSE in general.

6 Best Practice Guidelines

For secured systems, this paper identifies a set of common guidelines that are applicable to most of the secure software development:

1. Develop a list of security requirements checklists and classify them as: critical, medium, and moderate.
2. Bring in requirements inspection team to conduct the security requirements validation process
3. Identify, elicit, analyse, and manage security requirements
4. Specify and model misuse cases and derive security requirements from misuse cases
5. Cross-check operational and functional requirements against security requirements
6. Establish an organisational security culture (e.g., check to make sure proper use of email systems do's and don'ts).
7. Apply business process Modelling and simulation using BPMN tools such as Bonita soft which provides clear performance attributed for all selected security-specific processes.

7 Conclusion

Software security engineering offers several best practices, techniques, and methods to develop systems and services that are built for security, resiliency, sustainability. However, software security can not be just added after a system has been built and delivered to customers as seen in today's software applications. This keynote paper provided concise techniques and best practice requirements guidelines on software security and also discussed an Integrated-Secure SDLC model (IS-SDLC), which will benefit practitioners, researchers, learners, and educators.

References

1. McGraw, G.: Software Security: Building Security In. Addison Wesley, USA (2006)
2. Ashford, W.: (2009). http://www.computerweekly.com/Articles/2009/07/14/236875/on-demand-service-aims-to-cut-cost-of-fixing-software-security.htm
3. Allen, J.H., et al.: Software Security Engineering: A Guide for Project Managers. Addison Wesley, Boston (2008)
4. Jacobson, I.: Object Oriented Software Engineering: Use Case Driven Approach. Addison Wesley, Boston (1992)
5. Kotonya, G., Sommerville, I.: Requirements Engineering: Processes and Techniques. Wiley, New York (1998)
6. van Lamsweerde, A.: Requirements Engineering: From system goals to UML Models to Software Specifications. Wiley, London (2009)

7. Sommerville, I., Sawyer, P.: Requirements Engineering: A Good Practice Guide. Wiley, New York (1998)
8. Firesmith, D.: Engineering Safety- and Security-Related Requirements ICCBSS Tutorial. SEI, Carnegie Mellon University, 27 February 2007
9. Firesmith, D.: Engineering security requirements. J. Object Technol. 2(1), 53–68 (2003)
10. CERT-SEI: www.cert.org
11. CERT-UK: https://www.cert.gov.uk/
12. BSI: Attack patterns articles (2013). https://buildsecurityin.us-cert.gov/articles/knowledge/attack-patterns
13. Schneier, B.: Attack trees: modelling security threats. Dr Dobbs J. (1999). http://www.schneier.com/paper-attacktrees-ddj-ft.html
14. Schneier, B.: Secrets and Lies: Digital Security in a Networked World. Wiley, New York (2000)
15. Ellison, R.J., Moore, A.P.: Trustworthy refinement through intrusion-aware design (CMU/SEI-2003-TR-002, ADA414865). Software Engineering Institute, Carnegie Mellon University, Pittsburgh, PA (2003)
16. Howard, M., LeBlanc, D.C.: Writing Secure Code, 2nd edn. Microsoft Press, Redmond (2002)
17. Mead, N.R., et al.: Incorporating security quality requirements engineering (SQUARE) into standard life-cycle models. SEI Technical Note CMU/SEI-2008-TN-006 (2008). http://www.sei.cmu.edu
18. Caralli, R.A., et al.: Introducing OCTAVE allegro: improving the information security risk assessment process. Technical Report, CMU/SEI-2007-TR-012 (2007)
19. Alberts, C., Dorofee, A.: Managing Information Security Risks: The OCTAVE^{SM} Approach. Addison Wesley, Boston (2002)
20. Woody, C., Alberts, C.: Considering operational security risk during system development. IEEE Secur. Priv. 5, 30–43 (2007)
21. CLASP: OWASP CLASP, version 1.2 (2006). http://www.lulu.com/items/volume_62/1401000/1401307/3/print/OWASP_CLASP_v1.2_for_print_LULU.pdf
22. S-SDLC: Introducing Secure Software development Life Cycle (S-SDLC). Infosec Institute http://resources.infosecinstitute.com/intro-secure-software-development-life-cycle/
23. Ramachandran, M.: Software Security Engineering: Design and Applications. Nova Science Publishers, New York (2012). ISBN 978-1-61470-128-6. https://www.novapublishers.com/catalog/product_info.php?products_id=26331
24. Chen, J.A.: Security engineering for software (SES), CS996-CISM (2004). isis.poly.edu/courses/cs996-management/Lectures/SES.pdf
25. Belapurkar, A., et al.: Distributed System Security: Issues, Processes and Solutions. Wiley, New York (2009)
26. Ramachandran, M., Chang, V., Li, C.-S.: The improved cloud computing adoption framework to deliver secure services. In: Emerging Software as a Service and Analytics - ESaaSA 2015 in Conjunction with 5th International Conference on Cloud Computing and Services Science - CLOSER 2015 (2015). http://closer.scitevents.org/ESaaSA.aspx
27. Ramachandran, M.: Enterprise security framework for cloud data security. In: Chang, V. (ed.) Delivery and Adoption of Cloud Computing Services in Contemporary Organizations. IGI Global, Hershey (2014)
28. Graham, D.: Building security (2006). https://buildsecurityin.us-cert.gov/bsi/articles/best-practices/requirements/548-BSI.html

Conflicts Between Security and Privacy Measures in Software Requirements Engineering

Daniel Ganji$^{(\boxtimes)}$, Haralambos Mouratidis,
Saeed Malekshahi Gheytassi, and Miltos Petridis

University of Brighton, Brighton, UK
{d.ganji,h.mouratidis,m.s.malekshahi,m.petridis}@brighton.ac.uk
http://about.brighton.ac.uk/cem/

Abstract. The digital world is expanding rapidly into all parts of the physical world and our environment is shaped by the technologies we use. Majority of these technologies are user-generated content through browsing, emails, blogging, social media, e-shopping, video sharing and many other activities. our research considers how technology and software architecture in particular could be designed to pave the way for greater security and privacy in digital proceedings and services. The research treat security and privacy as an intrinsic component of a system design. The proposed framework in this research cover a broad approach by examining security and privacy from the requirements phase under a unified framework which enables to richly bridge the gap between requirement and implementation stages.

Keywords: Privacy · Security · Requirements engineering · Conflict management

1 Introduction

There is an increase awareness for the need for design for privacy from both companies and governmental organizations. Designing and building a privacy-preserving system is challenging since these systems have to realize conflicting security properties and system requirements to avoid any security vs privacy trade-off. It is about building products that protect not only the integrity of systems and data itself, but support users privacy as well [1]. A study [2] of 1300 organizations found that privacy and data protection was the main motivation factor for information security practices in 42 % of the organizations. This could be a step towards recognising privacy engineering as a valid profession in the minds of system developers and policy makers, this is about perception and cultivating a privacy mindset [3].

Building systems with solid privacy functions is difficult for many reasons, such as lack of privacy expertise in the development team and lack of methodologies to support developers without privacy expertise. Massey and Anton [2] states, an improve in understanding privacy requirements and communication

© Springer International Publishing Switzerland 2015
H. Jahankhani et al. (Eds.): ICGS3 2015, CCIS 534, pp. 323–334, 2015.
DOI: 10.1007/978-3-319-23276-8_29

between requirements engineers are a much needed process and to identify and model priorities and exception for privacy requirements is an area for exploration. Engineers in charge of building systems must be able to deal with a challenging and subtle concepts found in privacy legislation and policies [2]. If security and privacy are addressed together as a goal-driven requirements engineering, the resulting system have a security and privacy built-in rather than a bolt-on approach.

2   Privacy

Individuals rarely win lawsuits against private parties for privacy violations, because privacy like freedom means "so many different things to so many different people that it has lost any precise legal connotation that it might once have had" [4,5]. Privacy is about "the rights and obligations of individuals and organizations with respect to the collection, use, retention, disclosure, and disposal of personal information" [6].

Privacy, as a priority for security, means that we are free to carry a conversation with a fair amount of confidence that we are not leaking personal or business secrets to an unwanted third party. It is about choosing those we trust [7]. UK Information Commissioners Office (ICO) [8] categorises privacy into four sections of: (1) privacy of personal information, also known as data privacy and information privacy (2) privacy of the person, also known as bodily privacy (3) privacy of personal behaviour (4) privacy of personal communication.

2.1   Data Privacy

Data privacy as described by ICO [8] refers to the ability of a person to control, edit, manage and delete information about themselves and to decide how and to what extent such information is communicated to others. ICO also notes the risk of harm through use or misuse of personal information, the abuse may appear in various ways as tangible and quantifiable such as financial loss or losing a job. These threats [8] may arise through personal information being:

- Inaccurate, insufficient, out of date
- Excessive or irrelevant
- Kept for unnecessary amount of times
- Disclosed to unauthorised people
- Use for secondary and unacceptable purposes
- Kept insecure

Solove [5] states, if people's behaviour or data published on-line, it is very difficult to keep track of it and sometimes impossible to remove, their habits will not be forgotten. it is like a feather in the air.

By 2007, the amount of information created and stored each year was 161 Exabytes per year [9]. Eric Schmidt [9], Google's executive chairman, noted that "mankind now creates as much information every two days as it had from the dawn of civilization to 2003". A study by Gartner Inc. [10] indicate, that "by 2017, 80 % of consumers will collect, track and barter their personal data for cost savings, convenience and customization". A new business model such as "two-sided" or even a "multi-sided" introduced by many on-line services to allow consumers and users to access their services free of (monetary) charge as part of their business model, whilst their revenue is supported through advertising channels [11].

On the other hand a global survey of 3000 people in six countries carried by Fujitsu [12] with the aim of consumer attitudes towards personal data shows that 90 % of US consumers want to be asked to give permission for their data to be shared. They report that 88 % of people are worried about who has access to their data. 91 % of consumers want a system which enables them to control how their data is used. Fujitsu studies show that 88 % of people want simpler terms and conditions.

2.2   Privacy by Design (PbD)

It is in the interest of all academic scholars that privacy should be built as early as possible in the product development process rather than to bolt on privacy at a later stage in the design process.

A proposed privacy framework for business and policy makers by the US Federal Trade Commission [13] describes privacy by design as "companies should promote consumer privacy throughout their organizations and at every stage of the development of their products and services. Companies should incorporate substantive privacy protections into their practices, such as data security, reasonable collection limits, sound retention practices, and data accuracy. Companies should maintain comprehensive data management procedures through the life cycle of their products and services."

Cavoukian [14] notes that "rapid innovation, global competition, and increased system complexity" as challenges for information privacy which they should be approached from a design-thinking view. Cavoukian [15] views the future of privacy cannot be developed entirely depends on compliance with regulatory framework and this should be built by default into an organization's operation and culture. As Siani [1] declares, it should be default that every developer has a duty to follow a minimum set of development practises to avoid basic design flaws that lead to privacy breaches.

2.3   Privacy Impact Assessment (PIA)

The International Association for Impact Assessment (IAIA) [16] describes impact assessment as "the identification of future consequences of a current or proposed action" More specifically, a PIA "involves an assessment of the possible effects that a particular activity or proposal may have on privacy". PIA's core distinction is to give ability to companies to systematically assess and scrutinise their privacy implications of their operations and their customer's personal data handling [17].

Unlike Article 33 of the European Commission's proposed Data Protection Regulation, which focuses on only Data Protection Impact Assessment (DPIA) is not sufficient and organizations which use DPIA may satisfy data protection legislation but could still thirst into an individual's privacy [18]. It worth to note that PIA is not a legal requirements however it is often the most effective way to process personal data that complies with the Data Protection Act (DPA) [8].

Pearson [1] shows that a PIA should be established early at the design stage and supplied into the design process whilst ICO [8] indicates that PIA is a flexible process that should begin early in the life of a project however it can be incorporated with existing approach and run alongside the project development process. Trilateral Research and Consulting [18] studies indicate the following reasons for having a PIA:

- to identify and manage risks
- to avoid unnecessary costs through privacy sensitivity
- to avoid inadequate solutions to privacy risks
- to avoid loss of trust and reputation
- to inform the organisation's communication strategy and to meet or exceed legal requirements

2.4   Privacy Enhanced Technologies (PETs)

Privacy Enhancing Technologies is a system of information and communication technology measures protecting information privacy by eliminating or minimizing personal data thereby preventing unnecessary or unwanted processing of personal data, without the loss of the functionality of the information system [19]. PET allows the end devices/users to protect their identity (anonymity) from being monitored and tapped (unobservability) or from being identified by their activities and behaviour (unlinkability).

Part of quantitative benefits of PET are increase client satisfaction, streamline data processing, facilitate privacy, making services and data processing more efficient. It could include less correction and administration processing of personal data. In general it can help to reduce audit, supervisory and management cost and prevent fines for data breaches. Author describes the qualitative benefits of PET as supporting compliance with privacy data protection acts, it increase personal control over data, build trust with consumers of the systems and ensure risks of privacy violations remain manageable. Shen and Pearson [20] declare that PET on its own do not solve all privacy issues however it has a role in resolving privacy harms. Authors describe a number of reasons which include:

- Huge interest in gathering personal information such as for use of marketing
- Lack of regulatory and oversight on obtaining data and processing of personal information
- Lack of user awareness in protecting their personal information

- A rapid innovation and technical change
- Social computing or cloud computing
- The contextual complexity of privacy
- Increasing distribution and availability of personal information

3 Security Requirements Engineering (RE)

The system security is a complex process and a structuring methodologies are required to secure an overall security of an information systems, All security measures should concern: physical security, operating security, logical security, and telecommunication and network security [21]. Firesmith [22] states security is about preserving systems assets from harm due to various form of attacks that could be reached by the various attackers, It is critical to understand the underlying notions of security engineering and most importantly security itself in order to specify security requirements.

Lamsweerde [23] describes Requirements Engineering (RE) as "a coordinated set of activities for exploring, evaluating, documenting, consolidating, revising and adapting the objectives, capabilities constraints, assumptions that the system-to-be should meet based on problems raised by the system-as-is and opportunities provided by new technology."

One of the major sources of system security failure is not considering the security requirements of the complete system [24]. Pfleeger [25] states describes software engineers are rarely equipped to build in security from the scratch and it is mainly looked at the near the end of development. The best approach to design and protect customer data and privacy is unusable if it is deployed to an insecure environment [26]. Increasingly, regulations are requiring software security engineers to analyse, design and implement responsible systems to comply with laws and regulations [27].

Lamsweerde et al. [28] states, a general issue with requirements engineers are their expectation of first-sketch of goals, requirements and assumptions are to be too exemplary and this likely to cause an unexpected behaviour of agents such as human, devices or software components during the operation of system. authors [28] proposed techniques to manage exceptions at requirements engineering and goal levels, and providing formal techniques for resolving obstacles to the satisfaction of goals, requirements and expectations expected in the requirements engineering process.

De Gea et al. [29] claim development team should be able to access requirements specification easily with traceability throughout the project lifecycle, authors [29] categorized a series of capabilities in the current requirements engineering tools: requirements elicitation, requirements analysis, requirements specification, requirements verification and validation, requirements management, and other capabilities.

Firesmith [22] solution to security requirements engineering is for the security team to build a group of parametrized reusable templates that is achievable by requirements team to engineer security requirements to meet the necessary compliance.

4   Conflict Management

Pfleeger [25] instructs that a single strategy, technology or product is not sufficient to resolve the challenging and contextual privacy issues, it is useful to apply the history of security engineering for development of privacy engineering. Marsh et al. [30] studies show that "privacy requirements must be fed in at each of the four stages initiation, planning, execution and closure of a generic project life cycle".

The article by [31] observes that identifying and grasping conflicts among requirement specifications is important for ensuring that the final product will meet the user's needs without violating the consistency rules. The authors note, the conflict management have demonstrated a number benefits such as:

– Provide consistency in goal-driven requirements acquisition
– Ensure consistency of specifications across viewpoints
– clarify disagreements between different stakeholders
– validate scenarios

They describe, requirements engineering is the most important stage of software development, where failures in requirements engineering tasks are likely to bring a number of failures in other stages. As part of fault and error prevention, systematic consistency checking was introduced as a fundamental task of requirement engineering. On the other hand, it is a very rigid tasks to guarantee an utter consistency in the enterprise/system. It is often not desirable to enforce consistency where other interests of stakeholders are involved. Easterbrook [32] publishes sources of conflict, author identifies the obvious sources of conflict in requirements engineering are conflict amongst the user's perceptions of the problem, and conflict amongst the many goals of a system design. Author [32] states three broad types of conflicts with different level of severity: (1) conflicting interpretation, inconsistencies in interpreting descriptions differently (2) conflicting design (3) conflicting terminologies. Author [32] mentions other sources of conflict to include conflicts between:

– Suggested solution components
– Stated constraints
– Perceived needs
– Resource usage
– Evaluations of priority

Raian Ali et al. [33] note that advances in computing and communication technologies have built many computing novelties which are sensitive to the changes in their domain.

Detecting inconsistencies and resolving them at the requirements engineering process is vital for development of the software implementing the requirements [34]. A policy promote a conflict when its results contains a set of actions that the stakeholders has specified cannot occur together, the conflicts are represented as "violations of action constraints" [54]. Conflict can happen either when an action allowed by an agent are not allowed by another agent, or alternatively when the action an agent needs to take in handling a constraint task are not immediately permitted in handling another task [35]. Different type or set of conflicts need different conflict resolution strategies, according to their nature to resolve different sorts of conflicts.

5 Related Work

This section reviews methods and framework which was originally categorised by [36] and involves with identifying methods that adopt concepts from the field of IS security engineering and use them in order to explicitly represent security requirements that include privacy requirements and they define the way that these requirements can be transformed in specific policies for the system under construction. Some of the major framework and tools are described briefly in below:

Non-Functional Requirement Framework (NFR): Mylopoulos et al. [37] represent NFR in five major parts: a set of goals for defining non-functional requirements, a set of link types for relating goals, a set of generic methods for refining goals, a collection of correlation rules for inferring potential interactions among goals and lastly a labelling procedure which identifies the level a non-functional requirement is being addressed by a set of design decisions.

i* model: Yu [38] describes i* model for modelling and reasoning about organizational information systems, it includes Strategic Dependency model to define dependency relationships between actors and Strategic Rationale for describing stakeholders interest in information systems and organizational environment.

Tropos method: Bresciani et al. [39] describe Tropos as a methodology aims to cover all the early analysis and design activities in the software development process up until the system implementation, Tropos features include the concept of agent and all the related concepts such as goals and plans and the second feature include the support for the early requirements analysis and allow to understand the operation environment and kind of interactions that should occur between software and human agents.

KAOS method: Heaven and Finkelstein [40] describe the method provides a goal driven for a system-to-be, the method support the elicitation of further goals and the requisites, objects, agents and actions of the system. The method including including eliciting and reducing goals until requisites are determined, determining objects from goals description, allocating the requisites, objects, and actions to agents.

Goal-Based Requirements Analysis Method (GBRAM): Anton and Earp [41] describes GBRAM as a methodical approach to determine and refining goals of system and enterprise. It helps to manage trade-offs between goals and converting them into operation requirements.

Role-Based Access Control (RBAC) method: This method was proposed by He and Anton [42] as a framework for modelling privacy requirements for linking them to organizational access control policies. The framework includes a data model and goal-oriented role engineering process to bridge the gap between high-level privacy requirements and low level access control policies.

Mofett-Nuseibeh (M-N): Moffett and Nuseibeh [43] proposed a framework which unifies the concepts of requirements engineering and security engineering, the former provides the functional goals which are operationalised into functional requirements and the security requirements provides the concept of assets as well as the threats of harms to those assets.

Bellotti-Sellen framework: Bellotti and Sellen [44] proposed a framework for design and elicitation of privacy requirements during system design phase and requirement specification. Authors describe the framework three important parts: (1) guide to identify the privacy issues and social practises (2) introduce the possible design solutions and possibilities (3) analyse the new solutions and their effect on the system.

STRAP (STRuctured Analysis for Privacy) method: Jensen et al. [45] proposed STRAP as a structured analysis technique that include analysis, refinement, evaluation and iteration of privacy aware design and a method for deriving policy requirements from the analysis.

PriS (Privacy Safeguard) method: Kalloniatis et al. [46] describe PriS as a security requirement engineering method which incorporates privacy requirements early in the system development process.

Caprice: Omoronyia et al. [47] proposed the tool to enable developers to focus on particular privacy threats from changing context and the plausible category of adaptation action. It helps for design of applications that adapt their behaviour to mitigate privacy threats by suggesting mitigation action based on defined adaptation rules configured by the developer.

SecuriTas: Pasquale et al. [48] proposed the tool to support adaptive security and allow software developer to model security issues at the requirements level to analyse changes in security and provide a set of security recommendations to protect the system.

Easy Win-Win: It is a groupware supported methodology for requirements negotiation that is enhanced from Win-Win negotiation approach to improve the participation and interaction of major stakeholders by a set of activities guiding stakeholders through a process of gathering, elaborating, prioritising and negotiation requirements [49].

Majority of above mentioned methods serve requirements engineering at the design level and some of them are designed with specific presentation of security or privacy up to the implementation level, however there is a lack of holistic method to consider security and privacy together without any trade-off between them.

Table 1 is provided with comparison of above stated methods based on four criteria: (1) usage view: the methods applied on the level of requirements engineering (2) subject view: classification of security and privacy issues (3) type of mechanism for expressing security and privacy (4) development view: type of development tools for designers.

Table key:
++ = Fully support
+ = Partially support

Table 1. Comparison of security & privacy requirements engineering

	NFR	i*	TROPOS	KAOS	GBRAM	RBAC	M-N	B-S	STRAP	PRIS	CAPRICE	SECURITAS	EASY WIN-WIN
Usage (Requirements)													
Elicitation		++	++	++	++	+	++	++	++	++	++	++	++
Specification	++	++	++	++	++		++	+	++	++	++	++	++
Validation	++	++	++	++	++	+			++		++	++	++
Subject (Security)													
Overall requirements	+	+	++	+	+		++				++	+	
Goals of collaborating actors			++	+	+		++				++		
Support of policies			++								++		
Adaptive security											++		
Subject (Privacy)													
Overall requirements	+	+	+	+	+	++		++	++	++	++		+
Goals of collaborating actors				+	+	++		+	++	++	++		
Support of PET	+								+		++	+	
Support of policies		+			+	+			+	++			
Support of PIA													
Adaptive privacy									+		+	++	
Representation													
Graphical notation	+	++	++	++			+				++	++	++
Formal language	+	++	++	++							++	++	
Development													
Guidance process					++	+	++	++	++	++	++	++	++
Modelling tools	++	++	++	++	++						++	++	++

6   Conclusions and Future Work

Lee [50] aptly states, a suitable framework should be able to address issues such as legal, economic, social and ethical aspects as well as technological possibilities and limitations. Tools and methodologies providing a systematic approach to the design of security and privacy are much essentials [51]. Most of the system designers are not having sufficient expertise in security and legal aspects to protect and deploy systems to meet the security and privacy compliance, therefore a framework to guide them through the system development is crucial [52]. A framework should facilitate a collaboration of security engineers and legal experts at the organizational model and raise the security and privacy problems and identify the appropriate solutions to those issues [52].

Our comparison in previous section present that there is a limited available methodology to observe and provide requirement engineering to security and privacy together and there is no widely acceptable tools to help designing and engineering privacy. there is also no specific techniques to deal with identifying and implementing privacy requirements.

Our future development is based on secureTropos framework which includes of a language and a process concentrates on requirements engineering phase. The process follow the cycle of requirements engineering which includes requirements elicitation and the requirements analysis phases, the former focus that a system's requirements are elicited and understood and latter focus on specification and modelling requirements [53]. The proposed framework in this research cover a broad approach by examining security and privacy from the requirements phase under a unified framework which enables to richly bridge the gap between requirement and implementations stages. secureTropos framework indicates an important set of characteristics:

- Its meta-model integrate requirements, security and privacy concepts
- The process initiate a fundamental approach to the elicitation and analysis of security and privacy requirements
- Support the selection of cloud provider
- Support common understanding based on the security and privacy mechanisms required by the system
- Supports the analysis of security, privacy and system requirements under one integrated framework

References

1. Pearson, S.: Taking Account of Privacy when Designing Cloud Computing Services, pp. 44–52. IEEE (2009)
2. Massey, A.K., Antón, A.I.: A requirements-based comparison of privacy taxonomies. In: 2008 Requirements Engineering and Law (2008)
3. Schneier, B.: The importance of security engineering. IEEE Comput. Reliab. Soc. 88 (2012)
4. Thomas McCarthy, J.: The Rights of Publicity and Privacy, 2nd edn. Thomson-West, New York (2005)
5. Solove, D.J.: Understanding Privacy. Harvard University Press, Cambridge (2008)
6. AICPA and CICA. Generally Accepted Privacy Principles. Technical Report August, American Institute of Certified Public Accountants, Inc. and Institute of Chartered Accountants (2009)
7. Perrin, C.: Privacy is security (2007)
8. ICO. Conducting privacy impact assessments code of practice. Technical report (2014)
9. Schwartz, P.M.: Privacy, ethics, and analytics. IEEE Comput. Reliab. Soc. 11, 66–69 (2011)
10. Plummer, D.: Top 10 Strategic Predictions: Gartner Predicts a Disruptive and Constructive Future for IT. Technical report (2011)
11. Koponen, J., Mangiaracina, A.: No free lunch: personal data and privacy in eu competition law. The Comput. Internet Lawyer 31(6), 7 (2014)
12. Fujitsu: Personal data in the cloud: A global survey of consumer attitudes. Technical report (2010)

13. Federal Trade Commission. Protecting Consumer Privacy in an Era of Rapid Change: A proposed framework for businesses and policymakers. Technical report, December 2010

14. Cavoukian, A.: Privacy by design the 7 foundational principles. Technical report (2009)

15. Cavoukian, A.: Privacy by Design. Technical report (2011)

16. Clarke, R.: Privacy Impact Assessments (1999)

17. Oetzel, M.C., Spiekermann, S.: A systematic methodology for privacy impact assessments: a design science approach. Eur. J. Inf. Syst. 23(2), 126–150 (2014)

18. Trilateral Research & Consulting. Privacy impact assessment and risk management. Technical report, May 2013

19. PISA Consortium. Handbook of Privacy and Privacy-Enhancing Technologies (2003)

20. Shen, Y., Pearson, S.: Privacy enhancing technologies: a review. HP Laboratories 2739, 1–30 (2011)

21. Goncalves, G., Poniszewska-Maranda, A.: Role engineering: from design to evolution of security schemes. J. Syst. Softw. 81(8), 1306–1326 (2008)

22. Firesmith, D.: Specifying reusable security requirements. J. Object Technol. 3(1), 61–75 (2004)

23. Van Lamsweerde, A.: Requirements Engineering: From System Goals to UML Models to Software Specifications. Wiley, Hoboken (2009)

24. Haley, C.B., Laney, R., Moffett, J.D., Nuseibeh, B.: Security requirements engineering: a framework for representation and analysis. IEEE Trans. Softw. Eng. 34(1), 133–153 (2008)

25. Pfleeger, S.L., Pfleeger, C.P.: Harmonizing privacy with security principles and practices. IBM J. Res. Devel. 53(2), 6:1–6:12 (2009)

26. Microsoft. Protecting Data and Privacy in the Cloud. Technical report (2014)

27. Breaux, T.D., Anton, A.I.: Analyzing regulatory rules for privacy and security requirements. IEEE Trans. Softw. Eng. 34(1), 5–20 (2008)

28. Van Lamsweerde, A., Letier, E.: Handling obstacles in goal-oriented requirements engineering. IEEE Trans. Softw. Eng. 26(10), 978–1005 (2000)

29. Carrillo de Gea, J.M., Nicolas, J., Fernandez Aleman, J.L., Toval, A., Ebert, C., Vizcaino, A.: Requirements engineering tools. IEEE Softw. 28(4), 86–91 (2010)

30. Al-Fedaghi, S.: Engineering privacy revisited. Comput. Sci. 8(1), 107–120 (2012)

31. Dimitromanolaki, I., Loucopoulos, P.: Goal-based conflict management in scenario analysis. In: 11th International Workshop on Database and Expert Systems Applications, pp. 831–835. IEEE (2000)

32. Easterbrook, S.M.: Resolving requirements conflicts with computer-supported negotiation. Requirements Engineering: Social and Technical Issues, pp. 41–65 (1994)

33. Ali, R., Dalpiaz, F., Giorgini, P.: Reasoning with contextual requirements: detecting inconsistency and conflicts. Inf. Softw. Technol. 55(1), 35–57 (2013)

34. Van Lamsweerde, A., Darimont, R., Letier, E.: Managing conflicts in goal-directed requirements engineering. IEEE Trans. Softw. Eng. 24(11), 908–925 (1998)

35. Pham, M.T., Seow, K.T.: Multiagent conflict resolution planning. In: IEEE International Conference on Systems, Man, and Cybernetics, SMC 2013, pp. 297–302 (2013)

36. Kalloniatis, C., Kavakli, E., Gritzalis, S.: Methods for designing privacy aware information systems: a review. In: 13th Panhellenic Conference on Informatics, pp. 185–194. IEEE (2009)

37. Mylopoulos, J., Chung, L., Nixon, B.: Representing and using non-functional requirements: a process-oriented approach. IEEE Trans. Softw. Eng. 18(6), 483–497 (1992)

38. Yu, E.: Towards modelling and reasoning support for early-phase requirements engineering. In: 3rd IEEE International Symposium on Requirements Engineering, pp. 226–235 (1997)

39. Bresciani, P., Giorgini, P., Giunchiglia, F., Mylopoulos, J., Perini, A.: TROPOS: an egent-oriented software development methodology. Auton. Agents Multi-Agent Syst. 8(3), 203–236 (2002)

40. Heaven, W., Finkelstein, A.: A UML profile to support requirements engineering with KAOS. IEEE Proc.-Softw. 151(1), 10–27 (2004)

41. Antón, A.I., Earp, J.B.: Strategies for developing policies and requirements for secure electronic commerce systems. E-Commer. Secur. Priv. 2, 29–46 (2000)

42. He, Q., Antn, A.I.: A framework for modeling privacy requirements in role engineering. REFSQ 3, 137–146 (2003)

43. Moffett, J.D., Nuseibeh, B.: A framework for security requirements engineering. In: International Workshop on Software Engineering for Secure Systems (2006)

44. Bellotti, V., Sellen, A.: Design for privacy in ubiquitous computing environments. In: Third European Conference on Computer-Supported Cooperative, pp. 77–92 (1993)

45. Jensen, C., Tullio, J., Potts, C., Mynatt, E.D.: A structured analysis framework for privacy (STRAP) (2005)

46. Kalloniatis, C., Kavakli, E., Gritzalis, S.: Addressing privacy requirements in system design: the PriS method. Requirements Eng. 13(3), 241–255 (2008)

47. Omoronyia, I., Pasquale, L., Salehie, M., Cavallaro, L., Doherty, G., Nuseibeh, B.: Caprice: a tool for engineering adaptive privacy. In: 27th IEEE/ACM International Conference on Automated Software Engineering (ASE 2012), Essen, Germany (2012)

48. Pasquale, L., Menghi, C., Salehie, M., Cavallaro, L., Omoronyia, I., Nuseibeh, B.: SecuriTAS: a tool for engineering adaptive security. In: ACM SIGSOFT 20th International Symposium on the Foundations of Software Engineering, pp. 1—4. ACM (2012)

49. Boehm, B., Grünbacher, P., Briggs, R.O.: EasyWinWin: a groupware-supported methodology for requirements negotiation. In: 23rd International Conference on Software Engineering, pp. 720–721 (2001)

50. Lee, R.B.: Challenges in the design of security-aware processors. In: Proceedings of the Application-Specific Systems, Architectures, and Processors (ASAP03) (2003)

51. Liu, L., Yu, E., Mylopoulos, J.: Security and privacy requirements analysis within a social setting. In: 11th IEEE International on Requirements Engineering Conference (2003)

52. Compagna, L., El Khoury, P., Massacci, F., Thomas, R., Zannone, N.: How to capture, model, and verify the knowledge of legal, security, and privacy experts: a pattern-based approach. In: 11th International Conference on Artificial Intelligence and Law, pp. 149–153. ACM (2007)

53. Mouratidis, H., Islam, S., Kalloniatis, C., Gritzalis, S.: A framework to support selection of cloud providers based on security and privacy requirements. Elsevier 86, 2276–2293 (2013)

54. Chomicki, J., Lobo, J., Naqvi, S.: Conflict resolution using logic programming. IEEE Trans. Knowl. Data Eng. 15(1), 244–249 (2003)

Securing the Blind User Visualization and Interaction in Touch Screen

Mohammed Fakrudeen and Sufian Yousef(✉)

Anglia Ruskin University, Cambridge, UK
sufian.yousef@angelia.ac.uk

Abstract. Blind users cannot use visual CAPTCHA and review of literature suggest that the existing audio CAPTCHAs have task success rate below 50 % for blind users. In this paper, we describe how blind student's views external system (images) for academic purposes using an image map as a case study has been described. We proposed two interaction techniques which allow blind students to discover different parts of the system by interacting with a touch screen interface. An evaluation of our techniques reveals that (1) building an internal visualization, interaction technique and metadata of the external structure plays a vital role (2) blind students prefer the system to be designed based upon their behavioral model to easily access and build the visualization by their own and (3) to be an exact replica of visualization, the metadata of the internal visualization is to be provided either through audio cue or domain expert (educator). Participants who used touch screen are novice users, but they have enough experience on desktop computers using screen readers. The implications of this study to answer the research questions are discussed.

Keywords: Blind user · CAPTCHA · Image map · Digital security · Touch screen and visualization

1 Introduction

Interaction with touch screen is a complex process for blind users [1]. Understanding the internal visualization of cognitive activities is an important process for a designer to design external visualization. Scaife and Rogers [2] pointed out that more emphasis should be provided by "the cognitive activities when interaction takes place with external visualization, the properties of the external and internal structures and their benefits with different visual representation".

Under these circumstances, it is essential to understand internal visualization, their relation with external visualization and how physical activities help to bind these two visualizations. Without prior knowledge of these abstract concepts, it will be intricate for a novice designer to build external visualization. As a result, it is significant to make cognition a research agenda for building information visualization [3].

To address this research agenda, we propose the following research questions in accordance with mobile learning (m-learning): (1) What is meant by "internal visualization" for a blind user in terms of image map?; and, (2) For a given external

© Springer International Publishing Switzerland 2015
H. Jahankhani et al. (Eds.): ICGS3 2015, CCIS 534, pp. 335–347, 2015.
DOI: 10.1007/978-3-319-23276-8_30

visualization, how it can be related to internal visualization? Our paper is derived to discuss the answer for the above mentioned research questions. The answers to this questions, will immensely help developers to understand feasibility of developing visual CAPTCHA (Completely Automated public Turing tests to tell Computers and Humans Apart) for blind users without sacrificing security.

2   Internal Visualization

The researchers suggest that blind people have an internal representation for the information they hear. Most current research is on geometrical shapes and mathematical symbols, and has not touched the core representation of "abstract" information. In particular, the information visualization does not vary much within the sighted user. On the other hand, visualization varies widely among blind users depending on the description of narrator, comprehension and prior experience. Analyzing the mental model in the literature is the first step to investigate internal representation which may yield an effective theoretical concept.

2.1   Mental Models of Blind

A review of the relevant literature suggests that the mental model is an internal representation of real world phenomena, which is composed of many small-scale representations. Craik [4] claims that mental model predicts future action by constructing small-scale models, in his book "The Nature of Explanation". The Rouse and Morris [5] argue that the application of a specific mental model is necessary. The emergence of mental models has led to a decline in the theoretical concept to HCI [6].

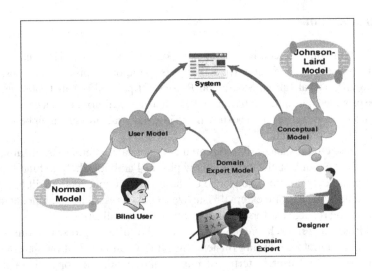

Fig. 1. Mental models

The literature also suggests that there are two potential and influential mental models: the Norman model and the Johnson-Laird model. Both models suggest that there are four agents which influence the interaction between the system and user: (1) The target system which refers to the device the user is intended to use.; (2) A conceptual model developed by designers in which the system is developed; (3) The user model developed by the user through interaction with the system. This user model continues to update whenever the user is exposed to the system; and (4) the model for the user model, as understood by the scientist (Psychologist or Usability Expert) [7].

Norman revealed that mental models are not usually accurate and are highly "volatile". Nevertheless, they are "runnable" to serve certain rationale. Although there are many lapses, it provides prognostic and expounding power in understanding the interaction.

The Norman model focuses on the user model while Johnson-Laird [8] focuses on the conceptual model of the system (Fig. 1). To put it more simply, Norman emphasizes the "behavioral" aspects of the user towards the system whereas Johnson-Laird defines the "Structural" aspect of the system.

Johnson-Laird views mental models as preserved entities and analogous of what they represent in the external visualization. The user can manipulate the system and configure his mental model with presupposing mental logic and formal rules. However, Norman believes that there are chances the user can pretend to behave with the system. As a consequence, users are forced to give a reason through verbal protocol, although they do not have one.

The Johnson-Laird and Norman models vary widely based on the emphasis and the nature of the problems being investigated. For instance, consider the premises "Tiger eats deer" and "Tiger eats rabbit". The user can conceptualize two different models where the relations between the entities are present as below:

Table 1. User mental model and their premises

Mental model	Premises1	Premises2	Premises3
M1	Tiger	Deer	Rabbit
M2	Tiger	Rabbit	Deer

Both models are coherent with the premises (see Table 1); however, the user cannot predict whether deer, eats rabbit or vice versa by merely exploring their mental models. The user cannot apply logical rules to infer, since it does not store premises based on logical predicates such as eat (Tiger, Deer).

2.2 Significance and Application of Information Visualization

To understand the problem related to interface design, it is imperative for designers to understand: (1) how the blind user imagines the external visualization (Sect. 2.2.1); (2) which tools are used to stimulate these images (Sect. 2.2.2); (3) the role of data in image formation (Sect. 2.2.2); and, (4) how the data are mapped together to form an image (Sect. 2.2.3). To address these questions, we will discuss this in the following section.

Image or Model. Although the items are scattered throughout the web page, the blind user considers all the items in a web page to be a vertical list [9]. The desktop screen reader processes all pages, and produces output in a sequential order that can be navigated by tab or up/down keys. Currently, touch screen technologies such as the iPhone and Android implement a static layout for the interaction [10]. With reference to this, two dimensional pages are collapsed to single dimensional to form a single horizontal list that contains a large set of items. It is burdened for the user to memorize the sequence of interest items. Furthermore, the relative position of item such as on the top or on the bottom is lost [11]. Although it has limitations, it is considered to be better than nothing.

Applying the interface design format such as size, position and color to the mental model, Johnson-Laird contends that mental models are essentially spatial representations and are more abstract. This inspection is in distinction with mental imagery. He emphasized that both the mental imagery and mental model can be used in logical analysis.

Such characterization makes it challenging to apply to the interface design, especially for blind users for two reasons: (1) The imagery varies widely between the sighted and blind user; and, (2) the designer cannot understand the imagery of the blind user. For instance, the designer can understand how the sighted user can imagine the size and shape of the checklist, but it is difficult to predict a blind user's imagination about the same fact.

In interface design, the blind user can understand the spatial layout of the screen based on the training. Instead, it seems unreasonable to provide audio cues related the color and length of the widget. Our own experience of developing courseware for the blind user indicates that a blind user has to be provided with cues about the position of the widget in the touch screen device. By continuous exploration, the blind user becomes familiar with the position of the widget [12].

Mental Simulation. The mental model is abstract and cannot be evaluated directly. The review of literature suggests that there are two types to simulate the mental models. In the first type, training the user to use the system and simulate the mental model. In the second type, the user is exposed to complex system without proper training and simulates the mental model [13]. Two factors are used to simulate the mental models: tools and data.

Tools. Different traditional tools can be applied to simulate the mental model for blind users [14]: (1) Task-based scenario: It requires users to perform a series of tasks to achieve the target. Generally, task acquisition time, number of clicks and error rate of the task performance are gathered. The user is prompted to think aloud during the experiment. It helps the investigator to extract the reason for performed errors; (2) Verbal and Hands on Scenario: It includes a task-based scenario, but it requires the user to respond to a query pertaining to the task performed with the system. Finally, toward the end of the experiment, the user has to explain the system; (3) Tutoring Scenario: The user is required to tutor about the system to another person. It is suitable if the user has enough experience to handle the system. Furthermore, the user has to depend on the learner. However, it encourages the users to articulate their knowledge; and (4) Exploration Scenario: Under this scenario, the user is involved with another person and investigates the application. In this way, the users were communicative and more involved. The main impediment to this type is a highly experienced user who dominates the session and less skilled users who will be controlled due to deficiencies in exposure. Additionally, it consumes much time to gather the data which is extracted through recordings.

Data. Mental models do not possess any data. The information about the external visualization is stored in the form of data which we termed as external data. The external data is used to simulate the mental model. The external data may be constructive data or passive data. Constructive data is data that is transferred from external visualization of the user in the form of audio cues to stimulate the next course of action. On the other hand, passive data is the acknowledgment sent by the system to users in the form of haptic feedback. Along these lines, data are transmitted to humans through the hands and ears of the human body. The transmission of data from external visualization of the user simulate the mental model by analyzing the data, selecting the task and choosing appropriate interaction techniques to accomplish the task. For instance, data named "Enter your name" invokes the user to search for the required information (name) in the internal data, select the data, and deliver the data using a voice synthesizer interaction technique. Finally, item level information is stored in the form of data. The information may be individual, such as "Click here" or may be aggregate information such as "error code".

Mental Map. The mental map is the internal representation of data in the mental model, the available data are mapped to each based on interaction with the system. The mental map is primarily related to item-level information. According to the schematic and semantic level, data are aggregated and the relevant task is performed to construct and simulate the mental model for different visualizations to get a feel of interface design. Thus, the mental model is more abstract than the mental maps.

3 Dynamics Between Mental Model and External Visualization

As discussed earlier, the blind user who uses the latest technologies, such as the iPhone and Android, views the external visualization as a horizontal list. Whatever the layout design is, a blind user navigates in the form of a queue keeping the layout static. The navigation is achieved through flung gesture, which supports both back and forward directions.

In the dynamic interaction that we devised, the blind user views the external visualization as dots in Braille located at fixed locations in the touch screen interaction. For each blind user, each dot acts as a stack (Data1, Data2 and Data3 as shown in the Fig. 2) in which items pile on top of each other. In this manner, the blind user can navigate through the items in the stack by click gesture. Since many stacks can be placed on the screen, many items can be accommodated which can be reached easily as compared to a static layout. The only predicament the blind user faces will be identification of the required stack. Navigation is supported by external data, such as audio feedback.

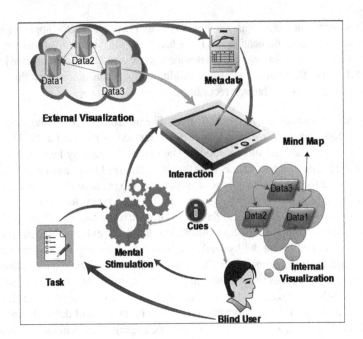

Fig. 2. Dynamics between the mental models and external visualization

From this point of view, the blind user does not have to hold the exact external visualization in their heads [15]. Since the internal visualization (mental model) does not contain item specific information about the data, internal visualization is simulated by using carefully designed external data in the form of audio cues.

However, in certain cases, the internal visualization should be an exact replica of external visualization. For instance, in the image map, it is imperative to understand the position of each section. In addition, there are limitations in visualizing the parts as either stack or queue. Thus, to understand the external visualization or to expand the internal visualization, focus should be on interaction and not on the brain. In specific, the events performed by different parts of the body, such as hand and ear, which interact with external visualization to construct, manipulate and stimulate the mental model have to be understood.

4   Parts of Brain – A Case Study

The interaction technique is the technique used by the user to communicate with external visualization. It is characterized by (1) initiating physical action, and (2) following alterations in the visualization state. Tufte [16] formulates around 57 interaction techniques to be used in the environment. However, most of the interaction is ignored in HCI research since there are no appropriate features to be implemented with it. Thus, many features are aggregated to a single group.

Generally, interaction in touch screen technologies is classified into tactile and non-tactile interaction. Whereas clicking the button and holding the device is considered as tactile interaction, listening to audio is considered as non-tactile interaction. It can also be generalized based on characterization of visualization (static or dynamic) and based on modality (such as hand or ear interaction). HCI research reveals that human events are often ignored, which results in usability problems.

We present a case study to understand how an external visual space is understood by the blind user using a touch screen device. As part of our courseware, an image map is created for exploring the parts of the brain. Our techniques do not require alterations to the underlying touch screen hardware. These techniques are entirely software based. Our design aims to improve the accessibility of existing touch screen hardware for blind users.

We formulate two techniques, namely the Touch technique, and the Control technique. The touch technique is based on the Johnson-Laird model giving more emphasis the conceptual model, where the blind user has adapted to understand the system behavior. In the control technique, more emphasis is given to user behavior (Norman Model) in order to facilitate easy accessibility of the system. The techniques which we devised are discussed in detail now.

4.1 Touch Based Technique

According to these techniques a blind user has to press the surface of a touch screen either from left to right or vice versa or in a zig-zag manner. If the blind user touches the surface and the target is located, then the audio will inform the user of the name of the target (Fig. 3a). If the target is not located, then no audio feedback will be received. Long tapping provides audio information about the target. Since we tested in small screen smart phone, if numbers of targets are more, then it is easy to locate more targets. If the target is less in the count and scattered wider around the space, then it is difficult to locate the target and time consuming. This technique needs a lot of patience and memorization of target location when used for the first time. Memorizing the target location will enable blind users to reach the target directly next time.

4.2 Control Based Technique

The control based technique is based on linearization of items while preserving the original layout of the screen. Blind users, on each tap over the widget placed on the bottom of the screen, will be provided with audio feedback about the name of the target (Fig. 3b). A long tap will provide the audio information about the target as in the above techniques.

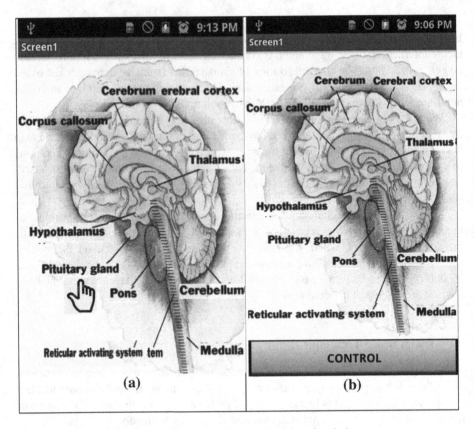

Fig. 3. (a) Touch technique and (b) control technique

5   Evaluation

5.1   Participants

We recruited 10 blind computer users (3 male, 5 female), with an average age of 50.2 (SD = 12. 4). No participants used a touch screen before. However, all of the participants are use a mobile using screen reader regularly in their daily life.

5.2   Apparatus

The study was conducted using Samsung Galaxy S2 smart phone based on Android. No hardware modification was made. We requested the blind users to identify the single widget above the home button in touch and control based techniques.

5.3 Procedure

The prototype is developed for each technique. The participants are tested to locate the item and understand the information about the item for each technique. Our prototype has an image map about parts of the brain. It has 9 items such as cerebrum, cerebellum, medulla, Pons and so on. The participants were given the target item and asked to reach the target item. While testing, we observe the following for each technique.

Task Acquisition Time. Time taken by the participant to reach the target was measured in seconds. The target is any part of the image. Task acquisition time is calculated as the time starts when the participant performs the first tap and ends when he reaches the target item.

Stroke Count. Stroke count is the measure of the number of taps the participants performed to reach the target item.

After performing each technique, participants rated the technique using a Likert-scale questionnaire. After all techniques had been tested, participants ranked the techniques in order of preference. Questionnaires were administered verbally, and the experimenter recorded the answers.

6 Results

Most complexity in dealing with touch screen by a blind user is in finding targets on the screen. A sighted user can quickly identify a target in a visual interface which uses empty spaces to design individual and group targets. Locating targets on the touch screen requires blind users to touch the empty area when they may not know where they are touching.

Each participant performed averagely 10 trials for each technique. The participant performance for each of the techniques and participant feedback is provided below. Our observation during the trials of each technique is also provided.

6.1 Descriptive Statistics

We examined the target acquisition time and stroke count to reach the target for both the techniques.

Stroke Count. On average, blind participants used 21.17 strokes in touch technique to reach the target which is higher than the control technique for which they used 4.25 strokes on average to reach the target (Fig. 4). In addition, the maximum strokes performed by the blind user to reach the target were 60 in the touch technique and 9 in the control technique.

Target Acquisition Time. We analyze how much time the blind users required to reach the target. The descriptive statistics reveal that on average, 9.7 s are required to reach the target for the control technique. While the mean time for the touch technique is

43.91 s. For the control technique, the maximum duration to reach the target is 16 s and minimum is 2 s. The maximum task completion time in the touch technique is 125 s and minimum is 4 s.

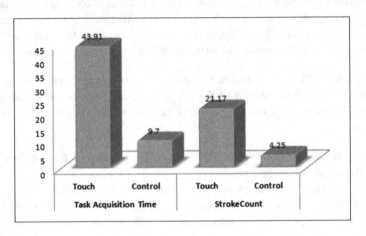

Fig. 4. Mean values for each technique

6.2 Technique Wise Comparison

The dependent variables are checked for normality by using Shapiro Wilkson (W) test based on techniques. The data are not normalized for touch techniques using duration (W(12) = 0.278, P < 0.05) or control technique using stroke count (W(24) = 0. 191, P < 0.05). Hence the Kruskal Wallis H test was performed for not normalized data to find the significance of each technique on the dependent variable.

From the result, it was concluded that there was a statistically significant difference between the duration of the techniques (H(1) = 9.6134, P < 0.05). It can be further concluded that the duration of touch (Mean rank = 26.17) was more than the duration of control technique (Mean rank = 14.67).

A statistically significant difference was also found between the techniques for a stroke count (H(2) = 9.943, P < 0.05). The stroke count for touch (Mean rank = 26.21) was more than the stroke count of the control technique (Mean rank = 14.65).

6.3 Feedback Analysis

The participants completed a questionnaire about the two techniques following the experiment. The participants show their compliance with each technique using a 5-point Likert scale (1 = Strongly Disagree, 5 = Strongly Agree) using a series of statements.

According to the Friedman Test, there was a statistically significant difference between the control and touch techniques, $\chi2(1) = 45.302$, p < 0.005. Pairwise comparison using Wilcoxon signed rank test found that the control technique is more preferred than the touch technique (Z = −6.232, P < 0.05).

Significant results were also found for the following measures: easy to use ($\chi2(1) = 5$, $P < 0.05$), easy to learn ($\chi2(1) = -2.60$, $P < 0.05$), familiar ($\chi2(1) = -2.232$, $P < 0.05$), easy to navigate ($\chi2(1) = -2.041$, $P < 0.05$) and intuitive ($\chi2(1) = -2.06$, $P < 0.05$).

7 Discussion

A qualitative difference between the touch and control techniques with touch screen device is observed. The primary difference between the two techniques was how the blind user visualizes the external visualization. In the touch technique, users are required to scan the entire surface to locate the target. This method was somewhat slow and time consuming. Considerable efforts and patience are required to accomplish the task. Our observation of this technique reveals that blind users were frustrated during attempts to find the target.

On the other hand, in the control technique, blind users were able to navigate items in a linear fashion. This allowed the users to iterate the items quickly. In addition, the interaction with the system is minimized.

Although participants were faster overall with the control technique, they are not able to visualize the system. They are able to extract the external data through audio cues. However, the actual mind map between the data is missing. Using the control technique, the mind map is linear. On the other hand, using the touch technique, the blind user is able to visualize the external structure.

Note that we adopted "not" describing the actual location of each part. One important consideration when comparing the duration and stroke count is the feedback from the user. The feedback reveals that the control technique is more favored irrespective of not achieving the visualization. In other words, the blind user prefers more behavioral aspects than conceptual aspects. Fortunately, they feel the visualization can be achieved through the domain expert (educators).

In the end, we can conclude that interaction plays a vital role in building internal visualization. The blind user expects easy interaction with the system. At the same time, the blind user prefers to build up their own mental model based on the external data. In order to maintain equilibrium with both the Norman and Johnson-Laird models, enough metadata has to be provided through external data either in the form of audio cues or through lecturing by educators. The metadata includes the actual location, size and shape of the external structure.

As a result, the external data are just converted to internal data and it is not of much utility in building the internal visualization equivalent to the external visualization. Specifically, the metadata about the external structure helps the blind users to build the internal visualization. By doing this, both behavioral and conceptual models can be kept in tandem.

8 Conclusion

In this paper, we inspect the characteristics of internal representation relevant to an external system. We also investigate the interaction techniques useful to building internal visualizations when external visualization is based on the image map. Our research explores the solution for the questions mentioned in the first section.

What is meant by "internal visualization" for a blind user in terms of image map?. We distinguish the mental model as behavioral, structural and internal. In addition, the mental model preservation data and mapping between the data or exact replicas of external visualization relies on metadata from external structures sent via audio cues.

For a given external visualization, how can it be related to internal visualization? The relationship between external and internal visualization depends on the interaction technique. The interaction should be simple and easily accessible to the external system. The interaction may be based on the behavioral model developed by the user for easy access or a conceptual model developed by the designer to build the system and the blind user has to adapt to the system.

How do physical activities relate external visualization with internal visualization? It is necessary for external visualization to augment with internal visualization so that they form a blended system. Internal-external blending is performed in terms of six purposes: project, select, precision, coupling, investigation and configuration.

By addressing the research questions, we set up a framework to design an image map using touch screen that merges external visualization, internal visualization, interaction and analytical process. We trust this framework can direct and notify future actions on the design, evaluation and comprehension for the developers to develop CAPTCHA for blind users.

References

1. Buzzi, M.C., Buzzi, M., Leporini, B., Trujillo, A.: Designing a text entry multimodal keypad for blind users of touchscreen mobile phones. In: Proceedings of the 16th International ACM SIGACCESS Conference on Computers and Accessibility (ASSETS 2014), pp. 131–136. ACM, New York, NY, USA. doi:10.1145/2661334.2661354
2. Scaife, M., Rogers, Y.: External cognition: how do graphical representations work? Int. J. Hum. Comput. Stud. **45**(2), 185–213 (1996)
3. Liu, Z., Nersessian, N., Stask, J.: Distributed cognition as a theoretical framework for information visualization. IEEE Trans. Vis. Comput. Graph. **2008**(14), 1173–1180 (2008)
4. Craik, K.: The Nature of Explanation. Cambridge University Press, Cambridge (1943)
5. Rouse, W.B., Morris, N.M.: On looking into the black box: prospects and limits in the search for mental models. Psychol. Bull. **100**(3), 349–363 (1986)
6. Saei, S.N.S.M., Sulaiman, S., Hasbullah, H.: Mental model of blind users to assist designers in system development. In: IEEE Conference Publications, pp. 1–5 (2010)
7. Norman, D.: Some Observations on Mental Models. Lawrence Erlbaum Associates, New Jersey (1983)
8. Johnson-Laird, P.N.: Mental Models: Towards a Cognitive Science of Language, Inference, and Consciousness. Harvard University Press, Cambridge (1983)
9. Murphy, E., et al.: An empirical investigation into the difficulties experienced by visually impaired Internet users. In: Universal Access in the Information Society, vol. 7, issue no. 1-2, pp. 79–91. Springer, Heidelberg (2008)

10. Fakrudeen, M., Ali, M., Yousef, S., Hussein, A.H.: Analysing the mental model of blind users in mobile touch screen devices for usability. In: Proceedings of the World Congress on Engineering 2013, London, UK. Lecture Notes in Engineering and Computer Science, pp. 837–842 (2013)

11. Abidin, A.H.Z., Xie, H., Wong, K.W.: Blind users' mental model of web page using touch screen augmented with audio feedback. In: International Conference on Computer and Information Science (ICCIS), Kuala Lumpur, pp. 1046–1051 (2012)

12. Fakrudeen, M., Yousef, S., Hussein, A.H., Ali, M.: Presentation design of e-assessments for blind users using touch screen devices. In: International Conference on Electronics, Computers and Artificial Intelligence (ECAI), Pitesti, pp. 1–6 (2013)

13. Zhang, Y.: The influence of mental models on undergraduate students' searching behavior on the Web. Inf. Process. Manage. **44**, 1330–1345 (2008)

14. Sasse, M.: Eliciting and describing users' models of computer systems. Ph.D. University of Birmingham (1997)

15. Brooks, R.A.: Intelligence without reason. In: Computers and Thought, IJCAI 1991, pp. 569–595. Morgan Kaufmann (1991)

16. Tufte, E.R.: Visual Explanations: Images and Quantities, Evidence and Narrative, 4th edn. Graphics Press, Cheshire (1997)

Behavioural Biometrics: Utilizing Eye-Tracking to Generate a Behavioural Pin Using the Eyewriter

Bobby L. Tait[✉]

University of South Africa, Pretoria, South Africa
taitbl@unisa.ac.za

Abstract. Biometric technology allows a computer system to identify and authenticate a person directly based on physical or behavioural traits. A human body is absolutely unique. Each human body on earth, if measured by composition on molecular level, is so unique, that the particular composition has never existed before. When that human cease to exist, that unique composition will never exist again. However the ability to measure a human to a molecular level of accuracy is not currently possible with existing technology. Biometrics refers to the science and technology that measure and statistically analyse human body characteristics and biological data. DNA, fingerprints, eye retinas and irises, facial patterns and hand geometry are used for biometric for authentication purposes. Apart from having unique physical traits, all human also exhibit unique behavioural traits. The way that a person talks, or the way that a person walks (a person's gait) can all assist in the identification of the person. Various research projects focused on the way that a person types a password. This behavioural trait can then be used to strengthen the security of a supplied password. This paper reports on research that investigates the uniqueness of eye movement. The way a person creates a pin, using his or her eyes are used as a behavioural biometric to strengthen the pin that is supplied. Eye tracking technology usually involves costly equipment such as the Tobii eye tracking system. For this research the Eyewriter system is used due to the affordability and the open source nature of the Eyewriter hardware and software. Earlier research concluded that the movement of a human eye is unique. Behavioural eye biometrics can be used to authenticate a human in a one to one match environment.

Keywords: Eye-tracking · Behavioural biometrics · Authentication · Eyewriter · Information security · Digraph

1 Introduction

Biometrics is not a novel technology at all. The notion of using a physical trait for authentication dates back over a thousand years. Potters in the east would make an imprint of their fingerprints in the clay as an early form of brand identity and to ensure the authenticity of the article [21].

© Springer International Publishing Switzerland 2015
H. Jahankhani et al. (Eds.): ICGS3 2015, CCIS 534, pp. 348–359, 2015.
DOI: 10.1007/978-3-319-23276-8_31

Humans rely on a person's physical traits for identification and authentication. A human will authenticate a person based on the person's voice, face, smell or even behaviour, to name a few.

Biometrics is the science of equipping a computer system with the necessary "senses" to allow the computer system to authenticate a person based on something that is part of the person, or exhibiting behavioral traits. Biometrics measures a physical or behavioral aspect that is inherently part of a person, to verify the authenticity of the person.

This paper presents a novel approach of measuring the unique movement of the eye to create a pin for authentication.

Eye tracking technology is central to the research conducted and reported in this paper. In Sect. 3 a brief overview of the working of eye tracking technology will be discussed.

The following section introduces biometric technology.

2 Biometrics

Biometrics: "(ancient Greek: bios = "life", metron = "measure") is the study of automated methods for uniquely recognizing humans based upon one or more intrinsic physical or behavioral traits" [4]. Ben Miller introduced the following definition for biometrics: "Biometric technologies are automated methods of verifying or recognizing the identity of a living person based on a physical or behavioral characteristic" [17]. The international bio-metric industry association defines biometrics as "automated methods for verifying or identifying the identity of a living individual based on physiological or behavioral characteristics" [12].

Various mechanisms have been developed to allow a human to be authenticated based on a physical biometric trait, a behavioral biometric trait, or a hybrid approach.

For the purpose of this paper, biometrics identification is divided into 2 major subsections, namely physical biometrics and behavioral biometrics.

2.1 Physical Biometric Characteristics

As mentioned in the abstract earlier, the construction of a human on molecular level is so unique that the combination has never existed before and will never exist again [20].

Various sensors are constructed to assist a computing system to measure some of these unique physical aspects.

A few of the physical aspects that can be used to authenticate a human will be discussed briefly. The physical biometric characteristics listed below are not an exhaustive list. It only serves as a brief list of technologies adopted in industry or technologies on which a lot of current research is being conducted.

- Fingerprints (Fig. 1A): The measurement of the physical ridges and valleys found the person's fingers can be measured using optical, thermal, capacitive or ultrasonic fingerprint scanners [15].
- Iris (Fig. 1B): The iris is the ring of colored tissue surrounding the pupil. The iris consists of pigmented fibro-vascular tissue known as the stroma. The unique pattern that is formed by the vascular structure of the iris is used to authenticate a person [11].

- Retina (Fig. 1C): The retina is found inside the back of eye. The blood vessels in the back of the eye have a very unique pattern and are used for authentication [22].
- Facial recognition (Fig. 1D): Various aspects of contribute to the uniqueness of the human face. These aspects are measured to allow the biometric decision algorithm to authenticate a person. Aspects such as distance between the eyes, size of each eye and distance from the nose to the edge of the mouth, are used for measuring uniqueness [5].
- Hand Geometry (Fig. 1E): The physical construction of the hand is used for authentication purposes. Aspects such as the length and thickness of each finger, the thickness of the palm, and the palm surface area are all metrics used in the authentication process of hand geometry [14].

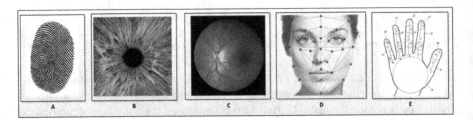

Fig. 1. Physical biometric characteristics

It is clear from the examples that the biometrics listed is all physical by nature. In many cases physical biometrics can be observed by the naked eye.

Physical biometrical characteristics are available for measurement, regardless if the human is alive or deceased.

The following section introduces behavioral biometric characteristics.

2.2 Behavioral Biometric Characteristics

The second type of biometric that can be used to uniquely identify a person is known as behavioral biometrics. This biometric characteristic is based on the unique way a person performs a specific action. Behavioral biometrics is based on the unique behavioral patterns that a person exhibits [2].

The behavioral biometric characteristics listed below are not an exhaustive list. It only serves as a brief list of technologies adopted in industry or technologies on which a lot of current research is being conducted.

- Key stroke dynamics (Fig. 2A): In this method a password is supplied by a user. A typical authentication system matches the supplied password to a reference password recorded earlier. When a behavioral biometric authentication system is used the way that the person typed the password is of fundamental importance. Keystroke dynamics aspects such as dwell time on each keyboard key, flight time between the press of one key and the following key, and time to type the complete password, are some of the aspects considered to determine the behavioral traits by which a person enters a password. Authentication is rejected if a person entered the password correctly, but the way that the password was entered was not biometrically matched to the behavioral template of the user [18].

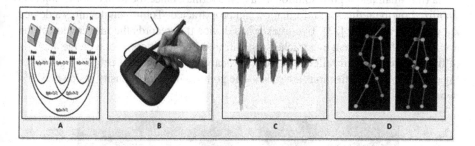

Fig. 2. Behavioral biometric characteristics

- Signatures (Fig. 2B): A signature is commonly used to sign documents and enter into a contract. A signature on a document is compared to a reference signature to test authenticity. In most cases a signature is not a 100 % exact match to the reference signature. If evaluation is done by an automated system, the system considers the behavioral aspect associated with creating the signature. Aspects such as pen-tip-pressure, acceleration and speed of creating lines, pen-up and pen-down times are all used in measuring the behaviour of a person signing a document [10].
- Voice recognition (Fig. 2C): To authenticate a person based on the person's voice, measurements are taken of the pitch, the dynamic range and the timbre of the voice. The combination of these factors is all used to determine the authenticity of the person. The behaviour of various aspects of the voice will directly influence the measured behavioral voice characteristic [13].
- Gait (Fig. 2D): The way that a person walks is also unique enough to be used for authentication. Accelerometers measure joint movement of the hip, knee and ankle. Aspects such as flight time of the leg and dwell time of the foot is also measured and contributes to the unique movement of a person [16].

Behavioral biometrics will evolve over time as the behaviour of the person's behaviour changes over time. The system is thus dynamic. It must adjust the biometric measurement factors as the person interacts with the system [24].

Behavioral biometrics cannot be measured after the death of a person.

Bednarik et al. conducted research in 2005 to establish the uniqueness of the movement of the eye for behavioral biometric purposes [1]. It was illustrated that 90 % accuracy was found during the authentication process of the eye movement of 12 subjects. Bednarik et al. concluded that due to hardware limitations the micro movements of the eye are difficult to capture with the technology available in 2005 [1].

The research presented in this paper does not exclusively rely on authenticating a person only on the behavioral movement of the eyes. It also incorporates the behavioral aspect into the creation of a pin.

3 Eye Tracking

Humans move their eyes in order to bring the image of an inspected object onto the fovea (the small and high-resolution area of the retina). Once the image of the object is stabilized on the retina, the information can be extracted. Tobii manufactures a device known as Eye-tracker [23]. Eye-tracker is a device that records the movements of the eyes. Most of the current eye-trackers use infrared light emitters, video image analysis of the pupil center and reflections from cornea to estimate the direction of gaze, see Fig. 3. The infrared reflections are seen as the points with high intensity inside person's pupil.

Fig. 3. Infrared reflection [1]

The movement of the pupil can be tracked with a fair amount of accuracy. It is possible to record exactly where the person is looking or how the person's eyes are moving.

Unfortunately current commercial eye tracking systems such as eye tracking systems available by Tobii are very expensive [8, 23]. Thus it was decided to implement the system proposed using the Eyewriter eye-tracking system.

3.1 EyeWriter Eye-Tracking

The EyeWriter project is an open source project. All software needed to allow the EyeWriter to function is freely available from the EyeWriter website. The complete instructions to create a DIY (do it yourself) Eyewriter, can be found on the EyeWriter website [7].

Tony Quan is a legendary LA graffiti artist, social activist and publisher internationally. He is known for his innovative artistic style and his efforts to build and nurture the California graffiti scene over the last three decades. In 2003, Tony was diagnosed with Amyotrophic lateral sclerosis (ALS). A degenerative motor neuron disease that has left him almost completely physically paralyzed. Tony can still move his eyes [3].

In 2008, Mick and Caskey Ebeling became familiar with Tony's illness. In 2009 the "Not impossible Foundation" and "The new school of Design" set out to create a low cost (~50 US dollar) open source eye tracking system that allows an ALS patient to draw by just using their eyes [3].

To utilize the EyeWriter, a software component must be installed, and linked to the EyeWriter hardware. The hardware and software component is discussed in the following sections.

Eyewriter Software. The Eyewriter software consists of three functional modules: eye-tracking, calibration and drawing. It is designed for drawing with eye movement using the Eyewriter eye-tracking glasses. The software for both parts has been developed using OpenFrameworks, a cross platform c++ library for creative development [7].

The eye-tracking software detects and tracks the position of a pupil from an incoming video image. It uses a calibration sequence to map the tracked pupil coordinates to positions on a computer screen. The pupil tracking relies upon a clear and dark image of the pupil. The designed DIY glasses use near-infrared LEDs to illuminate the eye and create a dark pupil effect. This makes the pupil much more distinguishable and easier to track.

The source code for the EyeWriter is public domain and can be found online [7]. Once the source code is downloaded, the source code must be compiled into an executable for the relevant operating system.

Eyewriter Hardware. The developers of Eyewriter set a goal to develop a hardware component of the EyeWriter project is to make the most simple and inexpensive eye-tracking headset possible to use with the EyeWriter software. The major benefit of the hardware component is the affordability. Furthermore the eye tracking headset is created from readily available components costing around US $50. Traditional commercial eye trackers cost between US $9000–$20,000 [8].

To create an EyeWriter headset, the following components are needed [7]:

- Pair of sunglasses (only the frame of the sunglasses will be used in the eventual headset
- PS3 eye camera
- IR wratten (Infrared filter, available from Kodak)
- IR LED's (Infrared Light Emitting Diodes)
- Aluminum wire
- Alligator clips
- Batteries

The complete instructions to create the EyeWriter as a DIY project can be found online [7].

The assembled Eyewriter Lens module is illustrated in Fig. 4.

Fig. 4. EyeWriter lens module.

The lens module is attached to the cheap pair of sunglasses, to align with one of the person's eyes, and is illustrated in Fig. 5.

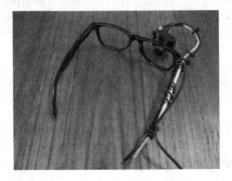

Fig. 5. EyeWriter with camera module

4   Application of the EyeWriter

In the initial design of the EyeWriter the system was developed for a person that is totally paralyzed, and thus has no head movement. The system was developed to assist a person who could only move their eyes.

In this research it was concluded that it is not accurate enough due to the movement of a normal person's head. An updated version of the EyeWriter was used. Placing the Camera module a bit closer to the eye and incorporating 4 IR LED's to increase the contrast between the pupil and the iris. The result of the contrast increase from the view of the PS3 camera is illustrated in Fig. 6. Note the contrast difference and the very dark nature of the pupil in the picture.

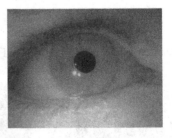

Fig. 6. Clear view of pupil from PS3 camera [9].

4.1   Using the EyeWriter to Enter a Pin

The first step in applying the EyeWriter is to ensure that a person can create a pin code by using the EyeWriter system.

The second step is evaluating the behavioral nature of a person's eye movement when selecting the numeric values of the pin. To test the ability of the EyeWriter to capture the pin, a template of a keypad is provided. The user must focus on the relevant numerical value on the keypad and blink to indicate a selection.

For the purpose of this paper, a colored dot is placed on the area numerical value that the person selected. For a secure application, the system will not indicate the value selected. It will only indicate that a selection was successfully made. As a test example this selection process for the numerical value 71753 is illustrated in Fig. 7.

Fig. 7. Keypad with values selected by EyeWriter

It is important to note that the EyeWriter allows a person to make a selection of a pin by only glancing at the keypad. However in the interest of this research a second step is applied as part of the authentication process. The manner the user glances at the keypad and selects the values from the keypad is important from a behavioral point of view.

In short, a person selects the pin form the keypad using the EyeWriter in the first step and in the second step, the behaviour that the user exhibits to create the pin, is recorded and used for behavioral biometric authentication.

4.2 Behavioral Biometric Measured in Creating the Pin Using EyeWriter

For the research presented in this paper, two approaches were considered to measure the behavioral aspects during the creation of the pin.

The first approach is to consider the path that the eyes follow between selecting the values from the keypad. However, this approach is beyond the scope of this paper, and currently still under investigation and research.

The second approach is based on the digraph behavioral biometric method, commonly associated with keystroke dynamics [6]. The working of a digraph is briefly introduced in the following section, followed by a discussion of the application of a digraph in the EyeWriter approach.

4.3   Digraph Measurement for EyeWriter Pin Selection

Keystroke dynamics is detailed timing information that describes exactly when each key was pressed and when each key was released. The recorded timing data is then processed through a unique neural algorithm that determines a primary pattern for comparison [2].

A digraph is used to measure the way that a person create a password or a pin rather than simply considering the actual password or pin supplied. The behavioral aspect of the pin creation is very important.

A Digraph considers two aspects to be measured against each other [19]. For example the time that the user took to select the first letter compared to the time that the user took to select the second letter, or the time it took from selecting the first key until the pin creation is completed (last key selected).

Figure 8 illustrates the working of a digraph for the example presented earlier.

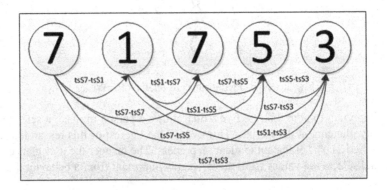

Fig. 8. Digraph for EyeWriter example.

The EyeWriter is used to select the values from the keypad to create the pin. To measure the behavioral aspect resulting from the creation of the pin, the time aspect is measured.

The measured times recorded using the EyeWriter is presented in the following table. Ten measurements were made as part of a proof of concept and listed under M1 to M10.

For the presented example, tsS7- tsS1 indicates the time taken from selecting key 7 until selecting the following key (key 1). The last measurement (tsS7-tsS3) refers to the total time that it took to create the full pin consisting of 5 digits. It is important to note that the measurements indicated in this table were created after the user was well trained and had sufficient practice in using the EyeWriter. 100/s is the time unit used to measure the time taken to select the pin. It is clear that there is a very strong correlation between the different measures (Table 1).

The following figure presents the 10 measurements over time (Fig. 9).

Table 1. EyeWriter digraph time capturing results

	M1	M2	M3	M4	M5	M7	M8	M9	M10
tsS7 - tsS1	0.7	0.89	0.65	0.71	0.59	0.71	0.76	0.61	0.81
tsS1 - tsS7	0.91	0.79	0.71	0.67	0.7	0.55	0.64	0.73	0.77
tsS7 - tsS5	0.6	0.61	0.77	0.75	0.66	0.66	0.81	0.69	0.8
tsS5 - tsS3	0.6	0.7	0.65	0.72	0.66	0.68	0.67	0.63	0.71
tsS7 - tsS7	1.61	1.68	1.36	1.38	1.29	1.26	1.4	1.34	1.58
tsS1 - tsS5	1.51	1.4	1.48	1.42	1.36	1.21	1.45	1.42	1.57
tsS7 - tsS3	1.2	1.31	1.42	1.47	1.32	1.34	1.48	1.32	1.51
tsS7 - tsS5	2.21	2.29	2.13	2.13	1.95	1.92	2.21	2.03	2.38
tsS1 - tsS3	2.42	2.19	2.19	2.09	2.06	1.76	2.09	2.15	2.34
tsS7 - tsS3	4.63	4.48	4.32	4.22	4.01	3.68	4.3	4.18	4.72

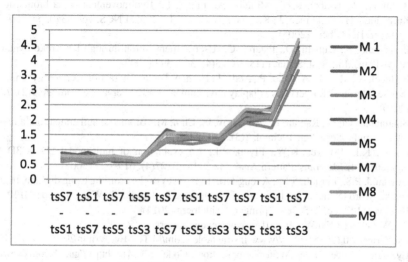

Fig. 9. EyeWriter measurements correlation.

Due to the behavioral aspect that is measured during the capturing process of the pin, the way that the user selects the pin using the EyeWriter will change over time. For this reason the reference biometric template must be adjusted over time to incorporate the slight behavioral changes of the user as the system is used.

5 Conclusion

The EyeWriter project is a project that was developed to provide eye tracking technology at an affordable price. The project was developed to allow people to draw figures by simply using their eyes.

The Eyewriter technology is used in this research to allow a user to enter a pin for an authentication environment by simply gazing at the numerical keys that correspond to the pin that must be supplied. Furthermore, the way that the person creates the pin is recorded. To test the behavioral aspect of the creation of the pin, a digraph approach is followed. Utilizing of a digraph is closely associated with testing the behavioral aspects when a password is. It is illustrated and tested in this paper that the same principals used for regular keystroke dynamics can be applied to eye tracking biometrics for the recording of a pin using the EyeWriter eye tracking system.

Future research will investigate the possibility to track the unique movements of the eye during the selection process of the characters of the pin. This research will investigate if it is possible to authenticate a person based on the eye movement recorded with the EyeWriter. Research conducted by Bednarik et al., proved that this is possible, using the Tobii eye tracking system.

References

1. Bednarik, R., Kinnunen, T., Mihaila, A., Fränti, P.: Eye-movements as a biometric. In: Kalviainen, H., Parkkinen, J., Kaarna, A. (eds.) SCIA 2005. LNCS, vol. 3540, pp. 780–789. Springer, Heidelberg (2005)
2. Bergadano, F., Gunetti, D., Picardi, C.: User authentication through keystroke dynamics. ACM Trans. Inf. Syst. Secur. (TISSEC) 5(4), 367–397 (2002)
3. Bellucci, A., Malizia, A., Diaz, P., Aedo, I.: Human-display interaction technology: emerging remote interfaces for pervasive display environments. IEEE Pervasive Comput. 9(2), 72–76 (2010)
4. Bhattacharyya, D., Ranjan, R., Alisherov, F., Choi, M.: Biometric authentication: a review. Int. J. u-and e-Serv. Sci. Technol. 2(3), 13–28 (2009)
5. Chang, K.I., Bowyer, K.W., Flynn, P.J.: An evaluation of multimodal 2D + 3D face biometrics. IEEE Trans. Pattern Anal. Mach. Intell. 27(4), 619–624 (2005)
6. Dowland, P.S., Furnell, S.M.: A long-term trial of keystroke profiling using digraph, trigraph and keyword latencies. In: Deswarte, Y., Cuppens, F., Jajodia, S., Wang, L. (eds.) IFIP WG. IFIP, vol. 147, pp. 275–289. Springer, Heidelberg (2014)
7. EyeWriter: The EyeWriter (2015). www.eyewriter.org
8. EyeWriter 2.0 (2015). http://www.instructables.com/id/The-EyeWriter-20/
9. EyeWriter code, Eye Writer Application Code (2014). https://github.com/eyewriter/eyewriter-1.0
10. Gamboa, H., Fred, A.: A behavioral biometric system based on human-computer interaction. In: Defense and Security, pp. 381–392. International Society for Optics and Photonics, August 2004
11. He, Z., Tan, T., Sun, Z., Qiu, X.: Toward accurate and fast iris segmentation for iris biometrics. IEEE Trans. Pattern Anal. Mach. Intell. 31(9), 1670–1684 (2009)
12. Higgins, P.T.: Introduction to biometrics. In: The Proceeding of Biometrics Consortium Conference (2006)
13. Kim, D.J., Hong, K.S.: Multimodal biometric authentication using teeth image and voice in mobile environment. IEEE Trans. Consum. Electron. 54(4), 1790–1797 (2008)
14. Kumar, A., Wang, D.C., Shen, H.C., Jain, A.K.: Personal verification using palmprint and hand geometry biometric. In: Kittler, J., Nixon, M.S. (eds.) Audio- and Video-Based Biometric Person Authentication. LNCS, vol. 2688, pp. 668–678. Springer, Heidelberg (2003)
15. Lee, H.C., Ramotowski, R., Gaensslen, R.E. (eds.): Advances in Fingerprint Technology. CRC Press, Boca Raton (2001)

16. Mäntyjärvi, J., Lindholm, M., Vildjiounaite, E., Mäkelä, S.M., Ailisto, H.A.: Identifying users of portable devices from gait pattern with accelerometers. In: IEEE International Conference on Acoustics, Speech, and Signal Processing, 2005, Proceedings (ICASSP 2005), vol. 2, pp. ii-973. IEEE, March, 2005

17. Miller, B.: Vital signs of identity [biometrics]. IEEE Spectr. **31**(2), 22–30 (1994)

18. Monrose, F., & Rubin, A. (1997, April). Authentication via keystroke dynamics. In *Proceedings of the 4th ACM conference on Computer and communications security* (pp. 48-56). ACM

19. Shepherd, S.J.: Continuous authentication by analysis of keyboard typing characteristics. In: European Convention on Security and Detection, pp. 111–114, 16–18 May 1995. doi: 10.1049/cp:19950480

20. Stern, D.P.: A Short history of nearly everything. Eos Trans. Am. Geophys. Union **86**(20), 198 (2005)

21. Thalheim, L., Krissler, J., Ziegler, P.M.: Body check. C't Mag. **11**, 114 (2002)

22. Usher, D., Tosa, Y., Friedman, M.: Ocular biometrics: simultaneous capture and analysis of the retina and iris. In: Ratha, N.K., Govindaraju, V. (eds.) Advances in Biometrics, pp. 133–155. Springer, London (2008)

23. Tobii: Tobii eye tracking technologies (2015). www.tobii.com

24. Wang, L. (ed.): Behavioral Biometrics for Human Identification: Intelligent Applications: Intelligent Applications. IGI Global, Hershey (2009)

Author Index

Printed in the United States
By Bookmasters